GENEALOGY OF A MURDER

GENEALOGY OF A MURDER

Four Generations, Three Families, One Fateful Night

Lisa Belkin

W. W. NORTON & COMPANY

Celebrating a Century of Independent Publishing

For information about permission to reproduce selections from this
book, write to Permissions, W. W. Norton & Company, Inc.,
500 Fifth Avenue, New York, NY 10110

For information about special discounts for bulk purchases,
please contact W. W. Norton Special Sales at
specialsales@wwnorton.com or 800-233-4830

Manufacturing by Lakeside Book Company
Book design by Lovedog Studio
Production manager: Louise Mattarelliano

ISBN 978-0-393-28525-3

W. W. Norton & Company, Inc.
500 Fifth Avenue, New York, N.Y. 10110
www.wwnorton.com

W. W. Norton & Company Ltd.
15 Carlisle Street, London W1D 3BS

1 2 3 4 5 6 7 8 9 0

To Alvin R. Tarlov,
who has always tried to do the right thing,
even—especially—when it was complicated

Thank you for entrusting me with your memories

You could not remove a single grain of sand from its place
without thereby . . . changing something throughout all
parts of the immeasurable whole.

Johann Gottlieb Fichte,
The Vocation of Man, 1800

✦

It always amuses historians and philosophers to pick
out the tiny things, the sharp agate points, on which the
ponderous balance of destiny turns.

Sir Winston Churchill,
If It Had Happened Otherwise, 1932

Author's Note

THIS IS A WORK OF NONFICTION. ALL QUOTES COME FROM PUB-lished news accounts, diaries, prison records, letters, autobiographies, and conversations as recalled by participants during my interviews with them. All facts came from primary or reliable secondary sources. Where an assumption or a supposition was made, it was grounded in these facts.

Because several characters share first names, I altered some in the interest of clarity. The woman I call Raisel Tarlov was in fact known as Rosa or Rose to her family. The woman I refer to as Rosie Cosentino used that diminutive only until she was married, when she preferred Rose; I continue to refer to her as Rosie throughout, however, since her mother was also named Rose. I refer to Charles Tarlov as Charlie, to differentiate him from Charles DeSalvo. Charles Troy, Sr., and Charles Troy, Jr., in turn, were changed to Patrick Troy to prevent confusion.

Introduction

I FIRST HEARD THE STORY OVER BREAKFAST. MY MOTHER AND HER new husband had poached the duck eggs they bought every weekend at the farmer's market and toasted the dense multigrain bread from their favorite Tucson bakeshop. Theirs was a relatively new marriage—she nearing eighty, he close to ninety—and they were delighting in this unexpected late-life chapter. We sat in their sunny kitchen, looking through the window at their cactus garden, sharing their Sunday morning tradition.

Our conversation meandered to a book I had written years earlier, one that my stepfather had read in anticipation of this visit. It reminded him of something that happened a long time ago, he said, way back in 1960. The story was compelling: a young army doctor is stationed at a research lab at a maximum-security prison and becomes friendly with a prisoner, one who himself is a subject of the doctor's research. The prisoner asks for the doctor's help, the doctor gives it, things go terribly wrong, a police officer is murdered.

What drew me from the first telling was not just the true crime, but the question of what had come before it. These three men—the prisoner, the officer, the doctor—had begun at the same starting line. They were all the same age, born in the early years of the Great Depression, and they all had parents or grandparents who'd left different homelands to pursue the same American Dream. How did they come to be who they were and where they were on that July night? How did one become the cop, one become his killer, and one become my stepfather, the doctor who inadvertently set this shooting into motion?

How any of us become who we are has long been a fascination of mine, a central thread in the knot of who *I* am. It is one of the reasons

I first gravitated toward journalism. "Take me back to the beginning," I ask early on in most interviews. "How did we get here?" And it's a game I play, when stuck in traffic, or standing at a boarding gate, or sitting in a hospital waiting room, scanning the collected strangers who, for the moment, occupy the same center of some cosmic Venn diagram. *What's your story?* I wonder. *Have our paths crossed before? Where did your path start?*

Finding that start is a lot like unrolling a ball of yarn. Not the kind that's round and plump, where a tug at one end quickly reveals the other, but the kind that's a colorful tangle, all knotted and entwined. My stepfather's was that second kind of yarn. Finding where it started was a journey backward, through coincidences and connections, deliberate choices and chance events, global forces and intimate interactions.

A few moments became signposts while I unraveled this epic string, and they shaped the book you are about to read. The first was the evening I messaged the police officer's children. "This may be one of the stranger Facebook notes you have ever received," I began. "I am a journalist, and I am researching a story from 54 years ago, about the night your father was killed. It's a night when my family and yours intersected, briefly and indirectly, and I am writing about the effect of that one night on three generations of three families."

The second moment occurred on the moonless evening when I stood in the crumbling ruins of an Illinois prison, shining a flashlight into the room where a warden's wife had been killed more than one hundred years before. I had come there with her great-great-stepgranddaughter, and together we retraced the steps of the woman for whom she'd been named.

While these children and great-great grandchildren were filling gaps beyond their memories, I was seeing how rarely we know the whole of a story, yet how directly we are the results of things we know nothing about. My stepfather changed the lives of the officer's children, but until I sent my note, they had no idea he even existed. The murder of the warden's wife had shaped the life of her great-great-step-granddaughter—and the next century of American prison life—but until we met, she didn't fully understand how.

And then came the pandemic. When Covid-19 first shut down the planet, I happened to be in the middle of writing the 1918 chapter of this book. Nineteen-eighteen was a ghastly year. More people died from the 1918 flu epidemic than from any other natural event in human history up to that point—far more than died in World War I, which was fought during the same year. And yet, I told my husband, "I would rather be back in 1918. I know how that ends."

History divides neatly into chapters only in retrospect. In real time, we experience it as a jumble, a hurtling through the darkness by the light of an inadequate lamp. Our lives are prologue to one version of a story, and epilogue to another. We don't get to see the "all of it"—or even the "more of it"—unless a family historian, or a fervent genealogist, or a somewhat obsessed author comes along to map the whole.

"One day closer to whatever comes next," my family and I would toast at dinner each night during most of 2020. I wrote this book in that same spirit, telling the tale as it was lived. The people in the early chapters are the forebears of the people in the later ones, but they don't know that yet, might never know. At the start they have no idea that a train crash in Altoona, a motorcycle race in Chicago, or a blazing fire in a prison tower in Joliet will start a cascade that will set the stage for a police officer's death. They can't know which family will eventually "create" the cop, which his killer, and which my stepfather. They could not know how some doors were closed to some children even before they were born.

Each one of us has a similar story, in which we will never be certain what part we play. We shape history even as we are shaped by it. We owe thanks (and blame) to our ancestors, and an explanation (and apology) to our descendants. We are actors without a script, travelers without a map, gamblers who don't know the odds.

We have less influence over who we are now than we believe. And much more power over the future than we think.

THE COSENTINO FAMILY

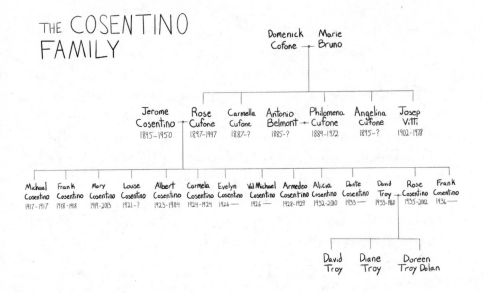

Domenick Cofone — Marie Bruno

Jerome Cosentino 1895–1950 — Rose Cufone 1897–1997
Carmella Cufone 1887–?
Antonio Belmont 1885–? — Philomena Cufone 1889–1972
Angelina Cufone 1895–?
Josep Vitti 1902–1978

Michael Cosentino 1917–1917
Frank Cosentino 1918–1918
Mary Cosentino 1919–2013
Louise Cosentino 1921–?
Albert Cosentino 1923–1984
Cormela Cosentino 1924–1924
Evelyn Cosentino 1926—
Val Michael Cosentino 1926—
Armedeo Cosentino 1928–1929
Alicia Cosentino 1932–2010
Dante Cosentino 1933—
David Troy 1933–1960 — Rose Cosentino 1935–2002
Frank Cosentino 1936—

David Troy
Diane Troy
Doreen Troy Dolan

THE TROY FAMILY

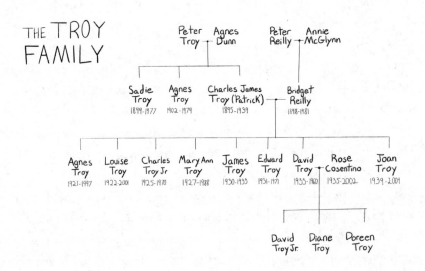

Peter Troy — Agnes Dunn
Peter Reilly — Annie McGlynn

Sadie Troy 1899–1977
Agnes Troy 1902–1979
Charles James Troy ('Patrick') 1895–1939 — Bridget Reilly 1898–1981

Agnes Troy 1921–1997
Louise Troy 1922–2001
Charles Troy Jr 1925–1970
Mary Ann Troy 1927–1988
James Troy 1930–1933
Edward Troy 1931–1971
David Troy 1933–1960 — Rose Cosentino 1935–2002
Joan Troy 1939–2004

David Troy Jr
Diane Troy
Doreen Troy

THE TARLOV FAMILY

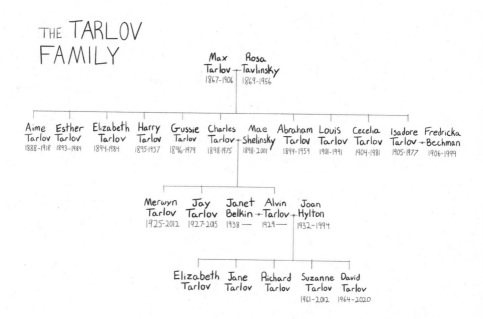

Max Tarlov 1867-1906 — Rosa Tavlinsky 1869-1956

Aime Tarlov 1888-1918 | Esther Tarlov 1893-1984 | Elizabeth Tarlov 1894-1984 | Harry Tarlov 1895-1957 | Gussie Tarlov 1896-1979 | Charles Tarlov 1898-1975 | Mae Tarlov — Shelinsky 1898-2001 | Abraham Tarlov 1899-1954 | Louis Tarlov 1901-1991 | Cecelia Tarlov 1904-1981 | Isadore Tarlov 1905-1977 | Fredricka Bechman 1906-1999

Merwyn Tarlov 1925-2012 | Jay Tarlov 1927-2015 | Janet Belkin 1938- — Alvin Tarlov 1929- | Joan Hylton 1932-1994

Elizabeth Tarlov | Jane Tarlov | Richard Tarlov | Suzanne Tarlov 1961-2012 | David Tarlov 1964-2020

THE DeSALVO FAMILY

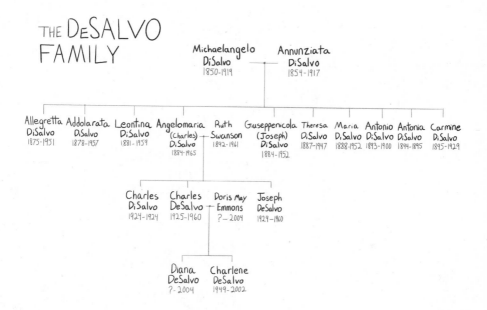

Michaelangelo DiSalvo 1850-1919 — Annunziata DiSalvo 1854-1917

Allegretta DiSalvo 1875-1951 | Addolarata DiSalvo 1878-1957 | Leontina DiSalvo 1881-1959 | Angelomaria (Charles) DiSalvo 1884-1965 — Ruth Swanson 1892-1961 | Giuseppenicola (Joseph) DiSalvo 1884-1952 | Theresa DiSalvo 1887-1947 | Maria DiSalvo 1888-1952 | Antonio DiSalvo 1893-1900 | Antonia DiSalvo 1894-1895 | Carmine DiSalvo 1895-1929

Charles DiSalvo 1924-1924 | Charles DeSalvo 1925-1960 — Doris May Emmons ?-2004 | Joseph DeSalvo 1929-1960

Diana DeSalvo ?-2004 | Charlene DeSalvo 1949-2002

Family trees by Talia Fishman

GENEALOGY OF A MURDER

Friday, July 8, 1960
The Tarlovs
Madison, Connecticut

THEY LOOKED LIKE ANY YOUNG MARRIED COUPLE AT THE CON-
necticut shore a few days after Independence Day. He, compact and
bespectacled, reclining in a sling-back canvas chair in the shade of a
striped umbrella that proclaimed THE MADISON BEACH HOTEL. She,
on a blanket spread for her by an attentive summer worker, her red
hair tucked beneath a floppy hat, book in hand, squinting in the brilliant midmorning sun. A casual glance would give no hint that he had
brought her to this beach because he could not think of what else to
do, how else to help.

So there he slumped, with a stillness that could have passed for
relaxation, though he didn't remember the last time he had felt
relaxed. He was leaden with exhaustion, the kind that usually comes
with being a new doctor, except he was not exactly new at this, and
his patients were not the usual kind. Back at home, he spent his days
not in scrubs but in an army captain's uniform. He did his work not
in a hospital but in a prison. His patients didn't come to him sick; he
made them sick, bringing tropical illness to a federal penitentiary on
the outskirts of a midwestern city as part of a military experiment. In
a few years his work would be called unethical, but he didn't know
that yet. On this summer day, he was certain his work was good, his
cause was right. He was a man who was very precise about doing the
right thing.

His was also the exhaustion that comes with being a new parent, his youngest just six months old. Decades later he would come
to understand that the birth of that child, the third of what would
soon be five children, was the beginning of the end. And that this

moment, shortly before noon on July 8, 1960, would forever mark for him a new beginning, the result of an unremarkable life choice that changed everything.

But that would come later, just as so much had already come before. Right now, all he could see was that the pretty young woman on the blanket to his right was fragile and unmoored. Since the newest baby, theirs had been airless days and sodden nights—postpartum depression, trickling milk production, endless breast infection. He'd come to fear for her sanity and their children's safety. Quietly frantic, he'd blocked off his two weeks of vacation time from the army and the lab, driven his family the 950 miles from Chicago to Norwalk, Connecticut (with an overnight, and spaghetti and meatballs, in Beaver Falls, Pennsylvania), and left the three children with his parents. ("A three-year-old, a two-year-old, and a half-year-old with the grandparents," he would say long after those children were grown with children of their own. "I still can't believe I did that. Cattle yes. Kids no.") Then he'd headed fifty miles farther east in that same wood-paneled station wagon, to this beach, where he'd hoped, though didn't really expect, that the sun, sand, and sea would bring back the woman he'd wed.

To tend to one cry for help sometimes means to turn away from another, and as his wife read and dozed, the doctor's thoughts returned to the insistent voice on the phone a few days earlier. The caller's words, as they now looped through the doctor's head, were benign, even banal, the usual kinds of questions asked by one who has learned a friend has arrived in town for an unexpected visit.

"You're here?

"For how long?

"Can I see you?

"When?"

"There's so much to talk about."

But behind the words there had been a discordant note of something more—a need, an attempt to veil an urgency. Now that tugged at the edges of the doctor's thoughts, bringing them back to his work when they should have been on his family. And that phone call, though draped in the trappings of friendship (the caller might even have believed it was a friendship) was about work. The caller, until three weeks before, had been in the doctor's charge in the prison lab. One serving his country, the other serving time. One hoping to find a cure for malaria, the other hoping to learn a trade and, with that, a way out. The man was a natural, the doctor quickly saw. "Not your typical prisoner," he would say, though were he to be as honest as he always tried to be, he had to admit that his life had not included exposure to a lot of prisoners and what he actually meant was *not like I expected any prisoner to be.*

"Smart," he would say. "The smartest I'd seen. A quiet man, but so smart."

And what he meant by that was probably *smart like me.* Or *I see some of myself in him.* Or *there but for the grace of God . . .*

The doctor had come late to embracing his own smarts, and the prisoner was a mirror in some unsettling ways. Conversations never got so personal that the doctor knew for a fact that the man had also felt like a seedling through the asphalt during his early years. But he could swear—or was he projecting?—that he heard echoes of his own life in the trainee's quiet tone, deliberate manner, and meticulous ways; saw something familiar in his bent for history, science, and poetry. What was a man like this, a man so like himself, doing in this locked and barred place? During the day, the two, doctor and prisoner, worked side by side. A team. Expectations clear. Machinery oiled. Differences blurred. Then the evening signal sounded, and one man was returned to his sparse cell, while the other returned to his suburban home, his sad wife, his young children.

One day the prisoner asked the doctor for help. The parole board would soon be hearing his case, which would be strengthened by a recommendation from a respected someone. Neither man expected that parole would be granted—the convict was only nine years into a ten-to-seventy-year sentence for armed robbery—but he wanted to feel satisfied that he'd given it his best try. Might the doctor be inclined to put in a good word?

The doctor considered this question as he did everything else: carefully, examining every possibility. Since he'd started work in the lab at the Stateville Penitentiary near Chicago, he had seen prisoners leave and then return. Every other Friday the doctor would have his usual haircut just before noon in the prison barbershop, where the barbers were also convicted of felonies, but trusted with razors and scissors. The doctor would take his usual seat before the glass wall that faced into the arrival hall, where, at the same time each week, a new crop of prisoners was brought from local jails to begin their penitentiary sentences.

Every week at least a few were returnees—and they waved to him as they marched past the barbershop window. "Hey doc," they'd say, oddly a little glad to see him.

In this way the doctor of medicine had become a student of recidivism, of the data, such as it was, about who returns to prison and who goes on to "make good" and lead a law-abiding life (or at least, not get caught). Three things, he found, seemed to make all the difference: a job upon release; a safe place to live; a move out and away from where you'd committed your crimes. Rather than just write the "good word" the convict had asked for, the doctor set out to find him the three things—the job, the home, the fresh start. Calling on friendships from his own years of training at a hospital near his parents' house in Norwalk, he secured a position for the convict in the medical lab there and a room to rent in a staff dormitory.

"He is ready to assume his place as a useful citizen in society," the doctor wrote. And he had believed it completely.

The parole board did, too, and just over a month before the doctor spirited his wife away to the beach, the State of Illinois handed the convict his freedom, along with a suit of clothes, fifty dollars in new bills, and a bus ticket from Chicago to Norwalk. Early reports were that he was a model employee, punctual, polite, good at his work. Then came that haunting phone call, the memory of which nagged at the doctor still.

He sat on his beach chair, still but agitated, watching the horizon but not focusing. On a nearby blanket were three men in bathing trunks and T-shirts—retired Catholic priests, it would turn out, a detail the doctor would remember for decades, though not one that mattered. One of the three was reading the morning's newspaper. Attempting to distract himself, the doctor scanned what he could see of the headlines: KHRUSHCHEV HINTS PACT IN FALL WITH EAST GERMANY and KENNEDY SNOWBALLS TO NOMINATION. But those were only the lesser stories of the day. Bannered above them both: CITY COMBED FOR SLAYER OF POLICEMAN, and in smaller type, BANDIT WHO HELD HIM UP A "PRO," BARTENDER SAYS.

In the crackling heat, Dr. Alvin Tarlov suddenly felt a chill. The shooting had happened in a town so very close to Norwalk. And armed robbery was what had put Joseph DeSalvo in prison in the first place. But no. His trainee—his friend?—was not capable of killing; he had learned his lesson, paid his dues, shown himself worthy of trust. And this cop, David Troy, whose photo gazed out from underneath the headlines—a man who, the doctor would learn, had been born less than ten miles up the coast from him, his youngest child also just six months old—he could not have died by the hand of a man the doctor had helped release.

Three men. Alvin Tarlov, Joseph DeSalvo, David Troy. How did one become the doctor, one the cop, one the convict? How did three lives loop, spiral, crisscross, and careen through the decades, then collide on this Independence Day weekend, with one dead, one at large, and one wondering whether he had somehow caused it all?

Dr. Tarlov sat on his beach chair, his body purposefully still, his eyes fixed on the pixilated image of Officer Troy, his mind swirling with seeds of questions, ones that would take root and grow over the years. How things that seem to be in your control, are out of your hands. How lives you know nothing about, even those lived generations before you were born, can completely change your own. How tiny moments, stacked and layered, become sweeping history. How sometimes what seems wrong can turn out to be unexpectedly right. And how trying to do the right thing—being careful to do the right thing—can go so inexplicably wrong.

1900s

May 1906
Max and Raisel Tarlov
On the No. 18 Train

THE NO. 18 TRAIN, ALSO KNOWN AS THE *CHICAGO MAIL*, WAS ON the wrong track at the wrong time and moving at the wrong speed on this otherwise unremarkable Friday night.

It had kept to its expected schedule for most of its eastbound run along the Pennsylvania Railroad's busy Middle Division: through Pittsburgh at 4:50 p.m., East Liberty at 5:00, Greensburg at 5:46, Johnstown at 6:57, all places where the whistle of the train still set the pace on this fourth of May 1906. It was still on time at Altoona, pulling away at 8:20, its seven cars loaded with twenty-two passengers, seven railway crew, eleven postal workers, and eighty-four horses, all due next into Harrisburg at 11:35. Minutes after that, there was a problem.

Not a problem on the No. 18. That would not happen for another hour. At 8:24 p.m., the problem was with a different eastbound train, seventeen miles away, near Union Furnace. The air hose running between the cars of that train began to leak, causing the Westinghouse air brakes to quickly apply. In a screeching cascade, twenty-one cars tumbled off and over the main line. Somehow no one was killed, but the derailment blocked one of the busiest stretches in the northeast on the busiest night of the week.

The No. 18 was headed toward that second train and would not be able to pass. More worrisome, if the No. 18 wasn't warned, it would run headlong into the twenty-one-car blockade, adding to the mess.

There was a plan for moments like these. Signal tower operators, responsible for routing trains safely through the busy rail network, would telegraph warnings to stationmasters, who in turn would write out new orders and hand them to the conductors as their trains came through. When No. 18 neared Elizabeth, the train was signaled to stop. Then the stationmaster handed engineer John L. Fickes instructions to retrace his steps and return the train to Altoona. The news must have frustrated Fickes, who was headed home to Harrisburg, this being his last run until Monday.

It takes some maneuvering to turn a train around. The crew uncoupled the locomotive, moved that engine up to a turntable, and rotated it 180 degrees. Once it was facing west, the locomotive ran past the train on a parallel track, switched back onto the main, then backed up and recoupled to the cars on the opposite end. The locomotive now faced west toward Altoona, but the order of the cars remained unchanged, so that what had been the rear of the train was now immediately behind the engine. Such runaround moves were not uncommon, but they were tricky to execute.

Even more complicated were the orders Fickes received upon reaching Altoona: keep the train reversed and head due south, detouring eastward over the Petersburg cutoff before rejoining the main line past the site of the derailment. Cut-offs were found throughout the Pennsylvania Railroad—branches off the main lines, some leading to a less traveled town and terminating, others ambling for a while then merging again. Many, like the one the No. 18 was ordered to take through Petersburg, were just a single track, and those were particularly dangerous. The most obvious risk was that "passing tracks," where one train could stop and wait "in the hole" for another to pass, were infrequent and required precise communication. On the Petersburg cutoff, this risk was magnified by the crooked, winding lay of the track and the many spots where visibility was limited to a single train-length. Which was why the No. 18 paused in Hollidaysburg and took on D. P. Shaffer, a local "pilot" who worked the cutoff regularly and knew it better than Fickes, who had never run that stretch before. Following the new orders, Shaffer headed slightly north into Springfield Junction, waited for a westbound train to pass, and finally, once a clear signal was given, shifted onto the Petersburg cutoff chugging due east, ostensibly on unimpeded track.

✦

MAX TARLOV WAS NOT supposed to be on the No. 18 at all. When he left his Connecticut home earlier in the week, he had told his family he would be back before sundown on Friday, the start of his family's Sabbath. His plan had been to travel only as far as Jersey City. There he would wait for his latest shipment of horses, then continue back east with them through Manhattan and up to the station in South Norwalk, Connecticut, which was just a few minutes away from the ten acres where he lived with his wife, Raisel, and their many children.

Max had a knack for horses. He had learned to break the wildest ones back in Russia, outside his home city of Grodno, back when he was Max Tarloffsky, the name that had been his family's for generations. Barely nineteen and almost completely on his own, he had found his way to the coastal town of Norwalk, Connecticut, in the late 1800s and surrounded himself with horses while waiting for Raisel and their firstborn to join him a few months later. In the two decades that followed, he had built a thriving business, traveling to Montana and Wyoming, corralling stallions and shipping them east where he could train them to pull buggies. He had an uncanny sense for which in a wild herd could best be tamed. Once they were, he sold some and rented out others.

Of the eighty-four horses in what had been the front cars of the No. 18 and were now bringing up the rear, twenty-six belonged to Max Tarlov. He had chosen them months earlier, then headed home on a faster passenger train and waited back in South Norwalk for his purchases to make their way out by freight. This shipment came east from the Badlands, resting a few days at the Consolidated Stock Yard in Chicago, before continuing through Pennsylvania. For reasons Max never learned, the animals were held up in Pittsburgh, which he discovered only after he had waited in vain in Jersey City. Since the horses were apparently not coming to him, Max got on a train and went to them, meeting up with T. J. Scott of Fort Wayne, the agent contracted to accompany this shipment. They untangled the problem, and by Friday afternoon, Max Tarlov, T. J. Scott, and all twenty-six horses were on the No. 18 going east, scheduled to reach Harrisburg before midnight. He hadn't telegrammed home about the change, probably because telegrams cost money, and he would only be late by less than a day. His Raisel would surely understand, after twenty years of marriage, that few journeys ever go exactly as expected.

Max made his living with horses, and by this spring night in 1906, he knew that the majestic animals, which had kept civilization running for thousands of years and had kept his own family housed and fed for twenty of those, were soon to become just a quaint bit of history.

The reason would be less that engines were faster and more that they were cleaner. Later generations would forget this in their romanticizing of the simpler past, but horses were the kind of threat that would one day be called an "environmental hazard." In a city like New York, where there were upward of 200,000 horses when Max first immigrated in the 1880s, more than 4 million pounds and forty thousand gallons of equine waste were deposited on the streets and in the stables every day. (In 1900 a futurist predicted that by 1930 the piles of horse manure in New York would reach the third floor of buildings.) This brought flies, which brought disease. The horses also caused accidents—more, per capita, than would cars in the twenty-first century—because not only did horse-drawn carts crash into each other, but the horses themselves bit, kicked, and trampled. And all that before accounting for the smell.

None of these dangers were new; Julius Caesar had banned horse-powered travel during daylight hours in ancient Rome due to the noise and congestion they created. But two things had changed very recently: a turn-of-the-century wave of immigrants—one that included the Tarlov family—made cities more crowded, which magnified all the above; and the mass manufacture of the automobile, which meant that for the first time in history, there was a door-to-door alternative to the horse.

In 1900 only eight thousand cars had been registered to drive on the mostly dirt roads of the United States. By 1906, as Max's train chugged through Pennsylvania, there were 108,000, and by 1920 there would be more than 8 million. The average cost of a new car that year was $500, against an average annual income of $879, and the former was dropping while the latter was rising. If it is a father's job to prepare his children for the world, how was Max to do that in a world about to be transformed? He and Raisel had spoken in the past year of their hope that their younger children could get an education that would allow them to be more than horse wranglers in a world of machines. Already Aime, nineteen, was on his way into his father's business; Esther, seventeen, would marry shortly; and Lizzie, fifteen, soon after that. Harry, twelve, would end his studies to earn some money, and nine-year-old Gussie and two-year-old Cecelia were just girls. But what of Charlie, eight, Abe, seven, Louis, four, and baby Morris, whose first birthday would be in ten more days? Max had started adulthood in America with nothing. How could he ensure that his children would not have to do the same?

As the No. 18 rolled through the darkness toward the Petersburg detour, Max Tarlov fell asleep. At about nine-forty-five, Scott walked down the center aisle to stretch his legs and saw his boss lying across the third row from the rear of the car, a coat rolled under his head as a pillow. Scott continued past, out to a small platform for a smoke.

Already outside was J. D. Conover, a traveling salesman from Manhattan.

"Do you have a stogie to spare?" Conover asked.

Scott did.

"Thank God," Conover said as he struck a match.

A few moments later, Mrs. W. N. Trinkle of Duncannon, Pennsylvania, came out for a breath of air. The group was soon joined by the train's brakeman, F. M. Harder of Harrisburg, who'd brought his own tobacco. That's about all the small space could hold, and the foursome smoked and chatted into the night.

✦

WHILE THE NO. 18 was coming east, the No. 21, known as the *Chicago and St. Louis Express*, was headed west, also toward the derailment, but from the other direction. It had left Harrisburg at 7:37 p.m. for Altoona, where it would have arrived at 10:54.

But at 9:53 the crew received instructions to detour over the Petersburg cutoff instead. "Go Slow," the orders said. Engineer John Lehr, who had been running the train thus far, had firsthand experience of how winding and dangerous that one-track cutoff could be, but he had never operated over it at night. So he surrendered the throttle of the No. 21 to fellow engineer James T. Dougherty who, at sixty-four, was the one of the eldest, most experienced men on the line.

Dougherty wore his tenure in his stooped posture and weathered face. He was a survivor in a profession where a long career was far from guaranteed. (In 1900, 2,550 railroad employees died on the job.) He credited that to his respect for his "presentiments," as he called them. Three years ago, he'd had a bad feeling while approaching a hill and had stopped the train just before the large pile of debris blocking the track on the other side came into view. Then only three weeks ago, he'd stopped just short of a tree across his train's path.

And now, half an hour after taking control from Lehr, he had the feeling again. Signal towers on this line had letter names, and the one where the westbound Petersburg cutoff narrowed to a single track was designated as Tower ST. Dougherty remembered the order saying that ST was where he was supposed to stop and wait for a clear signal to proceed. But as he approached, he noted that the tower operator at ST had set the lanterns to "slow," not "stop." Wondering if he had misread, Dougherty double-checked and saw that what he'd read as ST could also be SJ, which was the name of the next tower, the one where the track expanded again to two ways. That, coupled with the "slow" indication, led him to conclude that he had the right of way. His "presentiment" had been right again, he thought. There *had* been a potential problem; the No. 21 would have sat, perhaps for hours, waiting for another train to pass, while that other train waited, just as long, for the No. 21 to appear.

So he proceeded on ahead, running the eight-car train due west along Petersburg cutoff, carefully hewing to the instructions to "go slow."

✦

ON THE REAR PLATFORM of the eastbound No. 18, at about ten-forty-five p.m., T. J. Scott stubbed out his cigar and reentered the passenger car. He could feel the train heading up a hill—the large one just outside of Clover Creek Junction, a steep grade combined with a sharp curve. As the train climbed, Scott made his unsteady way past Max Tarlov, still asleep in the third row from the rear of the car. Then he continued up toward his own seat, in the third row from the front.

He was almost there when the No. 18 crested the hill and gathered speed downgrade. As D. P. Shaffer, the guest engineer in the locomotive, looked out at the darkness ahead of the boiler, he saw the headlight of another train burst through the blackness, frighteningly close.

"Jump!" Shaffer yelled, as the two locomotives collided.

"The engines reared up like fighting stallions and fell over on their sides," the next morning's newspaper would say.

Shaffer and the fireman next to him did jump, landing on rocky embankments to the north and south of the track. Fickes, the engineer who had turned this train around hours earlier, did not jump but was thrown through a window upon impact. (Later Fickes, with his right shoulder dislocated and his head wounds bandaged, would say proudly that he'd "stuck to his engines.")

Over in the No. 21—which had been accelerating to take the hill—Dougherty also jumped, his presentiment taking on new meaning. So did Lehr, the engineer who'd handed him the controls before the cutoff.

A shattered watch pulled from the rubble would show that the time was 10:46 p.m. T. J. Scott, still standing at the moment of impact, was thrown to the floor, and from there he could see the heavier mail car of the No. 18 rocket into and then over the rear of his lighter passenger car—peeling off its roof, essentially swallowing it whole. It stopped just a row or two short of where he lay.

Scott kicked a hole in the side of the splintered wooden car and crawled out. The crash had knocked out the lights on both the No. 18 and the No. 21, so he heard the anguish before he could see it. The vestibule where he'd smoked his cigar minutes earlier was completely gone. The acquaintances he'd smoked with were all dead. The mail car had landed at an angle, with its front end dipped toward the track and its rear end raised off the ground. Its contents—the mail, the men—spilled out. The five mail workers who survived were frantically digging through rail and timber for the six who would not.

A group of Italian laborers, living in a shanty encampment nearby, heard the crash and came with lanterns. A passenger, a traveling salesman from West Fairview, Pennsylvania, grabbed one of those lanterns and headed down the track, in the direction from which the No. 18 had come, because he guessed there was a train a few miles behind that had to be warned. There was. The engineer of that train, pulling freight but no passengers, saw the man and his lantern in time to stop. Together they cut the rear helper engine loose and ran it backward into the nearest depot, where all four doctors in town were roused from their beds and brought to the scene, along with axes, shovels, medicines, and blankets.

More help came from Altoona, from Williamsburg, from Huntingdon. The rescuers were soon covered with the blood of the dead and injured. Victims found alive were sandwiched between lifeless bodies. In a passenger car, a survivor, badly injured and intractably trapped, begged to be killed by those trying to rescue him. In the postal car, a doomed young man called out plaintively for his wife before he finally became silent.

In the third seat from the rear of the first car, Max Tarlov looked like he was sleeping. But his coat, still under his head like a pillow, was blackened with his blood.

It was Scott who found him, counting windows back to where he estimated his boss must be then chopping a hole in the side of the train car. Two other men had been thrown on top of Max by the collision, and they were unconscious but alive. Max was not breathing. Scott carried his body clear of the wreckage, wrapped it in a blanket, and laid it on the ground.

Twelve passengers died at the scene that night—six passengers and six postal workers. Four more died on the way to the hospital. Thirty-seven people were injured, most of them seriously. Nearly all the injured and all but one of the dead were on the No. 18, in the first two cars, which but for a leak in an air hose hours earlier and miles away would have been in the rear. Dougherty suffered only bruises but was forced out of his railroad job after an inquest determined that he misinterpreted a tower and misread a *T* as a *J*, causing the crash. Both locomotives were demolished, as were seven of the combined fifteen cars on both trains.

The three rear cars filled with horses did not leave the track. But for a few small scratches on their forelegs, not one of the animals was hurt.

✦

VERY EARLY IN THE MORNING of May 5, 1906, a reporter from the *Sentinel* newspaper arrived at the Tarlov home in South Norwalk, Connecticut. Louis Koslofsky, the apprentice employed by Max to help nineteen-year-old Aime care for the horses and mend the buggies, answered the door of the large white shingled farmhouse and learned that Max Tarlov was dead. Despite nearly two decades in America, Raisel had never become comfortable speaking English. When this visitor arrived just past dawn, it fell to her children to translate the news. Her disbelief was clear in any language. Her husband was due home shortly, she said. This must be a mistake.

The reporter showed the family the Associated Press alert that had brought him to the house. "Man answering description of Max Tarlov killed in wreck," it read.

Impossible, said Raisel. Her husband was in New Jersey retrieving his horses, not in Pennsylvania on an upended train.

The reporter returned to his office, double-checked with the Associated Press, and came to the door again. "Tarlov's death doubtless. OK" this telegram read. "He was on eastbound passenger train as a passenger. OK."

Max's body arrived at the South Norwalk station at 12:10 on Sunday morning, May 6. One of his own horse-drawn carriages brought his casket home. His funeral was held in the front parlor, followed by a procession to the Hebrew Cemetery in the western part of town.

MR. TARLOV'S HEAD CRUSHED IN TRAIN WRECK AT ALTOONA, read the headline in the morning edition of the *Norwalk Hour* newspaper.

"An honest man and a resident worthy of any city," read a eulogy written for the afternoon edition.

Morris Tarlov's first birthday came a week after Max died. The boy would not remember his father, but Raisel would make sure he had one last gift from him—an education. Days after Max's funeral, his new widow gathered their children together and set out the family's goal for the next seventeen years. Wherever the road ahead might lead, they would get Morris to college.

Then, having changed her littlest son's future, she also changed his name. Morris became Isadore, a name popular among Jewish immigrants because it sounded traditional, yet also modern and American—a name for an educated man. Another very new, very American custom, was to add a middle name. And a very old, very Jewish tradition was to name children not after the living but after the dead. Now that his father was gone, Raisel gave her youngest boy the middle name Max.

1914
Charles and Joseph DeSalvo
Chicago

IT WAS LIKE FLYING.

They swirled around the oval of track, a length of a quarter or a half of a mile, in a place that had been called the Velodrome back when it was for bicycles but was now called the Motordrome. They rode new-fangled contraptions called motorcycles, reaching speeds of eighty or one hundred miles an hour, until the crowds were a blur to the rider and the rider but a roar and a glimpse to the tens of thousands who came to see this newest of sports.

Originally invented to pace bicyclists during races, the machines were basically bikes that had been stretched so that a motor fit where the pedals used to be. They had no suspensions to absorb the bumps and rattles, no gears to shift upward or down again, and—the part that made it exhilarating or suicidal, depending on your point of view—essentially no brakes. Careening around pie-pan-shaped structures, where sides were banked up to sixty degrees, riders were all but parallel to the ground as they took the curves on oil-slicked wooden planks, the first humans to feel g-forces and, sometimes, to pass out from the effects. "Lords of the Boards," they called themselves. Spectators, standing on the rim of the pan, looked down onto the deities from above. Not infrequently a rider overshot the top of the wall and landed in the crowd.

The crashes—between motorcycles and other motorcycles, between motorcycles and the track itself, between motorcycles and onlookers—were spectacular. The crashes, in fact, became the attraction: *Buy a ticket! Witness death!* It wasn't long before headline writers renamed the arenas "Murderdromes," which only increased sales.

And the riders—why did they keep at it? Why does a man do anything that might end everything? Each generation has some version—duels, wars, sailing for uncharted lands, riding at unfathomable speeds on machines with no brakes—and each way of tempting death reflects the times. This one fit nicely in its moment, a symbol for a nation built by millions who were too restless, too striving, to stay where they were born. The Murderdrome racers reflected the same need for forward motion that propelled so many across the sea. They'd left behind an old world in order to usher in a mechanized and industrialized new one, where today had to be bigger, stronger, flashier—faster—than the day before. The metaphor was apt but left one question unanswered: Were the men atop the bikes racing away from something, or toward it?

Charles and Joseph DeSalvo were doing both. The twins had been born in 1884 in southern Italy, though back then they were called Angelomaria and Guisspecola. Their town was Pietrabbondante, which means "stones in abundance" in Italian, so named because it was tucked beneath massive boulders at the foot of Mount Caraceno, a place rich with archaeological wonders. But history doesn't make crops grow, doesn't keep cows fed, and doesn't undo a tradition that divides land again and again over the generations, until the slivers cannot sustain the households that called them home. The stark truth of life in Pietrabbondante was you are what your parents were—the work your father did, the land your father left—and in that way, the ancient ruins on the outskirts of their village were a reminder less of a grand past than of a dusty, crumbling future. For Michal and Annunziata DeSalvo, the only thing that remained to inherit was the urgency to leave.

They did so before their twins were a year old, crammed into steerage on the airless lowest decks of the SS *Italia*, where the metal bunks were three tiers high and fresh drinking water was rationed and monitored. The family settled in the densely packed Halsted neighborhood of Chicago, with ten thousand other Italian immigrants, the largest concentration in the United States. Michal DeSalvo found a job slaughtering cows in the city's stockyards. It was not pretty work, but it supported the five children he and Annunziata had brought from Italy, and the three others who would be born in America.

Although their parents might have seen the Halsted neighborhood as a destination, a goal, Charles and Joseph saw it as a place from which to escape. On this side of the ocean, you need not be what your parents were, and it was Joseph who took the first steps toward something bigger. He had been ahead since he'd been born—at 10:15 on the morning of June 19, waiting for Charles to show up at 10:20. Twenty-four years later he was the first of the duo to see his name in the newspapers, for coming in last—but finishing!—during a 1908 motorcycle ride from Chicago to New York. Next, he took first place in the first race of 1909: a hundred-mile, eleven-hour slog from Chicago to Aurora, starting one minute after midnight on New Year's Day.

Charles joined the sport a year later, once the action had moved from public roads to private stadium tracks and the point had shifted from endurance to daring. This was more his speed. Did it rankle that he was seen, at least at the start, as second to his minutes-older twin? "Charles DeSalvo of Chicago, brother of Joe DeSalvo, raced here today," said *Motorcycling Magazine* of the Independence Day competition at the Lima Driving Park on July 4, 1911. Before a crowd of four thousand, Charles placed first in four races, second in two, and third once, coming away with an extra twenty-dollar purse for most wins of the day.

By 1911, motorcycle racing was the most popular sport in America. Seen by more spectators than major league baseball (and certainly more than professional football because that league had not been created yet), it was an arena for gladiators with engines. Some of the blood was drawn by the track itself, which was built of rough-hewn pine slats and guaranteed to hurl splinters and pop tires. Bikes had open valves, and riders squirted them with oil midride, which dripped onto the track, creating slick spots. Periodically those pud-dles were scrubbed with lye, which did absorb the oil but also dried into a poisonous powder, to be spun into toxic clouds by spinning wheels. This made it even tougher to see on tracks lit by temperamental electric lamps, which flickered and often blew completely, leaving riders to race in the dark.

Much of the danger, though, came from the riders themselves. Winning required recklessness, so they wrestled while they flew, hooking opponents' handlebars, grabbing their sweaters, doing all they could to knock the next guy off his bike while wearing little to nothing that counted as protective gear. Advantages were short-lived in this arms race. When one rider added corrugated tires to his arsenal, the better to shoot sprays of pebbles at those behind him, everyone else soon did the same, until nicked goggles and bloodied faces became just another expected risk.

The justification for all the pain was possible fame and fortune. The new sport would tantalize Angelomaria/Charles and Guisspecola /Joseph with a way out, high risk for a slim chance of reward, just as boxing would do for Jewish immigrants in the 1920s, or the military for boys from farm hinterlands during the Second World War, or football and basketball for young Black men in the 1960s and '70s. In the world within the Motordrome, young men whose parents were Irish or Swedish or Italian or German, young men who were born in the United States and some who were not, all gathered, literally and figuratively, at the same starting line. They raced away from the drudgery of the factory or the farm, the insults, and the limitations of their parents' world. They raced toward a future of which their ancestors could not even have dreamed.

Daily newspapers covered every race in their sports pages, and weekly glossies like *Motorcycling Magazine* ran breathless stories about the biggest names, who were like the film stars of their day: "Texas Cyclone" Eddie Hasha, who entered his first race on a bike "borrowed" from the Harley Davidson shop where he worked in Dallas—one of the first in the nation—and won before his employers even knew it was missing; Charles "Fearless" Balke, who invited reporters along on his two-day train ride from Chicago to Los Angeles to propose to his girl "Snooks," whisking her into a taxi and then to the minister waiting at church: Balke's fiercest competitor, Quebec-born Jake DeRosier, who had a running tally of broken bones that made national news, with one reporter noting there were not "two inches of skin without a scar" anywhere on his body.

New though it was, the world of motorcycle racing was already a two-tiered system, with professionals like Hasha, Balke and DeRosier at the top, receiving lucrative salaries and first-class travel arrangements from the manufacturers who provided their machines. Below them, and gazing upward, were the "trade riders," amateurs who were thrown periodic treats by sponsors, usually merchandise rather than money, a tease that a real contract was around the corner.

Joseph and Charles were trade riders. The Excelsior Motorcycle Company, based in Chicago (and eventually to be bought by bicycle builder Ignaz Schwinn), gave them motorcycles (which cost about $200 at the time) and a chance to fight their way to the front. This gave them a taste of celebrity—greeted at the entrance of Chicago's brand-new fifteen-thousand-seat Riverview Motordrome by clusters of women, offering handkerchiefs as tokens of luck just as ladies had done for knights entering jousts. It was just enough of a taste to keep them returning, battered and bruised, for more. They were *this* close.

And so it went for more than a year. The DeSalvo twins elbowed fiercely against other trade riders and against each other, accumulating small victories, triumphant moments, scrambling to turn those into a new life. There was Charles in an ad in *Cycling* magazine listed as one of several "famous record making riders" whose Excelsior 7 motorcycles used Herz Magneto engines. Two days later the attention was on Joseph, in another Excelsior ad bragging he'd brought home "three more gold medals and one large cup" at a race in Toledo, Ohio. Then Charles again, rating a photo in the *Fort Wayne Daily News*, standing near his bike looking dour (though he likely meant to look serious) with the caption "DeSalvo with his speedy Excelsior on which he made a mile in 40 seconds."

The most attention either brother would receive in that first year came at the end of what had been a good day in Janesville, Wisconsin. Charles had taken first in an earlier three-mile, then come from behind to place second in a ten-mile so exciting that "the crowd stood up and cheered DeSalvo when he crossed the line" milliseconds ahead of the third-place rider. His last and final race that day was to be a "novelty" one, meaning Charles was enough of a name in the sport that the track's owner created a mini-spectacle in which he could star. The plan was that he and a hometown boy named O. Perry both complete a first mile, then jump off their bikes to down a full glass of fresh-squeezed lemonade, then get back on and complete a second mile.

Charles made it to the lemonade table first, quickly chugged his drink, and had just stepped back onto the track when Perry drove toward him at nearly ninety miles per hour, somehow losing control of his bike as he neared. Charles was thrown to the ground in the collision, his head hitting the wooden boards with a crack so loud it was heard in the stands. Perry flipped over his own handlebars, bleeding so seriously that two doctors in the crowd raced to his side and accompanied him to Mercy Hospital. Charles, somewhat dazed but outwardly unscathed, got up and finished the race. Describing the scene, the *Janesville Daily* anointed Charles the "amateur champion of the world," not a title that officially existed.

Still, the brothers remained trade riders, risking their necks while waiting for a call to the professional leagues that always seemed to be just one race away. Even as they became more reckless, the sport managed to outpace them. A short time earlier, jumping back onto his bike after his "lemonade crash" might have been enough to earn Charles a contract, but by the autumn of 1912 it was tame compared to the mayhem fans had come to expect. Just after Labor Day that year, chaos erupted at the Newark Motordrome in New Jersey, when nineteen-year-old pro star Eddie Hasha, overcome by g-forces, fainted at the wheel but did not fall off. His bike, still clocking ninety-two miles per hour, continued "riding the rail" at the top of the track for a hundred feet before being pulled downward. A young boy who had stuck his head out over that rail for a better view was decapitated as the motorcycle—unconscious rider still attached—flew past. Three more boys were killed as the bike slammed into a pillar, sending Hasha hurtling into the crowd, where he, too, died instantly. The bike continued to fly, falling back onto the track and hitting a rider in the shoulder; he died four hours later at the hospital, bringing the death toll for the night to six. Dozens more were injured as the crowd of five thousand spectators trampled each other trying to get to the exits.

By the end of 1912, Joseph DeSalvo quit—yet another thing he did before his twin. He was a newlywed by then and likely saw echoes of his own life in stories of how Eddie Hasha's young widow had wanted her husband to stop—had a premonition that he would be hurt—but he'd wanted to build their nest egg just a little bit more. Hasha's death likely influenced Joseph's departure in less direct ways as well. Public opinion was turning, increasingly seeing racing as something done not by daredevils and heroes but by brawlers and thugs. A man like Joseph, who would go on to build a business and raise three children, would have instinctively distanced himself from what editorial writers were calling a "bloodthirsty" sport.

Not so much his brother. Charles went all in, betting that at worst he would go out in a headline-filled, Hasha-like blaze of glory, and at best he would show them all and be a rich man someday. He did not calculate the odds of landing in the middle, spending his life as an almost-was and an also-ran.

Charles kept riding even as the motordromes that had been built in a rush were gradually closed, including the one in Newark, which never reopened after Eddie Hasha's death. Charles kept riding after Jake DeRosier, who'd briefly filled Hasha's spotlight, bled to death on an operating room table in early 1913. And he kept riding when "Fearless" Balke inherited DeRosier's place in the headlines. Ever a trade rider, Charles DeSalvo rode and rode, literally round in circles. Balke's contract earned him $20,000 a year (more than $500,000 in current dollars), with first-class accommodations for travel, while DeSalvo made, at best, fifteen dollars a week at the slaughterhouse plus whatever freebies manufacturers threw his way. Balke's 1911 wedding reception included a fifteen-piece orchestra, five silver champagne fountains, and coverage on both the sports and the society pages, while DeSalvo wore his Sunday suit in March 1914 to quietly marry Ruth Swanson, one of the few remaining women waving lace-trimmed handkerchiefs at the stadium entrance.

On June 7, 1914, Balke and DeSalvo were both at the track for practice runs. Balke had been tempted to cancel and spend the cloudless, summery Sunday with his wife, but his mechanic had been working on ways to bring his bike to full speed seconds faster, so Balke decided the safe thing to do was to check out the changes in advance of the next weekend's race. Charles DeSalvo did not have his own mechanic. But he rarely gave up a chance to practice, and by midday both he and Balke were at the stadium ready to roll.

Balke was among the first on the boards, and as he mounted his newly souped-up bike, the trade riders gathered in the stands to watch the man they all envied. Balke roared off, easily catching up to two other pros who were also doing a few laps. The smoke from their engines mixed with the dust from the track, limiting Balke's visibility to just twenty feet. He was used to that. In response, he did what years of racing had taught him to do—when you can't see, you just ride the mental image of where everything was before it was obscured. Then, from somewhere behind the smoggy veil, he heard an engine backfire. He was used to that, too, and kept hurtling forward.

That was when he hit it—head on, with no chance to brake. Inexplicably there was another vehicle on the track, a lumbering two-ton metal roller, pulled by horses, designed to pack down the dirt for upcoming races. Someone—years of lawsuits would not determine exactly who—had scheduled this maintenance in the middle of the test runs. The smoke and dust made the machine invisible; then the backfire spooked the horses, who reared up and stopped directly in Balke's path. The racing superstar slammed into a wall of solid metal at seventy miles per hour.

The track manager and his assistant barricaded themselves inside their office, while an angry crowd of dozens of riders, both amateur and professional, gathered outside. Somewhere in the group was Charles DeSalvo.

"Next they'll tell us to race through a minefield!" one of the racers shouted.

"Come out here, you son of a bitch!" yelled another.

Eventually the manager did come out, just long enough to deliver the message that "the show must go on."

Charles DeSalvo did not race that night. He did not race again. Like his brother years earlier, he had many possible reasons for quitting. Perhaps he was sobered by Balke's death, no longer willing to accept the risks. Perhaps his new bride, Ruth, seeing photos of yet another motorcycle widow, insisted that he stop. Maybe he realized that even in the vacuum created first by DeRosier's absence and now by Balke's, sponsors were not lining up at his door to redirect their riches his way. Now in his thirties, he might simply have felt too old.

For Charles, walking away from racing did not serve as a new start or a burden lifted. Always a step or two behind his siblings, he became more so, drifting from job to job—quitting the stockyards, working variously as a truck driver, a carpenter, a factory hand. He was always restless, always disappointed, often angry. His brothers and brothers-in-law were succeeding—as the head of a furniture company, a factory foreman, the founder of a thriving funeral home—but he was stalled. What made him different?

If that question had been asked a century later, geneticists would look to his DNA, which was identical to that of his twin, but also influenced by his different experiences. Psychiatrists would look to the toll each disappointment took, eventually creating a mindset, a personality, an entrenched direction. Forensic pathologists would wonder about his brain and the effect of years of blows to the head while wearing only a worn leather cap. They would use terms like *traumatic brain injury* and *chronic traumatic encephalopathy* while wondering how an energetic ambitious young man had transformed into one who was always listless and moody. A subset of all these scientists, the epigeneticists, would ask whether the changes to one brain, one genetic code, one single self, might be sent down to the next generation.

Whatever the catalyst—dreams denied or blows to the head; psychic disappointment or a single crash on a motordrome track after downing a glass of lemonade—something changed Charles DeSalvo, and the effects of that change would be felt beyond the next generation.

1914
Rose Cufone and Bridget Reilly
Rose, Italy, and County Cavan, Ireland

ROSE CUFONE COULD NOT WAIT TO LEAVE THE TOWN FOR WHICH
she was named. The Tarlovs had exited Grodno in fear (fleeing rulers who did not want them), and the DeSalvos had bid farewell to Pietrabbondante with regret (abandoning land that could no longer support them). But sixteen-year-old Rose Cufone—the most beautiful and most spirited of the many Cufone sisters—practically danced away from the three-thousand-soul village of Rose, atop a mountain in the province of Cosenza, in the region of Calabria, in the southeast of Italy.

At the heart of that village was a church, at the outskirts, a convent, and between the two a well-worn dirt road, dusty where not covered with fresh mule dung. To a child, the whole world seemed to fit in that village: the mills along the river, pressing olives and grinding flour; the piazza in the central square, where a band played for the midsummer feast of the patron saint Lawrence; the stone and slate house Rose shared with her mother, three sisters, and an assortment of chickens and goats. As soon as she was old enough, five, maybe six, Rose went to work, doing things like clearing rocks, gathering wood, or picking olives and learning to balance them in a basket atop her head. By the age of eight, she had graduated to employment by the local bricklayer, carrying bags of cement in place of olives.

She did all this without a father. Dominick Cufone had headed for America in 1898, the year Rose was born, the year Raisel Tarlov joined Max in Norwalk with their only child, two years after the

DeSalvos arrived in Chicago. What pittance Dominick might earn farming someone else's land would never be enough to make a good marriage for Rose or her three sisters, so he left his wife and daughters behind, with promises that he would send for them to join him.

At first, he kept his word. In 1903, when the eldest, Carmella, turned sixteen, Dominick booked her passage to a place called Connecticut, and she was married there two years later. He did the same when Philomena turned sixteen in 1905. But when Angelina reached that age in 1912, it was Philomena, now married and a young mother, who sent the money, not Dominick, who had not been heard from for several years. This left the youngest, Rose, alone with her mother, in a house that felt both too big and too small, the town both familiar and suffocating. She was more than eager to leave.

Then in 1914 came an answer to a literal prayer. Philomena reached out again from across the ocean offering to bring Rose to Connecticut, to join the sister she hadn't seen for half a lifetime, the brother-in-law she'd never met, and the father who was a question mark. No invitation had come for their mother, Maria, who at first forbade the trip. Rose took refuge in the village church and refused to come out until the Lord changed her mother's mind. When the girl left for the train station in Montalto Uffugo, more than an hour away by foot, she had to have guessed it was a final goodbye.

✦

WHILE SIXTEEN-YEAR-OLD ROSE CUFONE was begging to set sail in the spring of 1914, another girl, not quite sixteen, was begging to stay at home. The land Bridget Reilly did not want to leave was Ireland—the county of Cavan, parish of Drumlumman, townland of Clonloghan, barony of Clanmahan, a place of lakes and hills. She lived there with her father, Peter, her mother, the former Annie McGlynn, and her five younger siblings. All eight of them shared a two-room shack, with a thatched roof and mud walls, plus an outhouse, a piggery, and a cowhouse, on a small patch of intermittently arable land.

Bridget's father had been baptized in the Mullaghoran Church in

Cavan, and her parents had been married there. The couple had buried two babies in the Mullaghoran cemetery: Edward, dead of whooping cough at four weeks old, and an even younger infant boy, who had
died before he had been given a name. Those two tiny Reillys shared
the graveyard with so many who'd come before, including those who
had not survived the Great Hunger, the potato famine of 1845 to 1851,
when Bridget's grandparents were still small. The famine had caused
a steady exit that would continue long after the potatoes returned,
and County Cavan, which had almost 250,000 inhabitants at the start
of the hunger and just below 175,000 when it ended, had fallen to
fewer than 100,000 the year Bridget was born.

One of those out the door was Bridget's uncle, William Reilly, her
father's elder brother. He'd headed for New York in 1891, when he
was twenty-eight, and found work as a guard at a newly built golf
course north of Manhattan. At first Peter had stayed behind for his
elderly mother, who felt tied to the land where she raised her babies to
adulthood. Then he'd stayed for his wife, who felt equally tied to the
land where she buried two of her own.

Despite his inability to leave (or perhaps, because of it) Peter was
determined that his children would go. He had nothing for his sons to
inherit, since he leased rather than owned the land on which he lived
and farmed. And he had no dowry for his daughters. Irish girls needed
Irish husbands, and because of the exodus Bridget was more likely to
find such a man in America than in Ireland. This math was why more
than half the Irish who sailed for New York after the turn of the century were women, traveling alone, something not true of immigrants
from other nations.

It takes an urgent something to decide to leave your native land. A
sense of adventure, a feeling of desperation, the imagination to envi-
sion an unseen life, the clarity that the risks of staying are greater than
those of leaving. Max Tarlov had all these, as did the DeSalvo boys on
their motorcycles, and Rose Cufone staging a sit-in in her tiny church.
Bridget Reilly had none. Her home, cramped, miserable, and degrading as it may have been, was her home. The devil you know is better

than the devil you don't, she believed. And Bridget Reilly, a devout Catholic, had a healthy fear of the devil.

It was a few months after her fifteenth birthday when she made her way to Granard, the town nearest her family's house. From there she traveled to the port city of Queensland where, saying she was eighteen, she used money sent by her uncle William to book passage on the SS *Oceanic*—a fare of three Irish pounds, the price of a young calf at the time or a year's lease on a small farm.

Her ship set sail for New York on May 14, 1914, and she traveled as Delia Reilly, the last time she would use that nickname. She is described on the manifest as a petite passenger, five foot one, with fair skin, light brown hair, and blue eyes. While Rose Cufone would tell later generations how she prayed until her mother let her leave, Bridget would describe how her parents sent her away—and how she would never forgive them for it.

✦

WHEN ROSE CUFONE ARRIVED by train in Greenwich, Connecticut, her brother-in-law was waiting at the station. Antonio Belmont, who already went by Anthony when out among Americans, headed the household that Rose was about to join. Was she surprised that her father was not there to greet her?

Philomena, she learned, had not told Rose everything. That may have been because, having never learned to write, Philomena's words would have to pass through the hands of someone literate on the way to becoming a letter. Then, because neither Rose nor her mother had ever learned to read, those words would have to be read aloud by yet another someone. And a lot of what Philomena had to say was not an outsider's business.

First, there was their father. Sometime after Carmella, the oldest Cufone sister, arrived in America, and before Philomena, the next to oldest, came, Dominick had built himself another family. Leaving Carmella in Greenwich, Connecticut, he moved to Hackensack, New Jersey, with a woman named Anna Sabio, and he now called her his wife, though there was no record of a marriage, at least not one that his descendants would be able to find. The new Mrs. Cufone clearly knew about Dominick's family in Italy—his nearly grown daughters kept arriving by ship every two years, after all—but Rose's mother would never officially hear of Anna, nor of the ten children Anna and Dominick would have.

Then there was the sad state of Philomena's own marriage. Their father, the bigamist, had been uninterested in supporting his second newly arrived daughter, leaving Philomena to support herself. She did so as a weaver, working a loom at a woolens factory in Greenwich, becoming one of the twenty thousand Italian immigrants employed in the mills of Connecticut, Massachusetts, and Rhode Island in 1910. Philomena spent twelve hours a day, six days a week at the mill, and that was where she met a go-getter named Antonio Belmont.

Antonio also came from the village of Rose—a *Rosetano*, like Philomena. He'd arrived in America when he was seven and had been working at the mill since he was eight, with a starting wage of fifty cents a day. Over the next ten years, he taught himself how to repair the machines and was known on the floor for his knack at keeping the looms running, which kept the factory going.

Young Antonio Belmont was a romantic. Proposing marriage to Philomena—she was eighteen, he was twenty-two—he made promises. They would have children right away, first one boy, then one girl, at most two boys and two girls, but not so many that they wouldn't all be grown in twenty years. Then, as he turned forty, an age he was certain he would reach though few of his relatives had, he and Philomena would take the fortune he was sure to have by then, and they would travel.

Philomena agreed—two boys, two girls, explore the world—and they were married on October 27, 1907. At first everything went according to plan. Antonio bought them a home in the Cos Cob neighborhood of Greenwich, an Italian enclave that was 15 miles south and far more rural than the larger town of Norwalk, where the Tarlovs had settled. In Cos Cob Philomena gave birth to a son, Sabato Belmont, on the night before Independence Day in 1908. He was an adored child living in a joyful home. He could stand at the age of six months—or so his father boasted. His mother sewed outfits that made him look more like a little man than an infant—tiny vests and matching suspenders like his papa's—and he was all spiffed up and waiting every night when the trolley brought Antonio home from the mill.

Come winter, seven-month-old Sabato became sick; six days later he died. Antonio blamed Philomena because she had nursed the baby while she herself had bronchitis. Neighbors and friends filled the house in shared sorrow. "You're gonna make a lot more," they told the grieving parents, who did make more—in fact there would be eleven more—but none would be boys.

Year after year Philomena would become pregnant, and with each pregnancy, she would go to church every day, sometimes twice a day, and pray for a son. Rose's prayers to see America might have been answered in church, but Philomena's prayers to have a boy went unheard. In 1910 she gave birth to Carmella. In 1912, Yolanda. In 1915, Helen.

Along the way Antonio stopped talking about retiring at forty and traveling. He moved his family to a new house, on Harold Street, where there were no memories. He began to bring Philomena's sisters over from Italy, so his wife might have some comfort from home. As each one married, he invited the next. Rose was the last to make the trip, and it soon became clear she'd arrived to a planned life. She was expected to do as Philomena had done—work at a local factory, marry within two years. Philomena had already secured the job and chosen the man. The first—making hats—was fine with Rose, certainly an improvement over carrying cement back in the village. But the man . . .

With her thick auburn hair, gold-flecked eyes, ample curves, and the sparkle that comes from believing the best of your life is before you, Rose Cufone had come to America to have fun. There were always young men wanting to take her to dances and parties. There was at least one older man, too, nearly twenty years her senior, married with five children. A natural flirt, Rose would stand on the back wall that divided her yard from his and wave across the distance, sometimes adding a rustle of her skirt and a little bit of a dance.

None of these men would amount to anything, Philomena warned. Not like her own choice for her sister, a *Rosetano* named Gerolimo Cosentino. (He had not yet changed his name to Gerome.) A cousin of Antonio's mother's second husband, he counted as "family."

Miraculously, this available match had some money. The Cosentinos owned the mill back in Rose, grinding wheat from village farms into flour for local bread. In addition, Gerolimo was self-educated and brilliant, speaking several languages, though the exact number was unclear. He boasted of five or six; as his children grew, they learned this was but one of his many exaggerations. He definitely read at least four: Shakespeare in English, Dante in Italian, Nietzsche in German, and books about horticulture in French.

Best of all, at least to Philomena, he had steady work. Arriving in Greenwich the year before Rose, Gerolimo earned a reputation as a tree surgeon and landscape designer on nearby estates, becoming part of the cohort of Italian men who were building the foundations of a changed Connecticut. These masons, carpenters, gardeners, chauffeurs, mechanics, and plumbers made possible the new estates on what had very recently been farmland.

Rose was not impressed. She found him pompous. He didn't like to dance. He was too quiet. He always had his nose in a book. "I would rather cut off my right arm" than marry him, she said. Sometimes, for variety, she would threaten to "cut off both my hands." In return, Philomena would call her sister *capatost*, meaning one who is extremely hardheaded. It was not that Philomena didn't understand romance. To the contrary, she had married for it, and now she paid the daily cost of her own lost fairy tale. Much better that her sister make a sensible match.

✦

LOW EXPECTATIONS INOCULATE AGAINST disappointment, and Bridget adjusted to America more easily than Rose. She never counted on the embrace of family, the attention of suitors, or the achievement of dreams. She was prepared for menial work and few reasons for happiness, and so there were few surprises.

Her uncle managed to send money for her fare, but he had no intention of supporting her further, and she wound up finding the first of a series of domestic servant jobs way up in Stamford, Connecticut, where a rising Irish middle class was eager to hire less established Irish girls as household help.

Where Norwalk and Greenwich were still towns, Stamford was racing to become a city. By 1914 it boasted nearly 35,000 residents, a third of them foreign born. The Anglo-Saxon Protestants who had looked down on the first waves of Irish Catholics by now aimed their disdain toward those who were darker, poorer and from farther south. Italians, Jews, and Slavs were coming at their highest rates in history while the Irish immigration numbers were at a century-long low. The Irish benefited by seeming more familiar, less "other," less threatening, to the xenophobic eye. Copper-haired, blue-eyed, and quick to blush, Bridget Reilly would have benefited more than some.

Bridget, who had been among the most destitute and desperate back in Cavan County, was not displeased to find someone else in that role here in Stamford. She accepted what she was told by the newly middle-class Irish whose homes she cleaned and whose meals she prepared. Italians were lazy, unclean, and unworthy, her employers explained. It was an unexpected relief to take pride in her origins.

For six years she lived in a series of Irish homes, sending some of her salary back to support her mother and father and some to her uncle William to reimburse him for the transatlantic voyage she had not wanted to take in the first place. During her years as a domestic, she rarely talked about her life back in Ireland. Once she could put her domestic work behind her, she didn't talk about that much either. But the lessons she learned ran deep. For the rest of her life, she would believe that some immigrants, some people, were superior to others. And she would make clear to her children that parents deserved respect. She had obeyed her parents, despite her own wishes. Dutiful children did as their parents said.

1915
Warden Edmund Allen
Joliet Prison
Joliet, Illinois

THE BELL IN THE WARDEN'S PRIVATE BEDROOM BEGAN TO RING shortly after dawn on that warm June morning. Warden Allen was out of town, and 6:10 a.m. was far earlier than his wife, Odette, usually rose. Also out of the ordinary was the fact that her "houseboy," Joseph Campbell, wasn't answering.

The Allens' apartments occupied the third and fourth floors of the central tower at the Illinois State Prison at Joliet, fifty miles southwest of Chicago. More commonly called just Joliet Prison, it was built before the Civil War by teams of prisoners who would be its first occupants. The castellated building looked like something out of the legend of King Arthur or, perhaps, the imagination of Bram Stoker. Constructed of honey-colored limestone that glowed gold in a certain light, it had everything short of a dungeon and a moat, though the solitary cells in the basement might be considered the former, and the marshy mess left after each rain certainly resembled the latter. Joliet Prison had been designed back when the goal was to do more than prevent escape. Its evocation of gothic horror was meant to send a message to those looking in as well as out—to deter crime by being a place no sane man would want to enter.

It was not usual for a warden to live within the prison itself, but Edmund Allen was not a usual kind of warden. His father had been warden of the same prison twenty years earlier and had left disillusioned by his inability to reform the place; this was a chance for the son to succeed where his father had been thwarted.

Another woman might have been rattled to wed a wealthy widowed businessman only to find herself the wife of a jailer, but Odette Maizee Bordeaux Allen calmly packed up her household, her husband, her new teenage stepchildren, and Mike, her French bulldog, and created a comfortable home in the otherwise inhospitable place. In the cellblocks to either side, eighteen hundred men were stacked in cells so narrow that their armspan reached both walls. They had no heat, one bare bulb for light, and a tin bucket that they emptied once a day into an odiferous pit at the edge of the prison yard. Inside the warden's tower, however, there were large fireplaces, chandeliers, and indoor plumbing. Odette filled the eleven rooms with her husband's family heirlooms, and she softened the echoing stone with her tapestries and rugs. She even brought her own piano. The men took to calling her "the angel of Joliet"; her trained singing voice could often be heard through her large open windows, which faced the bare recreational courtyard.

Some prisoners came to know the Allens particularly well because the twenty-five-person staff of cooks, waiters, bakers, pantry men, linen room men, barbers, chauffeurs, and valets were all serving long sentences. A few brought practical experience—the butler had spent years working at one of Chicago's best hotels before killing his brother-in-law in an argument—but that was not a requirement for these jobs. They were all chosen because the warden trusted them.

How a nation treats its prisoners is a reflection of its soul. In Dickensian England, the "workhouse" movement saw hard labor as a way to repay the wages of sin. In colonial America, punishment was designed to send a public message, humiliation by way of stocks and pillories, and worse, by way of the hangman's noose. The Pennsylvania Quakers stressed prayer, isolation and penitence and began the use of the word *penitentiary* rather than *prison*.

The first Warden Allen, inspired by the prison reform movement of the late 1800s, saw punishment as secondary and reformation as primary. The reform movement of the early 1900s, which forced him out, emphasized punishment in the form of strict discipline. Allen's successor, "Iron Man Murphy," had ordered that prisoners walk in lockstep from place to place, that their heads be shaved, that silence be observed at all times, that uniforms be scratchy wool even in the summer. And now came a second Warden Allen riding yet another penological wave—the belief that simply being imprisoned was punishment enough, and that a man's time behind bars should be spent readying him to return to society.

Now two years into the job, Edmund Allen had infused Joliet with that worldview. He had implemented an honor system, dividing prisoners into three categories. The lowest level was for those Allen described as "defiant, desperate, untrustworthy," not (yet) ready to change. In the middle were men who wanted to be better but did not trust themselves enough to swear that they would not escape. The highest level was for men who did make that pledge—raising their right hands on a Bible before the warden. They were then moved to a two-thousand-acre farm a five-hour train ride away, where they lived in tents, grew crops, built state roads, and were watched over by guards without guns. Two flags flew over the property, the American flag, with its thirteen stripes and forty-eight stars, and a blue cloth onto which Odette had sewn white letters that read CAMP HOPE.

All Joliet's prisoners, therefore, were preparing for life upon release. Allen's policy of trust seemed well-founded, as not a single man had tried to escape from Allen's Honor Farm and not one member of his domestic staff had tried to leave or harm him. As the men readied for release dates, Allen took it upon himself to find them jobs, his recommendation based on the work they had done in one of the many "factories" he'd established within the Joliet compound. Of those for whom employment was found, more than 80 percent "made good" and did not return to prison for another crime. Local employers began writing to the warden offering to hire his "graduates."

Allen's success received national attention, and the first anniversary of his arrival at Joliet was marked by a visit by the rumpled, shaggy, and eloquent defense attorney, Clarence Darrow. Darrow's most historic cases—defending two brash young men who killed just to prove they could commit the perfect crime, and defending an embattled young teacher who taught what he believed was proof of the evolutionary origins of humans—were more than a decade away, but he was already a legend among the men gathered to hear this speech. He was seen as a champion of hopeless causes, winning some of them, and even in losing making his iconoclastic point that the law was too often used to bludgeon when it would be better used to uplift.

In his off-the-cuff hour-long speech during his Joliet visit, Darrow praised Allen for reaching the correct conclusion to an age-old question: Why do some men go bad, and what is to be done about it? Not coincidentally, Allen's was the same conclusion Darrow had reached.

"Most all the people here are poor and have always been poor, have never had a chance in the world," Darrow said of the hundreds of prisoners seated before him in the windowless basement chapel. "The first great cause of crime is poverty, and we will never cure crime until we get rid of poverty; until men have a chance to make a decent living in this world."

Prison, as traditionally designed, is certainly not the cure, he said. A doctor treating a patient with typhoid fever would "find out what kind of water the patient had been drinking, or what kind of milk, and if it was [infected] he would clean out the well so nobody else would get it." But the law, when called on to treat the same patient, "would give the patient sixty days in jail." If the prisoner "gets well in two weeks," the law "would leave him there until the sixty days were up; and if at the end of sixty days he was still sick, he would let him out anyhow because his time was up."

Darrow suggested each "patient" should instead be treated as a singular result of individual circumstance. "We didn't all of us exercise good judgment when we chose our grandfathers and our grandmothers," he said. "We all have peculiarities of character, disposition and feeling, as sent down to us through certain environment and certain surroundings that were all powerful, and we struggled along as best we could."

He went on to praise Warden Allen for understanding the complexity of the human condition, and for realizing that just as each convicted man's past led to prison, his time in prison could shape his life after he leaves. Then he ended with a stern warning: "If something serious were to happen under the system that the Warden is trying to carry out . . . it will hurt you. It will hurt every other person all the world over who is suffering in prison and looking for deliverance."

That warning haunted Allen for all the following year. He understood Darrow to mean that his changes were ephemeral, likely to dissolve with the first setback. One trusty gone wrong, one uprising, one scandal, and all would be lost—unless the warden could build a firm foundation under his reforms. Allen became obsessed with a literal foundation—a building that would stand as a philosophy rather than just a prison. His proposed Stateville Penitentiary, on a site four miles from Joliet, would not look like a medieval castle but rather would be a laboratory for the latest thinking in criminal justice. It would have indoor plumbing and central heating, fewer small spaces, more natural light, a modern infirmary, and an expanded library, amid rolling acres where prisoners could grow fresh vegetables for use by a nutrition-conscious kitchen.

He carried the designs for his new prison back and forth as he lobbied Illinois state officials in Springfield. His plans called for a prison unlike any other in the world: five circular structures—four cellblocks and one communal dining hall—connected by walkways and tunnels. The buildings were "panopticons," a word first used by philosopher Jeremy Bentham in the late 1700s to describe a tower with a circle of cells around a central watch station. *Panopticon* means "all seeing" in Greek, and in Bentham's vision a single guard could have eyes on hundreds of cells. Because that guard would be shielded behind "blinds and other contrivances," Bentham wrote, prisoners could never tell who was being watched at any given moment; they'd best behave as if someone were always watching.

Bentham was long dead, and panopticons were still mostly a theory when Edmund Allen became inspired by the idea that architecture could be used to make people better. Many Illinois politicians, however, were not as impressed. Facing entrenched resistance, Allen traveled often—arguing for funds in the state capitol, speaking to citizens' groups who protested the use of tax dollars to "coddle" criminals, touring other modern prisons. During the rare stretches when he was home, he rose early and retired late to cram in all he had missed while away.

He developed an ulcer. Odette worried as she watched her husband turn pale and gaunt, one fist constantly pressed beneath his ribs. Finally she insisted he take a break and arranged a ten-day stay at the West Baden Springs Hotel, built around the natural hot springs in West Baden, Indiana. The resort was remedy wrapped in luxury, with a soaring dome over its two-hundred-foot atrium and a fireplace big enough to burn fourteen-foot logs. The warden could spend his days bathing in medicinal waters and his evenings dining and dancing. Odette had ordered several new gowns from her seamstress for the black-tie dinners.

The new prison was the reason for the ulcers, the ulcers were the reason for the new gowns, and the gowns were the reason the couple did not travel together to West Baden on the morning of Saturday, June 19. Odette's seamstress had been ill, and the dresses weren't ready. It was decided that the warden would leave first, and Odette would follow the next day, her trunks filled with new clothes. He was not happy about the plan and would later recall the moment of fear that had nearly led him to turn around and return to Joliet. What had the conductor of Max Tarlov's train called it? A presentiment?

But he proceeded as scheduled, making one secret stop along the way. At Odette's favorite jeweler, he picked up a surprise he planned to give his wife as a thank you for her tender concern—a $3,000 ring, centered by two four-carat diamonds. She, in turn, completed the alterations on her wardrobe, and while her husband was on the nine-fifteen p.m. train to Indiana, she was at a double feature at the downtown cinema with her two stepchildren—seventeen-year-old Katherine and nineteen-year-old Jack—and a college friend of Jack's who was visiting for the weekend. At ten-forty-five, the warden's chauffeur drove the foursome back to the prison apartments, where they spent an hour in the parlor dancing to music from their new gramophone, which newspapers would later describe as "a talking machine."

At about eleven-fifteen p.m., Odette asked the "houseboy" on duty, a twenty-nine-year-old prisoner named Joe Campbell, to prepare a snack. Campbell was in the fifth year of a one-year-to-life sentence for murdering an employer who had fired him. Relatively new to the household staff but already a favorite of the family, he had been personally chosen for this job by the warden, who was taken with the "negro" man's manners. His work ethic had impressed Odette, who had written letters to the Joliet Prison parole board recommending that Campbell be released. She planned to testify at his parole hearing when she returned with her husband from the spa.

Campbell brought sandwiches, along with a sheet of paper on which the Allens wrote the times they wished to be awakened come morning. Then Odette announced she was heading up to bed.

The Allens' apartments were fitted with a network of bells. There were two call buttons in the couple's bedroom, one next to each of the twin beds. The warden's rang in the butler's pantry, to summon his valet, while Odette's rang in the servants' den, to summon Campbell. When the pantry bell began to sound early on the morning of June 20, the rest of the staff was, at first, annoyed that Campbell didn't respond, then alarmed when they began to smell smoke. A guard ran out to the prison yard and into the boiler room, where he grabbed the cord of the fire whistle and yanked it so hard, it sliced the skin on the palm. The fire siren began to wail, heard by the eighteen hundred inmates who had gathered for breakfast. Practice drills had become common at Joliet since Warden Allen arrived—men were being trained to fight fires upon release—and the breakfasting crowd assumed this was but another. The handful of prisoners assigned to the volunteer fire squad walked quickly to their rendezvous point in the boiler room, but the rest continued eating.

The fire team gathered axes and hoses and marched to the warden's tower. They followed the smell of smoke to Odette's bedroom and found the staff banging on the locked door. There was a shattering crash from within as a bedroom window blew out from the heat. Still, the bell kept ringing.

The men used an ax to break through the center panel of the door, then reached through and turned the key on the other side. The smoke that poured toward them was so dense and hot that the firefighters were driven back, gasping. Two of the group—the fire captain and the warden's chauffeur—inched inside, feeling their way. The posts of both beds were still standing, but the mattresses were badly burned. Shining their electric lamps downward, the men realized with horror that they were looking at the charred, lifeless body of Odette Allen.

During all this, the ringing continued. Now the men realized why. The wooden covering over the wire that ran between the call button and the gong in the outer hallway had been burned off, creating a short circuit. The fire captain reached over and clipped the wire. Finally, mercifully, the bells were silenced.

The Joliet coroner was out of town, but his deputy arrived quickly and reported that Odette had been hit over the head before she died, probably with the heavy earthenware jug found in pieces next to the bed. A jug of similar description was missing from the back of the closet in the Allens' bedroom, meaning it was likely an inside job. Odette's $2,000 wedding band was still on her finger, and her purse, with several hundred dollars inside, was still on her dresser, meaning robbery was not the motive.

Suspicion quickly focused on Joe Campbell, who admitted to being in the bedroom that morning. Mrs. Allen had rung for him shortly after six a.m., he said, with a request for the morning papers. He returned with Sunday editions of the *Tribune*, the *Herald*, and the *Examiner*, along with a cup of coffee and a pitcher of ice water, all of which he put on her nightstand and remains of which were found after the fire. Then she said she was going back to sleep and wished to be awakened again at nine. Campbell said he left with Mike, the French bulldog, for a walk across the prison yard, outside the prison walls, and about a hundred yards up the drive near the greenhouse,

meaning he could not possibly have heard the bell when it started to
ring at 6:10.

He knew where the alcohol jug was, he said, but he had not touched
it since the morning before, when he'd helped Mrs. Allen pack her
husband's grip and watched her mix a lotion of witch hazel and alcohol for after his shave. And no, he was not the only one with access
to that jug. And why would he ever want to hurt Mrs. Allen when she
had been so good to him, writing letters to the parole board for him
and planning to testify for his release in just one week? Anyone who
said he did anything wrong, anyone giving evidence against him—
why, they were just trying to curry favor and get paroled themselves,
he said. He loved Mrs. Allen as much as anyone.

While Campbell and the others were being questioned, the deputy
warden, Lawrence Ryan, reached Warden Allen via long distance at
the West Baden Hotel.

"We've had a little accident here," Ryan said. "A fire in the warden
house. Mrs. Allen is—is hurt."

"Will she die? Is it that bad?" he demanded. "Can you keep her
alive until I get there?"

"We'll try," said Ryan, thinking news like this must only be told
in person.

It took several hours to get a train out of West Baden, and then the
warden nearly missed the 5:44 connection in Englewood. Waiting for
him at the next station was a group of friends who broke the news
that Odette was dead. The warden reached into his pocket and took
out the diamond cocktail ring, the surprise his wife would never see,
and slipped it onto his own pinky finger. "Something told me not to
go without her," he said.

When he finally arrived at the prison, he had to be supported on
either side as he entered the apartment tower. He paused at the thresh-
old of what was left of his bedroom, entered for barely an instant, and
emerged in tears.

There was a riot in the dining hall the next morning.

After breakfast on Monday, more than two hundred prisoners,

whether out of grief for their first lady or fear that the liberties they'd come to enjoy would be curtailed, swarmed the yard chanting "Give us Campbell!" They would have lynched him if they could have reached him. By early afternoon they'd made their way to where he was being held in solitary confinement and tried to batter down the cell door, leaving only after guards fired shots into the air. Campbell was moved to a county jail cell across town for his protection. His parole hearing, scheduled for the next week, was canceled.

Odette was buried on Tuesday. The whole city all but shut down for the funeral. By day's end, seventeen hundred of Joliet's eighteen hundred prisoners had signed the pledge of condolence and loyalty to the warden. It read in part:

Dear Friend,

The eyes of the world are upon us, and we must succeed. We, each and all of us, pledge ourselves to wipe out the tragic stain by making your work here a success. The hour has struck and we cannot retreat. Come back to us and we will build together a real honor system as a fitting memorial to your dear departed wife that will be more lasting and enduring than marble or bronze. We will build men in whom honor is not dead and will not die.

Our hearts are heavy with grief and our eyes are wet with tears because of this sad tragedy.

For your wife and our friend, Odette Allen, words cannot express our thoughts nor speech contain our love.

YOUR BOYS

Soon afterward the warden quit, not directly because of his wife's death but because of a fight with the governor over the origins and effectiveness of the honor system. Joe Campbell, the only Black convict on the domestic staff, was convicted after a three-week trial and sentenced to hang, even though evidence was circumstantial at best and despite his protests that he had no motive.

Eventually Joe Campbell's sentence would be commuted to life in prison, and he would die at Joliet in 1950. Part of the reason for the commutation would be a public statement from Edmund Allen asking that mercy be shown to Campbell, whose guilt, Allen believed, was less than clear. "The man who killed my wife must die," Allen said. "But I must be sure that I have the right man." He still trusted his prisoner.

1920s

After the Great War
The Tarlovs and the DeSalvos
Norwalk, Connecticut, and Chicago

RAISEL TAVALINSKY TARLOV WAS TOUGH. IN THE STORIES THAT would be told from one generation to the next, by her children to their children and onward, that's the word they would use, distilling her, as family stories do, to the essence of herself. She looked tiny and fragile—she had not reached five feet tall next to her husband's five foot three—but anyone who thought she was a pushover never thought that more than once.

Raisel had made the journey from Grodno to America alone with her one-year-old son, Aime, and her descendants liked to share the story of that arrival as it had been told to them. When it was her turn to step off the ship, Raisel was stopped by an immigration officer who said she could proceed but Aime had to stay behind. She sat herself down in protest, wrapping her firstborn son under her coat and crossing her arms across the bulge to hide him. Finally, word reached the captain, and he came to intervene, insisting that mother and child be allowed to enter the United States together because he and his ship had places to go.

That was one version. There were others. That the ship had been sinking, or the ship had been aflame, or that Raisel grabbed Aime and fled down the gangplank, the crew in pursuit. She did everything but dive off the deck and swim for shore. The only problem with those stories is that there are no records of a ship foundering or burning in New York Harbor around the time when Raisel arrived. And even the most benign of the tales runs up against the fact that immigration rules did not separate babies from their mothers in the 1880s.

Something apparently happened to Raisel that day—something

frightening that made her fear she would lose Aime. But she spoke Yiddish, some Russian, no English, and the specifics seem lost in translation. Less important than what happened, though, is what generations of Tarlovs came to *believe* happened. There are the facts and the truths of our lives, and the distances between the two. We are built, in part, from the stories we are told, the memories we carry. Even when those are distortions or illusions, they can also be real. Charles DeSalvo was reckless on a motorcycle. Rose Cufone was stubborn and flirtatious. Bridget Reilly was long-suffering. Was it those traits themselves, or was it the belief in those traits that would be inherited by those who came after? Were these stories about who people were or about who others needed them to be? Whatever the specific *facts*, the *truth* was that Raisel was tough—so tough that her family thought it completely in character that she would refuse the orders of a man in uniform, face down the flames, and go down with the ship rather than risk separation from her son.

If Raisel had proved to be "tough," then Aime had grown to be "responsible." He had just reached adulthood back when Max died, and everyone—most of all, Aime—assumed he would fill his father's shoes. Instead, he watched as his father's legacy was sold. Raisel had inherited the twenty-five dollars in Max's savings account at the City National Bank of Norwalk and the $19.80 in cash on hand. Within a few weeks an auctioneer sold off the twenty-six new horses that Max had been escorting home on the No. 18 train, along with ten others he already owned and an assortment of buggies, wagons, and harnesses, assessed by the probate court to be worth $5,364. Within a few months, the farmhouse and the business were sold, too, for $4,350, to Max's brother, Meyer. Raisel kept her husband's diamond stud cufflinks, worth fifty dollars, and his gold watch, worth fifteen dollars. She was left with a modest estate (the nearly $10,000 would be nearly $300,000 today) with which to feed, house, clothe, and otherwise raise her ten children.

She and Aime rented a small house a few blocks away from the one that used to be theirs, with cramped bedrooms on the upper floors and space for a shop at street level. From there Raisel sold produce and groceries, her older children working alongside and her younger ones scrambling underfoot. First Aime provided most of the physical labor. When his younger brothers grew strong enough to step in, Aime, in partnership with Harry, opened a new business in downtown Norwalk, selling cigarettes and cigars.

By 1914 the Tarlov Brothers Smoke Shop was earning enough that Raisel could close her grocery. Only then did she take the money she'd collected after selling everything Max had owned and use it to buy a house. The one she chose, at 16 Grove Street, was a tall, narrow, three-story Victorian. It had eight bedrooms, a big bay window on each of the first two floors, a stone fireplace in the front parlor, and a front porch large enough for one rocking chair. Built in one of the earliest sections of Norwalk to boast municipal sewer and water lines, it had indoor plumbing in its kitchen and its three bathrooms, which made it a palace indeed. Every Friday night Aime and his siblings would gather for Sabbath dinner at the house they shared with Raisel. There they would put most of their pay into one communal jar for household expenses and a smaller percentage into a second jar, for Isadore's growing education fund.

✦

HAD SHE TRIED, RUTH SWANSON could not have found a man more removed from her own world than Angelo "Charles" DeSalvo. Or perhaps she *had* tried and purposefully found her complete opposite. Her Swedish-born parents were against the marriage of their high-school-graduate daughter—who loved poetry, music, and theater and even dared to dream of being an actress—to this motorcycle-riding, cow-butchering Italian man who had not completed sixth grade. By then, though, the Swansons were against most things that happened in America, and rather than attend Ruth and Charles's wedding on March 16, 1914, they had taken her younger brother and boarded a ship back to Gothenburg.

Charles was not Swedish. Nor was he native born. In the rough cultural currency of the day, their marriage was a step up for Charles and a step down for Ruth. When the couple married, two-thirds of Scandinavian immigrants wed other Scandinavian immigrants, and most of those were within their own national groups. In contrast, only one in ten Italian men married native-born women. Ruth and Charles were breaking, and therefore changing, the norms.

With a small church ceremony (she was not Catholic, to the quiet but clear dismay of her new in-laws), Ruth redrew everything in her life. She left her job as a housekeeper, which was the work Swedish girls did while waiting for a husband, even educated girls like herself. She also left the smaller city of Moline for the teeming Little Italy section of Chicago and traded a compact household of just her parents and her only brother for a family that resembled a tribe.

Newlywed Ruth DeSalvo became the sixteenth person crammed into the three-story ten-room building on which Charles's father, Michal, had taken a steep mortgage a few years earlier. Each payday the employed adults put their earnings in a communal kitty to pay that mortgage, as the Tarlovs had been doing in Norwalk since Max's death. Ruth and Charles shared the close quarters with his parents, his twin brother, Joseph (and Joseph's family), his younger siblings, Theresia and Carmello, and his older sister, Lucy (along with her husband and five children). It was a lot of togetherness.

Everyone in the DeSalvo clan, every in-law, every grandchild, was either born in Italy or had parents who were—except Ruth. She spoke virtually no Italian, and every Sunday when the extended family gathered for dinner, she was the tallest but also the one trying hardest to disappear. It was a running joke, one that never amused Ruth, that she never learned to cook or to tolerate all the red sauce and garlic. Decades later it would still be the way some in the family summed up the marriage—his mother's cooking gave her heartburn.

Ruth also would have been the only person in the household who had met her husband as Charles. The how and when of that meeting did not make its way to later generations, though it seemed understood that she was a fan of motordrome races and the riders who competed in them. What is very clear is that the man Ruth thought she knew was different from the one his family saw. Their Angelo was the one who hadn't the sense to stop this irresponsible sport even after he'd gotten whacked in the head. Her Charles, on the other hand, was the cocksure minor celebrity whose big break was just a race or two away.

After Charles quit the circuit, even Ruth clearly saw a man who was falling further behind. Charles left every morning for the Electromagnetic Tool factory and returned every night to the overfilled house, a place that felt oppressive both because it was cramped and because it was empty. Not only were his siblings building careers, they were also building families. Dora had five children by then, Lucy had seven, and Joseph had two sons, lost a daughter, then had another son. Bambina had four daughters, one of whom died at the age of two. Lauretta had six children, Theresia, three. Ruth and Charles had none. She had not been pregnant once, this narrow-hipped, book-loving blonde who, his relatives noted, only had one brother, and what kind of family was that?

✦

IN 1917 AMERICA WENT to war. The posters in the smoke shop windows changed from motivational requests earlier in the year (THE UNITED STATES ARMY BUILDS MEN) to staccato demands now (UNCLE SAM WANTS YOU). Like many immigrant parents, Raisel felt this was not her family's fight—she had fled Grodno with Aime so that he would never be conscripted by the tsar. But he believed that being born elsewhere gave him an added responsibility to defend the country, not an excuse to shirk. He and Harry were among the 10 million men between the ages of twenty-one and twenty-nine who reported to register on June 5, which was national registration day for the first draft since the Civil War. The brothers stood in the long line at Norwalk City Hall and described themselves as "Unmarried Registrants with no Dependents" on the official card.

It was not until April of the following year that Aime was ordered to report to Fort Slocum, New York, for basic training. He sailed for

France on the SS *Princess Matoika*, which had been a German mail transport on the Pacific route until the United States seized it and turned it into a troop ship. From June 15, 1918, onward, Aime was a member of the American Expeditionary Forces, Company L, 113th Infantry. His letters home were filled with exuberance about army life. "Get into khaki" as soon as possible, he wrote to his brothers. "It's the only clothes to wear nowadays."

Then summer turned to autumn, and for seven weeks there was no word from Aime. None to Harry, who himself reported for training to noncommissioned officers' school at Fort Oglethorpe, Georgia, on August 24. None to Charlie and Abe, who were still waiting to be called. None to Raisel, who last heard from her eldest boy in mid-August when he wrote to say his company had finished a full month in the trenches, doing the near-suicidal job of positioning barbed wire, and was now rotating farther back from the front lines.

They would later learn that he had been sent to the Alsatian village of Montreux-Château, a place for troops to rest in barracks built on the footprint of encampments from the Franco-Prussian War. Axis bombers left the region alone for the most part, firing only every so often in tit-for-tat response to an Allied attack on a German place of similar size and disposition. Hence, tiny Montreux-Château had never been seriously shelled during the four years of fighting. Secure in this knowledge, the 113th Infantry went to sleep on the night of September 13 as peacefully as was possible amid the Great War.

The bombardment began just before midnight. Of the two barracks, one was hit dead center, collapsing onto itself. The other was destroyed by the concussive force of the bull's-eye shell and the resulting storm of shrapnel. Those who escaped did so by a hair's breadth. One man's gas mask, lying on his pillow next to his head, was pocked and shattered, but he was without a scratch.

The barracks had landed on their sides, and stunned survivors had to climb over twisted, smoldering metal to pull out other victims. Fifty-four men were wounded that night. The injured were dragged to trucks and raced toward a makeshift first aid station in a nearby café.

Not until thirteen hours later, when the shelling stopped, could the survivors be transported to the nearest hospital in a neighboring village.

It would be even longer before the seven who died on impact could
be reached and removed from the rubble. One of those dead, found
lifeless where he slept in the barracks, a makeshift pillow still under
his head just as his father's had been before him, was Aime Tarlov.

There would be no funeral for him in Norwalk because there
would be no body. Just a flag with a gold star in the downstairs bay
window at 16 Grove Street and a letter from the president bringing the
gratitude of a nation.

Years later Raisel would be invited, as were all the gold star mothers and wives in the country, on a congressionally sponsored pil-
grimage to visit their lost soldiers' graves. For Aime, that was the
Meuse-Argonne American Cemetery near the site of the Battle of
Verdun; with 14,246 graves, it was the largest gathering of American
dead in Europe before or since. More than seven thousand women
would accept the all-expense-paid journeys, traveling to France and
back with army escorts, with time for some sightseeing in Paris. But
Raisel would decline and would never cross an ocean, or even leave
the country, ever again. Deep in U.S. military archives more than a
century later, a yellowing, typewritten list of the women and their
response to the proposed trip would still exist. Next to Raisel's name,
in capital letters: NO.

As the 1920s began to roar and Prohibition made celebrities out of
bootleggers and gangsters, Harry Tarlov, newly elevated to being the
oldest of Raisel's sons, returned to the tobacco shop he had run with
his brother. But Harry, a prankster and schmoozer, was not suited to
the role. Soon Charlie, the third oldest of the Tarlov boys, stepped up
to replace Aime as the "responsible one." Charlie might have liked
to further his education, but it was not in the cards. He would have
enjoyed law or politics, but those paths required schooling. A businessman he would be, giving some of his money to Raisel and putting
some aside for Isadore, just as Aime had done.

If Raisel was tough, and Charlie was responsible, Isadore was blessed. He was the unquestioned and surprisingly unresented prince of the Tarlov family, the one in whom the rest were invested. He spoke only English with his siblings, rather than the Yiddish they spoke to each other. He never had the chores the rest of the children had taken on when they were small, because his only task was to study. While they found jobs after school as they got older, he spent his spare time devouring books. The others did what they needed to do; Isadore did as he pleased.

Self-assured and charming, he was a favorite of most of his teachers, ahead of his peers in math and science. Was he the smartest of the Tarlovs or the only one given a chance? Was he freed from expectations or burdened with new ones? Was he the best equipped for the challenge, or did he rise to it? There is no control group in the life experiment, but whatever the cause, the effect was that Isadore flourished.

He began Norwalk High School in the fall of 1919, a tiny teenager with a huge personality. The Tarlov stature turned out to be in the genes, and at five foot four, Isadore fit right in. But in so many ways he was the family giant. He discovered tennis, and for lack of a practice court, he hit balls he'd borrowed from school against the side of the house at 16 Grove Street, *bonk, bonk, bonk*. Raisel, so quick to snap at Lou, Abe, and the others, never said a word. In time her youngest son would look back on his life and say, "There are people who are happy and people who are not happy, and most of the people who are happy play tennis."

He had the grades for Harvard, which accepted several of his less academically gifted classmates. But the year he applied was also the year Harvard began closing its doors to Jewish students, a response to postwar resentment of those who weren't "old American stock." The rest of the Ivy league did the same, adopting quotas that halved the percentage of Jewish students to 10 percent at Harvard, 20 percent at Columbia, and 3 percent at Princeton. The dean of Yale was quoted as saying, "Never admit more than five Jews, take only two Italian Catholics, and take no Blacks at all."

Whatever might have been in a different year, in 1922 Isadore enrolled at Clark University, in Worcester, Massachusetts, intending to go on to medical school. His tuition was one hundred dollars a year, room fees were $1.50 a week, and dining costs were six dollars a month, all paid by Raisel from the money the family had saved.

✦

SCIENCE ALREADY KNEW THAT it was biology, not curses or karma, that kept Ruth and Charles DeSalvo childless, but medicine did not yet know what to do about that. Ruth probably felt that she was to blame. Her new family likely thought so, too, seeing her as pitiable at best and frigid at worst. Charles could easily blame his wife, while also wondering quietly whether this was but one more way he did not measure up to the rest of his family.

In 1923, nearly ten years after they married, thirty-two-year-old Ruth was finally able to tell her forty-year-old husband that she was pregnant. It was their chance at a new start. They moved out of the DeKoven Street house and into an apartment three short blocks away. It was separation in the technical if not the practical sense, as everyone still gathered for pasta and meatballs every week. The only one allowed to be absent was Charles's sister, Dora, the midwife, as babies always seemed to be arriving during dinner.

On February 11, 1924, Dora delivered yet another of Joseph's sons, his fourth child and third boy. Little Paul was born at home, as were all the other DeSalvos before him. Seventeen days later Ruth's labor began. Dora was not at her bedside. One can only imagine how the revered midwife took the news that for Ruth's long-awaited child, only a hospital birth would do. The Columbus Extension Hospital on West Polk Street had been founded six years earlier by Mother Frances Xavier Cabrini to bring modern medicine to Italian immigrants. It was there, at six a.m. on February 28, 1924, that Ruth was delivered of a son. The new parents named him Charles Jr., after his father's Americanized vision of himself.

Modern medicine and a modern name were not enough. Within moments of birth, baby Charles became blue and listless, his tiny lungs unable to oxygenate his blood. Ruth and Charles Sr. never brought this son back to their small flat on Polk Street. He died at one a.m. on March 4, never having left the hospital. "Failure of closing of foramen ovale of the heart," the death certificate said.

That was not what killed him. The woman who would go on to establish the field of pediatric cardiology was still in medical school when baby Charles died, but already researchers would have known that patent foramen ovale is not fatal to a five-day-old, though that information had obviously not made its way out of academia and down to this doctor.

Whatever it was that damaged the tiny boy's heart, it also broke his parents'. The next day they buried some of their dreams and a bit of their marriage with him at the Mount Carmel Cemetery outside Chicago. Charles DeSalvo, Jr., was placed next to his grandparents beneath a five-foot-tall granite column onto which "Di Salvo" was carved into the bottom and an elaborate insignia of the letter D was etched at the top. A granite cross leaned against the base. REST IN PEACE, it read.

1929
Rose Cufone Cosentino and
Bridget Reilly Troy
Cos Cob and Stamford, Connecticut

IT WAS WELL BEYOND MIDNIGHT, AND GEROME COSENTINO WAS
not yet home. This could not have surprised Rose, as this night, in late
June 1929, was hardly the first her husband had spent out past closing
time at whichever was his favored haunt of the moment, one of the
barely disguised saloons that seemed to do even better business since
Prohibition began.

Theirs had been less a marriage than a compromise, with Gerome
giving in to his family's wishes (and resigning himself to the fact that
at least this girl was beautiful), and Rose submitting to hers (and
rationalizing that at least she could escape her sister's house of sadness). Their reluctance could be seen in the paper trail. A marriage
license was issued in late October 1915, but they waited eight more
months to wed.

Once married, they apparently focused on the things they did share:
distrust of his cousin Anthony and her sister Philomena, and resentment at being manipulated. The result was a game of one-upmanship.
When Anthony bought a home on Harold Street in the Cos Cob Park
neighborhood of Greenwich, Gerome bought one around the corner
on the Cos Cob Avenue, three rooms, paid for with his dwindling
inheritance from Italy and a $1,000 mortgage. When Anthony bought
a car, so did Gerome. Philomena gave birth to Eva, her fifth daughter. Rose gave birth to Michael Cosentino, who lived for six weeks
before dying of cerebral meningitis. A year later Rose had a second
boy, Frank, who was injured during birth and died two days later of

a cerebral hemorrhage. Anthony still had no son. Rose and Gerome still had no children.

✦

LESS THAN FIVE MILES from where Rose was reluctantly setting up her household in Cos Cob, Bridget Reilly worked in Stamford, cleaning homes, washing laundry, and cooking meals. Domestics—"girls"—worked six-day weeks, and on the seventh they went to church. For Bridget, that meant the Basilica of St. John the Evangelist on Atlantic Street. Established in 1850 by Irish immigrants, it was still where the Irish gathered.

Patrick James Troy worshiped at St. John's too. His parents had been married there in 1893, soon after they each arrived from Ireland, and Patrick had been baptized at the stately steepled building two years later. All this would have made Patrick seem familiar to Bridget, a reminder of home. Freckled and baby-faced despite years of wartime service, Patrick looked much like everyone back in County Cavan. But Patrick wore his Irish heritage lightly, almost as an afterthought. Bridget might have ascribed that to the fact that he was one generation further removed from her native land, but that wouldn't explain why his Irish-born parents felt the same.

Bridget's "kind" of Irish clustered together, looking outward—and down—on those who were from anyplace else. The women for whom Bridget worked were that kind, pleased to hire her rather than those Italian girls. "Eye-talian" was how these employers pronounced it, and so Bridget did, too. "Eye-talians" lived in neighborhoods like those that were home to Rose and Gerome Cosentino—places Bridget was told were "garlic towns."

The Troys, by contrast, moved easily, even eagerly, through other worlds. One morning in 1910, Patrick's mother, Agnes Troy, Sr., was sweeping her front porch when a frightened teenager, with the darkest skin Agnes had ever seen, came running toward her. He was being chased by two burly sailors. As one neighbor would later describe it, Agnes "lived up to the spirit of the Irish and kept the sailors off

with her broom." The fourteen-year-old she rescued was Edwin The-
ophilus Pompey, son of a North Carolina sharecropper. The boy had
jumped ship to escape indentured servitude, and after a brief stay in
the Stamford jail while his status was sorted out, he became a member
of the Troy household, calling Patrick "brother" and Patrick's parents
"Mother and Father."

The house where Pompey sought shelter, and then called home,
was at 379 Weed Avenue, in the part of Stamford known as the Cove.
The neighborhood was a world apart from the rest of the city, a cres-
cent of land along the mouth of the Noroton River. To be from the
Cove was not like being from anyplace else in Stamford.

At first it was called Bishop's Cove, home to two small mills grinding flour for local bakers and housewives. By the 1840s, railroads
made it possible to move larger shipments of grain in and flour out,
and the industrial age made it possible to convert large batches of one
into the other. Eventually the mills were running around the clock.
Now they produced not only flour but also dyes and medicines created from roots and barks imported from around the world.

By the time Patrick's father, Peter Troy, had come to work there near
the turn of the century, the mills encompassed the entire Cove. An
internal railroad moved men and material throughout the sprawling
complex. Coal was piled so high, it had its own elevator. And to cover
all eventualities, the Cove had its own on-site fire engine company.

Surrounding the mill, all along Weed Avenue, were houses for the
workers. Single men lived in dormitories, with bunk beds and shared
lavatories, while most men with families lived in small row houses.
There was also one single-family building, 379 Weed Avenue,
grander than the others and set off by itself. For several years, it was
the home of the foreman of Cove Mills, who moved out in 1901 when
he was promoted to president. His former residence was given to
Peter and Agnes Troy and their three young children, Patrick, Sadie,
and Agnes Jr.

The Troys had arrived at the Cove during its years of peak fortune. But revolutions eat their young, and the same Industrial Age

that made possible the large-scale manufacture of natural dyes and medicines also led to the creation of synthetic versions of these same things, leaving the mills unable to compete. When war began and the company's European market disappeared, workers suffered as their hours were cut.

Teenage Patrick, who had been apprenticing as a plumber, was let go. He joined the navy in the spring of 1917, one of relatively few who enlisted before the national draft. If he hoped to see the world, he was disappointed, as he spent most of the next two years as a ship's fireman, sailing no farther from home than Norfolk, Virginia. The day the Armistice was signed, while the Tarlovs were newly grieving Aime, Patrick was docked in Brooklyn. By January 1919, he was back in Stamford, living with his parents and sisters at 379 Weed Avenue, working once again at the greatly diminished Cove Mills.

It was dinnertime in the Cove on the night of February 19, when the fire bells at the mill suddenly began to clang. A spark had ignited vats of acid in a storage room, and flames quickly enveloped all twenty-five buildings in the complex. The Cove Engine Company was first on the scene, followed by firefighters from all over Stamford. Patrick, trained to fight fires in the navy, joined the failed attempt to save the place where his family lived and worked. For hours it burned, visible from a distance, with colors vibrant as fireworks. Vats popped, boilers blew, sparks cascaded. For days afterward, the site smoldered, heat radiating off the remains of the buildings, charred smokestacks towering over the wreckage. Of the five hundred men employed at the mills on the day of the fire, fewer than one hundred still had jobs a few weeks later, a skeleton crew to protect the premises and begin the cleanup.

When Patrick met Bridget a few months after the fire, he was working alongside his father as part of that cleanup crew, the job a reward for his bravery. His family had also begun taking in boarders to help ends meet, specifically men from South and Central America, with limited English and exotic customs, giving Patrick more exposure to the world than he'd ever gotten in the navy.

Would his embrace of differences and her wariness of them have eventually sent the couple separate ways? Impossible to know. By the spring of 1920, Bridget was pregnant. On August 26, Bridget and Patrick were married at St. John the Evangelist in midtown Manhattan, far from the home parish they shared back in Stamford. The witnesses who signed their marriage certificate—the only attendees other than Father Francis Shea—were two secretaries in the church office, both recent immigrants from Italy. Four months later, on December 19, 1920, their daughter was born, a third Agnes, named after Patrick's mother and sister.

All this served to confirm Bridget's view of her place in the world. Things happened *to* Bridget Reilly Troy, not *because of* her. Her father had sent her away, her uncle had sent her north to work as a domestic, her beau had gotten her pregnant, and by 1920 she was a housewife and mother. The family celebrated the couple's first anniversary by pretending it was their second. None of their children would ever know.

✦

ON THE NIGHTS GEROME did not come home, his family welcomed his absence. He had bought the house before alcoholism took hold, paying $800 for the neat corner parcel of land, and $1,050 more for the stucco bungalow with its woodstove for heat and the drafty outhouse in the back. The plan had been to expand when the time came, but that time had come, then gone. Whatever competition he might have imagined with Anthony and Philomena, he had lost, as the Belmonts now ran several thriving businesses and had moved their growing family to ever larger quarters. Gerome and Rose, in contrast, were stuck. Their three rooms were filled twice over by the five Cosentino children who had managed to survive as of this night in June 1929, the oldest nearly ten and the youngest just turning three. Four more were in St. Mary's Cemetery, most recently one-year-old Amedeo, who had died of whooping cough six months earlier. When Gerome was home, the small space could not contain his anger and disappointment. Things were better when he was gone.

Perhaps it was the pain of loss that led Gerome to drink. Maybe it was his way of softening the sharp reality of married life when it didn't compare with the adventure of the Shakespeare on his shelves or warding off the chill of a wife who did not think he compared to the men she was not allowed to have. Whatever the reason—is there ever *one* reason?—the marriage, from the start, was more combat than love.

At least at the beginning, Gerome was not an angry drunk. With every whiskey, the friendlier he became, and the more likely he was to sing "La donna è mobile," a favorite from Verdi's *Rigoletto*. "*Qual piuma al vento, muta d'accento—e di pensier*"—"Woman is fickle, like a feather in the wind, she changes her voice—and her mind." They heard him sing less often as the years passed.

It was when he was sober that he was a menace. On the evenings he was home, for instance, he demanded silence. Rose, who was in the habit of listening to more contemporary music in the late afternoons, sometimes even dancing around the kitchen with the children, would jump up to click off the radio the moment she heard Gerome at the front door. Even the youngest of them learned to be quiet once Papa returned.

During dinner, he claimed one of the few chairs that fit around the tiny kitchen table, leaving Rose and most of the children to stand while they ate. No one was allowed to speak, neither during the meal nor afterward, when Gerome turned his chair to face the wood-burning stove, which was the only source of warmth in the house. There he sat, waxing and waterproofing his work boots with lard, while holding his stockinged feet close to the fire. Next, he would spend a few hours reading one of his beloved books or his stack of Italian and American newspapers, while the children, once they reached school age, attempted to finish their homework. They had to do so without rustling any of the pages of their assignments because that sound would be met by the back of Gerome's hand against their cheek.

✦

THE MILL IN THE COVE never recovered from the fire a decade ear-lier, and the stock market crash of October 1929 extinguished the smoldering fantasy that it ever would. Only a skeleton crew remained, protecting the mostly shuttered buildings from vandals and the newly reclusive owners from former employees, who had taken to hurling stones and epitaphs as cars exited the gated compound. Peter and Pat-rick Troy were part of that last decimated guard, often as the chauf-feurs in those vulnerable vehicles.

The job kept a roof over their heads. While Peter and Agnes Sr. had thought of 379 Weed Avenue as home for thirty-eight years, the house had always belonged to the Mill, and employment was a requirement for occupancy. The same was true of 5 Cove Cottages, where Patrick lived with Bridget and, by 1929, their four children, a fifth on the way. A tiny Cape Cod, it was one of fourteen almost identical row houses built during the expansive growth of the late 1800s. Out front was a porch and an irregular brick path. In the back were paired outhouses, each side reserved for a separate family.

Unlike the Weed Avenue house, the Cove Cottages had no elec-tricity, just kerosene lanterns, and no hot water, just a single cold fau-cet. The cottages' yard tended to flood in heavy rain, and the small windows kept the interior dark. But despite these flaws, the six-hundred-square-foot home represented the most security, and the most independence, that Bridget had ever known. She tended flowers in her tiny garden, kept a small rowboat in the nearby lake, and could close her front door and be mistress of her modest domain.

Like so much else in the autumn of 1929, however, any feeling of security was about to end. Patrick's father died just as the Great Depression began, and his widow was informed that she would have to vacate the place she'd first entered as a new bride. Perhaps to soften the blow, it was offered to her son, Patrick, and his ever-expanding family. But if there was any discussion of combining both households—Agnes Sr.'s and Patrick's—it did not come to pass. Agnes evicted a tenant from the somewhat run-down home about a mile away on Leeds Street that she had inherited from her husband's sister and had been renting out as her only source of income in the months since Peter's death. She moved there with her divorced daughter, Sadie, while Patrick and Bridget replaced them on Weed Avenue.

The Weed Avenue house was bigger, with practical comforts and a worn, musty charm. It was a step up for Bridget, yes, but not a completely welcome one. To Bridget, the house would always still belong to her mother-in-law, even in her absence. Unlike the cottage, which had been hidden, this place was vulnerable and exposed, easily seen by the unemployed men who gathered every morning in front of the mill to throw stones and curse their fate.

✦

EVENTUALLY THE ARRESTS BEGAN. Gerome was picked up night after night in Greenwich, usually by Officer Flanagan or Connor, sometimes by Officer Piney, who was well known in the Italian neighborhoods for throwing coins at children on the playground saying he liked "watching those Dago kids fight over every cent." After spending the night in the city's tiny jail, Gerome would be arraigned before Judge Mead or Judge Finney and be released after paying jail costs and a fine. A total of $60.82 was due in July 1926 for cruelty to animals, after he drunkenly beat a donkey that had gotten loose from who knows where and wandered into his garden. He owed another $12.82 for driving while drunk on a July night in 1927. In June 1929 the charge was "intoxication and breach of peace"; in March 1931 it was "breach of peace and intoxication." In the summer of 1932, he was charged with assault. Three more times before the end of that year, public drunkenness. During the summer of 1933 he was sentenced to six months at a state-run "farm" for inebriates.

And so it would go for years, Gerome staying away from home, Rose staying away from Gerome, both crossing paths often enough for yet more children to arrive. Dante Amadeo, in 1931, was named for the writer who filled Gerome's shelves and the composer who haunted his Victrola; Lecia Pia, in 1932, was a name that meant "noble and pious" in Italian. Procreation paused briefly while Gerome was at the farm, but then in 1935 Rose Jr. was born. Her mother had planned to call her Rosemary, but Gerome insisted otherwise and won. Everyone but Gerome called the little girl Rosie.

When Rose Sr. became pregnant again in the summer of 1935, Gerome was furious. He had not wanted another child. This would be their thirteenth baby, which he considered unlucky, and he announced that he would throw the infant into the oven when it arrived. The shouting match that followed led thirteen-year-old Albert to physically push his father out of the house.

Gerome tried to exert control, even as Rose refused to allow him back. When he heard that number thirteen had been born, he sent the godparents to the city clerk's office with instructions to register the boy as Balboa Graziano Cosentino. But the godparents could not remember the name of the sixteenth-century Spanish conquistador, Vasco Núñez de Balboa, one of Gerome's historical heroes, or else they chose to forget. They knew Rose's choice was Frank, after her second baby, the one who had died in 1918, and that was what they entered on the birth registry. They also misspelled the middle name as Grariano.

All Frank's life, Rose would tell him that this was a misspelling of Graziano, which it was, and that it was in honor of the legendary Italian boxer Rocky Graziano, which it was not. *That* Graziano did not begin boxing until years after Frank was born. Rose had likely never heard of William Shakespeare's character Graziano, who appeared in both *Othello* and *The Merchant of Venice*, a sidekick who was "too wild, too rude and bold of voice." By the time Frank could have asked his father questions, Gerome was gone, and his youngest child would never learn what message he had wanted to embed within his name.

The Roaring Twenties
Nathan Leopold and Richard Loeb
Stateville Penitentiary
Joliet

IT WAS CALLED THE CRIME OF THE CENTURY, A TERM THAT BY 1924 was new yet already overused. It had previously been used to describe the 1906 love-triangle murder of architect Stanford White on the rooftop of Madison Square Garden, and the 1920 double-murder by anarchists Nicola Sacco and Bartolomeo Vanzetti, whose guilt is debated to the present day. But in May 1924 the crime that rocked the city and shocked the nation was this one, and even against a backdrop of one murder per day during Chicago's mob wars, singular adjectives were found.

"This cruel and vicious murder . . . this gruesome crime . . . this atrocious murder," said brand-new Chicago state's attorney Robert Crowe. "The most cruel and cowardly, dastardly murder ever committed in the annals of American jurisprudence."

Nathan Leopold and Richard Loeb were eighteen and nineteen years old when they kidnapped and murdered fourteen-year-old Bobby Franks just to prove they were too smart to get caught. Loeb had been fourteen when he'd entered the University of Chicago, which was where he met Leopold, who had an IQ above 200; in other words, their pride in their intellect was warranted. But they were sloppy—near Bobby's body, they left a dropped pair of eyeglasses, which turned out to be a rare frame (there were only three of its kind in the city) that was easily traced to Leopold. The two were also cocky (Leopold was fond of quoting Nietzsche and comparing himself to his *Übermenschen* or Supermen). Both were wealthy (they were scions of multimillionaires, as was their victim), and both had governesses who loomed large in their lives (Loeb's was domineering, Leopold's was sexually abusive). They were sexually attracted to each other.

Clarence Darrow appeared for the defense. In trying to spare his clients the death penalty, he spun a version of the argument he had presented to the assembly at Stateville back when Warden Allen celebrated his first year—that all human beings, criminal and free, were victims of factors they could not control.

Darrow was hardly the first to muse on such questions as "How do we become who we are?" and "Are we responsible for what we do?" They are as old as time—the basis of most religion, the foundation of ancient philosophy, the theme of much great literature.

Arkhe kakon, the ancient Greeks called it—"the beginning of the bad things." The moment deep in the past that leads to all the moments far in the future, the domino that topples the whole string of dominos, the lone first straw upon the proverbial camel's back.

"The mind is everything; what you think, you become," Socrates said, coming down on the side of free will.

"Destinies and accidents," are what "legislate" the lives of men, responded Plato, arguing for fate.

"Not in our stars, but in ourselves," Shakespeare wrote. Free will.

"Free will and the moral order of the world are lies," countered Nietzsche. Fate.

But what if it was neither will nor fate, but rather an internal blueprint, that made certain choices more likely, though still at the whim of chance? Modern scientists would go on to call it genetics and would recast free will versus determinism as nature versus nurture. Before they did, Clarence Darrow would use what would come to be called the Trial of the Century to put these existential questions on the stand.

The view that each man was the product of earlier generations originally appealed to Darrow for all the reasons he had laid out at Joliet: if outside forces, mostly poverty and ignorance, created criminals, that made any given crime easier to defend. His critics, of whom there were many, said he sympathized to the point of mollycoddling, and that the *reductio ad absurdum* of his argument would be the elimination of all punishment of anyone for anything. In fact, they said, Leopold and Loeb encapsulated what was wrong with Darrow's worldview. These defendants were neither poor nor desperate; they were highly privileged, supremely educated young men who had chosen to commit a horrible crime for fun.

Darrow's response to these inconvenient facts was to expand his argument. Those born into hopelessness were *most* likely to become criminals, he said, but other factors helped determine the trajectory of a life, even a wealthy and privileged one. And, he added, science could measure it all. It was a cunning argument because as much as Americans of the time wanted to believe in free will and pulling oneself up by one's bootstraps, they were also newly taken with science. And in 1924 science seemed tantalizingly close to cracking the code of all human action and reaction.

Darrow seized on that emerging science to argue that hormones, enzymes, brain waves, electrical currents, and genes shaped human behavior. "Each individual operate(s) as a machine might operate," he warned. "If the machine was defective then of course it would operate imperfectly. . . . No one is surprised when an automobile, equipped with a mechanism much simpler than the nervous system, refuses to respond properly."

Those defects, he continued, can be especially lethal when they encounter the wrong environment. "Endless discussions have been devoted to the relative importance of heredity and environment in human conduct," he wrote. "This is a fruitless task. . . . Heredity has everything to do with making the machine strong and capable, or weak and useless; but when the machine is made and thrown on the world in its imperfect shape, environment has everything to do in determining . . . its fate."

To make his case that Leopold and Loeb were "defective" creations thrown into a triggering environment, Darrow assembled an army of new thinking. The American Psychiatric Association had existed under that name for just three years when Darrow used the group's annual meeting in Atlantic City to recruit members who would appear for the defense. The prosecution had already hired mostly old-school alienists who thought Sigmund Freud's new theories were a fraud. Darrow wanted Freud's acolytes, who would testify that certain behaviors in adulthood can be traced directly to the experiences of early childhood.

Darrow then blindsided prosecutors and announced that his clients would withdraw their pleas of not guilty and enter ones of guilty, forgoing a trial and requiring a sentencing hearing in front of a judge. At that hearing, Darrow presented his novel theory that while Leopold and Loeb were sane, they were victims of the biological heritage that created them and the emotional upbringing that shaped them. Most specifically, he and his experts argued, neither young man would have committed the crime on his own.

"The psychiatric cause for this is not to be found in either boy alone," psychiatrist Harold S. Hulbert said, "but in the interplay or interweaving of their two personalities, their two desires caused by their two constitutions and experiences."

It was much like a chemical reaction, Darrow argued, with all the elements happening to collide in the exact ratios and at the right temperature for an explosion. His two young clients did not act or plan so much as converge. What happened would not have happened had they not happened upon each other.

Some of the expert testimony would not stand the test of time, but Darrow's broader argument would create a new legal template. Rather than explore the mitigating circumstances of a crime, he explored the mitigating circumstances of a self: lives shaped by factors beyond an individual's control, seeds planted generations and continents away. Defendants might not be *not* guilty, but they might be *less* guilty.

Defense attorneys would use the argument in coming decades when wives were accused of murdering their abusive husbands and children their abusive parents, when traumatized soldiers returned from battle with lethal tempers, when postpartum mothers drowned their infants, when wealthy teens raised with no limits were given leniency based on what was dubbed "the Affluenza defense." In 1924, however, the message was new and explosive. For Darrow's closing arguments, a crowd of hundreds stood outside the courthouse hoping to grab a seat. For those who did make it into the sweltering courtroom, Darrow did not disappoint.

"These boys, neither one of them, could possibly have committed this act excepting by coming together," he roared. And they could not have come together, he said, if not for all that came before. "Their parents happened to meet; these boys happened to meet; some sort of chemical alchemy operated so that they cared for each other; and poor Bobby Franks's dead body was found in the culvert as a result."

In the end, the judge rejected the death penalty, citing only the fact that the two defendants were minors and making no comment on Darrow's lofty discussions of fate. The teens were driven south during the night in a long caravan of cars, a mix of police and journalists. Flashbulbs popped as the young men entered the front gates of Joliet Prison, disappearing into the ground floor of the central turret for what was expected to be the rest of their lives.

✦

THE NEW STATEVILLE PENITENTIARY had opened in 1925, a decade after Odette Allen was killed and her husband resigned. The Stateville campus was huge, the single largest maximum-security prison in the United States. It sent a message of strength, sixty-six acres behind a steel-reinforced wall, two feet wide at the top, eight at the base, rising thirty-three feet above the ground, and rooted eleven feet deep. It was modern—a concrete and industrial vision of the future, deliberately unlike the medieval limestone of the old Joliet building three miles away. Most of all, it had the distinctive round cellblocks Warden Allen had championed—four stories of cells rising in a circle, with a guard's booth in the middle, so that the officers could theoretically see any prisoner at any moment.

But while it might have looked like Allen's vision, it did not operate as he'd planned. The venetian-style blinds that Allen had expected would shield the jailers from sight had not been installed; there were curtains, but the prisoners became adept at reading the shadows, meaning the inmates could watch the guards more effectively than the guards could watch the inmates. There was still an Honor Farm, but it was now used as a stopgap fix for overcrowding rather than a reward for trust. During Prohibition, the cells were filled with gangsters and rumrunners; then the Depression years brought burglars and pickpockets. Within a few years of Allen's death, the population of the old and new prisons together would reach nearly five thousand, twice their intended capacity, and the Farm would become a source of extra beds—outdoor living behind a ring of barbed wire for first-time offenders who were guilty of vagrancy or stealing food. Conditions in the old Joliet building, in turn, were by now so bad that it was officially condemned, yet stubbornly remained open, a place where bad apples were placed before earning their transfer to the relative comforts of Stateville.

The two very different campuses on opposite sides of the Des Plaines River were collectively renamed the Illinois State Penitentiary, though everyone still referred to them as Joliet and Stateville. The two, one new, one old, were overseen by a single warden, a series of successors of Edmund Allen, none of whom would bring his idealism or drive. Clarence Darrow's warning at the prison assembly decades ago, that a misstep by one inmate would end Allen's reforms for all the rest, had come to pass. The only hints that the Allens had ever been there were the periodic rumors of a translucent figure of a woman, all in white, seen in the windows of what had once been the warden's tower apartment.

✦

AT FIRST WARDEN John L. Whitman kept a close watch and a tight leash on his best-known "house guests," knowing the public was watching, too. Though Leopold and Loeb were certainly educated enough to do administrative jobs, Whitman assigned them manual tasks, like weaving rattan chair seats and cobbling the heels onto shoes. And although Stateville opened several months after they arrived, Whitman kept them at Joliet, with its cold showers, bare lightbulbs, and bucket latrines. Only one or the other would be permitted to live in the brand-new prison, at least at first.

Then Whitman was forced to resign when his deputy was found to be taking bribes in exchange for parole. The next wardens, Green and Hill, were both attracted to Allen's ideas of trust. But Green left when a new governor wanted his own team, and Hill essentially abdicated his authority after prisoners rioted to protest the tightening of parole requirements after the Whitman scandal. "We want a new parole board! Change the parole board!" the rioters had chanted, as they hurled whatever they had—band instruments, food scraps, furniture, paint-filled drums, homemade knives—at retreating guards and at each other. They also set fires in the library, the dining hall, the laundry, the factories, forcing Hill to leave his sickbed to tour the wreckage. Like Allen, Hill had a gastric ulcer, and on the day of the riots he was in surgery to remove part of his stomach. The next morning he surveyed the $500,000 in damage (which would be $8 million today), then he returned home and summoned a local surgeon to restitch his reopened surgical incision.

Warden Hill was broken by the 1931 riots, in much the same way that Warden Allen had been by Odette's death. In part, Hill became disillusioned by the penal system, when the final report by the state's prison board had been largely a buck-passing exercise rather than a proposal of reforms. Mostly, though, Hill was left broken by his prisoners. Like Warden Allen, Warden Hill had considered himself a defender of his men, believing that his kindness could pave their path to rehabilitation. And they repaid him with a riot. "This is a terrible thing our boys have done," Hill's wife wept, as she and her husband had toured the still-smoldering ruins. "I'm so deeply hurt." Her husband did not cry, at least not in public, but he did stop trying. During his remaining time in the job he chose the path of least resistance: just keep the convicts happy, keep the prison in the black and out of the newspapers, keep his ulcer in check.

As a result, the prison was run by its prisoners. Most of the rules were gone, and those that remained were barely enforced. Most work details were eliminated, too—the furniture shop, the shoe factory— the result of the Depression. State law required that items manufactured by prisoners be used within the prison. But state purchases of prison-made goods had been shifted to outside companies to avoid accusations that manufacturing jobs were being given to incarcerated men when law-abiding factory workers were losing theirs. Hence every day at Stateville was a day of leisure, as prisoners raised and raced canaries in their cells, built handball courts against the outer walls, and created a warren of tarpaper shacks in the recreation yard in which they fermented hooch and gambled, out of view of the guards.

Many could have escaped, but most did not seem to want to. Beyond the prison walls the Great Depression deepened, making life inside—"three squares and a cot"—look acceptable by comparison. "With a bitter winter ahead and thousands in the outside world cold and hungry, these men, well fed and warmly housed, have something to be thankful for," wrote a *Chicago Tribune* reporter who was given a tour of Stateville by Col. Frank D. Whipp, Hill's replacement, a few weeks before Thanksgiving 1932.

A career penologist with the reputation for not shaking up the status quo, Colonel Whipp, like Hill, chose to ride out the economic bad times, defining success as whatever it took to avoid another uprising. He painted this pragmatism not as a surrender but as a purposeful plan. The clusters of shacks built out of scraps? Those gave everyone something to do, he explained: the prisoners built, the guards tore down, the prisoners built again. The liquor stills the men operated in their cells? He chose to allow them, too, because it gave the prisoners a modicum of control, meaning they would not be so broken down by their time behind bars that they would be unable to function once they were released. This pretzeled logic was not his alone. When Gov. Henry Horner was asked about the shacks, and the liquor, and the fact that prisoners had taken to calling Stateville "The Gangster's Country Club," he answered: "The vast majority of prisoners ultimately gain their freedom and the society in which they live has the right to demand that we do not send them men who are broken down spiritually and mentally."

Two prisoners who benefited most from this resignation in reformative clothing were Leopold and Loeb. Finally assigned to the relative luxury of Stateville at the same time, they were given plum jobs. Loeb would run the Stateville greenhouses, while Leopold restocked the library, which had been reduced to ashes during the riots. They often did their jobs together. Leopold could be found replanting seedlings while he and Loeb brainstormed which books to buy with the library's hundred-dollar-a-month budget.

They saw each other daily, to talk about plants or books, to play bridge. During these many conversations they hatched a new project: to expand the prison's school. The one operating at the time went only to the eighth grade, and its classes were held during prison work hours, meaning any prisoner who managed to snag a half decent work assignment (and its related privileges) would not give it up, even for an education. Prisoners also had the option of enrolling in correspondence classes from universities around the country, as Leopold had been doing for years—by 1932 he had taken long-distance language and integral calculus classes with professors at the University of Iowa, studied philosophy with those at Columbia, and Etruscan inscriptions with one at the University of Chicago. But those were expensive and only accessible to men who already had a good deal of education.

Leopold and Loeb were certain that there was demand for more. Both were regularly asked for help writing letters, researching laws, or just choosing something to read. They knew that most of the inmates didn't understand the books about Nicomachean Ethics, or quadratic equations that they were regularly checking out of Leopold's library. They also knew that they *wanted* to understand those things.

Their plan quickly took shape. They would teach at the high school level, as the lower grades were already covered. Theirs would be correspondence courses, but rather than mailing back and forth with a professor at a university, students would correspond back and forth with Leopold, Loeb, and a small group of others with enough education to join in the teaching. Readings and homework assignments would be delivered and returned through the internal mail system. Everyone would do the work in their cells, on their "free" time, rather than gathering in groups in classrooms, something the administration was loath to allow after the riots.

They wrote a three-page prospectus that argued that schoolwork would give bored prisoners something to do. The cost to the state, they promised, would be zero. The in-house teachers would provide all the man hours, and the students would be required to purchase their supplies—pencils, notebooks—with their own commissary funds as a way of showing they were invested in their own education.

Finally, Leopold and Loeb addressed the question of what a criminal needed an education for anyway. When Leopold had first arrived at Joliet and volunteered to teach, the then deputy warden (the one who turned out to have been taking bribes) advised him that, at most, men behind bars should be taught to "read a little . . . figger a little . . . write a little. And not too much of that," lest they all turn to forgery. Anticipating a similar objection now, the prospectus ended with a discussion of the importance of knowledge if a man were ever to lead a lawful life.

By the 1930s, "a high school education was almost a necessity," compared with earlier eras, Leopold summarized. "Increased education meant increased earning power, and increased earning power meant decreased recidivism. . . . Many jobs require a high school education; often the fellow who writes the best letter of application lands the job."

By early December 1932, Leopold and Loeb had permission to start the first prison correspondence school in the country. Now in their late twenties, they sent letters to all their old teachers, professors, and tutors requesting syllabi and curricula, then used that advice to create coursebooks for their inaugural group of twenty-eight students:

high-school-level English composition and English literature, elementary algebra and plane geometry, American, ancient, and world history and first-year-level Latin, French, German, and Spanish.

By the end of 1933, nearly one hundred students were being taught a dozen subjects. By 1935, 204 incarcerated students were taking twenty-five courses. Leopold and Loeb ran all this from their own office suite, complete with typewriters, desks, filing cabinets, and blackboards, and equipped with its own bathroom and shower. They still "checked in" to their separate cells at night count, but during the day they had full run of the prison.

Such was Stateville in 1935. Two murderers happily in charge of their own school; a warden willing to pretend he did not see the ground troops of Capone, of Touhy, of Dillinger recreating a gang life that was not unlike the one they lived in Chicago; guards, earning just $112.50 a month, letting the capos come and go at will from their unlocked cells, flush with cash; prisoners raising pets in their cells—some cats, a few dogs, and tens of thousands of birds, canaries mostly, which they sold to pet store owners through the holes in the fences (giving new meaning to the term *jailbird*); a prison yard filled with more than eighty teetering, taunting shacks, which served as clubhouses, headquarters, and gambling dens complete with cards and chips and roulette wheels—physical embodiments of who was actually in charge.

And so it might have continued—a surrender to the limitations of the times—had Henry "Midget" Fernekes not made his sensational escape. In the summer of 1935, the five-foot-three bandit, convicted of five murders and several dozen bank robberies, simply walked out of Joliet disguised as a visitor. The public took notice. When he then taunted the warden by mailing a letter while on the run, saying he'd left because he'd found prison life too darn crowded, the audacity created outrage. "Dear Warden," Fernekes wrote in his grammatically spotty note. "You were good to me. Too many men my reason for giving more room. However, I still like Joliet." He signed it "Midget."

Newspapers delighted in the details of how Fernekes had outsmarted the prison system; among other things, he'd managed to play the stock market from his cell in the years since the crash, accumulating a small fortune. Governor Horner responded by offering a $1,000 reward for his capture. The Midget parried back with another signed letter to the warden: "I think a reward of $5,000 is more fitting."

Fernekes was spotted holding up several banks in the Chicago area but always avoided capture. Warden Whipp did what he could to look like a man in charge, but most of it backfired. When Whipp dismissed the guard who had tipped his cap to Fernekes as he walked out the door unrecognized, the old-timer refused to leave, saying he had worked at the joint prisons since 1908 and had more of a right to be there than did the warden.

The governor agreed, and Whipp was soon gone—the latest warden unable to tame Stateville.

1930s

Summer 1935
Joseph DeSalvo and Alvin Tarlov
Chicago and Norwalk

IT FELT AS THOUGH THE TROPHIES WERE STARING AT FIVE-YEAR-old Joey DeSalvo as he tried to fall asleep. Flimsy curtains hung on the front windows of the dining room that served as a bedroom, and the streetlights shone right into Joey's eyes. He couldn't move himself into a more "shaded" spot because he and his older brother, Charles Jr., slept head to toe on the single daybed, and there was no spot into which to move.

And so Joey lay still, looking up at the shelves of trophies reflecting the streetlights. All the medals, ribbons, loving cups, and framed newspaper clippings seemed to be mocking him through the night as his father and brother did during the day.

He had heard that his parents had once wished desperately for children, and that there had been another Charles Jr., an infant who had lived for only four days, then died of a sickly heart. Joey wondered if his father had used up all his love on that child. Charles Sr. didn't show much warmth or pride toward the second Charles Jr., either, but at least he tolerated that son, possibly because they shared a name, or maybe because all three Charleses had looked alike, dark and solid, rather than fair and delicate like Joey and his mother.

Perhaps it was because of Joey's name. He'd been called Joseph after his father's twin, the one who had once been a motorcycle racer, too, but had quit sooner—"chickened out," his father said. Later, after he'd read a lot of books, Joey would see this as the foundational myth of his family: to his aunts and uncles, his father was Icarus, a braggart who'd failed; to his father, Icarus was a hero, who'd at least given his dream a try. The twins, now in their forties, rarely saw each other anymore, and when they did, Charles Sr.'s mood became even darker. Everyone could see that the ten-minutes-younger twin lagged the older one, that the extra years spent trying to become a racing superstar had left Charles Sr. behind in the race to build a middle-income American life.

Charles Jr. had arrived in 1925, a year after the first Charles Jr. died. Then Joey—Joseph Eugene DeSalvo—was born into optimism in the summer of 1929, a moment when his father felt sanguine enough about his own future that he could be the bigger man and baptize his son with the name of a twin he'd failed to keep pace with his entire life. But the two boys, born just before everything imploded, would turn out to be more reminders of what might have been. By Joey's first birthday, around the time President Herbert Hoover reassuringly said, "I am convinced we have now passed the worst," the SpeedWay Manufacturing Company reduced its delivery force. Like Patrick Troy in Stamford, Charles DeSalvo, Sr., managed to keep his job—no small feat as unemployment would reach 50 percent in Chicago, double the national rate. Also like Patrick, he took a sizable cut in salary.

Then when little Joey turned two, Ruth, Charles, and their boys had moved out of their home. Like the Troys, they played the Depression game of musical chairs, and when the music stopped, they were left as boarders in a redbrick two-family building at 217 LaPorte, a dismal and dingy part of town. They came hat in hand to a building owned by Charles's widowed niece, who lived in the more spacious top apartment with her mother, Dora, the midwife whose services Ruth had by now spurned three separate times. The four DeSalvos roomed downstairs, with a single bedroom and a living room that doubled as a dining area; the boys' daybed pulled up to the table as seating for meals. The layout meant that every time the two women came or went from their home, they walked through the room where their charity-case nephews ate and slept.

There was, thankfully, indoor plumbing, but the washing machine had been lost to creditors, as had much of their furniture.

A large bookshelf, the only decoration in the room, was filled not with books but with all Charles Sr.'s motorcycle memorabilia. They were the last things his sons saw at night, and the first things they saw in the mornings.

✦

THE BEDROOM ALVIN TARLOV shared with his older brother was different in every way from the one where Joe DeSalvo tried to sleep. By 1934, Al's parents, Charlie Tarlov and the former Mae Shelinsky, had moved their three sons from an apartment near the old Tarlov Brothers Smoke Shop into a newly built two-story cape on a quarter-acre in Norwalk, a view of the water out back and a green and tidy lawn to the front.

The roughest and prettiest parts of every city are by the water, where the desire for the idyllic competes with the need for the industrial. In Stamford, the Cove had been given over to the business of the mill, but in Norwalk, eight miles north on the same Long Island Sound, tranquility had triumphed. By the time young Alvin Tarlov arrived with his parents and brothers, what had once been a marsh had been drained by a succession of eccentric owners and was now a development known as Shorefront Park. It was a first glimpse of the new suburbia to come, with its two stone pillars at the main entry point and postage-stamp-size beach at its northwestern arc.

The Great Depression was a capricious villain, an economic tornado that imploded 60 percent of American lives, but left 40 percent whose days went on as before, including the Tarlovs. Mae and Charlie had married in 1922, during the boom years, and when the stock market crashed, they were raising Merwyn, who was born in 1925; Jay, who followed 1927; and Alvin, born on July 11, 1929, exactly four days before Joey DeSalvo. Mae delighted in baking in the small kitchen of their tiny apartment back on West Washington Street, toddlers underfoot. Charlie, inspired by her industry and its delicious results, persuaded her she could be home but also help grow his business— their family business—at the same time. With Aime dead and Harry having left to sell life insurance, Charlie was now the sole owner of Tarlov Brothers, and he began selling Mae's pies—apple, berry—in addition to pipes and cigars. Then he added her sandwiches—tuna, pastrami—which proved to be the perfect grab-and-go lunch for downtown workers who still had work. By 1932 the ratio of smoke shop to snack shop shifted. Soon Charlie turned the whole thing into Tarlov's Luncheonette, stocking a few cigars behind the counter, mostly for old times' sake.

By 1934 they had moved that business again. Among the five thousand banks that failed nationwide by then, three were in Norwalk. None of those were where the Tarlovs happened to keep their money, which kept the family solvent. One of the failed banks was the South Norwalk Savings Bank at 50 North Main Street, which presented the family with a business opportunity. No one else in town could see any use for the cavernous marbled interior, so Charlie and Mae took out a twenty-year-lease and opened Tarlov's Restaurant. The varnished wooden teller cages became dining booths, the vault became a wine cellar, and the bank president's office served as the place the Tarlov boys would do their homework for the next decade or more. Tarlov's was open 364 days a year, closed only on Christmas. Charlie Tarlov would spend the next two decades working nearly every one of those days, not stopping for illness, or his children's high school graduations, or the Jewish holy days that his mother believed he still observed.

Of Charlie's and Mae's sons, Al's was the life most changed by the opening of Tarlov's. When Merwyn and Jay were Al's age, their mother was always around, even as she spent increasing amounts of time in her home kitchen cooking for the luncheonette. Hers was the first generation to see the new role of "housewife" as a luxury, a step up from their own mothers who had worked alongside their men—running the family farm or the family shop, taking in laundry or boarders. When Charlie first began to dream of a restaurant, Mae told him sharply and often that she would be home with and for her children until the last one went to school. So it was no coincidence that Tarlov's opened in the fall of 1934, just as Al began kindergarten.

The family's mornings did not change much. Charlie Tarlov still left for the restaurant at seven a.m., but Mae remained until all three boys had eaten breakfast and kissed her goodbye on their way out the door. Afternoons, on the other hand, were nothing like before. It would be a while before Al realized that not all children made the fifteen-minute walk from the Christopher Columbus Elementary School to the family restaurant every weekday afternoon (sometimes with a stop at Grandmother Raisel's for a snack). That not all children were served their dinner at a table in the corner of the dining room—monitored by their mother between making change for customers and printing out the next day's menus. That not every family had a rule saying children began to work in the family business when they turned seven, the age that Charlie had been when his father, Max, had been killed in a train crash (a story that the Tarlov children heard regularly).

Most of all, other children did not fall asleep to the sound of their outwardly cheerful mother weeping quietly through their shared bedroom wall at night because her family was not the planned and proper center of her life. Nor did they hear their father, tone sharp, answering that this was how a man loved his family, by working to give them everything they might possibly need.

◆

JOEY DESALVO ALWAYS FELL ASLEEP, eventually, despite the glaring trophies. And he was almost always awakened early when the light from the LaPorte Avenue streetlight gave way to that of the Chicago sun. On the rare mornings when he slept through sunrise, the sounds of his father's morning routine would serve as an alarm. Then his mother would appear in her housecoat, the signal for her sons to turn the daybed back into dining room seating.

After a quick breakfast, it was time for errands. By the summer of 1935, ten-year-old Charles Jr. was already finding reasons not to come along. He went, as his mother put it, "God knows where" with "God knows who," pods of neighborhood boys who filled street corners, vacant lots, and front stoops with everything from improvised sports to introductions to hooliganism. Perhaps Ruth could have stopped him, but she didn't. Perhaps Joey could have tried to join the big kids, but his brother would have only laughed at the idea and his mother would never have let him go. Most of all, Joey preferred his mother's company as much as she preferred his, and so most mornings it was just Joey and Ma. They went to the grocer. They cleaned the apartment. Once a week they went to the library, where Ruth spent hours reading stories aloud. Joey already knew how to read—had taught himself at this very library before he even went to kindergarten—so sometimes they read silently side by side. Joey preferred adventure tales; Ruth loved poetry and plays. They never brought their books back home.

On very special days they went on an adventure. One memorable kind was to a place called Moline, where Ruth had lived as a child. There were still dozens of Swansons in the local address directory there, though none were directly related to Ruth, and the corner newsstands still sold editions of the *Svenska Amerikanaren.*

Joey and his mother stood outside the gates of the International Harvester Farmall Works building where her father had worked before he returned to Sweden, back when the factory was called Moline Plow. Joey wondered what that grandfather would have thought of him. On these visits his mother often said Moline was where "my people" were from. Who, then, were Joey's people?

She would remind him that his middle name, Eugene, was a Swedish one, meaning "noble" or "well born." But that was not the only reason she chose it, she said. One of her favorite playwrights, Eugene O'Neill, had won three Pulitzer Prizes for Drama in the 1920s, and Ruth loved the theater. What she likely didn't mention was that Eugene O'Neill was much in the news for other reasons the year Joseph Eugene DeSalvo was born, as the playwright had just scandalously divorced his second wife and, weeks later, married his third.

On the way home, she would always remind Joe that the trip was a secret, something just for them. She needn't have worried; he wasn't going to tell. These adventures were the only times he saw his mother smile. And why should he share that with anyone else?

✦

AL TARLOV WAS AWAKENED one morning in the summer of 1935 by a series of sharp plinks of rock against glass. Opening the heavy curtain, he saw a figure he couldn't place, but who was clearly a Tarlov, with the short, compact stature shared by everyone in Al's family. He was cheerfully and relentlessly aiming pebbles at Al's upstairs bedroom window.

It was neither Uncle Abe nor Uncle Lou, and it certainly was not his father, who would never do something so whimsical as pitch stones before dawn. He quickly figured out that it was another of the brothers, Al's Uncle Isadore, who the boy knew least well but who was already a larger-than-life presence to his young nephew. Isadore's visits back to Norwalk were infrequent, meaning Al had heard *of* him far more than he'd heard *from* him: of how a chance train accident had killed Izzy's father but led him eventually to Clark University, the only one of that generation to get to college; of how he had gone on to medical school, graduating near the top of his class at the Johns Hopkins University School of Medicine in 1930; of how a chance attendance at a lecture there by Dr. Wilder Graves Penfield, known as "the father of neurosurgery," had led him to the rest of his life.

Penfield's lecture made such an impression that, upon graduation, Isadore moved to Canada, where Penfield was founding the Montreal Institute of Neurology. There Isadore became Penfield's first neurosurgical resident. If any of Raisel's other children had up and left for another country, she would have thundered her objections. But Isadore could still do no wrong.

And now he was beckoning Al from beneath a window. Isadore had spent several years in Montreal by this time and had just finished a few months of additional surgical training in London. Days earlier he'd arrived in New York Harbor on the SS *Aquitania* from Cherbourg, traveling first class. This would be the first visit where the boy was old enough to leave an impression on the uncle, and vice versa, and Al ran down the stairs to unlock the front door. A few minutes later the youngest of two generations of Tarlovs were off on the first of many adventures together—this one a short walk to the tiny beach at Shorefront Park, where they swam to the wooden platform anchored about a quarter-mile from land and lazed for a while in the sun.

Isadore stayed in Norwalk until early fall, and many a morning he would appear at his young nephew's window and take him for a swim. A grown-up Al would look back and see that his parents probably knew he was with his uncle, and that he had been chosen for these near-dawn swims as much because Isadore enjoyed his company as because he was the only one willing to get out of bed that early and let Isadore in. But six-year-old Al saw this as a secret shared, and he cherished it.

1936
Bridget Troy and Rose Cosentino
Stamford and Greenwich, Connecticut

ORIGINALLY A "HAPPY DRUNK," GEROME HAD BECOME A BELLIG-
erent and dangerous one over the years, leaving emotional and physical marks on his wife and children. The worst days of the Great Depression had passed, but Gerome's work prospects continued to dim. Prohibition had been repealed, and, in response, he drank even more. The country was attempting to move on. Gerome remained stuck.

On the night of July 14, 1936, he raged more than usual, or perhaps as much as usual but one time too many. Rose sent sixteen-year-old Mary to find a patrolman; she returned with Officer John M. Gleason, who would go on to become the chief of police in Greenwich but who at the time was a gangly twenty-nine-year-old with six years on the force.

The home the officer entered was not the one Gerome had bought back when he still had a job and a future. He had lost that house in Cos Cob Park in 1933, one among the blur of foreclosures that were happening nationwide at a rate of one thousand per day. Gerome's cherished Model-T Ford was repossessed at about the same time. Waving a document that Rose could not read, two men had hotwired the ignition and driven the car away. The family's two dogs disappeared that day, too, a coincidence that felt ominous.

Rose and Gerome could have sought help from Anthony and Philomena Belmont, who managed to thrive during the lean years and now owned a grocery store and several rental properties in Greenwich. But Gerome was too proud to ask. At about the same time that Charles and Ruth DeSalvo lost their Chicago apartment and moved in with family, Rose and Gerome Cosentino lost their house and found a small apartment on the second floor of a distant cousin's home on Valley Road in North Mianus, a section of Greenwich that some residents preferred to pretend did not exist. Even during the Depression, Greenwich was still one of the wealthiest enclaves in the United States; North Mianus was its desperately impoverished secret.

"We were among the poorest people in the country in the wealthiest town in the country," the Cosentino children would remember.

There was just one true bedroom, for the five girls, and a small dining room, which Rose used for sewing during the day and the boys for sleeping at night. Rose took the couch in the living room, sharing it with Gerome when he came home. The family also shared a three-seater outhouse with their landlords. The "bug-a-house," Rose called it, and her children thought she was referring to the stench and the flies. Decades later they realized she was saying "back of the house" in her heavy Italian accent.

When Mary led Officer Gleason up the back stairs that July night, he found a very inebriated Gerome arguing loudly with a distraught and angry Rose. As they fought, eighteen-month-old Rosie, their twelfth child, and two-month-old Frank, the "unlucky" thirteenth, wailed for emphasis. Gleason brought Gerome to the Greenwich jail, where the guards already knew him well. After a trial in town court the next morning, he was sentenced to six more months at the Norwich State Farm for Inebriates, where he had been once before. It hadn't dried him out that time, either.

"The Farm" was part of an effort to recast drunkenness as a disease rather than a crime, offering treatment rather than punishment and providing to the poor and working class what had previously been available only to the wealthy. Having opened in 1915, with beds for sixty patients, it shared philosophical roots with Edmund Allen's Honor Farm—the belief that meaningful work could rehabilitate a man and ready him to return to society. After several days of "rest" at Norwich Hospital (time that would now be called "detoxification"), patients were transferred to two-story brick barracks of the Farm, where they worked sunup to sundown maintaining the

property, cooking meals, stoking the furnaces, and tending crops
and livestock.

At first, Prohibition had a counterintuitive effect; rather than an
increase in the arrests for drunkenness, it brought a decrease, and the
number of men sent to the Farm correspondingly dropped. But then,
as bootleggers, rumrunners, and speakeasies perfected their methods,
and the Depression led more men to drown their woes, the Farm's
population began to tick steadily upward. Like Stateville, it became
overcrowded. Between 1930 and 1932, nearly three hundred more
men served time at the Farm than between 1928 and 1930. The 1934
head count was nearly twice that of 1933. With the end of Prohibition,
occupancy jumped further still.

Just as Stateville administrators allowed reality to dilute their
ideals, Norwich administrators allowed patients to run this asylum.
Joliet prisoners brewed moonshine in the yard; Norwich alcoholics
had thirty-seven-year-old Stella Oskin, a hospital attendant who operated a five-gallon still at her home and sneaked "hootch" to the Farm.
Both Joliet and Norwich tried to use parole as a tool to determine
when each man was ready to reenter society; both failed, because of
scandals at Joliet and a need to release patients early for space reasons
at Norwich.

During Gerome's first stay at The Farm, back in 1933, a series of
escapes had led to questions about the practice of allowing patients
to wander the grounds freely. No conclusion was reached, and the
roaming continued. During Gerome's second stay, the Public Welfare
Council began an investigation into whether the place should exist
at all, since no one seemed able to scientifically prove that what they
were doing there made any difference.

✦

IT WAS NEARING DINNERTIME at 379 Weed Avenue when the officer
arrived at Bridget Troy's door. The police had never come before, a
point of pride in a neighborhood that had its fair share of squabbling,
tempers, and intemperance. But on the evening of October 6, 1939,

there an officer stood. And like Raisel Tarlov more than three decades earlier in Norwalk, and Rose Cosentino just three years earlier in Greenwich, Bridget Troy would see her life upended by his knock.

Until that moment, her life had been reasonably good. Patrick had somehow held onto his job at Cove Mills, though it had been renamed the Cove Investment and Improvement Company, part of an attempt to make it attractive to potential investors. Thus far there were none. The Weed Avenue house was still in need of repair, but by now it had become home. There were ghosts and shadows, but Bridget had made peace with them: Her displaced mother-in-law, Agnes, who had died in a home not her own in 1935; her three-year-old son, James, who died of whooping cough in 1933. To keep them a bay at night, she prayed for their souls at church every day.

And so her lingering sadness was somewhat soothed by satisfaction. She had been heavily pregnant when James died. Ten weeks later she'd given birth to her seventh child, a boy she'd named David Daniel for the lyrical sound of it. Like the recently buried James, David had bright red hair from birth, and it became even redder as he grew—a way to spot him in any crowd. David was also fair like James, almost as fair as Bridget herself. But while James had been a sickly boy, David was robust and energetic. He was James with a second chance. David became Bridget's shadow, or, perhaps she became his. The others teased that he was her clear favorite.

Now six years old, David sprinted everywhere, and so he'd reached the front door just before Bridget, who came up behind, carrying her eight-month-old daughter on one hip. Both mother and son assumed it was Patrick knocking, as he often did when his hands were full. On this Friday evening, he had taken sixteen-year-old Louise to the dentist, and they were expected at any moment. Instead, there was a police officer.

"Do you have a daughter Louise, and is your husband Patrick?" he asked. "There has been an accident."

Patrick had been driving and had pulled over when the pain began. The car was fine. Louise was uninjured. Patrick had collapsed at the wheel and died. He was forty-four. Bridget, like Raisel and Rose before her, was left alone to raise so very many children, the oldest on the cusp of independence, the youngest not even a year.

Patrick was felled by biological happenstance—a miscoding of a bit of DNA, a scrambling on a chromosome. The word *hypercholesterolemia* would become well known to his children, and to theirs—it referred to a glitch in the system designed to clear the body of cholesterol, leading to heart attacks or strokes. Eventually scientists would invent a test that would find the gene in nearly all of Bridget's grandsons in time to treat them. It would not save her sons, however, most of whom would die in their forties like their father. And it certainly was not in time to help Patrick, nor protect Bridget from the cascade of events that followed upon his death.

Soon after her husband's funeral, Bridget, like her mother-in-law before her, was evicted from 379 Weed Avenue. That house was still reserved for the families of men who worked at Cove Mills, and for the first time in nearly forty years, no one in her family did.

Also like her mother-in-law, Bridget relocated to 39 Leeds Street. Whereas Agnes had displaced a paying tenant, Bridget displaced Patrick's sister, Sadie, who had recently remarried and who had been promised the house. But how was Sadie to turn away a grieving widow—even though this particular widow hadn't shown much remorse years earlier when displacing her own in-laws? What kind of monster would Sadie be to refuse?

With no other source of income, Bridget found a job as a lunchroom cashier in the local Schick Razor factory. She put her older children in charge of her younger ones, then headed to work six days a week, embittered yet resigned.

Nine months after her husband's death, on the night of July 4, another policeman arrived, this time at 39 Leeds Street. "Is David Troy your son?" he asked Bridget. "There has been an accident."

A police car was parked at the curb, and her Davey, who'd just turned 7, was seated inside, one hand wrapped in white gauze. He'd been playing with firecrackers during the celebration down at the park and suffered some mild burns. He was treated at Stamford Hospital and released. After that, Bridget insisted on holding an Independence Day barbecue on Leeds Street every year. Her children always thought she was particularly fond of the holiday, and perhaps she was. But it was a way to keep her loved ones home.

◆

FOR THE MONTHS THAT Gerome Cosentino was away, his family muddled along back home. When the weather was warm, Albert and Valentino would take Dante, Lecia, Rosie, and even baby Frank to play in the woods, while Mary, Louise, and Evelyn helped their mother drag basins and scrubboards into the front yard for laundry.

When it grew colder, Albert and Valentino would chop trees while their younger siblings collected sticks for kindling. It was Valentino's job to sift the ashes out of the stove just before bedtime every evening, and Albert's to start the fire in that stove every morning before sunrise. There was bread with weak coffee and some milk for breakfast; bread and coffee or tea for lunch (and if luck was with them, one thin slice of bologna for a sandwich); a dinner with little or no meat and a lot of fried potatoes and onions.

Gerome's absence meant no more required silence during or after dinner, and they chattered about what they would do if they came into money—not just any money but the amount in the welfare check they knew had been in Gerome's pocket when he was taken away to the Farm. They could not visit him there, could not communicate in any way, and so the moment when that check returned home became the stuff of fantasy. Their plans for the long-delayed funds shifted by day and by season, but among the most frequent was the idea of buying a tin of something exotic and dividing it up among the ten of them. The thought of one-quarter of a slice of sweet, syrupy canned pineapple per child, with none for Papa and three-quarters of a slice left for Mama, helped get them through the 180 days.

They had other ways of coping, too. Donated clothing appeared often at their door from neighbors and the church donation room.

Most of those clothes needed patching, and the shoes needed cardboard in the soles, but the family was more than used to that. They also received less tangible gifts. When Mary was readying to drop out of school in order to work, the librarian at the North Mianus branch stepped in and found an after-school job for the teen, as a nanny for the daughters of one of the librarian's friends. This librarian also took an interest in Dante, who had just started kindergarten and had fallen in love with learning the moment Louise brought him to his new classroom and introduced him to Mrs. Wilcox, who said, "Dante—what a beautiful name."

Gerome was released from The Farm exactly six months after he'd arrived. Given a rail ticket for the hundred-mile trip downstate, he reached Stamford in the early afternoon, cashed the welfare check he'd been holding on to since his arrest, and proceeded to get extremely drunk at a bar near the train station. His family never bought their tin of pineapple.

Rose filed for divorce three weeks later. Even the monsignor agreed, she would tell her children for years, justifying the decision. Her legal fees were paid by an anonymous donor to the Family and Child Center; her descendants would later wonder if it was Philomena, quietly trying to make amends. The grounds were "intolerable cruelty," which her petition said began in 1926, the year Gerome was first arrested for drunkenness. The divorce was granted on June 24, 1937. Gerome was to pay Rose fifteen dollars a week in child support and alimony with which to raise nine children between the ages of two and seventeen— money that she never saw.

She rarely saw Gerome, either. Nor did the children. Evelyn missed him, but the rest of the older siblings wanted little to do with him, and the younger ones were left confused, especially the boys. A few months after the divorce, Gerome took six-year-old Dante to visit a farm and gave him fresh milk from a cow, which he promptly vomited onto the barn floor. A few months after that Gerome took nine-year-old Valentino out for hot dogs and canned soup, a relative feast compared to meals at home, and even as an adult, Valentino felt guilty that he had eaten so well that day while knowing his mother was constantly hungry.

Two years after the divorce, in July 1939, a report by the Public Welfare Council to the Connecticut governor described the Farm as "absolutely useless" in curing alcoholics, saying "in reality it is nothing more than a jail." It was permanently closed.

1930s
Nathan Leopold and Richard Loeb
Stateville Penitentiary

JOSEPH E. RAGEN HAD ALWAYS WANTED TO BE A WARDEN. AS A child, he shadowed his father, who was a sheriff in Clinton, Illinois, on his rounds at the local jail. As a young adult, he succeeded his father as sheriff and in 1933 was appointed both the warden at the Southern Illinois Penitentiary at Menard and the superintendent of prisons for Illinois. He held the two positions at once while being paid for only one, because there was a depression going on; for most of his tenure in them, he would use his predecessors' stationery rather than spend to print his own. Every four weeks he would make a tour of all the prisons in the state, then write a summary of each for the governor.

Which was why Joseph Ragen most definitely did not want to be the warden of Stateville. Knowing how much was wrong with the place, he had already turned the job offer down twice. But the sensational escape of Henry "Midget" Fernekes meant the governor would not take another no for an answer. So began the legend of Warden Ragen of Joliet.

Ragen had been seventeen years old when Odette Allen died. He thought about her when he and his wife, Loretta, traveled with eight-year-old Jane and six-year-old Bill to their newest home in October 1935. They approached from the east on Highway 66A, the tops of the prison's panopticons rising like Oz from the surrounding fields.

The family would live not in the turret of the old prison, where Odette had burned, but on the new Stateville campus, in an eleven-room apartment that was comfortable, even opulent, and extremely well staffed. The Depression had returned the practice of "hiring" from within for the domestic household. The elevator operator to the warden's apartment would be a convicted murderer; his valet, a former bank president (in for embezzlement); his barber, a lifer, who—reassuringly?—had committed murder not with a razor but with a gun.

Ragen knew well who his prisoners were: 5,675 men in his charge between the two prisons, serving time for sixty-four types of crime. They were robbers, burglars, murderers, kidnappers, con men, embezzlers, extortionists, bigamists, and forgers, and one was a horse thief. More than a quarter of them had been incarcerated more than once, and fifty-five were imprisoned for the fifth time.

All were under the watch of a most ineffective group of guards. On one of his first days as warden, Ragen watched a guard march a work detail to an assignment. A dozen men were in the group when it set out across the yard, but one by one the men peeled away. As the guard reached the work location, just a single prisoner was still following, and the task was abandoned. When Ragen reviewed the file of that guard, and then of the four hundred others on his staff, he found no employment histories or background checks, just recommendation letters from the county political chair or local ward boss.

So he gathered the employees in the chapel of the Old Prison, a room that had not changed much since Clarence Darrow visited twenty years earlier. Dressed in his signature pinstripe suit and natty pocket square, he started with a list of rules. Guards would no longer deliver notes between cells for prisoners. Guards would not accept bribes from prisoners or their families. All officers should be in uniform when on duty—and should not be drunk while wearing that uniform, whether on duty or off. All staff had to pass a physical exam by the prison doctor. All staff had to be fingerprinted and cleared of any criminal record. Friendships of any sort between inmates and staff were prohibited.

By morning, there were twenty resignations on his desk, from men who preferred not to have either their fingerprints or the state of their health examined. Dozens more soon followed.

Having cleaned house, Ragen cleaned the yard. It took three days for guards to destroy the shanties and cart away the debris. Before dawn on the fourth day, all the lights blazed on suddenly in every cell-block of Stateville. In a coordinated swoop, prisoners of "influence" were given mere minutes to pack and then were marched away, shipped to other prisons around the state, effectively divided and conquered.

That done, Ragen addressed the problem of prisoner downtime. Early one November morning, those without other tasks were gathered in the yard and divided into twosomes. Each team was given a twenty-four-inch-square bread tin and a spoon and told to fill their pan with topsoil from the slopes at the edges of the yard and carry it to the low spots near the front of the building. The prisoners hooted and hollered, some sarcastically moving just one small spoonful of dirt per trip.

The job could have been done in a day using shovels and wheelbarrows. With kitchen implements, it took weeks. When guards questioned the warden, he pointed out that, grumbling aside, the men were spending seven hours a day walking back and forth from one end of the sixty-six-acre prison property to the other. They were sleeping better at night and had less time during the day to make trouble. He considered this a win.

Another win, of sorts, was the capture of "Midget" Fernekes, who, after 12 weeks on the run, was caught living in plain sight in Chicago as a boarder at a modest home on Erie Street. Alone in his cell at a local jail, awaiting transfer back to a place where big shots like himself were no longer in charge, the escape artist ripped open a secret seam in his pant leg, swallowed enough cyanide crystals to kill five men far larger than himself, and was dead within minutes.

✦

WARDEN RAGEN WAS NOT the only one studying the prisoners of Stateville. Nathan Leopold and Richard Loeb were, too. By the time Ragen arrived, the prison's two most famous prisoners had been running the school and the library for nearly five years. They were also working on another project, one they hoped would not get caught in the clean sweep by this new warden.

It had begun as a game of sorts. When anyone in their circle was about to leave on parole, Leopold and Loeb would make a friendly wager on whether the man would "go straight" or return to prison. They soon realized that they rarely disagreed, and they were similarly rarely wrong. For Loeb, a born gossip, this was mostly fun. For Leopold, though, it raised deeper questions. Why does one man succeed on the outside and another fail? he wondered. Is it due to what's within him or around him? Does it vary depending on what brought him to prison in the first place, or what happens while he's there?

Darrow's description at their trial of Leopold and Loeb as inevitable products of a capricious universe may not have influenced Judge Caverly, but it did have a profound effect on Nathan Leopold. Already a nihilist and an atheist, Leopold was moved toward fatalistic resignation by Darrow's words. Everything at Stateville confirmed that view, filled as it was with men whose lives were shaped by haphazard happenings a day, a year, or a generation before: prisoners who might have been free but for accidents of birth, or economic forces beyond their control, or chance encounters; jailers who could as easily have been criminals but for circumstances of which even they were unaware.

It was a convenient way for this notorious killer to look at life. Rather than thinking about what he had done wrong, he dissected how he had been wronged, how the eddies of fate had shaped him, and the prisoners around him, into the type of men who could do wrong. Listening to stories of how so many had tipped into lives of crime, Leopold came to see patterns that were "almost identical," he would eventually write in his autobiography. As each man began to describe his own life, Leopold realized he could "predict what would come next" in the story. As in any science, he wrote, finding a repeated pattern "is a pretty clear tip-off that there is a single underlying principle."

Leopold's first decade at Joliet-Stateville coincided with the rise of sociology as an academic field, providing a backdrop to all this thinking. The epicenter of the new discipline was his alma mater, the

University of Chicago, where one-third of all graduate students in the field were studying. Yet another of Darrow's fierce summations—this one at the Scopes "Monkey" trial in the summer after he defended Leopold and Loeb—had given traction to Darwin's theory of evolution. The "Chicago school" of sociology applied the theory of natural selection to societies, teaching that cultures, like species, evolve in response to external influences. Actions and beliefs that had been seen as individual choices—suicide, crime, even religious and political convictions—were viewed under this new lens as the outcome of a process of social competition.

Eager to prove itself a real science, sociology needed hard data, and both the Great Depression and New Deal provided that in abundance. The Gallup organization began polling in 1935, and while it got a lot of things wrong (its subjects were disproportionately male, wealthy, and white), it familiarized the public with the idea that a sample could represent a larger whole. The government, too, produced reams of statistics. A mini off-year census was conducted in 1931 to measure the depth of the unemployment crisis—the first census to be based on statistical sampling rather than complete head counts. Added to that, the "Alphabet Agencies," created as part of the New Deal—FDA, FHA, WPA, one hundred in all—monitored, measured, and published their results, dissecting the population as had never been done before.

What to do with all this data? The Chicago school was not content to simply collect and categorize facts. It sought to put those facts to use. In the sociological study of crime, for instance, it was not enough to identify what led a given man to prison. The next step was to forecast how that man would do once released back into the world. Rather than just analyzing the past, could sociology predict the future?

Parole is, at its core, a best guess about what a prisoner will do next and was therefore a magnet for the new generation of Chicago sociologists. Parole itself was relatively new at the time; introduced in New York in 1907, it would spread to every state by 1942. It paralleled the trend toward "indeterminate sentences," where legislatures empowered judges to hand down a range of years as punishment rather than a set number. Both parole and flexible sentencing were based on a belief that different prisoners were ready to reenter society after differing amounts of penitent time. It was unclear, however, how to identify the moment when any given prisoner was ready for release. If only there were a *scientific* way.

The earliest parole boards had had little use for science. At best, they went with instincts based on the impression a prisoner made during a brief interview, meaning that those who were well-spoken, genial, and calm tended to fare best. This described most con men. At worst, decisions were based on who could provide cash in exchange for early release. This described most gangsters. The pattern of favoritism and bribery was what led to the 1926 murder of the deputy warden at Stateville, who had been selling paroles for $500. That, in turn, had spurred the Illinois Department of Public Welfare to appoint a four-man commission to study how parole *should* work.

One of the members was Ernest W. Burgess, a Canadian-born professor at the University of Chicago, who had gotten his Ph.D. in sociology at the school in 1916, then returned to teach. He would spend his career creating tools with which to predict social phenomena— divorce, delinquency, difficulty in old age, urban growth—and parole. "Prediction is the aim of the social sciences as it is of the physical sciences," he wrote in 1929.

While the commission's specific goal was to figure out how to make parole bribe-proof, Burgess's own objectives were more sweeping: How to determine who deserved the early monitored release and who would do well by it? He turned for guidance to the rapidly growing insurance industry, which had begun to enter such factors as a man's age, drinking habits, and line of work into a formula to predict how long he might live or how safely he might drive compared with other men. To make a similar determination of how trustworthy one parolee would be compared with all parolees, Burgess began with data from the intake questionnaires completed by new arrivals to Joliet and Stateville. After that, he guessed. First-time offenders, he reasoned, would be less likely to violate parole than recidivists; a married man with family ties would be more likely to "go straight" than a single man with none; a man with a profession to which he could return would fare better than one with no history of (legal) employment.

Next, Burgess tested his hypotheses against real-world results. He looked at the records of the last thousand prisoners to have been released from the twin prisons: 716 had successfully completed parole, and 284 were back behind bars. Burgess gave each man a score between 0 and 21—one "point" for every "life factor" the prisoner had that Burgess believed should increase the likelihood of parole success. The final tallies confirmed his theory that the higher the score, the better the odds. Subjects with a score of 16 and above had a 98.5 percent chance of succeeding on parole; a score between 7 and 9 meant a 56.1 percent chance; a score of 2 to 4 brought the success rate down to 24 percent. The result was much like the insurance industry measurements on which this system was based—not a guarantee of any particular man's future but a general assessment of risk.

Burgess labored over his equations for years, but when the parole commission finally issued its final recommendations in 1930, the Burgess factors were not even mentioned. His three fellow members decided that the best way to reform the parole system was to make parole all but impossible to get. Their core suggestion was that "good behavior time" should no longer be subtracted from the minimum sentence before a prisoner was eligible for parole. An abstract concept to the board, this rule change translated into added days, weeks, months, and years for the state's prisoners.

The result was a precipitous drop in the number of parolees released, which led to an equivalent drop in inmate morale and a spike in anger and overcrowding, which triggered the riots of 1931. Those riots led Burgess to belatedly have his day as Gov. Henry Horner established the new office of sociologist-actuary at Stateville. Sociology professors and graduate students already spent their days embedded in other institutions around the city—hospitals, schools, stockyards, factories, tenement buildings. Now a sociologist would work full time within one of the nation's largest penitentiaries. Part of the new actuary's work would be to replace gut instinct with science when evaluating prisoners for parole by preparing a "parole prediction report," the key piece of which was a "Burgess score" from 1 to 21. The rest of the actuary's job was to conduct further research, using prisoners as subjects, to establish the accuracy of and potential improvements to the Burgess method.

Hired to fill this position was Ferris Finley Laune, who'd received his Ph.D. in sociology from Northwestern University. The forty-year-old began working at Stateville in the summer of 1933. One of the first prisoners he met was Nathan Leopold.

Leopold's interest in parole prediction was not (yet) personal; his ninety-nine-years-to-life sentence meant that, whatever the formula, he would not be eligible for a hearing anytime soon. As a philosophical and statistical question, though, it intrigued him. The more he talked with Laune, the more Leopold saw potential answers to the questions he'd been musing about for years. Burgess's twenty-one factors were effectively a map of how and why any given man went wrong. And they were very much like the ones Leopold and Loeb had been creating with their "hunches" as they watched fellow prisoners leave and return.

From his perch within the system, however, Leopold found a fundamental flaw in the Burgess formula: its predictions of the future were based on a static past. Of the twenty-one factors on the list, nearly all were things that could be known about a man from the moment he walked through the front gates. They were a measure of who that man was when he began his sentence, not of how he might have changed during it. If the purpose of parole is to return men to society once they were ready to be civil, shouldn't it be the purpose of prison to make them ready? If you don't believe men could change, what is the point of parole? And if you do believe in change, how then to measure it?

Leopold was a believer because he himself had changed. After nearly ten years behind bars, he was nearing thirty and looking back with feelings of grief and regret on "the arrogant monster" he had been in his teens. When he'd entered Joliet, the only thing he had been sorry for was the fact that he'd gotten caught. But by the 1930s, "remorse not only entered my mental life—it dominated it," he would write in his autobiography. In part, he'd changed because of his own losses while incarcerated, most singularly that of his father, whose death he had learned about when he spotted a newspaper headline in the commissary. Mostly, his were changes that came with age. He drafted several letters of apology to Bobby Franks's family but never sent any of them, thinking they would be seen only as selfish pleas for sympathy which, he realized, they probably were; that realization, in and of itself, represented growth.

As he'd aged, the way he was treated had also changed, and not only because conversations among others no longer stopped when he walked into a room. As he took and then taught ever more correspondence courses, he developed a network of friends in the academic world, accomplished men who came to treat him as a cross between a trophy and a specimen, one who attracted even as he repelled. In him they saw a path not taken, a man who in so many ways was just like them—brilliant, studious, educated, privileged—but also the embodiment of what they adamantly were not. Men whose expertise was criminology had often wondered what separated them from those they studied. In Leopold, they had a living example. There but for the grace of—something—go they.

Academics began to correspond with Leopold, and more than a few made the trip to Stateville to meet him. When he'd wanted to learn integral calculus, he wrote to Helen Williams, the director of the University of Iowa home study department (and the only woman in his brain trust), who advised him to take plane analytic geometry and then differential calculus to prepare. They exchanged letters so regularly that he began to call her Aunt Helen, and she was pivotal in the creation of the prison school, providing him sample Iowa coursework as a guide. When Leopold found himself struggling with the theory of relativity and needed guidance on choosing background reading that would help him understand, he again went directly to the source. An answer came in the mail in January 1934, postmarked Princeton, New Jersey, and remained tacked above Leopold's workspace for the rest of his prison life:

> *May I advise you not to attempt to achieve your goal too directly, but first to read a scientific book on Mechanics and Electrodynamics. They should preferably be books which use higher mathematics (calculus) and which are not too long; for instance the lectures by Planck. I am sorry that I do not know the English textbooks, but you should ask someone who is familiar with them. When you are through with these books, it should be easy for you to study relativity.*
>   *Sincerely yours,*
>   *A. Einstein*

Perhaps the most important reason Leopold believed in change, however, was not what he saw in himself but what he had seen in others. By now, hundreds of incarcerated students had passed through the prison school, and while some were just filling time with the classes, others left fundamentally altered. One con learned enough French on the inside to be sent to Officer Training School when he joined the army on the outside, then rose to the rank of captain while a translator in North Africa. Another came in barely able to decipher a newspaper but learned to read and write well enough to serve as a secretary in the chaplain's office, then went on to work a desk job when he was released.

One particularly powerful success story was of the longtime inmate who was working in the Stateville soap factory but dreamed of a life outside as a chemical engineer. The Stateville Correspondence School did not teach chemistry, because it was not a good idea to give potentially explosive substances to men behind bars, but it did teach math, a foundation of chemical engineering. Leopold had humored the student as he made his way through seven math courses, ending with college algebra. Upon parole, the man enrolled in a small local college, earned his tuition working as a janitor, and got his degree.

None of those men returned to crime. And none would have been considered a good risk under Burgess alone. "Men do change in prison," Leopold would write. "They are reformed—that is, re-formed."

During near weekly conversations with Ferris Laune, Leopold expressed admiration for Burgess's goal but continued to take issue with what he saw as the limitations of the twenty-one factors. Laune agreed, to a point. Since change was the stated requirement for parole, he said, it would be best if it could be accurately measured. What, though, to measure? Was a man changed because he said he was? Because he was trained in a useful profession? Because he apologized for past actions? Burgess had chosen factors that were objective and confirmable. Whatever the flaws of his formula, at least it provided a fact-based checklist. Could Leopold do better?

Leopold believed he could. All the attention he'd received from intellectuals around the country had only amped his opinion of himself. He was as smart as these men who were treating him as a peer, he reasoned, and on one subject—the mind of a criminal—he was arguably smarter.

Overseen by Laune, Leopold and Loeb set out to codify the hunches they'd been batting around in the school offices. As a first step, they created a list of 150 fellow prisoners whom they both knew reasonably well. Then they separately wrote their estimate of the odds that each man on the list would stay out once paroled. They confirmed what they already guessed: that their senses of who was a safe bet and who was too high a risk were essentially the same; they were responding to an undefined "something" about any given man.

The next step was to define it. For months the duo spent two hours a day on the task, parsing what had led to each rating, with Leopold transcribing their conversations. The "good risks" were those who had a "willingness to work" or had "learned [a] lesson," or demonstrated "religiosity." The poor risks were those who had an "excessive interest in clothes," or who bad-mouthed their parents for not enclosing cash in their letters, or who demonstrated a "lack of love for family," "stupidity," "timidity," and "argumenta-tiveness." Eventually they had compiled fifty-four "hunch factors" for the 150 men. They turned that into seventeen hundred questions aimed at eliciting those factors: *Were you ever so taken by an article of clothing in a shop window that you walked right in and bought it? Would you work if you had enough money to keep you comfort-able for the rest of your life? Are your brothers and sisters ignorant? Do you respect your father? Do you love your mother? Would you be here if your parents had brought you up differently?* And they found dozens of men to complete the first iteration of that question-naire, appealing both to their altruistic inclinations (the good that today's prisoners could do for "convicts yet unborn") and to their more practical concerns (the promise of anonymity, and free ciga-rettes on testing day).

In the end, fifty-seven volunteers answered all seventeen hundred questions. Leopold entered all 96,900 responses using giant charts and thousands of five-by-eight file cards. Then he repeated the test-ing several more times, trying to determine which of his hunch cat-egories were most predictive and which of his questions were most likely to elicit honest answers. Using statistical analysis that had not yet been taught back when he was a student (for instance, Thurstone factor analysis—Thurstone himself made the trip from the University of Chicago to provide advice), he culled the list of factors to thirty-six and the total number of questions to 426, resulting in a shorter (but by no means short) questionnaire.

Leopold was exhilarated by his new academic bona fides and even began inquiring about earning a Ph.D. while incarcerated. His first toe in those waters was a 1935 article for the *Journal of Criminal Law and Criminology* about the short history of parole prediction, essentially a review of the two dozen works of scholarship by eight scholars in the new field. *Parole Prediction as a Science* appeared in the September 1935 issue under the (pseudonymous) byline William F. Lanne. Two months later the *Chicago Tribune*, in a front-page story, outed Leopold as the author and suggested that his interest in parole was to create a system that would benefit him when he was finally eligible for a hearing—in twenty-two more years.

When the *Tribune* ran its "gotcha," Warden Ragen had been at Stateville just a few weeks. He put a Band-Aid on the problem by transferring Leopold out of the sociologist-actuary's office but allowing him to continue the work in his cell. Then Ragen turned his attention back to things farther up on his to-do list: the yard full of shanties, the lack of useful things for the rest of the prisoners to do. As he checked all those boxes, though, he'd kept Leopold and Loeb on his mind.

✦

JOSPEH RAGEN BELIEVED IN prisoner education. But he had long insisted that all his prisoners were equal and that freedoms gained from good behavior were equally available to all. Now here were Loeb and Leopold, who had virtually free run of the entire Stateville campus and even had their own correspondence school office, including a private bathroom with a single shower. The bathroom had two doors, one of which opened into the office and the other into the prisoner dining hall. Both could be locked from within.

How, Ragen wondered, was this different from the gang bosses who had run their businesses from the prison yard? He did not immediately revoke any of the duo's work-related privileges, but he did, as a start, put a clamp on their cash. Leopold had almost no access to money. Loeb, though, had started with $500 on permanent deposit, an account replenished regularly by his father and then his uncle. In addition, whenever his brothers visited, they gave him another fifty dollars in cash. Loeb was generous with his funds, stocking up on far more tobacco, candies, and sundries than he could use, sharing the wealth in exchange for friendship and a wide variety of favors.

The ban on cash was not aimed solely at Loeb—nearly $25,000 in bills and coins was seized throughout the prison after the ban—but it hit him hard. In the weeks afterward, he began to argue loudly with James Day, his cellmate at the time. The twenty-three-year-old Day was four years into a ten-year sentence for a gas station robbery that had netted him either $9.75 or $26, depending which documents you believed. Day's family gave him nothing while he was inside, making Loeb's largesse more than welcome. When Loeb's spigot was cut off, Day lashed out with such frequency and at such volume that shortly after Christmas, Ragen ordered Day moved to a cell a few floors away.

It was because of Day that Ragen never did have to decide what to do about the other perks Leopold and Loeb had been given. On January 28, 1936, just past noon, Ragen had only just begun his lunch in the family quarters when the telephone rang.

"A bad stabbing," the warden was told.

He walked briskly to the correspondence school offices, where Loeb, naked and barely conscious, was being lifted onto a rolling stretcher that had been rushed from the prison hospital. The thirty-year-old had been cut so viciously that he was shredded. Blood gushed from dozens of stab wounds; doctors would eventually count fifty-seven in all. His throat had been slashed from behind, four deep gashes creating a ghastly, smiling wound that ran ear to ear.

A few feet away stood James Day, pale and dazed, half dressed and covered with blood—which would turn out not to be his own. Moments earlier he had handed a barber's razor to guard Capt. Austin Humphries, saying, "This is what I did it with, Cap."

While surgeons tried to save Loeb, Ragen questioned Day, who insisted it was Loeb who'd brought the knife. Ragen didn't believe him. If it happened as Day said, Day would have been fighting for his life; had the knife switched hands multiple times, as Day insisted, Loeb would have had his chance to cut Day. But while Loeb had cuts everywhere on his body, including defensive wounds on his hands and arms, Day had not suffered a single scratch or bruise.

Ragen did not like Day. The young man was the kind Ragen saw as nearly impossible to reform—one who had been on a road to a criminal life since birth, one who was "a bad actor. Erratic. Given to wild temper tantrums." Day's prison file, which Ragen scanned quickly before questioning him, contained the story of a boy who had never known his father, whose mother died when he was eight, and who was raised by relatives who considered him a burden. After years of fistfights and petty crime, he was sent to the St. Charles School for Boys at the age of fifteen, and then to the Cook County Jail, both on charges of theft. He would never qualify as a good parole risk, by either the Burgess or the Laune/Lanne/Leopold standards.

Ragen also knew that Loeb—whom he liked more than Leopold—was hardly a saint. He was manipulative and cunning and, unlike Leopold, had never expressed a word of remorse for what he had done. Still, his modus operandi was to influence with charm, not muscle, and he had gotten his way for more than a decade without threatening anyone. Ragen thought it was far more likely that Day had been hounding Loeb for sex and commissary goods rather than the other way around, and that it was Day who had sought to settle things with a knife when Loeb's generosity ceased.

At 3:10 p.m. that afternoon Ragen's phone rang again, with word that Richard Loeb had died.

There would be a funeral, of sorts. A hearse, with police escort, whisked the body to a Chicago funeral home where, after his mother briefly visited, Loeb was cremated and secretly buried somewhere other than the Loeb family plot. There would be headlines. King George V of England died that same day, but at least in Chicago, Loeb's death was bigger news. There would be a trial, but it would not come close to determining what happened in the bathroom that morning.

It took the jury less than ninety minutes to find Day not guilty. Outside Stateville, opinion was that Bobby Franks's murder had been avenged and justice had finally been served. Inside Stateville, Warden Ragen was displeased. Day, he thought, had succeeded in doing what Loeb himself had not—he had gotten away with murder. Months later Ragen proved the premeditation he suspected when he coaxed a confession from Day's cellmate George Bliss, who admitted to stealing the razor from the barbershop and slipping it to Day to bring to the meeting with Loeb.

Double jeopardy laws meant Day could not be retried with this new evidence, but Ragen had other tools, specifically the parole system. He ordered that Day's "good behavior time" be forfeited, requiring him to serve the full ten years of his sentence, rather than being eligible for parole in six years and three months. Day sued to have that time restored, a demand that was eventually rejected by the state's highest court. Day never appeared before a parole board. He never qualified because he had too many demerits, as Ragen instructed Stateville guards to hold Day accountable for every infraction. He would finally be released from Menard in 1942 but would return to prison decades later after terrorizing a babysitter and three children with a shotgun on Chicago's North Side.

Nathan Leopold would eventually forgive James Day, who he saw as "just a kid." But he would never forgive Warden Ragen. Leopold's study of parole was a study of cause and effect. When Ragen banned cash, he had not intended to cause Loeb's death, but he did. In the same way, Day had not intended to increase Leopold's clout at Stateville, but that was the result. Before Loeb died, Ragen had been poised to remove both Leopold and Loeb from their unique perches within the prison. Now he just let Leopold be.

1940s

The War Years
Al Tarlov and Joe DeSalvo
Norwalk and Chicago

IT WAS THE FIRST SUNDAY IN DECEMBER 1941, AND TWELVE-YEAR-old Alvin Tarlov was listening to the radio. The New York Giants versus the Brooklyn Dodgers was arguably the least consequential of the three football games played that afternoon, since the Giants had already secured their playoff spot. Still, the fact that it was a local rivalry made it a must listen for the Tarlov brothers, who were home between the luncheon and dinner service at their parents' thriving restaurant.

Al knew more than a little about football. There were pickup games at the makeshift field at Shorefront Park, where Al, though tiny and with a mild case of scoliosis, was an intrepid regular. His oldest brother, Merwyn, had made the Norwalk High School team just this fall and would be joined there in two years by Jay. Eventually Al, too, would play football for Norwalk, at quarterback, though he wouldn't be a star like his bigger, meatier brothers.

"Tarlov," the coach would tell him when awarding his varsity letter, "you can't run, you can't kick, you can't pass, and you're not very good at blocking. But you can think."

Even as Al played, followed, and talked football (and basketball, and baseball), he understood that his relationship to sports was not like his brothers'. It was just one of the many ways that he was different, and his brothers noticed it, too.

"How did you DO that," they would ask when his fifth-grade teacher decided he needed an extra project to keep him engaged, and so he spent the year translating *Huckleberry Finn* into Braille and donating the resulting book to the Norwalk Home for the Aged.

"How did you KNOW that?" they would ask, when Al would know the names of world leaders or the fluctuations of the stock market or the workings of the human nervous system.

How *did* he know? Mostly, he read. The Tarlov boys were still spending most of their time at the restaurant, where Al was now busing tables, having reached the point in his father's training timeline where he was strong enough to lift barrels of lobster, burlap sacks of potatoes, and cases of whiskey. Merwyn and Jay were full-on waiters, having learned to balance a laden tray on an open palm while navigating between tables. On weekends they all worked the lunch and dinner shifts. On weekdays they still walked from school to the restaurant, still ate dinner in the dining room with Mae, still did their homework in their father's office. They also found time for chats with the regulars and for reading copies of *The New York Times* and the *Norwalk Hour* that the lunch crowd left behind. Alvin always started with the news and ended with the stock listings. He had noticed that this was what the successful businessmen did while they ate lunch. He also noticed that his brothers began with the sports section.

As Al read, he pondered, lining up the facts of the outsized world with that of his smaller one, trying to fit the scattered pieces into a picture. Back in 1938, he'd read of *Kristallnacht*, the two-day pogrom during which mobs destroyed Jewish property while the German authorities looked on. In the spring of 1939, he'd read about the *St. Louis*, a ship carrying 925 Jewish refugees from Germany that was denied entry to both the United States and Canada. Al knew that his family was Jewish. He had spent much of the previous year visiting a local rabbi once a week to learn the prayers and Torah portion he had chanted at his bar mitzvah this past summer. The service was held at the synagogue that his grandfather had helped to build, and during the service Al sat in a straight-backed pew that bore a brass plaque with Max Tarlov's name. All his relatives had come, and Al knew they were all Jewish, too. Except, also, they weren't. All his father's sisters had married Jewish men and were raising their children as they had been raised; but all the brothers had married women of other faiths, and their traditions were a hodgepodge that Max would not have recognized. Isadore, most of all, was, as his son would later describe it, "oppressed by his Jewishness." And although Al's father, Charlie, had married a Jewish woman, and all three of their boys had bar mitzvahs, no other religious rituals were practiced in Al's home.

The only real conversation Charlie had with his boys about religion was when he told them they had to observe certain customs (Passover seders, bar mitzvah ceremonies) out of respect for Raisel, and that they had to be "exceptional" in their daily lives. If they misbehaved, he said, it would reflect poorly on the entire Jewish community. If they had dreams—a fancy college, a prestigious profession—doors would open only for Jews who were exceptionally qualified. Was that why some in his family chose not to be Jewish? Al wondered. Could the refugees on the boat or the residents of demolished neighborhoods have chosen likewise and had a different fate? Were you born who you are, or did you choose it?

During his bar mitzvah service, he had looked around the synagogue, as aware of those who were not there as of those who were. The pickup games in Shorefront Park included everyone in the neighborhood, yet the only neighbors in the pews were the ones who were Jewish. It was simply understood that his Christian classmates would not attend, just as it was understood that some students he'd known his whole life went to weekend parties at country clubs to which he was not invited.

This tendency of people to sort themselves and then stick together became more visible to Al the more he spent time with Isadore, who communicated his critique of the status quo in his every action. When Isadore finished training in Canada, his mentor, Dr. Penfield, had written a glowing recommendation for a coveted job in Manhattan, adding the handwritten postscript "I must tell you, he's a Jew." Isadore did not get that position and began work at the Brooklyn Jewish Hospital, where he made a name for himself as a neurosurgeon with exceptional hands and an even more exceptional mind. There was no neurosurgeon in the city of Norwalk, so Isadore became the de facto one, setting aside Monday mornings to operate on local patients at Norwalk Hospital, then borrowing his brother Charlie's car to make afternoon house calls.

He often took young Alvin along on those rounds, and the nephew was struck by how the uncle's manner did not change from house to house. His patients were of all races, nationalities, and religions; those who could not pay did not. Isadore came into each home as though it were that of a friend, accepting the cups of tea or ginger ale he was offered (though never coffee or whiskey, which he believed were bad for one's health). If anything, he lingered longer and spoke more warmly in the "colored" homes—houses that Al passed on his walk to school but had never entered. A few of his classmates, several waiters, and one chef from the restaurant lived in these, but Al was invited inside only when he was with his uncle.

In 1940, Isadore had been named a professor and chairman of the department of neurosurgery and neurology at New York Medical College—apparently, Al reasoned, because he had finally proven himself exceptional—and moved with Fella and their three young children to a sprawling apartment on Fifth Avenue, near 96th Street, right by the entrance to Central Park. In 1941 he acquired a two-tone gray Cadillac for the trips he still made every Sunday night to Norwalk in advance of Monday's surgery and house calls. Al began to take the train down to Manhattan one weekend a month, arriving Friday night and often being awakened before dawn on Saturday morning by a light knock on the guest room door.

Dressing quickly—and, in the winter, warmly—he and Isadore would walk to a grocer at Lexington Avenue and 80th Street, where the owner would be waiting by the back door. The man would hand out two crates loaded with fruit and sausages, which Al and Isadore would carry onto the subway, disembarking at Coney Island. As they reached the boardwalk, they would see the usual circle of men around a makeshift fire, who would treat the surgeon, whom they called "Doc," like a long-lost brother. Isadore once described them to Al as "down and outers," but when he greeted them, he called them "my friend" and "my good man." Pleasantries exchanged, Isadore would shed his heavy fur coat and hat, scramble out of all the clothing underneath, and go for a nude swim in the frigid winter surf. As he emerged, the men would hand back his coat, which they had been warming next to the fire, along with one of the sausages that they had lightly charred on a stick over the flame.

Al studied Isadore as he was learning to study everything else—paying close attention to what he could use to guide his own life choices. Isadore found a way to give those who would judge him what they needed to see—his Cadillac, his country home on sixteen acres in Protestant Litchfield County, his love of tennis, the pipe he smoked because it made him seem less boyish—while staying true to the eccentric and opinionated man beneath. That man subscribed to the *Daily Worker*, contributed to the Socialist Party, and parked his Cadillac wherever he saw fit, earning himself a place on Manhattan's list of biggest scofflaws. He kept tea in a whiskey bottle on his liquor cart so he could appear to be having a cocktail with guests, and he kept an ax in his tennis bag. If on his way back from his regular game in Central Park he saw a fallen tree, he would turn it into logs—for firewood for any passing "down and outers," and also for some added exercise.

It was a way of being that appealed to Al's essential nature. At the restaurant, he pretended to care about the workings of restaurants, even while he cared far more about the workings of the world. With his brothers he talked sports, and he truly liked talking sports, while also liking politics and policy. Merwyn acted on impulse, shooting out the streetlight in front of his window because it was shining into his eyes at bedtime, and Jay was a jokester, rigging up his car so that it played organ pipe music—loudly—when he honked his horn (leading one surprised driver to come at Jay's windshield with a baseball bat). But Al acted only after long, detailed thought, almost always choosing the more deliberate path. His parents were too busy to pay close attention, he concluded, so what he did with his time was less important than what they *saw* him do. They measured his behavior by his grades, and he made sure his grades were excellent.

When they weren't watching, he chose routes from here to there that took him through the poorest parts of town. He attended church, a different denomination every week, to see if unfamiliar rituals would spark meaning. He gambled after school, mostly poker, sometimes dice, with kids his father would not have considered good role models.

What he did not hide was his delight in the camaraderie that came with sharing his brothers' world. That was the reason he was rooting for the Giants on the afternoon of December 7, 1941, listening to the radio at the house in Shorefront Park, his father still at the restaurant, his uncle Lou making his usual batch of meatballs in the kitchen. The Dodgers would beat his Giants 21 to 7 that day, but long before the fourth quarter, when the Giants would score their only touchdown of the game, a radio reporter would break in:

"We interrupt this broadcast to bring you this important bulletin.... Flash. The White House announces Japanese attack on Pearl Harbor."

◆

THE YOUNG WOMAN, a girl really, was not much older than Joe DeSalvo, who, on this morning just after Thanksgiving in 1942, had recently turned thirteen. It wasn't the girl herself who caught his attention, it was her purse, a tempting target, dangling loosely over her wrist.

"Why?" his mother would ask him. Joe never had an answer that satisfied either of them. In a way, it was as simple as he wanted what someone else had—the pocket money of a classmate in the school-yard, the pocketbook of a stranger on a sidewalk. Eventually he would come to understand that he took things because he could and for the look of surprise and fear as his victim realized what they were about to lose. He never stole quietly or surreptitiously. He wanted to be seen.

His father was horrified, which Joe understood to mean his father was embarrassed, and Joe made a huge show of not caring. What right did Charles Sr. have to be embarrassed? Charles, who himself was an embarrassment to his children, with an accent so heavy he was often difficult to understand, and a drawerful of documents that said his name was Angelomaria? Charles, who talked incessantly about what a big deal he had been on a motorcycle way back when but now made a modest living at the Speedway Manufacturing Company, where he had barely progressed in nearly thirty years?

And yet Charles constantly belittled his children for not doing big things. Young Joe might not yet have learned the words *irony* and *hypocrisy*, but he understood that a man who earned a paltry twelve dollars a week, a third the national average, should not heap scorn on his youngest son just because the boy preferred reading books to building muscle, watching movies to tinkering with cars. His father regularly told him that a life counted only if the world took notice, but he also dismissed every dream his children might have because they were not as grand as his own had been. Joe saw the same qualities in his older brother—a love of motors and speed, a disdain for those who didn't. Together his father and his brother made Joe feel other and odd. He was fair and painfully skinny, with a sunken chest, a long narrow face, and a wide forehead, giving his head a triangular look. All this, and with adolescence, a bad case of acne, made him a target at home and at school.

As Charles Sr. came to favor one son, Ruth teamed up with the other. She sneaked Joe books and introduced him to jazz. She told him he was smart, which he knew was true, and handsome, which he knew was not. Her protectiveness came off as the desperation that it was, and it only made Joe all the more determined to show his father he was tough. When Joe started skipping school, Ruth looked the other way and did not tell Charles Sr. about the visits from the truant officer. When Joe began strong-arming other students for money, Ruth kept that to herself, too. But Joe would not be kept secret. The more Ruth excused or hid his behavior, the more flagrant it became. By age twelve, he had been to Boys' Court in Chicago half a dozen times for truancy and petty theft. And in 1942, after snatching a girl's purse, he was sentenced to the St. Charles School for Boys.

The school was created early in the 1900s, the pet project of philanthropist John Gates, Chicago Daily News editor Nelson W. McClain, and Judge Loeb Stanley Tuthill, the first judge to preside over the first juvenile court in the country. Tuthill wrote his best-known opinion in a lawsuit over a movie about Shakespeare's life, when he ruled that Francis Bacon was the true author of the plays. He wanted a different legacy, hence the school. Tuthill saw no distinction between boys who committed crimes and those who were orphaned, abused, or neglected. They all needed the kind of parenting they clearly had not had—a firm but benevolent kind that he was confident the state could provide. He found farmland thirty-four miles west of Chicago, a half-day trip by train, and purchased 130 acres using large donations from philanthropists Charles M. Schwab and J. P. Morgan. Then he sold it to the State of Illinois for one dollar on condition that the legislature appropriate $360,000 to build his imagined school.

The founders' dream was realized in a circle of ten dormitory-like cottages, each designed to house forty to forty-five boys plus one mar-ried couple who served as house mother and father. Each "family" shared a living room and a kitchen, and the children spent half their day in the eight-room schoolhouse and half in vocational training on the working farm. Religious attendance at the small chapel was mandatory. There was a pool in the gymnasium building and a four-hundred-seat auditorium with a stage.

But by the time thirteen-year-old Joe arrived on November 27, 1942, and was assigned to the cottage for the youngest children, those in charge of the school were simply going through the motions. First the depression and then the war effort left little energy or money for penal innovation. St. Charles was a place to put a growing wave of "juvenile delinquents," and Joe hated his seventeen months there. It was degrading to be among the youngest of the residents, and he reminded the "little kids" that though he had been *caught* stealing just one time, that was not his whole story. He hinted at mob con-nections and ins with the cops and said his brother had taught him to use a gun and his father had taught him how to hotwire a car engine.

He bragged about his father a lot, describing him as a world-famous motorcycle racer.

"He [is] inclined to exaggerate in order to attract attention and [is] almost considered to be a pathological liar," one psychological evaluation of Joe would read. This tendency toward braggadocio, the evaluator theorized, was likely because he "has been much over-indulged by his mother and that his attitudes [have] also been affected by his acne, which made him feel self-conscious."

No one thought Joe had broken the bragging habit by June 1944, but he had kept his record clean and moved up the tiers of the merit system, so he was released. Back home, his father still raged, his mother still wept, his brother, now nineteen, still went to work with his father at Speedway Manufacturing Company during the day and prowled the streets at night, never getting caught for the many things he told Joe he had done.

The St. Charles rules of parole required Joe to enroll in ninth grade at Austin High School. His grades and attendance were good—and then they were not. He dropped out to work a series of part-time jobs—resetting pins at a bowling alley, jerking sodas at a drugstore— but didn't keep any of those for very long. They were all beneath him and boring.

As Joe made his way in Chicago, an ever-evolving set of facts was making its way out of St. Charles. Speaking to the Kiwanis Club of Southwest Chicago, Superintendent Eddy justified the existence of the School for Boys by saying, "Seventy-five percent of the graduates of the school make good in life despite their heritage." At about the same time, the lieutenant governor of Illinois, Hugh W. Cross, told the Illinois Sheriffs' Association, "A check-up of six hundred former inmates who had been sent to St. Charles School for Boys, discloses that more than 72 percent of them continued afterwards to lead a life of crime." Joe was but a subject in a penological experiment, one where there was no real agreement on the results.

The War Years
Dante Cosentino and David Troy
Stamford

DANTE COSENTINO DID NOT TELL HIS MOTHER ABOUT THE appointment. Rose was already beside herself with worry over Albert, her eldest, who had been wounded at the Battle of the Bulge, and Dante saw no reason to worry her further. He certainly didn't say that he was headed all the way downtown in Stamford, nor that his appointment was scheduled at a time when he should have been in school. To explain would have required bringing up other things he had neglected to mention: that he had been "absent" for more than half of the required 180 days of school last year; that even though he'd passed all his final tests anyway, he was required to repeat ninth grade when classes began this past September; that he hadn't shown up terribly often to this do-over version either.

On one of the rare days when Dante was present for morning attendance at Burdick Junior High School, the guidance counselor had handed him a note telling him to report to the Family and Child Center, which was likely the same charity that had helped Rose pay for her divorce. He knew downtown well (something else he had never told his mother) and arrived at the appointment right on time. Because fourteen-year-olds are built of contradictions, the inwardly obedient child arrived punctually for a meeting to discuss why the outwardly rebellious teen was so unreliable.

A psychologist greeted him and administered an IQ test, explaining that its goal wasn't so much to measure what Dante knew as to look at how his brain worked, so he shouldn't worry about getting a grade. But Dante never worried about grades. Even though he failed to show up for classes last year, he had passed every subject, which was why he was angry that he had to repeat a year.

The IQ questions were followed by a series of pictures—splotches, really—and Dante was instructed to describe what he saw. What he "saw" was nothing but a black inkblot on a white page, so he decided to "have some fun" with the test, creating the most absurd scenes he could imagine. There were witches and monsters, he told the psychologist, all threatening to harm him.

After that they just talked. How was life at home? the man began.

Dante was not one to think about his lot in life, so he wasn't quite sure how to answer. He knew his family had once been "well off," but then his father, Gerome, became a drunk and his mother was granted a divorce, and the neighbors in North Mianus had looked down on them for years. He knew his mother had moved out of North Mianus to get away from the gossip. It certainly wasn't for the accommodations. At Rose's first post divorce house on Pacific Street in Stamford, she had to hold a cheesecloth over the kitchen spout to filter out the worms that lived in the pump. For Thanksgiving dinner in that house, each child was allotted one boiled potato and one hard-boiled egg.

That made their current house, a few blocks away on Holly Place, an improvement. Dante still shared a bed with Valentino and Frank, but now the heat worked well enough that they didn't pile their winter coats over the blankets. This move had coincided with the start of the Second World War, and the Cosentinos benefited from the surge in national economic fortunes. Louise, Evelyn, and Mary all had jobs, and Albert had sent his army pay home to Rose.

The younger Cosentinos also brought in what they could. Dante was selling newspapers and shining shoes on street corners downtown. He sometimes took Frank along with him, teaching his youngest brother to snap the polish rag in the way that showed customers he knew his stuff. The two would come home with their shoeshine box on one shoulder, and if the weather was nice, they would see Rose sitting on the front porch, watching the cars pass by, sometimes humming to herself. They would hand her their earnings, counting the coins out into her palm, and she would give them back a few for a triple-scoop cone, one vanilla, one chocolate, one strawberry.

As for their father, he was like a ghost in their lives, an apparition, appearing out of nowhere and disappearing again. He would fall in step with them as they walked down a random street. Or they would hear him rustling on that front porch at night. He took to hiding half-empty whiskey bottles in their bushes, which the youngest children would find and shatter on the sidewalk. That didn't stop his visits.

A younger Rose might have responded to his intrusions with anger, but this matronly version, who sat on the porch in her ankle-length dresses and neat cap of white hair, mostly shrugged. Her need to fight had left with Gerome, as had her energy to keep everyone in line. The woman who had once clocked Dante over the head with a cast iron frying pan because he argued with his younger sister now pretended not to know that he held back some of his tips.

And so the children became the parents, caring for each other, relishing their freedom. Which was how Dante managed to miss half a year of school and be held back a full year without his mother knowing.

How was life at home? the psychologist had asked.

"It's okay," Dante answered. "No complaints."

Did he like living in Stamford? the man continued.

Fact was, he loved it. He felt more comfortable in the big city than he ever had back in the relatively rural part of town. North Mianus was just three miles away from Stamford, but one was sprinkled with farms and crisscrossed with dirt roads, while the other was filled with bustle and traffic. The city, he learned, allowed anonymity. Back in North Mianus every shopkeeper had known his name—including the one who'd caught him trying to fit a few too many comic books into his jacket without paying and threatened to call both the police and his mother should he ever try that again. But in Stamford he was just another young teenage boy, and if he kept moving he need never become familiar anywhere.

"I like it fine," he answered.

And school? What did he think about that?

He thought it was easy. In algebra he figured out most of the answers in his head, so why take tests or do homework? A voracious reader, he'd already finished most of the books before his English teacher assigned them. He never said any of this aloud because his father had loved books and his mother had hated that fact. When Gerome left, Rose burned thousands of volumes—for warmth, she said, though Dante would have gone and chopped more wood. The loss of all those books made his heart hurt, but he had gotten the message. Books did not put food on the table.

How did he like school? "I like it enough," he answered. "I have no problem with it."

Eventually the psychologist seemed to run out of questions, and he came around his desk and shook Dante's hand, as he would a grown man's. Then he destroyed the illusion by saying "Come back next week, at the same time. And please make sure to bring your mother."

✦

ON SUNDAYS, THE TROYS went to church. The family attended St. Mary of Stamford Parish, the Catholic church in the Cove. Bridget could most often be found in one of the forward pews, with all her children but her youngest son, David. He was up front, serving as an altar boy while his mother beamed and prayed—for the soul of her husband and for the safety of her children.

There were as many reasons to be sitting in that pew as there were Troys. Bridget attended because her religion was something constant when so much else in her world had changed. Since her husband's death, she spent each day leading her life as it was, ever aware of a parallel life, the one she would have had were he still here. Every morning she left the house at 39 Weed Avenue for her job at the Schick razor factory in Stamford, knowing that if Patrick were alive, she would be home getting the children off to school at that hour. Every day she served and cleaned in the company's cafeteria, and sold the pies she'd baked at home the night before, aware that if Patrick hadn't died, she would be cooking and cleaning only for her family.

Bridget still found no joy in working. No liberation or pride that she could make her way on her own. There were women who felt those things, who had taken on the jobs men left behind during the last war, and who seemed sad, even angry, that they'd had to give it all back when the men returned. Bridget already knew she could support herself; she had done so for all the years between being sent out of her father's house and brought into her husband's. Marriage had allowed her nearly twenty years of certainty that someone else would keep a roof over her head and food on her table. She had relished relinquishing that burden. Why would any woman want it back?

Deep in prayer at St. Mary's, she could forget all that. The Latin of the mass, the vestments of the priests and the altar boys, the familiar hymns, the icons, bells, and communion wafers, they were all as they had always been. If she closed her eyes, she could even be back in her home parish in Ireland, reciting the same words with her own parents and sisters.

Most of her children attended because their mother said they had to; a few would stop when they had children of their own. Agnes, now a nurse at Stamford Hospital, regularly worked Sunday shifts. Louise was soon to be married and would join her new husband's congregation. Patrick Jr., just back from his years as a gunnery instructor in the navy, accompanied his mother out of duty, not devotion. Twelve-year-old David, though, was not at St. Mary's against his will, and while he was there, his mind wasn't elsewhere. He did not see mass as something to be endured. He attended because he believed.

David often saw signs, connections, and tests of faith in his daily life. His God was one who wanted him to be good and who sent him signs in the form of recurring dreams, numbers that popped up regularly, and coincidences that must have meaning. He was a sunny young man by nature, had been since he was born, and the appearances of these tiny messages made him happy. When he moved up the ranks in the Boy Scouts, collected scrap metal and paper during the war, and served as an altar boy, it was partly because it made his mother proud but mostly because it made him feel he was fulfilling his destiny. He had only gauzy memories of Patrick, but Father Ganley was as kind and wise as he imagined his real father had been.

He looked like his Pa—red hair, blue eyes, ruddy complexion, and stocky build. His chatty nature seemed to come from Patrick, too. David could talk to anyone and loved nothing more than making a stranger his friend. Also like Patrick, he was a tinkerer. Bridget believed her husband could fix anything and had he lived, he and David might be doing so together. While she was fantasizing, she wondered if Patrick might have nudged their son into a practical purpose for his inherited skill—plumbing, perhaps, or electricity. Because while pipes and fittings had been Patrick's favored puzzle, David was entranced with dirty, dangerous automobile engines. A neighbor on Leeds Street worked at a gas station near St. Mary's, and in his free time, David would hang around the repair bays, wishing he were old enough for a car of his own.

Or maybe a motorcycle. In the postwar world, motorcycles were having a moment. Their popularity had declined some after World War I, but during the Second World War, American GIs used Harley Davidsons to move messages in Europe while the Germans used BMWs. At first the German motorcycles went farther and had foot pedals that could shift gears so drivers could keep both hands on the bar. But as the fighting went on and U.S. troops captured more enemy hardware, the Harleys were upgraded. By war's end, so many Harley Davidsons escorted U.S. convoys into newly freed territory that the locals nicknamed them "The Liberator."

Returning soldiers brought their love of the machines back home with them, and young men embraced the bikes and the victory they'd come to represent. During the postwar boom, the roaring motors were the sound of the future. For boys like David, they were a way to ride like heroes, providing a hint of danger while also being steadfast and true.

It was a plan best broken to Bridget in stages, however. As it was, she loathed cars, having lost her husband in one. She walked nearly everywhere in the Cove and took the bus to the Schick factory for work. It would be a leap for her to approve of motorcycles, which were certainly not what the God-fearing rode. If David were meant to have one, then one would make its way to him. Good boys did not pray for toys for themselves; he should focus his prayers on helping those he loved. The rest he could leave to fate and faith.

✦

DANTE RETURNED TO THE psychologist's office right on time. He "forgot" to bring Rose.

The psychologist raised an eyebrow, then introduced him to a woman whose title was "social worker" and who had still more questions for the boy.

If he enjoyed school so much, why was he absent so often? she asked.

That had nothing to do with school and everything to do with money, he answered. He could make more of it when he was not in school. When he didn't have to wait for the school day to end, he could get to the *Stamford Advocate* newspaper office earlier and pick up as large a pile of papers as he could carry. The late editions were still warm at that hour, and he bought them for two cents a copy to hawk them on the street for their cover price of three cents.

The earlier he did this, the larger the pool of customers who hadn't already bought from another newsboy. Sometimes the businessmen would give him a nickel and tell him to keep the change. Next, he said, he hoped to get a delivery route to the houses with yards; the tips were even bigger in the neighborhoods where the "rich" people lived.

What, the psychologist wondered, did he spend all this money on?

He gave some to his mother, he said, then admitted he kept some for himself. He bought candy and movie tickets, and clothes like the others at school had. He had his eyes on a pair of new shoes. He'd been to a doubleheader at Yankee Stadium once, a paying customer, which was much more fun than when he'd gone for free, arriving in a bus sporting a banner that read UNDERPRIVILEGED CHILDREN.

This made the social worker smile. He was smart, she said, and his future was bright—but only if he stayed in school. To help him do that, the organization she worked for was offering him a scholarship, not for school itself, because that was public and therefore free, but to replace the money he made while working. He would receive $3.75 every week of the school year, if he attended every day and set a good example for other students. And if he stayed the course and graduated, they would provide a scholarship to college.

He was tempted for several reasons. First was the money. Rich kids got allowances, and how could he pass up the chance to be treated like a rich kid? This was a hefty sum, more than he made every week hustling newspapers and collecting beer bottles and snapping shoeshine rags. The Thom McCan store downtown had a most excellent pair of brown leather lace-ups for $4.20. Those would be his first purchase.

The other reason, though, was what the social worker said about setting a good example. With his older siblings grown and gone, he was now "the biggest of the littles," and he knew he had been falling down on that job. It wasn't only his mother who he'd been keeping things from—his truancy, his shoplifting. He had also been lying to Frank, Lecia, and most of all to ten-year-old Rosie, who thought he was her hero in the same way he had looked up to Albert before he'd come home darkened and damaged from the war.

Heroes did not let their adoring crowds down. And if you had to lie about it, Dante figured, maybe it wasn't so heroic. His father had turned out to be all too human; Albert, too, had been drinking and withdrawing. Maybe it was his job to at least pretend to be a role model until they didn't need one anymore.

The psychologist and the social worker were waiting for an answer. "It's a deal," Dante said.

The War Years
Warden Ragen, Alf Alving, and Nathan Leopold
Stateville Penitentiary

THE MEN OF STATEVILLE REGISTERED FOR WAR AND WERE screened in the prison infirmary. Their X-rays—eight hundred of them in three days—were taken by Nathan Leopold, who had recently been reassigned to the radiology lab after spending eight more years at the correspondence school without Richard Loeb. Though convicted felons were required to register, most were not allowed to serve—in part because, as one member of FDR's draft board put it, the mothers of law-abiding young men would be "understandably upset" that their sons might be serving with criminals. Over the course of the war, only 133 Stateville inmates would be inducted; all of them had been imprisoned for relatively minor offenses and were released early to go fight.

Those who remained had a few limited ways to contribute. They could give blood in the mobile Red Cross units that arrived periodically in the prison courtyard, and they donated 4,200 pints over the years of war. They could use canteen funds to buy war bonds, and they invested $6,200. They could be assigned to churn out shirts, jackets, trousers, and blankets in what used to be the upholstery shop, or to build military cots in what used to be the furniture factory; they filled four hundred train cars with these materials between Pearl Harbor and VE-Day.

For Warden Ragen, the war provided an administrative headache. He had left his prison job briefly, during the walk-up to the fighting, moving to Washington, D.C., to help the Department of Justice create detention camps for immigrants whose allegiance to America had been questioned. He had returned to Joliet-Stateville in the autumn of 1942, and the terms of that return had theoretically solidified his power. Now, for instance, he had complete authority over the hiring of guards, but he could not find guards to hire. The men who would otherwise fill those positions were either off at war or working at munitions plants for better pay. Ragen stretched his smaller staff by closing some cellblocks and doubling and tripling the number of cellmates in others.

By far the biggest changes to Stateville, though, were yet to come. In September 1944, Ragen walked through the campus with a short, sandy-haired, bespectacled physician-scientist named Alf Sven Alving. Born in Grängesberg, Sweden, but living in America since the age of seven, Alving was a nephrologist at the University of Chicago, an expert in diseases of the blood and the kidneys. Warm and jovial, with a disarmingly crude sense of humor, Alving was best known for creating a system that made it possible to remove one kidney from inside a dog and attach it to the outside of the body, where it was available to researchers who sought to observe and manipulate it. His work might have seemed like something out of science fiction, but his manner was the opposite, and touring the hospital wing he looked more like Santa's elf than Dr. Frankenstein.

Alving was not at Stateville to talk about kidneys. He was there to talk about malaria. Not because anyone at Stateville had malaria, but because Alving was there to give it to them. The mosquito-borne tropical disease was as old as history—pictured on ancient Babylonian tablets, described by Hippocrates, and thought to have contributed to the deaths of King Tut, Alexander the Great, and Genghis Khan. During World War II, the malaria parasite was as much an enemy of the United States as were the Axis powers. Just as more soldiers were killed by the 1918 flu than by warfare, the toll of malaria on American troops in Asia and Africa was worse than that of enemy weapons. An estimated 8 million "man days" were lost between 1942 and 1945 while soldiers fought soaring fevers, teeth-chattering chills, excruciating headaches, and constant vomiting. Gen. Douglas MacArthur warned in 1943 that "this will be a long war if for every division I have facing the enemy, I must count on a second division in hospital with malaria and a third convalescing."

It was not the first time U.S. goals had been threatened by malaria. Although uncommon within America itself—there were but a million cases a year in the Deep South, compared with 300 million globally— the grueling illness regularly crippled U.S. interests when Americans ventured into swampier lands. The building of the Panama Canal was almost halted because so many workers fell ill. Theodore Roosevelt saved the project by authorizing $20 million to drain wetlands and cover standing water with kerosene. That killed mosquitos and their eggs, which reduced the rate of infection, but it did not eliminate the disease. Nor was it a cure for those who still fell ill, whom doctors treated with mustard baths, kerosene massages, and alcohol (administered internally and externally).

Until the mid-1920s, the only drug known to have any effect on malaria was an imperfect one. Quinine did not prevent the rolling relapses that were a part of the disease, and it had unpleasant side effects, including blurred vision and ringing in the ears, but it mitigated the worst malarial symptoms. Through the first decade of the 1900s, it had been a reliable moneymaker for Cove Mills—which, beside extracting dyes from exotic trees in those years, ground cinchona bark from Peru for quinine. Then cheaper farmed substitutes from Java and Sumatra caused demand for naturally derived quinine to plummet. Even cheaper synthetic versions followed, invented by German scientists during the Great War, when Germany was cut off from Indonesian suppliers.

At first the German offering, called pamaquine or plasmoquin, was heralded as having no side effects. Further testing found some potentially life-threatening ones—specifically the onset of severe anemia, particularly in patients of African descent. It was shelved. In 1932 a next "miracle" drug, atabrine, entered the marketplace, but it had the unfortunate tendency to turn patients' skin bright yellow while causing debilitating headaches and vomiting that were almost as bad as malaria itself. Soldiers were instructed to take a dose weekly as a preventative. Compliance was low, falling even further when Japanese propaganda leaflets claimed (erroneously) that it caused impotence and sterility.

The downsides, real and rumored, became a moot point because soon there was little atabrine to be had. American stockpiles could not be refilled since the drug was manufactured primarily in Germany. Nor could U.S. forces revert to quinine, because the Dutch East Indies had fallen to the Japanese. Meanwhile documents were discovered showing that the Nazis were aggressively experimenting with new malaria drugs for their own soldiers, while planning to flood battlegrounds and breed malaria-infected mosquitoes to cripple Allied troops. It would not be the first time an army had used malaria as a microbiological weapon. Ancient Romans, who had developed immunity to malaria from lifetimes of exposure, survived several invasions by simply hiding out within the city's walls while the disease decimated whichever army was trying to fight its way in.

The outcome of this modern war, too, could depend on who solved the malaria puzzle first, and by September 1944 the U.S. Armed Forces were desperately looking for a new treatment. President Roosevelt created the U.S. Committee on Medical Research to fund medical and scientific programs related to national defense. Of the nearly $25 million the CMR spent during the war years, nearly one-quarter went to malaria research.

By the time Alving toured Stateville, army researchers had narrowed thousands of candidate drugs to several dozen, some developed in American labs over the prior two years, some seized from German strongholds in North Africa. Nearly all had been tested for toxicity on animals and were ready for efficacy testing on humans. These next trials had to be conducted on human subjects because of the unusual way malaria works. The female anopheles mosquito needs human blood to nurture her own eggs, and she bites to get it. When she happens to bite a human who is infected with malaria, she ingests the larval form of the malarial parasite along with the blood. Those larvae incubate within the mama mosquito's salivary glands and are introduced into the bloodstream of whichever human she bites next. Once the organisms are in this new host, they migrate to the habitable environment of the human liver, where they take about two weeks to multiply and mature before entering the red blood cells and moving throughout the body. This is when symptoms begin. The invaders burst the cells in which they travel—waves of parasitic explosions, forty-eight to seventy-two hours apart, each causing a new round of fever, sweats, and chills. Sometimes the parasite remains dormant in the liver or blood for months or years, reemerging seemingly at random.

Malaria does not act this way in any of the usual lab animals, so the army needed a large number of humans on whom to test its candidate drugs. Ideally, those humans would be as similar as possible— all eating the same food, breathing the same air, following the same routine. Once they were all infected with the same strain by the same mosquito, the only variable would be whether they received drug A, B, C, or a placebo. That standard was easy to meet in animal studies but nearly impossible with people. Two groups came particularly close: prisoners and institutionalized psychiatric patients. This was what brought Alf Alving to Stateville.

Preliminary malaria trials had already begun in psychiatric hospitals, including one outside Chicago run by University of Chicago scientists. Decades earlier the Nobel Prize in Medicine had been awarded for the discovery that infection with malaria can reduce psychiatric symptoms in some patients with late-stage syphilis. (Fifteen percent died from the malaria itself, but that was a lower rate than those who died from the arsenic and mercury that had been the previous treatment.) The fact that malaria cured some schizophrenics led one government bureaucrat to authorize giving the disease to a wide swath of patients with "other neurological and psychiatric disorders," reasoning that the infectious cure had "*not* been proven *not* to help" nonsyphilitic subjects. Such was the double-negative logic of war.

It was in part philosophical discomfort with this twisted rationalization that led Alving to meet with Ragen. Primarily, though, it was the more literal discomfort with conditions at the Manteno State Hospital for the Insane, twenty-seven miles from Stateville, where Alving had been overseeing early trials. Such research requires cleanliness, but at Manteno there was filth, with regular outbreaks of food-borne disease and a recent epidemic of typhus. The research also requires consistency, but Manteno patients were noncooperative, and the research nurses on staff kept quitting, fearing for their safety.

Alving turned his attention west, one in a long line of researchers to see prisoners as ideal subjects. "First, do no harm," Hippocrates wrote circa 400 B.C.E., and for generations that has been understood to mean that doctors should not hurt their patients. But even in Hippocrates's day, the protection did not apply to prisoners; using them for research, even when it approached torture, was considered part of their punishment. Circa 325 B.C.E., Herophilus and Erasistratus created the field of anatomy by dissecting the bodies of condemned prisoners. Whether those prisoners were still alive at the start of the dissections is debated by historians, but what is clear is that prisoners in ancient Greece were not considered patients—they were barely considered people.

That logic persisted for centuries and was the justification for the cholera research by American researchers at Bilibid Prison in the Philippines in 1906, pellagra experiments at the Rankin Prison Farm in Mississippi in 1915, "sleeping sickness" trials in St. Louis, and tuberculosis vaccine trials in Denver in 1933. The only public objection to these over the years was not that the prisoners were being mistreated but that they were being treated too well, since some were being offered early parole in exchange for being deliberately infected with a deadly illness.

The start of World War II changed public sentiment. The public was still fine with prisoners suffering, but not for possibility of a pardon, which could be considered self-serving; suffering for the benefit of the troops, however, was considered selfless. It was in that spirit that Alving had come to Stateville. Per army rules, he explained to

Ragen, one hundred dollars would be added to each volunteer's canteen fund and an official letter of thanks to their prison file.

Alving showed Ragen the form the "human subjects" would be asked to sign: "I assume all the risks of this experiment and declare that I absolve the University of Chicago and all the technicians and researchers who take part in the experiment, as well as the government of Illinois, the directory of the State penitentiary and every other official, even as concerns my heirs and representatives, of any responsibility." He also gave Ragen the script to be read before each signing—one that warned that death was possible, though not likely.

The warden and the doctor did not discuss whether an incarcerated man's signature truly qualified as "consent." Nor did they ask whether a prisoner within the walls of a prison had the right to say no to a "request" coming, even indirectly, from a warden. Or if the hundred dollars, the laudatory letter, and the knowledge that others had been pardoned in other places over the decades, slipped over the line into bribery or coercion. The coming decade would increase the urgency of those questions, in part because of the work that was about to begin at Stateville. But in September 1944, Alving was certain that his own aims were ethical and therefore that his experiments would be, too.

Ragen offered the entire third floor of the hospital wing for the research, with space for sick wards, mosquito incubators, and chemical and hematological laboratories. Rather than hiring a staff of nurses from outside, Alving could train prisoners to be both nurses and lab technicians, work that had the added benefit of preparing them for life after release. Alving's one remaining concern was whether he could find enough prisoners willing to be infected with malaria, then treated with an experimental drug.

The capos of the yard were long gone, but there were still prisoners with influence at Stateville. The carceral organism responded best to persuasion from within, and rather than have a man in a suit or a lab coat make this case, Ragen would spread the word through several of their own. On his tour that day with Alving, the last stop was a meeting with seven such prisoners, all gathered in a prison office at the invitation of the warden.

Alving tried to hide his discomfort when he saw Nathan Leopold among the seven. Ragen tried to pretend he didn't see the doctor flinch. Ragen still disliked Leopold, finding him pompous and cocky. He assumed the feeling was mutual, although over their nine years of acquaintance, the men had learned that each could be helpful to the other, and they behaved with exaggerated civility. Ragen had become so accustomed to treating Leopold with respect, however feigned, that he was surprised when men like Alving reacted with fear. When it came to Leopold, there were two kinds of academics: those like the sociologists at the University of Chicago, who delighted in seeing him as one of their own, and those like Alving, who was visibly repulsed. But Ragen pressed on, because Alving needed to meet the smartest and most influential men on campus, and Leopold, nearly forty years old by now and entering his twentieth year at Stateville, was both.

Alving explained his mission, then asked whether these men thought there would be willing volunteers. To Alving's surprise, though not Ragen's, everyone in the room turned toward Leopold, who answered with a question of his own.

"How many volunteers will you need?"

Alving estimated two hundred.

"I think you'll get at least twice that many."

Days later Ragen announced the trials on the internal prison radio. By afternoon, 487 men had signed up to participate.

The toxicity test at Stateville went so well that the U.S. Office of Scientific Research and Development soon centered all of the army's malarial research at the penitentiary. Alving stayed too, and within the first month, he built a staff that included a dozen prisoners, all training as nurses and technicians, all of whom came with the recommendation of Warden Ragen.

These trainees were a hardened bunch. Among them were three men who had murdered police officers, one who had beaten a man to death during a quarrel, and another who'd killed while robbing a restaurant. Kenneth Rucker, who was serving 199 years for the brutal murder of a garage attendant, and who once protested that he should not have been convicted at all because his victim was Black, turned out to be a gifted lab technician; Alving would go on to list him as a co-author on several research papers generated by the malaria trials. Charles Ickes, serving a life sentence after a career of robbery and car theft, also had a knack for the lab bench, despite having barely finished the third grade; Alving came to consider him a friend and would eventually work to help him get paroled.

Alving knew *of* these men's pasts, but he didn't know *about* them. Ickes and Rucker, to him, were simply the techs who worked with him each day, men dressed in starched white orderly jumpsuits, not their prison blues. He managed a similar lens for the men who enrolled as subjects in the experiments. They, too, were murderers and rapists, but Alving saw only pajama-clad patients in hospital beds. This ability to view the present man while remaining blind to his past was a trick that worked with all but one prisoner, one who badly wanted to be part of the team.

Nathan Leopold certainly had the education and intellect for the job and kept asking to join. But Alving couldn't square the smirking teenager on the front pages in 1924 with the balding man asking to be trusted with a top-secret government program in 1944. He could not imagine how the dandy who had stalked young Bobby Franks would take temperatures and urine samples, fetch juice for fever-parched patients, change sweat-drenched beds, and check that medications had been properly ingested. ("Open your mouth, lift up your tongue.") True, Leopold had helped generate volunteers for the program in the first place, seemed to run the prison X-ray lab single-handedly, and was apparently nearly as smart as he believed himself to be. But his very presence made Alving uncomfortable. Was that discomfort Leopold's problem or Alving's? Did every felon really deserve a chance to change?

Alving finally turned to Warden Ragen for advice. "Can Nathan Leopold be trusted?" Ragen's view of trust was more complex than

Edmund Allen's had been thirty years earlier. Allen had given his trust until he had reason to do otherwise. Ragen withheld his trust until it had been earned.

As far as the warden knew, Leopold had never directly lied to him, and that, he had concluded, made him worthy of trust. So Ragen called Leopold into the hospital wing for a meeting with Alving and presented the situation candidly. There was some concern, Ragen began, over whether Leopold could keep any secrets he might learn should he be permitted to be part of the army's work. There was even more concern that Leopold might not follow directions from scientists with whom he disagreed.

Leopold answered with a few qualifiers. "If you mean that I will keep anything I learn absolutely secret," he was happy to make that promise, he said. "As to the scientific parts of the project, I will do my level best to see that they are carried out honestly and to the letter. If, for instance, I learn of any volunteer trying to cheat by not taking his pills or by taking other medication, I will see to it that it stops—though I probably won't report it to you.

"But," he continued—and Ragen didn't like *buts*—"if by full cooperation you mean that I will report who steals an extra slice of bread from the chuck wagon, then you'll have to find yourself another boy."

This was a *but* that Ragen could live with. He looked to Alving, who nodded in agreement. Leopold joined the malaria trial team.

1945
Al Tarlov and Joseph DeSalvo
Norwalk and Chicago

FINALLY, AL TARLOV HAD A BEDROOM ALL TO HIMSELF AT SHORE-front Park. Merwyn had left home in 1944 to join the Army Air Corps, but just as he finished training as a bully gunner, the war ended, and he moved out to Long Island to sell life insurance, as his uncle Harry had done. Jay turned eighteen during the postwar years, joined the navy, and never saw action. When his tour was over, he eventually opened a Cadillac dealership in Maryland.

Neither Merwyn nor Jay would ever run the restaurant. Charlie had shaken both boys' hands just before they left for basic training and asked whether they might like to take over the business one day. Both declined. This left Al as the only potential heir to all his father had built, and with his brothers away, his responsibilities increased. Most of the regular waitstaff had gone off to fight, so at age thirteen Al became a full-time waiter and part-time bartender, taking orders for a table of eight from memory, mixing martinis, Manhattans, side-cars, and whiskey sours from a book he kept hidden behind the bar. He served drinks he could not legally taste (technically he could not legally serve them, either, but in this time of crisis, the authorities were inclined to look the other way). He never once took a sip because he had already decided to abstain from the stuff. He'd seen how alcohol was so often present when things went wrong. Also, his Uncle Isadore did not approve of drinking.

The war ended as Al began his junior year at Norwalk High School. His class quickly became the largest ever at the school— 350 students—as the youngest of the returning GIs picked up where they had left off. Al's weeks took on a regular rhythm. Tuesday through Friday afternoons he stayed late at school, busy with team practices or meetings of the many clubs that had paused during the war. Tuesday, Wednesday, and Thursday nights he arrived at the restaurant in time for dinner with his mother, now just the two of them at the table in the corner that had once been set for four. Friday nights he visited his grandmother, Raisel, once the formidable matriarch of his large family, now physically stooped and frail but still emotionally tough. Her cooking was terrible, her English minimal, and so their Sabbath dinner conversation was mostly her gesturing toward seconds of overdone meat and underdone potatoes while he pantomimed being full. Every so often she got up to yell at the cat in Yiddish.

Saturdays he worked at the restaurant. The banquet space at Tarlov's could seat 125, and after the war the room was booked nearly every weekend. Sundays were all about the car. When Jay left for the navy, he had given Al his beloved 1936 Ford four-door. It had been a clunker once, but Jay had reassembled the engine and shined the exterior until its black paint gleamed. Jay had also left Al the simonizing business he'd started. Regulars would drop off their own Fords, Cadillacs, and Chevys in front of Tarlov's, and Al would take each car to his parents' driveway; for eight dollars he would wax and buff and live up to his brother's reputation as the best in town.

On Sunday evenings, Al used the car to pick up his dates at their homes, where he would make small talk with Mr. and Mrs. Lamb, or be grilled by Mr. and Mrs. Bloom, or receive a warm welcome from Mr. and Mrs. Stephanak before leaving with Mary or Eleanor or Barbara for a movie and a bite to eat. Often he would be invited to Sunday dinner at a classmate's home, and he would eagerly accept. To Al, Sunday dinner offered a glimpse at how other households approached being a family: how they ate together most nights, at a dining table, the meal cooked by the mother and presided over by the father, the parents talking *with* their children, not *at* them.

✦

BY THE SUMMER OF 1945, while Al Tarlov was simonizing cars, David Troy was itching to repair cars, and Dante Cosentino was saving his scholarship money to one day buy himself a car, Joe DeSalvo was doing time for stealing one.

He'd been caught by what should have been a routine ticket for ignoring a stop sign, but then a young man with a "swarthy complexion" leaped out of the passenger seat and got away. Joe, who was driving, did not. He'd been a few months shy of sixteen years old on April 25, 1945, meaning he did not have a license. Also, it turned out the car was stolen. Police never could prove who the passenger was that day, though they strongly suspected Joe's older brother, Charles.

"Are you taking the rap for him?" they asked repeatedly, and Joe repeatedly insisted—with a calm that exasperated his questioners—that the officer was mistaken and no one else had been in the car. At nineteen, the elder brother was an adult and would have been charged as such. Just sixteen, the younger brother was still a minor, and a juvenile court judge returned him to St. Charles.

At first Joe was miserable to be back. His father had not even come to court for his hearing, his brother had hightailed it to Florida, and his last glimpse of his mother was when she crumpled into a chair, crying, as he was led away. He spent his first night at St. Charles in the infirmary, telling the cottage "parents" that he was suffering from severe stomach pains, but he was really hoping for medication to help him sleep. When the night nurse brought it, Joe wrestled the bottle away, aimed a handful of pills at his mouth, and started to chew. Her screams brought the guards, who pinned Joe down, pried open his jaw, and emptied what was left of the Seconal. The next day he insisted that he had never meant to kill himself, that this was just part of a plan he'd cooked up to escape. The staff chose to believe him and sent him back to his cottage. This time he bunked with the oldest boys.

It was a reunion of sorts. Two of Joe's cottage mates, William Clair and Edgar Keck, had been at St. Charles during his first stay. They were both doing time for stealing cars, and it was a bit of a boost for Joe to be charged as a car thief, too. The three became a tight posse, though not one that lasted for long. First Clair escaped, when he and four housemates pummeled their resident "father" into unconsciousness and stole a car. Then Keck was paroled, and that was the last Joe ran with a "group" at St. Charles. As the months passed, notes in his file described ways he had changed with his friends gone. He did not exaggerate as often, was less prone to flashes of anger, and approached his schoolwork with an interest and commitment he hadn't had the first time around. During his free periods, he could often be found in the cottage's small library, where he was fond of detective stories and biographies of world explorers. When not reading, he was at the piano. He had taught himself to play by recreating popular tunes he'd heard on the radio. His real love, though, was jazz, a favorite of his mother's, and he put the few records he found at the cottage onto the aged player.

In his biweekly discussions with social workers, they theorized that these changes meant he was becoming a responsible man. He outwardly agreed but inwardly doubted. He didn't feel mature—he just felt trapped and bored. The books and music helped him keep his head down and get through each day.

When his case came up for review a year later, there was nothing to flag. No more suicide attempts, no disciplinary citations, just solid grades and steady work habits. On April 26, 1946, he was released. The newest superintendent, a military man who had fought two world wars, saw him off with a salute and his usual parting words: "I hope not to see you here again."

✦

OF ALL THE DAYS of Al Tarlov's week, Mondays were the undisputed highlight. That was when Uncle Isadore would travel to Norwalk. He'd spend the morning seeing patients at the hospital, where he was still the only neurosurgeon, and afternoons making house calls. After school and on holidays or vacations, Al was invited to follow along.

Isadore had come to loom larger over the years, not only in his youngest nephew's life but also in the medical world. During the war, he had researched a way of repairing nerves by "gluing" severed ends together with clotted blood plasma. The technique had allowed wounded GIs to retain at least some feeling and function. Isadore would write a book about the process, his first of four. With his mentor, William Cone, Isadore would also pioneer the "knee-chest" position for lower spinal surgery—placing patients in what yogis would call the "child's pose" while receiving anesthesia. The position created less pressure on the abdomen and the chest, which reduced pressure on epidural veins in the spine.

Watching Isadore work, Al learned about the anatomy of the spine and the dynamic of doctor and patient: how to listen, to hear what might be unspoken, to be a reassuring presence at a time of vulnerability while steering clear of false hope. Between house calls, uncle and nephew would talk—about what Al had just seen, but also about much more. The two youngest sons of practical families were joined by their shared intellectual streak, sharing thoughts that were grand and sweeping.

Isadore was interested in everything, and his intensity was contagious. To Al, whose conversations with his father were almost always about grades or the restaurant, talking to his uncle was a revelation. The rare times Isadore did discuss Tarlov's, it was to note that the waitstaff were mostly Black while all the customers were white, and to convey that he did not think this was okay. Even a literal nuts-and-bolts subject like Al's simonizing business, Isadore turned into an elegy: on the beauty of automobiles, their transformation of society, the inability of man to create a machine as durable as the human heart, and his pride in his own heart, which on X-ray was decidedly larger than average, something Isadore attributed to his robust schedule of daily exercise.

They talked about the news of the day, which, as 1945 became 1946, was often about the rebuilding of Europe, and the lessons of the past that would—or in Isadore's opinion, *should*—shape the future.

Sometimes their discussions followed the front-page headlines: the liberation of the Nazi concentration camps in April 1945, the official surrender of Germany in May; the dropping of the atom bomb in August, the Japanese surrender ceremony in September. But Isadore was also drawn to the news that was deeper down in the papers, especially stories about medicine.

Two separate war crimes trials were underway in Europe by late 1945. In Nuremberg, Germany, twenty-four high-ranking officials, including Hermann Göring and Rudolf Hess, were being judged by an international tribunal. The other trial, less covered but of more interest to Isadore, was taking place within the gates of the Dachau concentration camp. There forty doctors were being tried by an American military court, among them Dr. Claus Schilling, who had been an internationally respected physician prior to the war. He had trained at institutes well known to Isadore and written papers in important journals. Now he stood accused of conducting what prosecutors described as "hideous" experiments on prisoners at Dachau—deliberately infecting them with malaria, then dosing them with potentially toxic medications. Of the one thousand Dachau prisoners who were used as subjects, nearly four hundred died, including many Polish priests who had been imprisoned for refusing to collaborate with the Nazis.

Military prosecutors charged Schilling with violating long-standing international norms of medicine. Schilling's defense relied in part on his assertion that there were no such norms, no agreed-upon list of what was and was not accepted medical practice. His was legitimate medical research, he said.

Nonsense, Isadore believed. Of course there were rules. No respectable doctor intentionally sickened a patient. Any responsible doctor explained what he would do and got permission. That victims of experiments at Dachau were in no position to give permission was just one reason why this was not medical research.

Sometimes their conversations were about health controversies closer to home. Five-year-old Rose Castelluzzo, of Stamford, for instance, had been born with something called "blue baby syndrome."

A percentage of her blood did not return to her lungs for oxygenation, turning her fingertips and toes a purplish blue. Even the smallest of exertions—walking across a room, climbing into bed—could leave her exhausted. Two doctors at Johns Hopkins Hospital in Baltimore had found a surgical cure for some causes of the syndrome, and *The Stamford Advocate* created a "Blue Baby Fund" to pay her expenses to travel there. Every day the newspaper published the most recent donors by name and amount given. Reaching $2,384, the fundraising more than covered the costs of the trip, with much left over to donate to infant heart research.

It would turn out that little Rose Castelluzzo was not a candidate for the surgery, and she returned home to Stamford. City residents were heartbroken that they could not cure her; Isadore was piqued that they had thought they had to. Whether your child lived or died should not depend on how rich you were, where you lived, and whether your community had a generous soul, he said.

Isadore practiced as he preached, operating on any patient who came to him. One Sunday night, when Al was having dinner with his classmate Ann Marie Lamb and her family, Mr. Lamb took him aside and asked a favor. Mrs. Lamb, he said, had been having severe back pain and was diagnosed with a herniated disk, yet no evidence of herniation—no problem with any disk at all—showed up on an X-ray. Her orthopedist had declared it a mystery. "Do you think your uncle would examine my wife?" Mr. Lamb asked.

Within a week Mrs. Lamb was lying on a testing table at Norwalk Hospital under a fluoroscope through which Isadore peered at her spine. He had injected a liquid contrast into a space between her lowest vertebrae and looked for shadows that would show liquid being displaced by a bulge that would indicate either a tumor or a slipped disk. The table on which she lay was designed to move, like a seesaw, and Isadore began with its head end elevated between ten and thirty degrees, encouraging the liquid, which was less dense than spinal fluid, to float up her back, allowing him to see the entire lumbar spine and then the lower part of the thoracic spine as well.

There was no shadow. Nothing was wrong with the disks in her lower back.

What then was causing her pain—sensations she described as a fire shooting down the back of one leg, interrupted by periods of numbness, all making it difficult to walk? On a hunch, Isadore tilted the table backward, one degree at a time, until Mrs. Lamb's feet were higher than her head. He watched the liquid migrate back through the lumbar region and continue into the sacral zone. When looking for disk problems, doctors didn't venture their fluoroscopes this far down, because there were no disks, just the bony protuberance that ended the spine. But there it was, a mass the size of a baseball, sitting atop the cluster of nerves where they exited out to the thigh, calf, and foot.

Mrs. Lamb's cyst was removed, leaving her pain free. Soon afterward Isadore would write the first medical journal description of what he called the sacral nerve cyst but would become known in textbooks as the Tarlov cyst. It wouldn't be his most important discovery, and time would show him to have been wrong about whether operating on it was always wise. But it would always bear his name. Which meant it would bear his nephew's, too.

✦

AFTER HIS RELEASE FROM the St. Charles School for Boys, Joe DeSalvo moved back home to 217 LaPorte Avenue. His brother was still in Florida, working as a truck driver, so Joe shared the small space with just his parents, the ones his thick penal file described as "hard working respectable people who made an effort to control inmate but were unable to do anything with him." He lasted eight weeks, much of it working on the factory floor at the Airway Finisher, and all of it fighting with his father, who believed he'd come back from St. Charles as less of a man than when he'd been sentenced. He'd gotten taller (now five foot ten), heavier (128 pounds) and paler while he was away, his acne giving way to deep rutted scars. Sallow looks mixed with a love of music that wasn't Italian opera and books that weren't the Bible provoked Charles more than his son's growing criminal record.

In July 1946, just before his seventeenth birthday, Joe stormed out and joined the navy. He said goodbye to his mother but not to his father before heading to basic training near San Diego. The impulsive move was not surprising to those who had reason to read his entire file, which described him as a "stubborn, self-willed individual who acts with little thought to the consequences and generally in a direction that will bring gain to himself without thinking of the loss to others."

California was a revelation to Joe, who had never left Illinois. He was so thrilled with the place that he regretted joining the military to get there. He went AWOL in August, having developed a business plan of sorts. He stole a car, sold it on the black market, stole another one, and drove up and down the coast, repeating whenever he needed cash. It was a game, and he was winning. He would later remember it as the happiest period of his life.

In late October 1946 he appeared in the front driveway of St. Charles, driving a brand-new Nash automobile. His clothes were "well-tailored, though a little on the flashy side," the *Chicago Tribune* would write when the whole visit went south. "There was a roll of bills in his pocket, and he was the youthful prototype of the 'old grad' returning to the ivy-covered walls of his alma mater." Administrators were suspicious, and the same superintendent who had wished him farewell in April now came and frisked him. Joe was insulted. "I don't see why they thought that car wasn't mine," he protested. "I would not have called the police if I saw the head of the school driving a new car."

When the search of his person turned up a German Luger revolver (which he had purchased days earlier in an Iowa pawnshop for fifty dollars), he was unfazed. "You never can tell when you'll need one of those things," he said. And when a search of the car found it really belonged to Harold B. Wilson of 508 Leclaire Avenue, the staff called police.

The deputy sheriff of Kane County brought Joe to the small local jail where five other "graduates" of St. Charles happened to be awaiting trial. Alone in his cell, Joe managed to fashion his belt into a noose and hang himself without anyone hearing. He was unconscious when he was found by a guard delivering a supper tray. Cut loose and brought to the prison infirmary, he came to several hours later. Then he was simply sent back to his cell without a belt.

The story made a brief splash in the Chicago papers, and what seemed to outrage the writers most was not that Joe had nearly died in police custody, but that he would not be properly punished. One *Chicago Tribune* article ended with this prediction: "Since Illinois has no reformatory for its teen-aged criminals, the odds are about even that if DeSalvo is convicted of car stealing or carrying a concealed weapon he'll again be a student at the training school."

That was not a good bet. Joe was not returned to St. Charles. He was convicted. The state's attorney argued that the school clearly could not reform him, and he was sentenced as an adult to a term of two to ten years for auto theft.

All criminals then sentenced in southern Illinois were brought to the Diagnostic Depot, across the street from the original Joliet building. They were given a battery of medical and psychiatric evaluations and were classified by their personality, capacity for improvement, and treatment needs. Joe filled out form upon form in his perfect flowing script. In the space asking for his nationality, he wrote "Italian, Swedish"; he said he drank moderately and smoked but didn't chew. When asked for former employers who might vouch for his work history to help place him in a prison shop, he made clear that his relationship to work had been casual.

"I absolutely do not know the names of the officials for whom I have worked, nor can I recollect any specific incident which would recall their attention to myself," he wrote. And when asked for the names of people who had known him for ten or fifteen years, he listed his father's twin brother and two of his father's sisters. Then he asked that officials not contact any of them. "I do not wish to have any of the relations I have mentioned, know that I am incarcerated, as my parents have led them to believe I am still in the Navy," he wrote.

Depot staff corresponded with all his relatives anyway, on Bureau of Prison stationery. In the end he was classified as a "questionably improvable offender. Guarded prognosis. Very superior intelligence." Even the possibility of change, however, meant that Joe was assigned to the Pontiac penitentiary, which was mostly for young offenders who were considered "improvable." The Menard prison was for psychotics, sexual psychopaths, and the criminally insane; the twin prisons of Joliet and Stateville were for "incorrigibles," and Joe was not considered that far gone—yet.

Joe arrived at Pontiac on November 23, 1946. He was transported from the depot on the same bus with Edgar Keck, his former bunkmate at the St. Charles School for Boys, who would be serving five concurrent sentences of three to seven years each for an armed robbery spree. Keck had good news: William Clair was already at Pontiac, serving time for escaping from St. Charles. The gang, such as it was, would be getting together again.

1946
Dante Cosentino and David Troy Stamford

WHEN DANTE COSENTINO PROMISED THE SOCIAL WORKER AND psychologist that he would take their money to stay in school, he had meant it. He'd left the Children and Families offices thinking he'd gotten a hell of a deal, but he also left with their words looping through his head. He could set a good example for the rest of the children. He recited that to himself as he repeated the ninth grade, wearing his brand-new Thom McCans and the first store-bought clothes he'd ever owned. For a while the clothes and words had helped. Eventually they didn't.

If he'd been bored the first time around, he was all but asleep this second time, and his informal mantra took on a less heroic meaning. Exactly what role was he modeling? He was still lying to everyone, acting the part of a good student while hating every minute, taking charity when a real man would have gone out and earned money on his own. It wasn't a specific moment that broke him, but rather the steady grind of his wants against everyone else's expectations. One cold night Frank headed to the bedroom he shared with Dante and found it locked from inside. With a shrug, Frank took his pocketknife and shimmied the hook out of its eye to let himself in.

"Why'd ya lock the door?" he demanded of his brother, who was already in bed, blankets over his head. Miffed, Frank yelled the question again, then shook Dante—getting an answer when the mound under the covers turned out to be a pile of pillows. Fifteen-year-old Dante had been gone for hours.

Looking for adventure, he found it. For a while, he made a home in an abandoned shack on the edge of Durham, North Carolina, which was as far south as anyone in his family had ever been. But eventually officers knocked on what passed for a door, asked how old he was, didn't believe him when he said he was eighteen, and told him to leave the state or go to jail. They amiably drove him to the northern county line. From there he hitchhiked toward Connecticut. Nearing Stamford, a middle-aged gentleman offered him a lift and asked why he wasn't in school. Tired of puffing himself to seem older, or more experienced, or less frightened, he answered honestly. The man considered his story for a few moments and said, "What you *earn* they can take away from you. What you *learn* they can never take away."

Dante would think back on that advice often over the years. But in the winter of 1946, at fifteen, he rejected it. The guy was well-meaning, sure, but Dante knew for certain that boys like himself—Italian boys with immigrant parents—had four possible paths out of the working-class life. Three of those—sports, entertainment, and crime—led to fame and fortune. Look at Joe DiMaggio, Frank Sinatra, and the local Stamford bookies. The fourth—the military—brought adventure and the possibility of dealing with the rest later. College was not for kids like him; nor were jobs that required suits and ties. He'd seen his father make a mistake and live in his head. He would not fall for that same trap.

✦

AT ABOUT THE SAME AGE, in a different part of the same city, David Troy was receiving similar advice. His guide was not a stranger at the wheel but his great-uncle Thomas making his daily rounds. The message was the same: you choose your own path. Thomas was the youngest brother of a grandfather Dave had never met, and the uncle of a father he didn't remember. The afternoons Al spent following his uncle Isadore to house calls, thirteen-year-old Dave spent walking a beat with Stamford officer Tom Troy. Both were glimpses into another world.

Your views of the causes of crime and criminality—of whether humans are essentially good unless led astray or essentially bad unless reined in—depend on what you bring to where you stand. Tom Troy was a beat cop in a chummy city, and his corner of the criminal justice system was a friendly, open-hearted one. He started and ended his shifts as a crossing guard at the elementary school in the Cove, and in between he walked, popping his head into small businesses and local playgrounds, greeting passersby by name. His message to his grand-nephew was that this job was to keep the innocent safe and to steer the less than innocent toward safety.

Tom's worldview dated back to his earliest days on the job, and he was full of stories from before young Dave had been born. As a rookie in May 1926, for instance, Tom had been walking past the Stamford harbor at three a.m. when a man approached, his clothes dripping wet.

"Looking for me?" he asked.

"Not that I know of," Troy replied. "Why?"

"Oh, I thought the voices might have sent you down here," the wet man said.

While wringing droplets out his sleeves, the man explained that he'd awoken from a fitful sleep and distinctly heard a disembodied someone tell him to go to the canal and throw himself in. He jumped into the water but found it to be uncomfortably cold and decided not to drown himself after all, so he swam back to shore.

The officer brought him to headquarters, warmed and sobered him with hot coffee, and had him examined by a police physician. Come morning, the doctor told the judge that the defendant suffered from "prolonged consumption of poor liquor," and he was sent to a sanitarium.

Twenty years later Tom Troy's view of policing was little changed: he still saw it as a whimsical world where men emerged from canals in the middle of the night and officers were eager to help. That view appealed to teenage Dave, who himself was big-hearted, optimistic, and kind. These were traits he got from his "pa," or so the older siblings who remembered Patrick told him. They shared stories only when their mother was not around; talk of her late husband, even eleven years after his death, still brought anger that he would up and leave her like that.

It was Bridget who encouraged Dave's regular meetings with Tom, for a complicated tangle of reasons. Her relationship with her husband's family was still strained, with bitterness on both sides because of the tussle over 39 Leeds Street. Bridget still lived in that house, Sadie still considered it her own, but it was not a desire to fix the rift that led Bridget to push Dave toward Patrick's uncle. Nor was her goal for him to hear treacly stories about his father. Her far more tactical aim was to have Dave take a liking to police work.

The Stamford Police had been a welcoming home to Irishmen since its earliest days, and the first roster of recruits included names like McMahon, O'Brien, and Lunney. Bridget saw policing as a secure place with a regular paycheck, along with a pension and no small amount of respect. The secret to stability in America was a profession, not just a job, she had learned, and so she'd steered her older children toward that goal. She aimed to ensure that her daughters had skills to fall back on, that they would not have the nonchoice she'd been forced to make between domestic work and working the cash register at the Schick cafeteria. Both Agnes and Mary trained as nurses, which satisfied Bridget. Her sons, in turn, would not exit this earth abruptly without providing a cushion for those they left behind: Patrick Jr. and Eddie found union jobs on factory floors, steady work. David, though, was talking about starting a business of his own, repairing cars and tinkering with machines as his father had done. That had left Bridget with nothing but a small monthly stipend for each child from the welfare office, and brought on a decade of her selling pies during lunch hour. Her youngest son, and whichever nice Irish girl was lucky enough to become his wife, would do better.

In the late 1940s, when Bridget arranged for Dave to shadow Tom, policing in Stamford was still a safe line of work. The crime waves of the Prohibition and Depression years were over, and the racial tension and urban blight that would later scar the city had not quite begun. Instead, the current postwar prosperity meant that most police calls were of the "colorful drunk" or "cat up a tree" variety. The "seedier" parts of town were not ghettos of despair; any African American in Stamford had stories of being mistreated or disrespected, but white citizens, who made up 94.6 percent of the population, still had the privilege of pretending that inequality was a problem only in the South.

Still more an overgrown town than a big city, Stamford saw few murders, and none of those were of policemen. The first shooting ever of a Stamford officer would not happen until 1948, when Angelo Sabia was hit three times while interrupting a restaurant safecracker; his injuries, though chronic, were not life-threatening. Only two officers had ever died in the line of duty, both during the summer of 1938 and both in motorcycle accidents while on patrol. One skidded and was thrown under a truck; the other was struck by a car at an intersection.

Those deaths had dimmed department enthusiasm for motorcycles, and they were still in minimal use by Stamford Police. They'd had a surge in popularity during the war years, when gasoline was strictly rationed, but though sales to civilians spiked after the war, officers were eager to get back to their comparatively luxurious, weather-proofed sedans. This was fine with Bridget, who did not want her son anywhere near the machines. Dave, though, was itching to ride, which was another reason his mother was eager for him to spend time with Thomas.

Her plan was of questionable success. Dave was more than happy to shadow his great-uncle, but that would not keep him from taking a part-time job at Woldan's Service Station after years of hanging out around the service bays. It was a dream made real—the paycheck, yes, but even more so the rows of tools waiting for a problem to fix, the rush of doing a road test on a newer model he couldn't afford, the glad-handing with customers. His craggy smile (Bridget could not bring herself to send her children to the dentist after Patrick had died en route) was extra broad whenever a motorcycle growled into the shop. It was a sound that hinted at risk, but also one that he aimed to tame. He even loved coming home from work stinking of sweat and grease. Bridget did her best to launder the smells from his clothes and, with less success, to knock his cockamamie plan to own a station of his own out of his head.

So many paths were open to a muscular teen with a good work ethic, but as Dave was heading toward high school, his choice was, by his own process of elimination, already binary. He could become a cop, like his uncle Tom, which seemed like a worthy adventure and would also please his mother. Or he could build and fix and operate things that moved and belched and roared. Either way, he could have a grand old time.

✦

BACK HOME FROM HIS WANDERINGS, Dante Cosentino did not see his life as filled with possibility. Mostly, he felt like a stranger in his own family. While his mother had greeted his return with relief, his younger siblings had responded with a bit of a cold shoulder, particularly the youngest two. Frank and Rosie had once viewed him as a role model, but then they'd watched him chafe, wanting to be free of them, to be a hotshot in the big world. He'd become insufferable after he got his scholarship, and his brand-new clothes felt like a sneer at their hand-me-downs. While he was gone, they found it surprisingly easy to close the circle, and they carried on as if he'd never played a part.

Frank was ten months younger than Rosie, but he treated her like his little sister. They were the only two Cosentinos still in elementary school, and they walked there and back together. In their classrooms, she was the good student and he was the uninterested one. Outside of school he was the protector, and she was the free spirit. By the time Dante came back home, Rosie and Frank had become a tight, self-contained twosome, which left their older brother an orbiting satellite, visible but distant.

He'd returned physically changed—stronger, browner. To Rosie and Frank, he seemed older and more confident, the way their oldest brother, Albert, had been before the war had diminished him. Over the next few years, he moved from one job to the next—mail boy, dishwasher, short order cook, delivery man, soda jerk. If Dante's "allowance" had made him cocky, his paycheck amplified his strut. Working the soda fountain, wearing the ridiculous white paper hat, he acted like a big man amid the childish students. Yet even as he lorded over his small dominion, it was clear these were just temporary gigs. His desire to be gone, to have adventures, to leave his old life behind—these wants radiated off him in the small Cosentino household, creating ever more distance.

Soon after his sixteenth birthday he told the National Guard recruitment office that he was 18, and they chose to believe him. Then, when he turned 17, he used his National Guard discharge papers to persuade an Air Force recruiter that he was old enough to join. He was surprised, however, when life in the military failed to meet his need for excitement. He kept bumping up against the rules, being restricted to base for small infractions, finally committing a major one—going AWOL and hitchhiking from Lowry Field in Denver to the seedy side of St. Louis. Two local police officers thought he matched the description of a suspect in a string of recent robberies; for the next two weeks, he spent time in a series of civilian and military jails, then was escorted back to Denver for a summary court martial and ten days in the stockade.

In postcards home, he made light of the "adventure." He warned Frank and Rosie, "Stay out of confined guarded places which can only be unlocked from the outside."

1946
Warden Ragen, Dr. Alving,
and Nathan Leopold
Stateville Penitentiary

WHEN THE ARMY DEMANDED SECRECY AT THE START OF THE
Stateville malaria drug trials, Warden Ragen had been happy to comply. He was surprised, therefore, in the spring of 1945, when army officials agreed to allow a team from *Life*—the most popular magazine
in America, with a circulation of more than 13 million—to visit Stateville and observe the experiments. The reporter and photographer
came on "bite day." Sixteen volunteer patients were photographed in
bed that morning, each with an arm extended. To the patient's left,
an army researcher held a baseball-size plastic cylinder with the top
and bottom cut flat, a piece of gauze covering the open ends. A single female mosquito occupied each small "cage," and the researchers
placed the gauze against the subject's skin and waited for the insect to
bite. Each patient received a total of ten bites from the same ten mosquitoes, as technicians carefully charted the order in which they were
bitten, creating a map of how the malaria parasite was carried from
one "human host" to the next.

Both Ragen and Alving stayed out of range of the camera lens.
This was fine with the *Life* photographer, who was more interested
in Nathan Leopold. The session took an entire grueling day, with the
mosquitoes uncharacteristically uninterested in biting, and the men,
to Ragen's eye, mugging for the cameras. The result was three full
pages in *Life*'s June 4, 1945, edition.

"Men who have been imprisoned as enemies of society are now

helping science fight another enemy of society," the article began, alongside an obviously staged photo of Leopold holding a clipboard amid a group of volunteers, some with thermometers clamped in their mouths.

The army was thrilled with the coverage. Ragen was not convinced it had been worth the trouble. Still, when officials asked again months later, he allowed another reporter, this one from WGN radio in Chicago, into the third-floor laboratory at Stateville.

The live broadcast in January 1946 came at a sensitive moment in the history of the malaria trials. Much progress had been made toward a drug that relieved the symptoms of the disease (a fact that the army was ready to announce), and great promise was being shown in the search for a drug that would prevent relapses (a fact that was not yet ready to be made public). Why hold a live media event when you were still actively keeping secrets? The Second World War was over, and the malaria discoveries had not come in time to play a part in the victory. The army was looking ahead to a postwar era when military budgets would face more scrutiny and "for the war effort" would no longer be justification for everything.

To ensure that none of the participants said anything unhelpful during the live broadcast, the army worked with WGN to pre-interview everyone and turn their answers into an eight-page script, which was written in the gee-gosh-golly tone so popular at the time. Thirty minutes before the scheduled start, the warden met with his prisoners and warned them, yet again, to read their lines as written. At seven p.m., sharp, the "on air" light went on in the laboratory that had been temporarily turned into a studio.

"For a firsthand report of the malaria research project, we take you now to Stateville," an announcer said.

Ragen need not have worried, as every man stuck to the plan.

"I'm George Johnson, Number 22798."

"Johnson, I've heard you ran a pretty high fever as a result of those tests."

"That's right. At one time my temperature was 108 degrees."

"One hundred eight degrees! And you're here to tell the story! Johnson, what was your main reason for volunteering for these tests?"

"I served in the United States Army during the First World War and figured by going through the tests, I'd help some of my buddies in the war just ended."

Next up was Charles Ickes, Number 13187, the murderer who was now Alf Alving's co-author on some of the project's research papers.

"My brother was killed in the crossing of the Saar River," he said. "That made up my mind for me. We weren't being shot at here. It was the least we could do."

Finally, reporter Ward Quaal said, "Here's a man who is one of the many inmate nurses helping out in the ward. What is your name?"

"Nathan Leopold, 9806-D," Leopold answered. "I was a malaria volunteer, and now I am acting as a nurse."

"How do most of the patients react under these tests?"

"All the men are good soldiers. Their morale is high."

At exactly seven-fifteen, Quaal signed off with a hint at even better news, very soon, about a "secret" drug that was "in the experimental stage."

"The army doesn't give up, and neither do the many men of science associated with this project," he concluded.

Ragen breathed a sigh of relief. The broadcast was over—but it was not the last Ragen would hear of it.

✦

TRIALS OF THE LEGAL kind were still going on in Germany, two years after the war, and they, too, involved malaria. American prosecutors eventually created twelve separate tribunals, trying a total of 207 defendants over the next three years. On January 27, 1947, testimony was underway in the second one, officially known as *United States v. Karl Brandt et al.* and unofficially dubbed "the Doctors Trial." The lead defendant was Hitler's personal internist, and twenty of the twenty-three defendants were physicians. The proceedings would span eight months, 139 court days, and 11,538 transcript pages. Many of those pages would mention Stateville Penitentiary, five thousand miles away.

The first prosecution witness was Dr. Werner Leibbrand (sometimes spelled Liebbrandt), a German psychiatrist and medical historian who had been persecuted by the Nazi government for rejecting fascism. He testified that there were clear and accepted guidelines for medical research on human subjects: Subjects must understand what would be done to them. They must be able to change their mind at any time. And they must give their free, uncoerced consent. Concentration camp inmates, he said, did not meet any of those requirements.

Brandt's lawyer began his cross-examination with a hypothetical question. If a prisoner did agree to participate in an experiment, he asked Leibbrand, "do you consider such approval voluntary?"

"No," replied Leibbrand, explaining that a prisoner by definition cannot volunteer because "(he is) basically brought into a forcible situation by being arrested. . . ."

"Are you of the opinion that eight hundred prisoners under arrest at various places who give their approval for an experiment at the same time do so voluntarily?"

"No," Leibbrand said again, assuming the defense attorney was talking about eight hundred concentration camp prisoners.

"If such prisoners are infected with malaria because they have declared themselves willing, do you consider that . . . admissible?"

"No," repeated Leibbrand, still believing these questions were about Dachau. "As prisoners, they were already in a forced situation."

The defense attorney then handed the prosecution witness a clipping from *Life* and asked that he read the story aloud into the court record. It was about malaria drug trials at Stateville Penitentiary in Joliet, Illinois.

"The experimenters . . . have found prison life ideal for controlled laboratory work with humans," Leibbrand read.

Next the attorney produced the script for a radio program

carried live from Stateville a year earlier, and he read that one to the judges himself.

The dual messages were clear in all four of the languages into which the Nuremberg testimony was being instantly and simultaneously translated: experiments on prisoners were unethical—but Germany was not the only nation conducting them.

The prosecution could have simply moved on. There were clear differences between the American trials and the Dachau ones. The concentration camp subjects were not asked to volunteer—they were selected. They could not drop out, and no thought at all was given to their health, comfort, or survival. Those details would be entered into evidence shortly, and the horror would speak for itself.

But an observer named Andrew Conway Ivy was not content to let the accusation go unchallenged. The fifty-three-year-old physician-scientist had been sent by the American Medical Association to advise the prosecution team. During the war he'd been the civilian scientific director of the Naval Medical Research Institute, where he conducted experiments on pilots, aiming to determine how they could use salt water to survive when downed at sea. After the war, he helped found the National Society for Medical Research, to defend the use of animals in medical experimentation. A native of Illinois, he taught both at the Northwestern Medical School and at the University of Illinois. *Time* had called him "the conscience of U.S. Science."

Ivy thought Leibbrand's answers were damaging to more than just the prosecution's legal case. Germany was not guilty because it had experimented on prisoners; it was guilty because it had tortured those prisoners in the name of experimentation. He could not allow American researchers to be smeared with the same brush. He did not consider it sufficient for Nazi research to be condemned at Nuremberg. American research also had to be exonerated.

Ivy's answer to accusations of unethical conduct at Stateville was to lie. First he postdated the creation of a state panel to examine the ethics of malaria research at Illinois prisons, then wrote a report himself in the name of the committee. He took the stand at Nuremberg to testify that said committee had established rules for ethical human research (voluntary consent, prior toxicity research on animals and oversight by medically trained personnel) and had determined that Stateville's experiments met all requirements. Prisoners could be used as subjects, he continued, quoting "the Green committee report," if they were given full information, were allowed to back out at any time, and were rewarded for their participation, though rewards should not be so great as to become coercive.

At no time during his testimony did Ivy mention he was the de facto author of the documents he was citing, or that the "Green committee" had not yet actually met. That fact would remain secret for fifty years, until a journalist unearthed it on the anniversary of the tribunals.

In cross-examination, Ivy's lies of omission veered into commission.

"May I ask when this committee was formed?" the lead defense attorney asked about the governor's panel.

"The formation of this committee, according to the best of my recollection, occurred in December 1946," Ivy answered, even though he had first proposed it in February 1947.

"Did the formation of this committee have anything to do with the fact that this trial is going on?"

"There is no connection between the action of this committee and the trial," Ivy said, though of course there was.

Ivy's testimony was hardly covered in the United States, as Americans had moved on from the war. Newspapers did give front-page play to the eventual conviction of fourteen of the twenty-three Nuremberg doctors (including Karl Brandt, who was executed by hanging in 1948), but those stories made no mention of the few dozen paragraphs in the tribunal's 254-page decision that would, over time, come to be called "the Nuremberg Code." Ivy did not directly write the ten-principle code, but he might as well have, based as it was on his testimony.

The Nuremberg Code could have sparked a moment of introspection for U.S. researchers, causing them to reevaluate their relationship with imprisoned subjects and recognize the complexity of obtaining consent from subjects who were confined. Instead, the code was seen as license to continue. Because the differences between Nazi and American actions were so jarring, so profound, it was unnecessary to face the similarities.

"Uncle Isadore and I talked about it briefly, I think," his nephew, Al Tarlov, would remember years later. "The Nuremberg Code said what we already knew—the Nazis didn't get consent, but American researchers did."

What followed Nuremberg was what medical historian David Rothman called a "gilded age" of medical research. American scientists made ever more prisoners their subjects, so much so that for decades nearly all research on healthy volunteers would be done at least partly in prisons. Men and women behind bars would be used in treatment trials for everything from athlete's foot to syphilis, from the seasonal flu to the flash burns that result from atomic weapons. All were justified by patriotism, or its cousin, military strength. The wartime Committee on Medical Research became the peacetime National Institutes of Health. "Continuous systemic research is an evident necessity," said Secretary of the Navy James Forrestal. "It may be regarded as a kind of military insurance."

Governor Green embraced the conclusions of "his" committee and announced that any participants in the Stateville malaria trials would be entitled to an accelerated parole hearing. On the scale from coddling to coercion, it was a middle ground—not the pardon that some might have envisioned, but an expedited chance for parole.

Warden Ragen was proud of the trials. Among the few decorations on his office walls was a proclamation created in the prison printing shop, declaring him an honorary malaria volunteer, signed by several hundred prisoners. Ragen believed that most of the men had joined the research for patriotic reasons and that the suffering of the volunteers was real; he had visited the clinic regularly and seen for himself.

Yet he had seen something else there as well. As in any experiment, changing one factor changed the result. When Ragen announced that no inmate could be thrown into solitary while participating in the malaria trials, enrollment went up. When he added that volunteers would not lose their work assignments while they were volunteering, enrollment increased further. When Governor Green approved early parole hearings for every volunteer, men who had scoffed at the trials stood in line to join.

The scientists on the third floor of his prison building were not just measuring the behavior of the malaria parasite. They were effectively conducting an experiment on the behavior of the human volunteers. The governor granted early parole; men got patriotic, got malaria, got released. All of which led Ragen to wonder, was volunteering to get malaria good citizenship? Or a new way to play the system?

September 1947
Al Tarlov
Hanover, New Hampshire

IT DID NOT OCCUR TO CHARLIE TARLOV TO COME INSIDE WHEN he dropped his son off at college. He parked his black Buick in front of the Fayerweather dorm at Dartmouth and waited on the sidewalk as Al took his large black trunk from the back seat. Though Hanover was chillier than Norwalk on this early September day, Al felt warm and itchy in his new suit. From nerves about facing something new? Or because he knew what his father was about to say?

Charlie, who had taken a rare day off from the restaurant to make this trip, wished his youngest boy well and told him to study hard and write to his mother regularly. Then he repeated the question he'd previously asked of Merwyn and Jay.

"Son," he said, "do you see yourself wanting to take over the restaurant one day?"

Alvin Tarlov had rarely been asked what he wanted during his eighteen years. Not about the big decisions. He did not want to be here at Dartmouth, but that choice had been made for him one afternoon a year earlier, when the school principal had arrived at Tarlov's between the lunch and dinner shifts. Mae, standing at her usual place in the front of the house, was more than a little worried that something was wrong. Had her boy not gone to school that morning? Had he caused some kind of trouble? She had no chance to ask, as Mr. Malmquist took off his hat, nodded in her direction, and without breaking stride, strode through the empty dining room, then marched down the short corridor and into the kitchen.

Fortunately for everyone, Charlie had already awakened from his daily nap on the wooden banquet table in the basement. Surprised

to see the principal, because no one ever simply walked into the Tarlov's kitchen, he did his best to appear as if this were the most usual
of visits.

Mr. Malmquist was not one for pleasantries and came directly to
the point. "Good afternoon, Mr. Tarlov," he began. "Your son Alvin
shall apply to Dartmouth College."

Charlie nodded. "He shall," he replied.

Later that evening, Charlie repeated that pronouncement to Al and
handed him the piece of scrap paper on which he'd carefully written
the name of the school so he would not forget. Al put it in a pocket.
He'd hoped to go to Amherst College, a small liberal arts school in
Massachusetts, which he had found when he took it upon himself to
research schools in the Norwalk Library.

Unlike Dartmouth, Amherst was not in the Ivy league. But it was
rigorous and prestigious, and most important to Al, its sports were
less competitive than Dartmouth's, which would have given him a
chance to join the baseball or basketball teams. He would have been
equally out of his element socially at either, as both schools had long
histories of admitting the sons of wealthy white Protestant families
with quotas on "others." That was the subtext of Mr. Malmquist's
pronouncement. As a Dartmouth graduate himself, he could assure
his alma mater that young master Tarlov was an acceptable Jew.

Al did not speak up about his own preferences; he had never in his
life argued with his father. Nor did he correct Mr. Malmquist months
later when he brought Al his acceptance letter and told him he would
make a fine physician someday. Everyone but Al assumed he would be
a doctor. DR. TARLOV MAKES REPORT ON NATION'S HEALTH, read the
pretend headline in the section of the yearbook that predicted where
graduates would be in twenty-five years. "Al hopes to be a successful
doctor and if he continues as he has here, he cannot possibly fail to
establish himself in his chosen field," read the "article" beneath.

But Al did not hope to be a successful doctor. He hadn't decided
what he wanted to be just yet. He loved his outings with Isadore and
the intellectual world in which his uncle lived, but he was intrigued by

the idea of planning a life rather than falling into one. His uncle Isadore was one of the few people Al could think of who had done that, and while this was one of the many appeals of medicine—a bright, linear road to a clear, defined future—certain realities of the profession gave him pause. He'd continued his "field research" into the status of family life in Norwalk and concluded that there were jobs that allowed for one and jobs that did not. His father's didn't; no occupation where you needed to be at work when other people were eating, sleeping, or celebrating was a good fit for family time. Nor did Isadore's; much as he idolized his uncle, Al saw that Isadore spent most of his time on patients and papers, leaving relatively little for his wife and three children.

Crafting a life means either doing things as your parents did or doing the opposite—affirming, or rejecting, what you know. And here was his father, delivering him to a new chapter and asking him to choose. For most of his eighteen years, Al had assumed he would not have to make this particular choice. Certainly the restaurant would go to one of his older brothers. But both had said no when they'd had one foot out the door. Now it was Al's turn.

"Do you see yourself wanting to take over the restaurant one day?" Charlie had asked, and he was still grasping Al's outstretched hand.

"No, sir," he answered. "No, I do not."

September 1948
Joe DeSalvo
Pontiac Prison
Pontiac, Illinois

ON SEPTEMBER 8, 1948, NOT QUITE TWO YEARS AFTER HE ENTERED the Illinois State Penitentiary at Pontiac, Joe DeSalvo sat in the drab conference room adjacent to the administrative office. His parents had left just before he'd entered. He didn't expect to be granted parole just two years into his two-to-ten-year sentence, and he hadn't done much to prepare for the hearing.

Taking one of the chairs his family had occupied, Joe sat ramrod straight, as he had been taught at St. Charles, in the navy, and in prison. He looked across the table at Mr. Harris and Mr. Reed and glanced only occasionally at the stenographer in the corner. This was how he'd spent much of the past twenty-two months, staring straight ahead, focusing on what was in front of him, trying not to be distracted by the future so he could get through the present.

That did not mean he was unaware of the future. In fact, he had big plans. At Pontiac, he had enrolled in a correspondence school based at the Stateville Penitentiary in Joliet, sixty miles northeast. Rumor had it that one of the prisoners grading the lessons he mailed back every week was the infamous murderer Nathan Leopold, who had committed an unspeakable crime the year before Joe was born but whose name he knew nonetheless. There were a lot of rumors in prison, and Joe tried not to dwell on things he could not confirm.

His goal was to earn his high school diploma. What would come next was less clear, though he knew it would *not* be what his father wanted for him, which was work in the repair of engines, automobiles, and machines. Charles was loud in his disappointment that his younger son didn't play sports, or tinker with cars, or do any of the things that Charles himself had done at the same age. This puzzled Joe. Why was his father determined that Joe duplicate his life when he wasn't happy with how that life had turned out?

Joe aimed to be the opposite of his father, the photographic negative. He was only just forming a vision of what such a life might look like, but his time at Pontiac had given him the first glimpses. GED in hand, the correspondence school would allow him to "graduate" to college courses, and while he hadn't signed up for any yet, he had started to think of himself as someone who could. He'd been reading his allocated book a week from the Pontiac library and found he gravitated toward poetry, which his mother loved and his father thought was for girls, and science, to which he had not given much thought before. He was fascinated by biology and anatomy—the mysteries of the human body. Enzymes, hormones, electrolytes, swirling together to make something glorious and unique—visualizing this was like listening to those jazz albums he had left behind at St. Charles. Elements fit together in ways that were both unexpected and meant to be.

Soon Mr. Harris began the meeting. "Give us your name, age and number please?"

"My name is Joseph DeSalvo. I am nineteen years old, and my number is 16232."

"Joe, you were sent here for larceny on November 26, 1946 . . . under a sentence of two to ten years, on a plea of guilty. . . . Were you guilty?"

"Yes, sir."

"Your parents appeared here for you. . . . Your father . . . appeared to be a fine man. He said that in the event that you were paroled, you could live with him, and he could get you a job where he is employed, at the Speedway Manufacturing Company, and I guess he conveyed that information to you, did he not?"

"Yes sir, he did."

Mr. Harris went on to review Joe's record aloud—his first arrests at age twelve, his nineteen months at St. Charles, the fact that he was "paroled, violated, returned, paroled again." His very short stint in the navy. His dishonorable discharge when he went AWOL, stole some cars, and brought a gun back to St. Charles.

Joe continued to stare straight ahead.

"Why is it, Joe," Mr. Harris asked, "you can't keep out of trouble?"

"Oh, I think it was when I was younger, I think I liked to show off. I think I have matured since then, and I think I am more of a man now than I was then."

Had he? Was he? What was a man, anyway?

"Could you abide by a parole agreement if you were given one?"

"Yes sir, I know I could."

"Is there anything else you want to add to your interview?"

"Well, no. Just that if I did make parole, I am sure I would make good, and I would work hard and get a good job and earn a living and try to be a man."

That job would not be at the Speedway Manufacturing Company. He'd rather be in jail—and he really didn't want to be in jail. But there was no need to say that out loud.

The whole interview lasted less than fifteen minutes. Then he was dismissed, and the conversation between Mr. Harris and the heretofore-silent Mr. Reed was equally quick. They read into the record the report by sociologist-actuary Gordon Beers, which used a slightly streamlined version of the Burgess/Leopold prediction formula to rate Joseph DeSalvo's parole risk. He was what was known as a "60 percenter"—"in a class in which 60 percent may be expected to violate the parole agreement. 29 per cent may be expected to be minor violators, 31 per cent may be expected to be major violators." An adjectival summary concluded, "This inmate [is] an occasional ne'er-do-well, moderate user of alcohol, superior mental rating, ego-centric personality, doubtful prognosis."

"Until this inmate has matured considerably more there will still be danger of his old habits of unpredictableness and all of his behavior reasserting itself," Beers had written, "which will inevitably result in further delinquencies possibly of a serious nature. Rather firm supervision will be necessary at present and this should include provision for some type of recreation outlet which will assist in draining off some of his energy. He is a questionably improvable offender, with egocentric personality and superior intelligence, for whom the prognosis is doubtful."

Based almost completely on that report and the few minutes Joe spent in the board's presence, Harris wrote his conclusion: "It is my opinion that DeSalvo is absolutely incorrigible, anti-social, vicious, mean and a schemer. I believe he intends fully to follow a life of lawlessness and every indication up to the present moment is that he is a dangerous character. It is the recommendation of the Subcommittee that parole be denied."

January 1949
Nathan Leopold
Stateville Penitentiary

NATHAN LEOPOLD HAD BEEN SENTENCED TO "LIFE PLUS 99 YEARS." Whether by omission or commission—a much debated question— Judge Caverly did not stipulate that the sentences be served consecutively (first life, *then* 99 years), so they were being served concurrently. Had Caverly ordered consecutive sentences, there would be far less chance that Leopold would ever be released. The simultaneous sentences, however, created a mathematical game.

Under Illinois law, a prisoner was eligible for a parole hearing after serving a percentage of his minimum sentence. The "life" part of Leopold's sentence would have allowed him a hearing in 1944, after twenty years. But the minimum for his additional ninety-nine-year-sentence was thirty-three years, meaning he would not be eligible for his first hearing until 1957.

Then Governor Green announced that malaria volunteers could apply for expedited parole, providing Leopold a glimmer of hope that his equation might change. Army administrators prepared reports on the 441 trial participants, including how many attacks of malaria each man suffered, how high his fever had spiked, and what drugs he had been given. Each file also included the standard letter Alf Alving sent to every "human subject." Leopold's, dated December 30, 1946, read: "This is to certify that Mr. Nathan Leopold, Inmate No. 9306D at Stateville Prison, has rendered valuable assistance in the malarial research sponsored by the Board for the Coordination of Malarial Studies and the U.S. Public Health Service. This research was carried on under my direction. The medical officers who were assigned to assist in this work by the Surgeon General of the U.S. Army join me in expressing their appreciation of the help that Mr. Leopold rendered as a technician and secretary from January 1945 to the present."

Also in each file was a white-on-black photocopy of the "Certificate of Merit" given to each man, "In Acknowledgement of Appreciation of his Contribution to the War Effort through his services as a Volunteer Subject in Experiments on the *PREVENTION AND CURE OF MALARIA* Involving Discomfort, Risks of Health, and Personal Sacrifice."

The 441 files made their way to Springfield, where the parole board reviewed two hundred of them at its February meeting. Those were of men who had already served their minimum sentences, and most were granted either immediate parole or a cut in remaining time to be served. It took nearly a year before the remaining 221 cases—men who had not yet served the minimum—were invited to submit a second application. This was not for parole but for executive clemency. Should the panel members be so inclined, they could recommend that the governor shave the initial sentences, effectively moving up the dates at which these prisoners became eligible for their first parole hearing.

Leopold applied, then spent months being evaluated by a prison psychiatrist, psychometrist, criminologist, and sociologist-actuary. He was not worried about the sociologist-actuary, who would simply apply Leopold's prediction formula to his own life; Leopold knew he would be a "97 percenter," as good a risk as possible using his questionnaire. What concerned him was the psychiatrist's report. While most of the commutation applicants spent less than fifteen minutes with the man, Leopold's first interview lasted three hours the first day and an additional three hours the second. In the end, the psychiatrist is said to have confided to a prison employee, who in turn relayed the comment to Leopold, "Hell, I'd take that boy into my own home."

Not satisfied with providing only the requested information, Leopold sent addenda. His brother Mike had spent years collecting letters of support from professors Leopold had worked with, and it was time to put them to use. By that time Mike had changed his last name, to Lebold, to spare his wife and child the stigma. Still, he was a loyal sibling, visiting Leopold every other week in the twenty years since their father died. He and their third brother, Sam (also by now a Lebold), wrote their own letter to the board, saying they were willing to bet their carefully protected reputation that Leopold could be trusted. "We have no desire to relive the events of 1924, and we would be the ones to bear this onus in the event that there were any repetition," they said. They also promised to support their brother financially.

Mike was Leopold's partner in the clemency application, working with him over the months to solicit additional letters, with mixed success. Leopold hoped Alf Alving would step forward with a more personal endorsement than the boilerplate every participant received, but Alving had never warmed to Leopold, never overcome his initial recoil. Alving told friends and colleagues that Leopold tended to exaggerate his own role in the trials. He responded with silence to all requests on Leopold's behalf, which continued to mystify Leopold.

Also on the Leopold/Lebold wish list was a letter from Warden Ragen. They did not get that either, although it is unclear how hard they tried. Rules dating back to Odette Allen's fiery death forbade anyone who worked for the prison system from speaking for or against a parole applicant's release—a practice designed to prevent prisoners from placing pressure on, or seeking revenge against, the staff.

Although many turned Leopold down, a few requests were met with an unexpected yes. The most notable came from Carl Sandburg, the legendary poet and author, who had never met Nathan Leopold. Sandburg had written a book about Abraham Lincoln, and Mike Lebold was a collector of Lincoln artifacts. They were both members of a round table of Lincoln scholars that met regularly at the invitation of Ralph Newman, a collector and seller of rare documents. Hearing Mike's stories about his brother over the years, Sandburg assured the parole board that were "Nathan Leopold a neighbor of mine, I would want to see him often, if only for benefits from association with a great and rare intellect. I would have him, on the basis of numerous reports I consider unquestionable, as a guest in my home, whose companionship would be valued."

All the affirmations and predictions were of little use if the parole board didn't read them. The board met every three months, reviewing a few cases at a time, but never Leopold's. The April 1948 meeting came and went, then July, then October; among those granted sentence reductions were Alving's favorites, Charles Ickes and Kenneth Rucker (though his was essentially symbolic, dropping his sentence to 99 years from 199). The case of Nathan Leopold still did not make it onto the agenda. Governor Green was defeated in November, replaced by Gov. Adlai Stevenson. Finally, on April 12, 1949, the board reached the last folder in its pile.

At that meeting, which was held at Stateville, the state's attorney for Cook County argued against shortening the sentence of the man who was still the state's best-known prisoner. Some of Leopold's letter-writers (though not Sandburg) came in one at a time to read their statements in person, while other letters in the file (including Sandburg's) were read aloud into the record. Finally, it was Leopold's turn to speak, the most he had said in public since his trial. He sounded like the weary middle-aged man he had become.

The board members reserved most of their questions for the malaria drug trials since those had made him eligible for this hearing in the first place. They gave particular attention to Leopold's health struggles; he had been diagnosed with diabetes, two coronary occlusions, and chronic kidney disease in recent years. Were these aftereffects of the experiments? The timing was certainly suspicious, Leopold said, but he added that he did not regret his participation.

"It is a little hard to condense twenty-five years into twenty-five minutes," he concluded. "I should like to say that when I came here, I was nineteen years old—not old enough to vote or make a valid contract. Now I am forty-four. I feel that I have matured. I was a wild, irresponsible kid when I came here. At least I am not a kid anymore.

"I realize that there was great publicity in my case. I hope that this will not prevent me from receiving the same consideration as the other men on the malaria project. That is all I have to say, gentlemen. Thank you."

It took five months for the board to reach a decision. Leopold learned of it while listening to the radio in his cell. "Here's a bulletin from Springfield," the announcer said. "The parole board has announced that the sentence of Nathan Leopold has been commuted. He will be eligible for parole in January 1953."

Leopold did the math. Eligibility in 1953 meant his sentence had been reduced to "life plus eighty-five years," requiring him to serve twenty-eight years and four months before requesting a hearing. That meant he still had three more years to wait, but also four fewer than had been ordered by Judge Caverly.

1950s

1950
Cosentinos
Cos Cob

AT FIRST ROSE INTRODUCED ANTHONY SICILIANO TO HER CHIL-
dren as an old friend from Cos Cob, just someone she knew from back
before she'd married their father and who she hadn't seen in years. She
didn't mention that her sister Philomena's yard had backed up against
Tony's years earlier, and that she would dance on the low stone wall
between the two, her skirts flouncing, his eyes following. The *hows*
and *whens* of their reacquaintance were never clear to her children.
All they knew was that this gruff, jowly, bald-headed man began stopping by with some regularity, and that his status somehow changed
from "old friend" to "the wedding is the third Saturday in October."

It could not be a church wedding. The priests at St. Catherine's
might have encouraged Rose to divorce her abusive first husband,
but they could not bless a marriage to her second one. The bride and
groom went together to the Stamford justice of the peace and completed their marriage license, which described Anthony as a sixty-five-
year-old widowed laborer and Rose as a fifty-three-year-old divorced
housewife. They each placed their X on the signature line, even though
Rose could have signed hers. She had, very recently, learned how to
write "Rose Cufone Cosentino." But Anthony had never learned to
write much at all, and if Rose used her newly learned skill, it would
show up her newly acquired husband. An X it was.

The Cosentino children were confused. Who was this old man
who had attached himself to their mother? At least Gerome, for all his
faults, had been an intellectual, a landscape designer, an artist. Tony
had been a gravedigger at the Putnam cemetery for thirty-seven years.
All Tony wanted was someone to cook his meals, wash his clothes,

and keep him company. His oldest daughter had done so since he'd been widowed. Now it would become Rose's job.

The Siciliano children, meanwhile, were angry. Who was this woman who had clearly trapped their father? She was younger, but you wouldn't know it to look at her, with her shapeless housedresses and gray-white hair. Anthony was not rich, but he was not dirt poor like this divorced woman and her brood of shabby kids. Behind her back they called her a *puttana*, a whore. To her face they ignored her.

What neither set of children could see was how the return to Cos Cob looked to Rose. She had walked these same roads—Harold Street, Valley Road, Cos Cob Avenue—when she first arrived from Italy. She had fantasized a new life while she walked, then watched those fantasies disappear. The house where she'd first stayed with Philomena was still visible through Tony's back windows, though the Belmonts had moved to fancier digs years earlier. The house she had briefly owned with Gerome was also the same, but different. Gerome's garden had been replaced by a patio, the woodstove by central heating, the bug-a-house by indoor plumbing. A late-model car stood in the paved driveway, one that was not likely to be repossessed in the night.

Rose, though she had never been to school, had long amazed her children with her knack for doing calculations in her head. Life has many kinds of math, and Rose had run a similar equation for what would turn out to be the remaining two decades of Tony's life. She would take care of him—fill his lunchbox every morning as he left for work, chat with him in their ancestral dialect every evening while he smoked an after-dinner cigar. In return, just as his children feared, he would change his will. She made sure of that, because she was good with numbers. The house on Harold Street would be hers to live in for as long as she wished after his death, and when it was sold, half the proceeds would be hers.

It was a lovely house. She had thought so for more than thirty years. Outside there was a wraparound porch, a grape arbor, a chicken coop, and a fig tree grown from a cutting brought over from Rose. The three bedrooms were on the second floor, and as Tony and Rose arrived after their reception, his eldest daughter hurtled down those stairs, suitcase in hand, refusing to stay if "that woman" was now in residence. She stormed out, nearly knocking down Frank and Rosie as she swept through. As she left she passed the wedding portrait of Tony and his first wife, Carmela, that had hung near the front door for forty years and that no one had thought to remove before Rose moved in.

The departure left more space for Rosie and Frank, the only two Cosentino children still at home. The exodus of their other siblings had begun when Dante first ran away; by now he was stationed in postwar Europe. Then Mary, Evelyn, Louise, and Lecia moved out, each into their own households and their own worlds. Albert and Valentino, too, were reduced to infrequent letters, and even rarer long-distance phone calls, from far-flung locations. The biggest loss for fourteen-year-old Frank and fifteen-year-old Rosie, though, was each other. Until the move, they had walked the mile or so to Cloonan Junior High School in Stamford together every morning, he in seventh grade, she in ninth; they'd return home together, too.

In Cos Cob, though, they were in different school buildings. For Frank, that meant effectively being placed "back" in elementary school because the neighborhood had no junior high. He didn't even have hope of reuniting with Rosie when he finally made it to Cos Cob High School, because she would not be there. She had enrolled in a three-year cosmetology course at a vocational high school in Stamford, for which she left early every morning and returned just before dinner every night. During her rare hours in Cos Cob, she was more likely to be with her first boyfriend—until he broke up with her when his mother, who had known Rosie's mother from back in Italy, told him he could not date the daughter of a woman "like that."

And so the siblings continued to widen their orbit around each other in Tony Siciliano's big house. Frank told Rosie less about his frustrations; Rosie talked less to Frank about her dreams. They never spoke about their actual father, either. It quickly became clear that Gerome had followed his shrinking family back to Cos Cob and was still watching his former wife, and her new life, from the shadows. His children didn't see him, but they saw *evidence* of him just as they had back in Stamford—in the emptied bottles he would stash in the bushes and under the stairs. They'd heard rumors he'd been living in the nearby Riverside neighborhood and was drinking nightly at the Diamond Bar and Grill.

The article on page ten of the *Greenwich Time* newspaper on Tuesday, November 14, was headlined FORMER COS COB MAN FOUND DEAD IN CAB OF TRUCK. The story quoted the medical examiner saying the cause of death was "exposure to the elements" and that "Mr. Cosentino had been dead approximately two days" before his body was discovered. The best guess of the coroner's office was that Gerome had crawled into the truck in the lot of the Stamford Truck Sales Company, next door to the Diamond, on Saturday night. He'd gone unnoticed until business opened on Monday morning.

When he was finally found, he was slumped behind the wheel with his shoes off and a "partially consumed bottle of wine" by his side, the news story said. "He leaves several sons and daughters. Funeral arrangements are incomplete."

One of those sons, Dante, could have requested bereavement leave and come home from where he was stationed in Austria, but he didn't even think to ask about that. Another of those sons, Valentino, managed to find the room Gerome was renting and quietly cleaned the signs of frustration from the walls—stains where his father had thrown bottles and holes where he had thrown punches. Frank and Rosie went back to school the next day, the same as always. Evelyn's husband settled accounts with the mortuary, and Gerome Cosentino was buried without a funeral in an unmarked grave. He was fifty-five years old.

1950
David Troy and Rosie Cosentino
Al Tarlov and Joan Hylton
Stamford and Norwalk

SEVENTEEN WAS TOO YOUNG TO BE A POLICE OFFICER. BUT IT was not too young to fix and build, and Dave Troy happily left the boring academics at Stamford High School for more hands-on vocational training at the J. M. Wright Technical School in downtown Stamford. It required a slight compromise with his mother. He agreed to forgo the automobile major and enrolled in the carpentry track instead. In return, he got to keep his job at Woldan's Service Station, which brought him both spending money and joy.

Wright was established back in 1919 as the Stamford Trade School, an idea born of the moment when the Great War met the Industrial Revolution. The factories sprouting in Stamford needed skilled workers—plumbers, machinists, carpenters, electricians. At the same time, soldiers returning from the fight needed jobs. For a short time, individual factories created separate training programs—Dave's father, Patrick Troy, had been enrolled in the one at the Cove Mills when he came back from the war. Soon owners hit on the economies of scale that would result from a centralized school. James M. Wright, for whom Wright Tech would eventually be named, was not an educator, but rather the president of the Electric Specialty Company and a vice-president of the Chamber of Commerce.

The building had been shiny and modern back in 1919 when Wright chose the site, but by 1948, when Dave enrolled, the four-story brick school was a fire hazard, a plumbing nightmare, and badly in need of a new roof. There were nearly twice as many students as there had

been twenty years earlier, and by the fall of 1951 the city would petition the legislature for a new Wright campus. Until then, the students
saw the drafty building as a bonding experience—and a chance to
practice their skills anytime something else needed repair.

Dave thrived at Wright. He learned to read blueprints and building
codes, finish floors, walls, and ceilings, create tables and cabinetry.
He also learned to read people, to handle a spotlight, and to lead others. Easygoing by nature and a natural athlete, he was quietly popular, a three-season sports star with baseball far and away his favorite.
When he earned his varsity letter in June 1950, his name was in the
newspaper for his mother to paste into what would become a bulging
scrapbook. The *Daily Advocate* covered his pitching victories for the
Techmen, his election to the student government, and the fact that he
was a tour guide at the yearly open house held each spring for pro-
spective students.

Most of all, Dave felt respected and heard. This was the ethos of
Wright—known as the "Wright attitude"—and it shared pedagogical
roots with iterations of honor systems at places like the St. Charles
School for Boys and the Stateville Penitentiary. "We're going on the
idea that if we treat them like adults, they act like adults," said Paul
J. Cubeta, the school director. Wright teachers, he explained, didn't
proctor tests or maintain order at recess; it was left to students to
monitor themselves.

By the fall of 1950, Dave was a relatively big man on the relatively
small campus. He arrived back from summer break driving a convertible that he'd bought with money he earned working for Woldan's
and that he'd restored to peak performance in their service bays. The
car drew admiring looks from the boys. Its owner drew similar looks
from the girls.

There was no specific moment when he and one particularly special girl first met; they just knew each other the way classmates in
small schools do. Later they would retrace their lives and figure they
had probably been in the same place at the same time often over the
years, their routes crisscrossing but not overlapping. Once they did,

she came to see him as the funny red-headed athlete, with the big ears and crooked teeth, which somehow, combined with the square of his jaw and the kindness in his eyes, made him handsome. He saw her as the dark-haired newcomer, an Italian beauty who, he learned from the grapevine, was moving to Cos Cob because her mother was remarrying.

Dave almost didn't ask Rosie Cosentino to the Christmas dance in December 1950. He certainly waited until nearly the last minute. He would later say he was sure she already had a date, how could she not? When he finally asked, she accepted, even though the "rules" of the day said a nice girl should be insulted by a late invitation. Rosie wore a dress her mother helped her sew. Dave wore white tie and shiny black shoes; he carried a corsage as he walked between the stone pillars and for the first time, up the stairs to her stepfather's house.

✦

AL TARLOV WAS HOME from Dartmouth one autumn weekend, grabbing a slice at Phil Baker's with a friend who recognized the slim, graceful redhead as she waited for a table. "This is Joan Hylton," the friend said, inviting her to pull up a chair. New to Norwalk, Joan had never been to Phil Baker's restaurant, hadn't heard of the famous boxer who owned it, and didn't much like pizza, but a long day and lack of anything to eat back in the student nurses' residence hall at Norwalk Hospital had led her to give the place a try.

Joan was not like any other girl Al had dated. While Al descended from Russian Jews on both sides, Joan's paternal great-grandfather had been a rakish British plantation owner in the West Indies who sold off his slaves to finance his move to California during the gold rush. Eventually he fathered two children and deposited the son—Joan's grandfather—in a New York orphanage in order to marry a wealthy widow who had no interest in raising the boy. That abandoned young man vowed to be the opposite of his father and grew into an industrious railroad worker, a teetotaler, and a regular at the Episcopal church. Because generations have a way of thumbing their noses at each other, one of his sons—Joan's father, Walter Hylton—then became a drunk who had a hard time holding on to a dollar or a job. Joan's mother, Eleanor, had married him when she was nineteen, against the wishes of her strict and humorless German Catholic parents. Eleanor then died of "female complications" six years later, leaving Walter to somehow raise five-year-old Joan and her eleven-month-old sister Carole.

He did so by marrying his dead wife's younger sister, Lucille, who loved both her nieces/stepdaughters but seemed to detest their father. Their descendants would wonder how their union ever came to be. Perhaps Walter felt incapable of caring for two little girls without a wife? Perhaps Lucille felt sorry for her widowed brother-in-law or motherless nieces? It could be that Walter and Lucille had fallen in love, but no one in the family seemed to believe that. There were hints that Walter had found his way into Lucille's bed (without her consent) while Eleanor was sick and that when his mother-in-law found out she insisted they make things right. But no one present for these decisions ever talked about them much. Whatever the catalyst, the marriage was not a happy one, and it effectively ended when Walter left to serve in the Philippines during World War II, never again to live under the same roof as his second wife and his first wife's daughters.

Lucille divorced him a few weeks after he returned, and she married a naval officer days later. Carole, who was eleven, agreed to join the newlyweds for a new life in California. Joan, who was fifteen, did not want to leave her high school. For the next three years Joan lived with her grandmother and aunt, both of whom earned a meager living taking in sewing work. As soon as she could, Joan enrolled in a nursing program in Norwalk, borrowing the tuition money from her father's sister.

By the night they'd met, Al and Joan had both arrived at the same goal for their lives—to right the wrongs of their own childhoods by building the family they'd wished they'd had. Ten children, Joan told Al early in their relationship. Maybe twelve, a huge loving brood that she could dote upon and mold.

Al was thrilled. He had continued his informal survey of how other

families did things, paying close attention when invited into his classmates' homes, and while he was grateful for what his own childhood
had given him—independence, a work ethic, a feeling of security—he
was also aware of what he did not have. Other families ate dinner
together, took vacations, and saw their father outside of work. Other
children talked to their dad about more than just a restaurant.

Al knew he wanted a life different from his father's and as meaningful as his uncle Isadore's. He certainly hadn't found it at Dartmouth.
As he'd feared, the school's Division One teams had no room for his
limited talents; most fraternities would not consider him because he
was Jewish, while the one Jewish fraternity did not feel welcoming
because he was not Jewish enough. As a result, he spent many weekends off campus, often visiting Isadore at his country house in Litchfield, Connecticut. They chopped logs in the woods, fed them to the
fire in the library, then spent hours in silence as Isadore wrote articles
about neurosurgery and read ones about socialism, and Al did schoolwork. Al began spending his summers in the outdoors doing land surveying, work that was part art and part science, blending physics and
law. After twelve hours of mapping nature and the buildings man
built upon it, he came home tired and tanned.

The night Al met Joan, he was at a crossroads. In his fourth and
final year of college, he needed to decide what to do with his life.
During his freshman year, his father had taken him at his word and
sold Tarlov's Restaurant, so that path was out. At the same time, Al's
uncle did not think he should become a doctor—at least not until he
had more thoroughly explored other options. He had applied anyway, a single application to Dartmouth Medical School. It was a half-
hearted gesture because, at the time, Dartmouth's was a half-hearted
medical school. Out in rural New Hampshire, there were not enough
patients to provide well-rounded training for new doctors so Dartmouth no longer granted medical degrees. It had been reduced to a
way station, a two-year program, after which students transferred to
a four-year school to get their M.D.

Al was more than a little perplexed, therefore, when he was rejected.

He was not sure he wanted Dartmouth, but it had not occurred to him that Dartmouth would not want *him*. When asked for a reason, a friendly professor on the admissions committee told him that it was because the school already had "our two Jews."

For the rest of the school year, Al spent his weekends in Norwalk, taking Joan to the movies or to dinner, and sometimes to shows in New York. Dating her was a comfort, a relief. She wanted what he thought he wanted. She saw work as he was trying to see it—as a means to a nice life, rather than as an identity or an obsession. Joan graduated from nursing school in the spring of 1951 and became a practical nurse in the pediatric ward at Norwalk Hospital. Al graduated from Dartmouth a few weeks later and started his own business, Land Survey Markers. It was honest, steady work. And it would ensure that, when the time came, he would be home for dinner every night with his many children.

November 1950
Joe DeSalvo
Pontiac Prison

JOSEPH DESALVO WAS BETTER PREPARED FOR HIS SECOND PAROLE hearing than he had been for his first. This time he had a story to tell—the kind of redemption tale that the Illinois parole board seemed to want to hear.

On the question of rehabilitation, some people believe that men can change and some do not. Like any group of political appointees, the parole board members tended to hold views that reflected the views of those who had appointed them. Governor Green, a Republican, had campaigned as a law and order man, suspicious of parolees. Even as he'd authorized parole hearings for malaria drug trial volunteers after Nuremberg, he had required that applicants prove that they'd truly suffered during the trials. It was Green's board that had heard Nathan Leopold's request for a commutation, decided he had suffered sufficiently, and reduced his sentence. That same board heard Joe's first parole request, decided he had not been duly punished, and turned it down.

In 1948 Green had lost in a surprise landslide to Democrat Adlai Stevenson, who saw himself as a reformer. Stevenson inherited Green's decree that all malaria volunteers be given a hearing, but he did not fully approve of the idea. He would have preferred that parole be awarded due to evidence of rehabilitation, not as compensation for pain suffered, and soon after he took office, the practice of moving up hearing dates for drug trial participants quietly ended. (Nathan Leopold's was the last of them, in April 1949.)

By Joe's second hearing, therefore, the membership and mindset of the board had changed. It now consisted of two Green holdovers and four Stevenson picks, and its members were much more interested in the ability of parole candidates to function in society than in whether they had been sufficiently punished. The new focus resulted in less granting of parole. Fewer could prove they'd changed than could prove they'd suffered. Back in 1940, 76 percent of those released from prison had been paroled, while only 24 percent had served their entire sentence. By 1950, just 36 percent departed on parole, while the rest were required to complete at least their minimum sentences.

Still, Joe had reason to hope that he would become one of the freed. To do so, he would tell the board a story. It would start with the rattling cough he had developed soon after his last hearing, one that shook him out of sleep so often that his cellmate complained, and the guards sent Joe to the Pontiac infirmary to end the squabbling. Confined to the prison's TB ward for much of 1949, Joe came to enjoy the niceties of hospitalization—the real sheets and blankets, the relative peace and quiet, the actual darkness at night, all the things Stateville's malaria volunteers had come to know well. The perk he liked best was the headset he was given to listen to whatever he chose on the radio; he drew himself a piano-size keyboard and played along with jazz oldies and current popular songs, remembering the sound of each key from his time at St. Charles. He would tell the board about how this time on the ward allowed him to read, study, and think. By 1950 he was considered cured of TB but not yet strong enough to go back to work in the machine shop. He was given a clerical assignment in the sociologist-actuary office at Pontiac, filing interview transcripts and parole prediction reports.

As he filed, he read, noting the stories other prisoners had to tell and how they compared to his own. If this parole board was looking for a redemption arc, then it was up to Joe to provide one from the narrative of his own life. For a prisoner seeking parole, act one was about what had come before—the distillation of chance and choice that had led him to jail. Act two was about what happened to him while incarcerated. Act three, then, was about what would happen next, and that was for the parole board to decide, envisioning the logical denouement based on the plot thus far. Had this character truly changed, or was he a criminal at his core? It was Joe's goal to make a happy ending seem possible.

His first act, he knew, did not give the audience much reason for optimism. The mathematical formula that had originated with Nathan Leopold and that was still used by the sociologist-actuary would deduct points because this was not his first encounter with the law, because his father was distant and his mother overly enmeshed, because he was single and a loner, because he had never learned a real trade. His second chapter, though, was more hopeful. In the two years since his last hearing, Joe's discipline record had been nearly perfect. This good behavior was in part because his only friends, Keck and Clair, had been released, and because he had been bunking mostly in the infirmary, he'd had little chance or inclination to make new ones. Mostly though, or so Joe could argue, it was because he had made the choice to put his energies into his education. The tests he'd taken when he was at Stateville showed his IQ to be 142, genius level. His file at the prison library showed he had checked out his maximum allotment of books each week, mostly science, philosophy, and poetry. His parole report from the sociologist-actuary would describe him as an intelligent man whose education was belatedly catching up to his abilities, one who "has reoriented . . . along more conventional channels."

The all-important number on his parole prediction report would list him as having a 56 percent chance of failure if granted parole. Though not ideal, it was a full four percentage points lower than his odds were said to be at the prior hearing, enough to move him from a "moderate risk" to a "fair risk" on the official forms. Even the statistical instruments seemed to agree that he was headed in the right direction.

Joe made his case on the afternoon of November 9, 1950, in the same Pontiac conference room where he'd been two years earlier. The questions were almost identical to the first time around, and Joe gave essentially the same answers. But this time his replies formed a story in which he was the humbled and penitent hero.

"Do you think you could stay out of trouble?" asked the parole board chairman, Joseph Lohman, who was a professor of sociology at the University of Chicago.

"I am positive of it."

Eventually Lohman got to what Joe had come to realize was the real point: would his behavior on the outside make them—the parole board—look good?

"We don't want any violators on our dockets," Lohman said, giving a version of the speech given to most who came before his board. "The reason we don't is not because it is a problem to us or to you, but it is a problem to the parole system. We are supposed to pick the right ones. That is what the parole system is for. Are you one of those?"

"Yes sir, I think I am."

"Are you one of those that will not come back?"

"I will do my very best."

Within the month, Joe received a letter signed by Lohman on behalf of the board. He had made a "favorable" appearance before the subcommittee, it said. "His creditable work record and the presence of an acceptable home and job opportunity in a free community," it continued, "augurs well for a successful adjustment on parole. Since there is no useful purpose to be served by further incarceration of this inmate . . . the recommendation of the Subcommittee is that he be paroled at this time, effective December 11, 1950."

The Tarlov family in front of their Norwalk home, c. 1905. Morris/
Isadore is the infant in Raisel's arms, and Max is seated next to the
family dog. *Photo courtesy of the Tarlov family.*

Aime Tarlov, c. 1918, when he
went off to fight in the Great War.
Photo courtesy of the Tarlov family.

Alvin Tarlov, c. 1943.
Photo courtesy of the Tarlov family.

Joan Tarlov with (left to right) Suzanne, Jane, Richard, and Elizabeth. David had not yet arrived.

Photo courtesy of the Tarlov family.

Rose and Gerome Cosentino wedding portrait, 1916.

Photo courtesy of the Cosentino family.

The four Cosentino
boys in 1948.
Left to right: Dante,
Val, Frank, and Albert.
*Photo courtesy of the
Cosentino family.*

Dante Cosentino in the army,
c. 1950, U.S. government
photo. *Photo courtesy of
the Cosentino family.*

Anthony Siciliano and
Rose Cufone Cosentino at
their wedding in 1950.
*Photo courtesy of Evelyn
Cosentino Davidson.*

Rosie Cosentino as a young teen.
Photo courtesy of the Cosentino family.

David Troy graduating from
Wright Tech, 1952.
Photo courtesy of the Troy family.

Lifting the bride's veil, July 4, 1954. Left to right: Rosemary Curcio,
Rosie Cosentino, and Rose Cosentino Siciliano.
Photo courtesy of the Troy family.

Bridget Troy at her son
Dave's wedding.
Photo courtesy of the Troy family.

Rosie and Dave Troy in
their new home at 33 Palmer
Avenue, c. 1954.
Photo courtesy of the Troy family.

Officer David Troy,
c. 1959, from his
Stamford Police file.
*Photo courtesy of
the Troy family.*

The Troys' third child, David Jr., was so young when his father died that Rosie did not have a photo of the family of five to give to newspapers. The *Stamford Advocate* ran this instead.

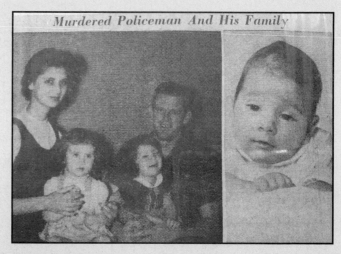

Murdered Policeman And His Family

THE FORT WAYNE DAILY NEWS

WILL RACE SUNDAY

De Salvo With His Speedy Excelsior, on Which He Made a Mile in 40 Seconds.

The Fort Wayne Daily News story about Charles DeSalvo before a race, October 7, 1911.

A jumble of DeSalvos, date and names unknown.

The original School
Building at the St.
Charles School for
Boys, in a photo taken
before 1925.

Joliet Prison,
1915.

Stateville
Penitentiary, c.
1944.

*Photo courtesy
of the Joliet Area
Historical
Museum.*

Warden Joseph Ragen with a cache of weapons found in a cell shakedown on November 24, 1944.

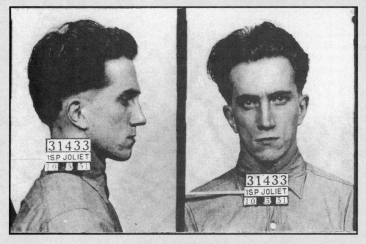

Joseph DeSalvo, 1951 mugshot.

Joseph DeSalvo awaiting trial, 1960.

April 1951
Joseph DeSalvo
Chicago

JOE DID NOT SAY A WORD AS HE THREW OPEN THE BACK DOOR of his parents' house at 217 LaPorte, the same house where he'd spent his childhood, though by now his family occupied the both floors. He clomped up the uncarpeted stairs on this April morning, rummaged in his bedroom for a few minutes, then left as noisily as he'd entered. His parents had been asleep when he first arrived, but Ruth, awakened by all the slamming, reached the top of the staircase in time to see Joe exit with a duffel bag slung over one shoulder. She called after him; he didn't look back.

Ruth was concerned but hardly shocked. Joe had been out on parole for four months, and for the first two of those, life had come as close to calm as she ever recalled it being in the DeSalvo home. Charles Sr. had gotten Joe a job at the Speedway Manufacturing Company and the two had ridden the bus to work and back every day—companionably, it seemed to Ruth—for about six weeks. Then Joe quit the company where his father was a manager and took a similar position as a drill press operator at Northern Metal Products, meaning he and Charles headed for work in opposite directions every morning, but still returned home to eat with Ruth every evening.

Early in March, Joe had stopped coming home for dinner. Some nights he didn't return until dawn. He said he had reconnected with an "old friend" and they were catching up; Ruth guessed this reunion had taken place when Joe went to a required meeting with his parole officer in downtown Chicago. The regular check-ins were a condition of parole, and for the first one the officer had visited Joe at home, quizzing his parents about how he was behaving. The officer opened the bedroom closets and asked which toothbrush was Joe's in the only bathroom, all to verify that he was living there. The officer also made a sketch of the apartment's layout, noting the two exits and entrances, a routine bit of caution should he ever have to arrest Joe for a parole violation.

After the home visit, though, Joe was expected to go see the officer. It was after one of those downtown meetings that Joe let slip that he'd met the "old" friend. By March 27 Joe told Ruth he'd quit his job at Northern Metal to explore better-paying opportunities. On April 17 he packed up a few things and left to "stay with a friend," though he didn't give a name. And now, on the morning of April 30, he appeared out of nowhere and left almost immediately, taking everything he could carry.

A few hours later Joe's parole officer knocked on the front door while two uniformed patrolmen stood at the back entrance, just in case.

"Mrs. DeSalvo, I am looking for Joseph. Is he home?"

"Not right now."

"When was he last here?"

"He left early this morning."

"I have a warrant here to search the house. Please step aside."

A look at Joe's upended room made it clear that he had fled, so Ruth told the officer everything. That he'd quit his job (a parole violation) and that he'd left no hint of where he'd gone (another parole violation). Her worry spilled out like rage, and she blamed the man asking all these questions for creating the problem in the first place.

She described Joe's shift in behavior and her belief that a chance meeting in the anteroom of the parole office had undone all his good intentions.

"He was doing all right until he met this fellow," she said. "I think if you had not made him come downtown, there wouldn't be any trouble today."

"He must report to our office within three days," the parole officer said, brushing the accusation aside. "If he doesn't, he will be declared a parole violator and a warrant would be issued for his arrest."

The officer never said what brought him to look for Joe in the first place, but whatever it was, Ruth was certain it was the fault of whoever he had run into a few weeks earlier. "If only he hadn't met that boy," she told Charles over and over again. "If only he hadn't met that boy."

✦

THE "BOY" JOE HAD met was Edgar Keck, who had come out of his parole officer's closet-size office in early March as Joe sat waiting to go in. Joe was thrilled to see his St. Charles bunkmate and Pontiac floormate, and after Joe's own quick check-in ("Are you keeping your nose clean? Has your address changed? Are you still employed?"), Joe emerged onto the street to find Keck leaning against the brick of the parole office building, suggesting they go for a drink.

Joe would describe this as the day he realized he'd been lonely, a thought that had surprised him. He considered himself a loner, keeping his own company, not needing anyone else. That was how he'd gotten through St. Charles after Keck and William Clair left, and how he'd gotten through Pontiac years later, after Keck and Clair left again. Now, downing whiskeys with Keck (a parole violation for them both), he widened the lens on his memories. He saw not only the rules and deprivations of prison life but the structure and companionship as well. There was loneliness in prison, but also a community. Back in his childhood home, with his brother still off somewhere, Joe felt very much alone. His father's glares, his mother's sighs—he had no one to witness those, to suffer alongside him.

Keck, too, seemed bored, misunderstood, and surprisingly nostalgic. They talked and drank for hours that first night, dropping prison slang, each enjoying the company of another who spoke his language. Keck had been paroled from Pontiac nearly four months before Joe and had been working alongside his mother at a cafeteria in Melrose Park. Every so often he spent time with William Clair, who had been released a full two years before either of them. Clair, too, was living with his parents and was working as a plasterer, a steady union job he had found through some buddies of his father.

DeSalvo, Keck, and Clair began to drink together nearly every night. They traded "war stories," told jokes, and mostly complained that they were stuck in jobs that wouldn't earn them the life they believed they deserved. They saw those they worked with as soft, not having had to handle prison. Joe believed his bosses were not nearly as smart as he was and bristled that the world saw him as a man with a record, not a man with a hard-won GED and a genius-level IQ. One night Clair lifted his trouser cuff to give the others a look at the handgun strapped to his ankle (a serious parole violation). "A guy can never be too careful," he said.

They would never agree whose idea it had been. They would all go on to blame one another, insisting they had been uninterested in anything but talk until the others manipulated them into action. They were probably right. Like Leopold and Loeb, their crimes were less an individual decision than the combustive effect of their personalities. Alone, DeSalvo, Keck, and Clair had observed the rules of parole, gotten satisfactory write-ups at work, allowed their parents to believe that the bad seeds might perhaps have turned into responsible men. Together, they magnified each other's tendencies toward recklessness and swagger.

Whatever its origins, a plan evolved. A fourth member joined the "club"—a twenty-one-year-old television repair apprentice named Arthur Hultin who, fresh out of the navy, was still in uniform the night they befriended him in a bar. He had never been in trouble but was put off that playing by the rules had landed him nothing but a seeming dead-end. His clean record was helpful when they decided to buy a few more handguns from area pawn shops, "just in case."

On April 16 they "acquired" a car, a 1949 Chevrolet sedan that Hultin took at gunpoint at four in the morning from an engaged couple who thought they were very much alone while necking on their deserted residential street. It was his initiation of sorts. Hultin also took the driver's wallet, which contained a disappointing fifteen dollars. That night the foursome rode for hours around Chicago, Hultin at the wheel, "just talking," they would later say. At ten-fifteen p.m. they pulled up to a tavern on West 47th Street, and DeSalvo, Clair, and Keck entered, seating themselves at the bar while Hultin idled at the curb.

"What will you have?" bartender Joseph Jurcaszak asked.

"This is a stick-up," they replied, each pulling a gun.

By 10:20, they were back in the Chevy, Hultin making random lefts and rights through the city as the others counted out the bills. There had only been eighty dollars in the register.

Hultin drove aimlessly while the group argued about how to find a more promising next target. They couldn't go to any of their usual haunts, for fear of being recognized. A few of the random pubs they passed were closed on this Monday night. Eventually they settled on the Share Inn Tavern, a pub and liquor store on Devon Avenue.

This time Clair stayed in the car. DeSalvo, Keck, and Hultin entered and took seats at the far end of the bar, where four others were already sharing a round of drinks. One was Sol Greenberg, the owner of the Share Inn; the man immediately to his right was Robert S. Bremer, a thirty-three-year-old political newcomer who had won a surprise victory as alderman for the fiftieth ward, where the Share Inn was located. He'd stopped in to talk with Greenberg, who'd been complaining that trash pickup in the area was neglected. Next to Bremer were thirty-five-year-old James Ott, a wealthy businessman who was president of the Chicago Name Plate Company, also in Bremer's district, and Ott's wife, Tessie. The Otts happened to be having a nightcap when their new alderman arrived, and Greenberg and Bremer both joined the couple, ordering beers.

At first, they hardly noticed the three young men.

"Are you fellows of age?" Greenberg heard his bartender ask.

Whatever was said in return prompted the bartender to open the register and place a stack of bills on the well-worn wooden counter. Greenberg slid off his stool and started to walk the several steps toward that money, when the tallest of the young men—the one with the long face, high squared-off forehead, and deep acne scars—raised a gun and said, "This is a stick-up."

The next minutes were a blur. One of the trio struck Bremer in the back of the head with a rifle butt. "Give me your wallet!" the man shouted, and the alderman said he was not carrying one. Seeing spots and losing consciousness, Bremer heard several gunshots. Bullets struck a soft drink vending machine and hit James Ott, who shouted "my God!" and slumped forward. His wife was thumped on the head by the gun that had wounded her husband.

"Come on, let's go!" the tall man yelled, grabbing the money off the bar. As he loped out the door, he warned his victims: "Don't anyone move for five minutes, or I'll kill you."

The Share Inn holdup netted less than $300, still far from the windfall the foursome had planned. The group squabbled about why they hadn't worn any sort of disguise and accused each other of being sloppy. Those with records were concerned that a good sketch artist would make it possible to identify them since their mugshots were already in the system. Hultin went hoarse from screaming about why these supposedly experienced thugs were thinking of all this only after the fact.

They agreed to lie low for a few weeks, staying away from their usual routines. Joe spent the time in grungy hotel rooms, leaving only to buy the Chicago papers, looking for news of the arrest of any in his small gang. He read that three of the victims had been taken to St. Francis Hospital, where Tessie Ott was treated for a scalp laceration, Alderman Bremer was treated for a possible concussion, and James Ott underwent surgery for injuries from a bullet that entered through the right side of his back and exited through the left. There was nothing about Keck, Clair, or Hultin.

Time passed, and the pull of guilt, relief, or thrill was strong enough that Joe reunited with the others on the late afternoon of April 29. Stores were closed as usual on this Sunday, and there were few pedestrians walking along South Laramie Avenue toward Cicero. It was not a chilly evening, but all four men were wearing woolen caps pulled

low over their foreheads. When they spotted a man parking his gray
Chrysler coupe, they moved the caps down even further.

Not five minutes later Joe was at the wheel of that car, driving
north on Laramie and speeding up at the yellow light at Lake Street,
turning right just as the signal turned red. Officer Charles Winkler
and his partner assumed this was just a routine violation when they
pulled behind the coupe and were surprised when the driver didn't
stop. The officers gave chase, a young man leaned out the rear window and fired on the cruiser, and both automobiles screeched around
the next corner, where the coupe crashed into a parked car.

Three men jumped out and ran in different directions. Officer
Winkler chased one through an alley south of Lake Street and captured him. That was Arthur Hultin, who was carrying a loaded 9-mm
automatic Luger. Officer Connolly chased another onto Lake Street
and made him freeze at gunpoint. That was Edgar Keck, who was
carrying a shotgun and an automatic pistol. Both were taken to the
28th District police station and held overnight. The next morning the
Share Inn victims identified them in a lineup.

In separate interrogation rooms, they admitted there had been
two more accomplices in the car. The first, William Clair, had hidden in the back seat when the others jumped out. Three well-armed
officers were dispatched to Clair's last known address, and while he
wasn't there, his parents told the policemen where he might be found.
He was arrested within the hour. The second, Joe DeSalvo, had run
south when the others ran north, and a squad car was sent to his home
address as well. That was where Ruth described how her son had
come and gone before dawn, and said she blamed all this on whoever
it was that he'd met at the parole office.

✦

WHILE THE LAWMEN SEARCHED his parents' house, Joe was headed
west in a stolen Cadillac. He hoped to reach California, but his plan
was slowed by the need to pay for gas, food, and a place to sleep. He
still had a gun, and he could have used it to get what he needed, but he

was already a wanted man, and the thought of multiplying the number of states where his face was on a wanted poster did not appeal. He spent weeks earning tips for playing the piano in bars in small towns of Wisconsin, Iowa, and Missouri, places abutting his home state and where there would not be warrants out for his arrest. His practice on his paper keyboard at Pontiac turned out to be good training, and he found he could even take customer requests. He earned enough to eat. He slept in his car, showered at men's shelters or the occasional church, and considered what to do next.

Joe did not think of himself as a thief. He believed he was a good man who had been dealt some bad hands, and he still saw a future for himself in a job that used his brain—maybe one like the sociologist-actuary at Pontiac, or one of the psychologists at St. Charles. He just needed a boost, that was all. The jobs he could get with a prison record were hand-to-mouth and would not allow him to go back to school. Now that he was on the run, it would be even harder to get a leg up, enough of a cushion to live on while he sorted the rest out. Just a few well-planned robberies, he reasoned, and then he could move on. Yes, he got an adrenaline rush from the act of taking what should be his, and he would miss that when it was gone. But he could quit at any time.

How then to make this final spree perfect? What lessons could be learned from the last ones? They should have worn disguises. They should have obeyed traffic laws. They should have chosen their targets more strategically and found places where the payoff was worth the risk.

As he moved from state to state, trading in one car that was not his for another, a plan began to form. It began with memories of visiting his mother's hometown of Moline as a youngster and of passing the massive factories in nearby Rock Island, with lines of tired men streaming out at the end of a shift. Ruth had pointed to the strip of taverns a short distance away, where CHECKS CASHED signs hung in the windows as they had in her father's day. A place like that would need to keep a lot of cash on hand. Were they still there?

They were. Joe cased several, nursing whiskeys while noting the rhythms of the joints. Payday was on Friday. Most establishments filled their safes on Thursday nights, so Joe arrived early on a series of Friday mornings, a bandana tied over his mouth and nose as a disguise, his hair now curled over his brow and down his neck since he had not had a haircut since he'd fled Chicago. Week one he took $1,091 from Johnny's Tap, and week two, $970 from the 400 Club. Week three was by far his biggest score. At seven a.m. he entered the Viaduct Tavern, a Rock Island institution since the days when his grandfather worked at the plant next door. Bartender John Delp told police that the robber had been a man about twenty-five years old, "badly in need of a haircut," wearing blue jeans, a corduroy jacket, and a peaked cap. He'd gotten away with an estimated $5,500 in cash.

That afternoon Joe was in the nearly empty Fifth Avenue Club, just down the block from the Viaduct, which made it a brazen place to loiter. Sitting at the tavern's rinky-dink piano, eyes closed, improvising jazz tunes, he was mentally calculating his totals, figuring he had almost enough to leave for a new start out west. He did not hear Rock Island Police chief Claus C. Miller approach with two fellow officers until they were standing behind him, guns drawn. Joe had a fully loaded .45 caliber Colt automatic pistol strapped beneath his armpit; there was an extra clip in his pocket. But he simply raised his arms and said, "You got me, boys."

He spent nearly four months awaiting trial in the Rock Island County Jail. Early in his stay a search found hacksaw blades in his cell, which he swore had been left behind by another prisoner. Later in the summer he managed to get his hands on an electric lightbulb, and he cut his wrists deeply enough to bleed but not to cause real harm. He insisted that he had only been trying to warrant a transfer to the infirmary, and the local sheriff believed him. He was being held on $15,000 bond, which his parents could not begin to pay, and he refused to see Ruth when she tried to visit. How to look her in the eyes knowing that her desire to share her childhood memories had given him this idea?

He could not avoid seeing her, though, when she took the stand as a character witness after he pleaded guilty at his nonjury trial in October. There she begged Circuit Judge A. J. Scheineman for mercy, saying Joe had tried to be good, but a chance meeting had led him astray. If he hadn't been told to come down to the parole office, she insisted, and if he hadn't met those ne'er-do-wells while he was there, he would not have gone bad.

The judge expressed "a deep sympathy" for the clearly distraught mother, but he was far more swayed by the testimony of the prosecutor. State's Attorney Bernard Moran described all of Joe's Rock Island holdups, noting that during one he had "punctuated his requests for money" by firing three shots over the bartender's head into the back bar. "He is apparently a good shot," Moran said wryly. "He brought each of the three shots closer to the bartender's head to emphasize his demand."

"If he isn't put behind bars for a time," the state's attorney continued, "he may use that gun to kill somebody someday."

Judge Scheineman agreed. All three of Joe's compatriots back in Chicago had been captured by now (the first Joe knew of that); Keck was ordered to serve seven to ten years, Hultin three to seven, and Clair one to three. Joe's additional spree demanded a stiffer punishment, the judge said.

"Such a man necessitates police officers to risk their lives," he warned, then handed down a sentence of ten to seventy years, meaning Joe would have to serve a minimum of 6.5 before he was eligible for parole.

He would not spend those years as he had before, at the more lenient Pontiac campus. He would be held at the state's maximum-security prison—Stateville Penitentiary.

1951 to 1953
Nathan Leopold
Stateville Penitentiary

WHEN JOE DESALVO ARRIVED AT STATEVILLE SHORTLY BEFORE Christmas 1951, Nathan Leopold took his chest X-ray. Every December the prison conducted a health screening of all 3,500 inmates and employees, and in the three years since the program began, Leopold had participated in snapping nearly every four-by-five-inch film. He enjoyed the work. It got him out of the building and into the large mobile unit in the driveway, which held a portable 200-milliamp photofluorography machine. He was even permitted to accompany the truck for a week of X-rays over at Joliet, which was still open and operating, though indoor plumbing and central heating had not yet been installed and would not be until 1956. That meant Leopold's week of X-raying at Joliet was a double reward: first the adventure of leaving Stateville (seeing new-model cars on the road), then the relief of coming back to warm food and flushable toilets.

To Leopold, Joe would have been just another in a long parade of lungs, someone he would not have noticed at all. This X-ray work was rote, allowing his mind to wander to other things. And by the time Joe entered Stateville, Leopold was thinking mostly about getting out.

Not by escaping. He'd had his chances over the years yet never run, concluding that he could not disappear into the larger world, could not blend. Nearly three decades after he kidnapped Bobby Franks, Leopold's face was still too well known, appearing atop the news articles that ran on anniversaries of the crime, and on his birthday every November 19, and whenever a member of the Leopold, Loeb, or Franks families made news, usually by dying.

No, if Nathan Leopold were to take his famous face and leave

Stateville, it would have to be in a coffin or on parole, and for most of his life he had feared it would be the former, as he could not imagine that public opinion would permit his release. Then came the malaria trials, the commutation of his sentence, and the scheduling of an actual parole hearing date for January 1953. Now Leopold allowed himself to believe that release on parole might be possible.

Just as his commutation hearing had been like no one else's, however, he assumed his parole hearing would be one of a kind as well. Those who vouched for him in his 1949 clemency application had focused almost entirely on his participation in the drug trials, as that was what the committee was instructed to consider. But while being bitten by mosquitoes was enough to earn him a hearing, it was not enough to win his release. He would have to prove that he had not only been "re-formed" in prison but had done a lot of good for others along the way. Having committed the crime of the century he would have to demonstrate an equally singular transformation.

A "war council" of relatives and friends gathered to brainstorm non-Stateville names who might speak well of Leopold. Mike Lebold was again in charge. The requests had begun with professors and academics—Burgess, Laune,—but the circle quickly expanded. Friends of friends provided introductions to the radio and TV star Sophie Tucker and to Bishop Fulton J. Sheen of the Archdiocese of New York, because both were not only well known but were also friends of Governor Stevenson. (Neither Tucker nor Sheen wrote a letter.)

When Leopold and his team were not soliciting letters, they strategized about what work he might do when he got out. Parole rules required that a parole applicant show proof of a place to live and an offer of employment should they be released, and Leopold found himself considering something that he'd not thought about as an adult: what he wanted to be when he grew up. He would never be the lawyer, professor, or scientist that he might once have become. His sociology work might have been worthy of journals when he was using his database of prisoner questionnaires, but a Ph.D. was necessary to continue the work on the outside, and he didn't think that likely. And the

academicians who had considered him a pet project while in prison—
would they be as eager to consider him a colleague upon release? He
was not naïve enough to think so.

He could use his X-ray training in the "real world," and so he
applied for certification from the American Registry of X-Ray Technicians. He was told that his eleven years of experience in the prison
radiology lab did not meet the organization's requirements of two
years of training under a certified radiologist because the prison doctors had always been general practitioners. He had more luck with
the Registry of American Medical Technologists. After sending proof
of his lab experience, he was permitted to take a proctored exam at
Stateville, which he passed. His certificate of admission to the group
was slipped into the growing parole hearing file.

Casting a wider net, Leopold's advocates sought offers at such
places as the War Department's Counterintelligence Corps ("you
could do a job as a translator or in coding or decoding codes,"
one friend, Abel Brown, suggested) and the office of the U.S. surgeon general ("where they could use your experience as a malarial
researcher"). They investigated such groups as the American Prison
Association and the American Probation Society. "Just as each of us
strives to become the best in our field in civil life, Leopold has in
all probability become the best convict in our penitentiary system,"
read one letter on his behalf. Said another: "If granted parole, it is
our belief that few men are better qualified to render service in the
important field of penology than Nathan Leopold."

He received eight job offers and narrowed them down to three for
inclusion in his parole application. His favorite was from a hospital for
the poor in the mountains of Puerto Rico, run by the Church of the
Brethren. They had an opening for a lab technician and would provide transportation to the island, food, housing, laundry, and medical
care—all of which had been given to him at Stateville and that he had
no experience arranging for himself—plus a stipend of about $7.50
a month. "Any of these three would [take] me far from Chicago," he
wrote, which was also of importance to the board.

On January 8, 1953, a morning so cold and wet that proceedings were delayed while parole board members navigated the icy roads to Stateville, Chairman Lohman and two other members sat at the front table, listening as nine speakers spent hours making the case for and against Leopold's parole. Eight of them spoke in favor, stressing how Leopold had been a model prisoner and how even Clarence Darrow had predicted, during his trial summation, that time might make "these boys" fit to return to society once "life and age [had] changed" them. Only one witness disagreed. State's Attorney John Gutknecht of Cook County professed not to care whether Leopold had been rehabilitated; this murderer was now a symbol, Gutknecht argued, and his release would send a dangerous message.

Leopold was finally called into the room in the early afternoon, after the lunch break. Unlike his clemency hearing, it was not mostly board members in attendance. As he approached his seat, he passed a crowd of more than forty reporters, one of whom was holding the first television camera Leopold had ever seen. He could hear it whirring and felt the hot lights on his back as he was asked for his name and prisoner number.

Lohman began with a few questions about Leopold's early years at Stateville, then about his plans should he be released.

"I would be willing to sell neckties or jerk sodas," Leopold joked, realized it landed flat, then elaborated on his three job offers.

Did he feel he could adapt to the outside world after all this time? Lohman wondered. Leopold answered that he'd have an easier time than most because he'd been less "cell-shocked" than many other prisoners. "I have spent less time counting the cracks in the wall than some men in here, because I have had the opportunity of doing some more interesting things," he said, alluding to the prison school, the parole research, and the malaria project.

Eventually Lohman asked if there was anything Leopold wanted to add. "I was a nineteen-year-old youth," he began, sounding a bit too rehearsed. "Today I am a forty-eight-year-old man. Nearly sixty-five percent of my life has been spent in prison. I feel that I have changed completely in personality and character. . . . I've learned my lesson. I am convinced that, should I be granted parole, I would never be of any trouble to the Parole Board."

He stopped, and then blurted, "Even physically there is not a cell in my body that was there in 1924. And certainly emotionally, I am certainly mature. I hope you will believe that . . . I can only tell you what happened in 1924 could not happen again. I know that, but how I can convince you, I don't know."

Board member Sam Arndt spoke for the first time. What, he asked, had led Leopold to kidnap and murder Bobby Franks?

Despite nearly three decades to prepare for the question, Leopold had no answer. "I can't give you a motive which makes sense," he stammered, no longer sounding rehearsed, only confused. "It was just a damn-fool stunt done by a child. A child without any judgement. It seems absurd to me today, as it must to you and all other people. I am in no better position today to give you a motive than I was then."

Four days later, on January 12, Republican William Stratton was sworn in as Illinois governor, succeeding Adlai Stevenson, who had stepped down to run a presidential campaign against Dwight Eisenhower. Two hours after his inauguration, Stratton announced the removal of Lohman and Arndt from the parole board and the appointment of two replacements. The members who had been at Nathan Leopold's hearing would not be the ones to decide his case.

Lohman's replacement would be Victor Knowles, who had been a printer at a Chicago newspaper before moving to Elkville (pop. 934) and buying a weekly of his own. "I had known him for years," Stratton said of his appointee, "and known his son. He was the type of man I thought we needed in that spot—the old country editor with all the virtues they stand for."

Knowles told reporters that he had met the governor only once and that he was likely given the position because his son was a generous Stratton supporter.

The newly configured board met as originally scheduled on January 22 and ruled on ninety-five of the ninety-six cases before them.

One, Nathan Leopold's, was postponed until the next meeting in May. No new hearing would be scheduled, meaning the committee would have only the written record. But as it happened, on May 1 Knowles and three other board members were at Stateville on other business and invited Leopold to appear before them at the last minute. It went as poorly as it had in January.

"Is there anything else you wish to say?" Knowles asked.

Leopold replied that he thought he had covered everything at the original hearing.

Then Knowles asked, once again, about a motive, a reason.

Once again, Leopold stammered. "As far as motivation and causation are concerned, I have racked my brain through the years," he finally said. "I honestly cannot today give a better explanation, a more reasonable explanation than that the thing was completely senseless, completely foolish, a stupid act, completely outside of my normal course of behavior. There is no answer; it was just insane."

Back in his cell, Leopold kicked himself because he had not expressed remorse. In the middle of the night, he wrote a letter in which he said he was deeply sorry for his actions and in the morning asked that it be sent to the parole board.

The board met in Springfield at noon on May 14. At three p.m., Leopold lay down on the bunk in his cell, put on his headphones, turned on his radio, and closed his eyes. At four p.m. an announcer read the bulletin: "Leopold parole is denied."

After the news bulletin ended, Leopold clicked off his cell radio, and a guard appeared to escort him to the warden's office. "Well, they didn't parole you," Ragen said, and handed Leopold the official teletype. Reading it, Leopold realized that not only was his request denied, but his case was "continued until 1965." He was not entitled to apply again for twelve more years.

He had steeled himself for a denial, and for the next step, which would be submitting a new parole application a year later. During the first twenty-five years he spent at Stateville, those were the rules— once a prisoner was eligible for an initial parole hearing, he was automatically permitted to apply for one every year. Those rules had been tweaked in 1949, and since then 3 percent of the board's decisions included continuances longer than twelve months, mostly for fifteen or eighteen months. Only twice had a prisoner been told to wait three years, and once—the longest continuance in modern parole history in Illinois—was for five years. Twelve years was unprecedented. There was no explanation accompanying this decision, just the one short phrase that meant his next chance at parole would come when he was sixty-one—eight years later than if his sentence had never been commuted by Stevenson in the first place.

April 1954
Dante Cosentino and Al Tarlov
Detroit and Manhattan

DANTE COSENTINO PINNED THE EMERALD-GREEN CHICKEN feather onto his winter jacket before heading out to the State Hall building on the campus of Wayne University. It was still cold in Detroit in April, particularly in the evenings. Dante had been much chillier during his twenty-three years, however, and this event was too important to even think of staying home.

As he walked, he looked for what he assumed would be a robust number of others, also wearing defiant green feathers. At the University of Michigan, there had been hundreds. At the University of Indiana at Bloomington, there had been thousands. At UCLA, more than two hundred students had paraded through campus in full costume, posing as Robin Hood and his band of Merry Men.

That was where it started—with the story of Robin Hood. Back in November 1953, Mrs. Thomas J. White (news reports never once used her given first name) called for the removal of Robin Hood stories from Indiana public schools. Mrs. White, a member of the state's textbook commission, didn't have actual authority to ban a book, but that didn't stop her from declaring that "there is a Communist directive in education now to stress the story of Robin Hood . . . because he robbed the rich and gave to the poor."

Mrs. White was a follower of Wisconsin senator Joseph McCarthy, who had been leading a charge against what he described as a Communist infiltration of society and government. McCarthy hadn't invented the accusation. Alger Hiss had been accused of spying for the Soviets in 1948; Julius and Ethel Rosenberg were arrested two years later for giving atomic secrets to the Russians. But McCarthy rode the issue as no one else had. He began with a speech to the Women's Democratic Club in Wheeling, West Virginia, in 1950, an event expected to be so mundane that no television cameras were present.

"Today we are engaged in a final, all-out battle between communistic atheism and Christianity," he had thundered. (McCarthy's speaking style was often at full volume.) "The modern champions of communism have selected this as the time."

He'd finished with the words that would lead historians to call the Wheeling speech one of the most consequential in history. "I have in my hand 57 cases of individuals who would appear to be either card-carrying members or certainly loyal to the Communist Party, but who nevertheless are still helping to shape our foreign policy," he said.

Or maybe he said 205. In the absence of recording, word-of-mouth accounts differed. Whatever the number, it would become clear over time that McCarthy had no names. He was, as often as not, waving blank pieces of paper. The ripple effects of his accusations, though, were very real. Loyalty oaths were demanded of teachers in nearly forty states. Employees in industry, entertainment, and academia were fired on suspicion of holding left-leaning opinions. Books were removed from the libraries of American embassies around the world and declared suspect by the House Un-American Activities Committee: Henry David Thoreau's *Civil Disobedience*, the poems of Langston Hughes, the works of Thomas Paine.

McCarthy never directly mentioned Robin Hood, but a group of students in Bloomington, Indiana, saw a clear link between the senator and Mrs. White. On March 1, 1954, they drove to a nearby poultry farm, filled six burlap sacks with chicken feathers, and dyed them green in a dormitory bathroom. Under cover of darkness, they pinned the feathers to every bulletin board on campus with messages such as "They're your books; don't let McCarthyism burn them."

Before long the five who originated the plan shed their anonymity, gave interviews to the campus press, and distributed feathers to any student who asked. Within weeks, the campaign spread to schools in Wisconsin and Illinois. In Michigan, it reached Ann Arbor and soon,

Dante hoped, Detroit. He and a small group were doing their best to bring the feathers to Wayne State.

✦

SPRING CAME EARLY TO New York City in late April 1954. Three days of temperatures in the seventies had coaxed open buds on the path from west to east. Al Tarlov all but bounced as he crossed Central Park, feeling like someone who knows he is exactly where he is meant to be, doing exactly what he was intended to do.

That something was *not* land surveying. He had enjoyed his year "off" after graduation—building a small business by day, dating Joan Hylton on her evenings free. They dined at Phil Baker's, or other favorite places in town, but rarely at Tarlov's Minute Chef, his father's new luncheonette on West Avenue. Spending time in the spare but welcoming diner made Al uncomfortable, though he wasn't sure if it was out of guilt for forcing his father to scale back his dreams or awe because his father was certain of what those dreams were. Charlie had tried to retire but failed, making it clear that he'd spent all those years rising before dawn and working nights and weekends not because he'd had to but because that's how he was made. He was happy doing work he loved.

Al was left wondering what kind of work would make him feel that way. For years he had believed his father had given over his life to his business for the wrong reason—to hand it along to his son. Now he found himself envious that his father *had* a reason. The perfect one for a man whose own father could not have handed him anything. Ditto his uncle Isadore, who, while he still hadn't said so directly, thought Al was not doing enough to change the world. During Al's year "off" from school, Isadore suggested he enroll in noncredit coursework at a place called the Thomas Jefferson School of Social Science and decide not only what he wanted to do with his life but why.

The Jeff School was one of several that the American Communist Party founded in the 1930s. The New York building was a nine-story former furniture warehouse at the corner of Sixth Avenue and

Sixteenth Street. The school's heyday had been right after the war, when upward of five thousand students took more than three hundred courses. During Al's time there, enrollment had dropped dramatically as even a whiff of socialism became suspect. Most of the Jeff School teachers had been dismissed by other colleges for refusing to sign loyalty oaths.

Al certainly knew the school's reputation when he began to attend night classes once a week. The connection to the Communist Party did not give him pause, as he was there not for the politics but for the instruction: Mystery Writing (taught by Dashiell Hammett!), the Art of Cartooning, the Greek Classics in Translation, and the History of Women. He never felt he was being fed propaganda or was involved in anything unpatriotic or subversive. He wasn't being trained to revolt, just to think.

As Al widened his view of the world, his fledgling land survey business began to look increasingly small. Swallowing his pride at having been rejected from Dartmouth, he applied to two medical schools known as welcoming to Jewish applicants: the University of Chicago, where, not coincidentally, Uncle Isadore had done a neurosurgery fellowship several years earlier; and New York Medical College, Flower and Fifth Avenue Hospitals, where, also not coincidentally, Uncle Isadore had just been named a professor of neurology and neurosurgery and director of the neurology department. Al never heard back from Chicago. So in the summer of 1952 he sold his business for $2,300 and moved to a rooming house on the Upper West Side of Manhattan with dozens of other New York Medical College classmates. For two years he took medical courses by day and attended classes at the Jeff School in the evenings. He also found time to see Joan Hylton most Saturdays.

On this April day in 1954, he had been summoned to the office of medical school president Dr. Jacob Adam Werner Hetrick. Al had no guesses about the purpose of the meeting, but he wasn't nervous. He was the top student in his class for the second year in a row and was a favorite of his professors, with whom he was just beginning to discuss

what he might specialize in upon graduation. His only certainty was
that it would not be neurology. He wanted to blaze his own trail.

✦

DANTE COSENTINO WAS NEW to campus life in the spring of 1954.
He had started classes at Wayne University that February, as a twenty-
three-year-old freshman, and he still marveled that he was there at all.
Aside from the few months of his middle school scholarship, college
had never crossed his mind. College was for the rich. He had earned
his GED during his four years in the army, where he had also learned
how to say "another beer please" in most European languages, and
how to play chess and pinochle. Mostly he learned that he did not
want a military career; when offered a three-year extension with a
chance to go to officer candidate school, he turned it down. He would
look back on that as the luckiest decision he'd ever made. The Korean
War began in earnest that year, and second lieutenants, which he
likely would have been, had the highest mortality rate by rank.

What he didn't learn in the army was what he *did* want. Discharged
in the fall of 1951, he'd found himself at his newly remarried mother's
house in Cos Cob, feeling worlds older than his siblings, Rosie and
Frank, drifting through the same kinds of jobs that had bored Joe
DeSalvo. He was a drill press operator in a factory. He packed boxes
of multicolored ribbons in a warehouse. He built fans and ventilators
on an assembly line. In the fall of 1952, Congress authorized $300 in
"mustering out" pay for every discharged soldier, and Dante spent his
on a 1939 Pontiac. Almost immediately, he got a speeding ticket but
talked his way out of it because "Veteran" was stamped on his license.
He felt only a little chagrined that the biggest battle he'd seen was
some fisticuffs at a bar outside Munich.

Restless, he drove to Washington, D.C., became a fry cook in a late-
night diner, then followed an attractive and flirtatious tourist from
Michigan out to Detroit. The relationship with the young woman
didn't last, but his connection with the city did. He worked as a short
order cook at the S&C Restaurant across the street from the General

Motors Building (where he eavesdropped on the businessmen talking deals and politics at lunch) and spent his free evenings in jazz clubs (where he nursed the kinds of drinks his father would have downed in great gulps) or libraries (where he read the kind of writers his father had loved before his mother burned all those books).

After about a year of this, Congress extended the GI Bill to include those who had served during the Korean conflict. Dante would receive $110 from the government every month, which, added to his hours at the S&C, would be enough to pay for tuition and books, room and board. He had the same "too good to be true" feeling he'd felt back when the social worker and the psychologist had offered to pay him to stay in school. This time he was determined not to run away.

When he'd taken all those mind-game tests in the psychologist's office, he'd been told he was good with numbers and should become an accountant, so at Wayne University he registered for accounting and business courses. He hated them but plodded on. And while he was bored in the classes that had to do with numbers, he came alive in the ones that had to do with words.

In his psychology class, his professor said, "The difference between a good, responsible young man and a troubled one is someone who believed in him as a child." Dante pondered who his own someone had been. Why was he here in a college classroom, while his father was dead, his brother Albert was drunk and despairing, and too many of the pals with whom he played hooky, stole comic books, and went AWOL were in jail or worse?

In his literature class, the professor asked, "Have you ever written an English paper before?" Dante braced for a critique of his grammar. Instead, the professor shouted "Congratulations!" and handed back his first college essay, marked with a large, circled *A*.

By the time Dante walked across campus wearing a green feather on a frigid April night, he felt almost as if he belonged. No longer an imposter in the classroom. More confident of his opinions outside of class. His growing cluster of friends tended toward the political, and for weeks the talk had been of McCarthy and how someone had to do something. So they spread the word that a resolution in support of the Robin Hood protests would be introduced at the next student council meeting.

The meeting was called for four p.m. Only fourteen of the eighteen voting members of the council were present when it was finally called to order at 4:37, along with one school newspaper reporter and twenty-two spectators. Just a handful were wearing anything green. The resolution was finally introduced, passed, and almost immediately tabled, because a minority of the council invoked an arcane bit of parliamentary process that allowed for that.

Dante headed back home in the cold, warmed by anger. He had found his voice, but how to get someone to listen? Taking out the secondhand typewriter on which he wrote his school papers, he banged out a letter to the editor of the *Wayne Collegian*.

"I attended the Council meeting, anticipating a big crowd, but I was sadly disillusioned," it read. "Obviously I have overestimated the political awareness of the students. I hope I am wrong in assuming that this political apathy will eventually sign the death warrant of a democratic country. I am interested in learning, and plan to form a club embodying the principles of the Green Feather organization, with or without the approval of the student council."

He dropped it off at the newspaper office the next morning. A week later he hosted a meeting in his cramped apartment to plan the Wayne State Green Feather campaign, which would never become as large as it had been in Indiana, but it made a good deal of noise for Detroit. Not long after that he switched his major from business to philosophy.

✦

AL TARLOV ARRIVED AT Fifth Avenue and 105th Street right on time. As he entered the president's outer office, he realized he was not the only visitor present for the meeting. Two men in dark suits were already standing with Dr. Hetrick, speaking in hushed tones.

"Mr. Tarlov, please take a seat," the president said.

Al did. None of the others sat down.

"These gentlemen are from the FBI. They tell me that you are enrolled in a school with Communist associations?"

It was not the first time that Al Tarlov's life had been spun off course by the times in which he lived, but it was the first time he'd been keenly aware of it. And while he would later understand that every path can be changed by distant, indirect whim, in the moment this felt deeply personal. It would be fifty years before he would see the FBI's records on his uncle, but even in 1954 he assumed that the agency was interested in Isadore and his subscriptions to the *National Guardian* and *New World Review*, his memberships in International Workers Order, and his attendance at dinners for the Committee for a Democratic Far Eastern Policy.

Would they ask him to turn on Isadore? Or did this mean someone already had? A few months earlier Norwalk had made national news when first the *Norwalk Hour* and then *The New York Times* reported that the local chapter of the Veterans of Foreign Wars had created a committee of members to investigate "activities of residents that were not related to a strong America," as the *Hour* put it, and to forward to the FBI anything determined to be possibly "communistic." Translation: the Norwalk VFW was spying on Norwalk citizens and reporting them to the government. "Unamerican," the *Times* called the tattling committee members. The VFW branch backpedaled furiously, saying that they had passed along the name of only one single suspected Communist.

Sitting in the president's office, Al's first thought was that the name submitted had been Isadore's. His next thought made the room spin. Was it his own name that had been smeared?

Dr. Hetrick was waiting for an answer.

"Yes," Al said. He was taking classes at the Jefferson School for Social Research.

"Are you aware that the school is funded by the Communist Party?" one of the FBI men asked.

Al said he knew Marxist theory was taught, but that was not why he was attending. He enjoyed their humanities classes, he said, and the fact that he could take them for eight dollars a course without pursuing a full degree. He was filling in the gaps in his knowledge, he explained, to be a more rounded doctor and human.

Dr. Hetrick did not appear impressed. "You can continue as a student there, or you can continue as a student here," he said. "You cannot do both."

"Yes sir," Al answered, but he did not consider this a promise to do anything, just a way to get out of the room. And he needed to get out of the room, lest these men see his rising anger. The VFW in Norwalk was called the Mulvoy-Tarlov-Aquino Post. That is, the VFW chapter that Al suspected of spying on Isadore, of spying on Al, was named after Isadore's eldest brother, Aime.

Arriving back at his rooming house, Al took out the new typewriter he'd been given by his uncle when he began classes at the Jeff and wrote a half-dozen letters to prestigious medical schools around the country. He explained that he was at the top of his class in New York and that he was looking to transfer. Soon he received a call from the dean of students at the University of Chicago, asking why Al hadn't replied to their original offer of admission. Apparently, he had been accepted two years earlier, but somehow the letter had never arrived.

If it had, Al would have gone to Chicago. It was the progressive slightly counter-culture place where he felt he belonged. The undergraduate program there was known for its rigorous "Great Books" approach that stressed broad learning over specialization, and the medical school was known for its ambition and clout. Postwar Chicago researchers were pioneers in nuclear medicine, chemotherapy, and infectious disease prevention—assisting the army in the development and testing of a drug called chloroquine, which proved to be a long-elusive treatment for malaria.

And by the 1950s, the university was increasingly a gathering place for "radical" thinkers. One law school professor had conducted the appeal for Julius and Ethel Rosenberg in the weeks before they were executed for spying. Another history professor had resigned rather than testify about his colleagues at one of McCarthy's hearings. Al did not consider himself radical, but he was intrigued by the idea of being in such company. When he came clean to the Chicago medical school admissions office about his "conversation" with the FBI, they assured him he was still welcome.

Al was a believer in facts and science, not fate. But as he packed his few belongings and prepared to move out of Manhattan, he could not shake the feeling that somehow the universe had recalibrated to bring him to where he *really* should have been all along.

July 1954 and June 1956
The Troys and the Tarlovs
Cos Cob and Chicago

ROSE CUFONE COSENTINO SICILIANO STOOD IN HER FRONT LIV-
ing room surrounded by brides. Only one—her radiant daughter,
Rosie—was real and standing next to her. The others were in photo-
graphs and memories.

The earliest of these brides was frozen in a photo on the wall by the
door, still in its gold-toned frame. It showed Tony and his first wife,
Carmela, she in her prairie-style dress and heavy veil, he in his black
suit and white shirt, looking more like a mourner and an undertaker
than a bride and groom. They were flanked by two flower girls, wearing veils of their own. Everyone wore a frozen expression, as the technology of 1910 demanded, leaving the impression that no one in the
distant past was ever happy.

Were they happy back then? In her own first wedding photo six
years later, Rose looked just as dour, her face round and pale, a
match for her new husband's. Then, when her eldest daughter married in 1940, Gerome and Rose had recently divorced, there was
barely enough money for food or heat, and worms were crawling
out of the pump in the kitchen. Somehow Rose had scrounged for
the cascade of satin and hint of lace Mary wore down the aisle of
St. Catherine's. Had Mary been happy? The next daughter, Evelyn,
was wed in the living room of a justice of the peace, because the
parish priest refused to allow her to marry at the church altar since
her groom was not a Catholic. And Lecia had eloped. Did the whole
town chatter about that, too? Rose had not been one to pay attention
to gossip then, but she was listening now. Her Rosie would have a
perfect and proper wedding, one that would pass muster not only

with the neighbors in Cos Cob but with the soon-to-be in-laws over in Stamford.

Rose had wanted to marry for her version of love but had been forced to marry for her sister's vision of security. Her daughter, miraculously, had managed to find both. From the night of that first school dance, Dave had been an adoring constant in Rosie's life and a regular presence in the Siciliano house on Harold Street, including nearly every Sunday dinner (which, by tradition, started in the afternoon), when he demonstrated an appreciative appetite for southern Italian cooking.

Dave was a year ahead of Rosie at Wright Tech. Upon graduation, he had taken the police force civil service exam and scored high, but there would still be a wait before he rose to the top of the list. So he bought himself a gas station. Or at least that was how both the Troy and the Cosentino families understood it—that the station belonged to Dave. The eccentric owner of Woldan's had died and left the business to his children, who had even less interest in the day-to-day management than their father had. The family had made a generous offer to Dave, their father's employee of several years. In place of an hourly wage, he would run the business and receive 50 percent of the profits after Texaco took its cut. Within a few months of Dave's graduation, the WOLDAN's sign was replaced by one that said TROY's TEXACO. Rosie had nabbed herself a businessman.

Rosie graduated from Wright on June 17, 1953. On July 4, Dave proposed. Independence Day was a favorite of the Troy family, and every year they celebrated with a big backyard barbecue—hamburgers, hot dogs, sparklers, and bunting. For years, Dave's mother had insisted on hosting the gathering, but by now it was held at the home of one of Dave's older sisters. Dave and Rosie arrived late to the party that year, bursting with news that they were engaged. He did not give her a ring. She had already told him she'd prefer a hope chest, a first piece of furniture for the home they would share, to fill with memories and hand down to their children.

Before the fireworks began that night, Bridget Troy produced her checkbook. With great fanfare, she handed the betrothed couple

$5,000 with which to buy a house. The gift was generous (the equivalent of nearly $50,000 today) but also baffling (where had Bridget gotten that kind of money?) and, in a certain light, controlling. (She would make it clear that they could use the funds only for a house within walking distance of her own.) Years later it would cause an irreparable rift, but even at the time it created tension. Bridget's sisters-in-law were still smarting from the fact that Bridget had laid claim to 39 Leeds after Patrick's death, even though it was supposed to be given to his sister Sadie. Then in the more recent past, Sadie had asked Bridget for financial help when buying a home of her own, but Bridget had said she didn't have the money. Yet somehow she now had $5,000 sitting in a bank account, waiting to be withdrawn?

The brouhaha put even more pressure on Rose. As much as she loved Dave, she was wary of his mother. Rose and Bridget had not met often over the years their children were dating, but when they did, the new Mrs. Siciliano had found the widowed Mrs. Troy to be a harsh, brittle woman who commented a bit too often about her son's fair complexion and Rosie's tawny one.

Rose certainly admired her counterpart's grit, knowing what it took to raise children in poverty after their father was gone. But she sensed that at Bridget's core lay complaint, not compassion. Waiting for her Rosie to emerge from her bedroom in her wedding gown, Rose thought of the brides who'd come before and saw the $5,000 as the throwing of a gauntlet, a raising of the bar, a declaration, a dare.

◆

AL HAD THRIVED AFTER his change of medical schools and was soon at the top of his new class. Having done the textbook part of his training back in New York, he arrived in time for the clinical years in Chicago, rotating between specialties, shadowing doctors, examining patients. The thirty-six-hour shifts took their toll, but he wasn't overwhelmed. He spent nearly every free hour doing research for a faculty member who had taken him under his wing and introduced him to laboratory science.

Al had first met Dr. Alf S. Alving when assigned to the nephrology service. He was drawn less to the subject matter than to the professor, who could be brusque to people he didn't like but supportive and loyal to those he did. He liked Al Tarlov and had welcomed him into the laboratory space in the basement of the medical school building and into an unofficial apprenticeship at a lab bench. Al worked for Alving and others in the department for two years, during which time he had his name listed as an author on his very first journal article, "Subclinical Diabetes Mellitus in Patients Presenting with Clinical Chronic 'Glomerulonephritis.' "

That research had nothing to do with malaria. None of the experiments on campus did, though Alving did continue to oversee the work at a nearby penitentiary, where a rotating series of physician-researchers reported to Alving, who in turn reported to the army surgeon general's office in Washington, D.C. Al read up on the Stateville experiments nonetheless, in the event of a pop quiz, though none ever came.

Al's conversations with Dr. Alving were most often about Al—the work he was now doing, and the work he hoped to do when he graduated. The final two years of medical school were about finding a path. Specialist or generalist? Single practice or partnership? Students weighed everything from the number of years of required residency, to the eventual pay scale, to the mess, competition, and hours. Al had concluded that though he didn't want to be a neurologist like Isadore, he did want his uncle's mix of patient care and research. As it happened, that was his new mentor's equation, too.

When Al told Dr. Alving this one day—"I want to be a professor of medicine, I want to teach, I want to run a research lab"—Alving gestured to a chair and closed the office door.

"Do you know that there are very few Jews within academic medicine?" he asked. "Here, at one of the most liberal universities in the country, we only have maybe three—and one hides it."

Al did not know this. He and Alving spoke many more times over the next two years—about Isadore's snubs from Harvard and Al's encounters with quotas at Dartmouth, about how there were even fewer "Negroes or Italians or Orientals" in academic medicine than Jews, of how this discrimination distressed Dr. Alving, and how he pushed back where he could.

By June 1956, Al had been named a valedictorian of his class, and on the advice of Dr. Alving, he accepted a two-year fellowship in the general field of internal medicine at the University of Pennsylvania. He and his co-valedictorian (Robert Druyan, who would go on to discover the cause and treatment of a rare disease called porphyria) led the procession, wearing the University of Chicago's traditional maroon robes and black and burgundy velvet tams. In the audience, the assembled Tarlovs sat with Al's "friend," Joan—who had followed him from New York, enrolling in the graduate school of library science and taking a job as a housemother in an undergraduate women's dorm at the University of Chicago.

After the ceremony, Al's small cluster of relatives, plus Joan, greeted him giddily as "Dr. Tarlov," and they all headed off for an early dinner.

"Too bad you aren't staying a few more days," Al told his mother offhandedly, between courses. "We're getting married on Tuesday."

◆

ALL WEDDINGS ARE BASICALLY alike—a legal union—but no two weddings are the same because they take the shape of the families being joined. For Rosie and Dave's, the ceremony was to be held at the Cosentinos' very Italian church, St. Catherine's, with Father Ganley officiating, and the reception would be at the very Irish Hibernian Club, where the Troys had long been members. There would be five bridesmaids, including Dave's sister Joan, all wearing orchid organdy dresses with lilac wreaths in their hair, and five groomsmen, including Rosie's brother Valentino and Dave's brothers Edward and Patrick, all in white jackets and black ties. There would be wedding rings—thick solid gold bands that reaffirmed Rosie's view that engagement diamonds were a waste of money. Toasts would end with the Irish

"*Sláinte!*" the Italian "*Salute!*" and the American "Cheers!" Bagpipes would play as the couple passed around the traditional tower of cookies—*sfingi, cannoli, pignoli.*

The ceremony was to start at ten a.m. on Saturday, July 5, 1954—another Independence Day weekend—and by nine-thirty Rosie's wedding party was in the living room, waiting. Tony, in his white dinner jacket, was pacing, worried about the time. Rose, in emerald silk brocade with a white crocheted shawl and matching hat, was calmer, though worried about appearances. Rosemary Curcio, the maid of honor, was not worried at all. She had just left Rosie's room after helping her dress, and the bride's joy was infectious. Indeed, when Rosie came down the stairs in her pristine satin gown with a billowing tulle overlay, she looked like Elizabeth Taylor on Spencer Tracy's arm in *Father of the Bride,* and like Elizabeth Taylor a few months later, marrying Nicky Hilton in real life. She looked just as every 1950s bridal magazine said every bride should look.

First the photographer had Rosie pin the corsage to her mother's dress. Next, he asked the women to stand next to each other in the living room—Rosie in the center, her mother to her right, her best friend to her left. On his count, Rose and Rosemary raised Rosie's fingertip veil from behind, holding it aloft like a peacock's tail. The shutter clicked as they lifted. Unnoticed in the moment, they were standing directly in front of the portrait of Tony and Carmela Siciliano at their wedding all those years ago. The result was a photo of a beaming bride in front of the ever-present portrait of a dour one, obscured by a curtain of lace and tulle.

✦

MAE, JAY, AND MARINA TARLOV changed their train reservations. Their presence at Al and Joan's wedding nearly doubled the number of guests, and that's if you included the priest who performed the ceremony.

The groom wore a black suit, white shirt, and a midcentury modern geometric tie as he walked down a makeshift aisle in a Chicago park. The bride wore a tea-length dress of white satin brocade that she'd sewn herself, with a matching cap shaped like a half-moon and finished with a small net veil. The mother of the groom wore the same dress she had worn to the graduation because, not expecting a wedding, that was all she'd packed.

The picnic lunch was provided by two of the guests, friends from Norwalk who had recently moved to Chicago and opened a grocery store. The newlyweds took no honeymoon to speak of—they just drove from Chicago to Philadelphia, where Al began his new job on the second day of July. He didn't get a day off on the fourth. He worked through his birthday on the eleventh. Hence Dr. and Mrs. Tarlov—who had bonded over their shared wish for a houseful of children and a belief that family came first—began their married life by forgoing a vacation. The irony would not occur to them for years.

1957 to 1958
Joe DeSalvo and Nathan Leopold
Stateville Penitentiary

THE RULES SEEMED DESIGNED TO CREATE DISCOMFORT. OR PER-
haps to trick inmates into making mistakes, for which they could
then be punished. Or maybe they were a response to incidents now
long forgotten, when less rigid rules had led to escapes. Whatever
the intent, the result for Joe DeSalvo at Stateville was that he did not
have to navigate the question of how to greet his parents. Neither
hugs nor handshakes were allowed during family visits, and violation
could result in time in solitary confinement. (Nathan Leopold had
once spent ten days in the hole for forgetting the rules and shaking
his brother's hand.) This solved a dilemma for the nondemonstrative
DeSalvos. Joe's father and mother sat on one side of the long wooden
table, Joe on the other. It had been years since the three had been comfortable in each other's presence, so this was all oddly familiar.

Charles and Ruth had not visited Joe at all during his two stays at
the School for Boys. During his two years at Pontiac, they had come
only for his parole hearings. They had been absent during his early
years at Stateville as well, but then Ruth began to appear every few
months, her husband accompanying her sometimes, but not always. By
1956, though, their visits had become more frequent—once a month,
perhaps more, with both parents making the trip almost every time.
Charles Sr. had been ill, they'd said, by way of explaining his years of
absence, though they named no disease or symptoms. They certainly
both looked frail across the table—pale, worn, and old.

Joe, on the other hand, looked hearty. Prison had a bolstering effect
on him, physically and emotionally. His acne had cleared, his posture
had improved, his skinny frame had filled out a bit, and he carried

himself with quiet self-assurance. He still had a strikingly high fore-head, exaggerated by his upsweep of hair, but overall, he had become more comfortable in his skin.

Some of that was due to the passage of time. Now twenty-seven, he had outgrown the age of macho and bluster and matured in the ways he had merely parroted to psychologists and parole board members over the years. Some was due to experience. Burned by being part of the gang, he now kept to himself. His only real companions were the books he took from the library as he had back at Pontiac, though Stateville was far better equipped. Nathan Leopold no longer ran this library, but his imprint remained. In addition to his initial choices from the 1930s, numerous volumes from his own collection that no longer fit in his cell were "donated" to the penitentiary. Through them, Joe could follow Leopold's trail of intellectual breadcrumbs—books about sociology, parole prediction, malaria, microbiology. All of Leo-pold's journal articles were available for any prisoner who wanted to read them, along with one unpublished paper. Titled "A Statistical Interpretation of the Concept of Causality," the forty pages were a musing on the cause and effect of any given life, something Joe had thought a lot about while at Stateville.

Joe crossed paths with Leopold the way nearly everyone at State-ville did by the mid-1950s, indirectly and from a distance. Leopold might appear at another table in the visiting room, talking with his team about his next shot at parole, though it was at least a year away. He was often in the library, though he had outfitted his cell like an office. He still worked in the X-ray lab and had some involvement with the malaria team, though not during the weeks when Joe himself was a volunteer in the ongoing drug trials.

These trials were slightly different from the ones Alving had begun a decade ago, back in 1944. Those had technically failed. Lost in the laudatory descriptions in *Life* magazine and *The Saturday Evening Post* (and even in the accusatory ones at Nuremberg) was the fact that while the goal of the trials had been to find a cure, no cure had been found. The best that science could offer American soldiers during

World War II was chloroquine, which was not a new drug, having first been discovered in 1934. The Stateville group had given it new life, but though it was better than anything else available, it still did only half the job, suppressing symptoms but not preventing recurrences, while causing some miserable side effects. The malaria project had been launched to keep U.S. servicemen from becoming too sick to fight, yet there had been half a million cases of malaria in American troops in Africa and Asia.

Not until 1947, two years after the war had been won, did one of the fifteen thousand compounds being tested in army labs begin to look like it might be a cure. It was the one hinted at in the radio address from within Stateville in January 1946, the "secret" one "in the experimental stage." Known then as SN 13,272, the synthetic drug had been produced at a lab at Columbia University based on data captured from the retreating Nazis. Two years of human experiments at Stateville (a version was tested on Nathan Leopold) showed that it not only suppressed symptoms in infected subjects but it also prevented relapses.

This drug—named primaquine—was the cure the army had had in mind when the prison experiments began. That it had taken a bit longer to develop than desired was forgiven, as military officials marched Dr. Alving in front of congressional boards and television cameras to declare victory (and justify the $10 million spent thus far).

"Malaria has been conquered," Alving had said. Primaquine was "not toxic and just as harmless as a sugar pill."

The problem with all the boasting and celebrating was that primaquine *did* have "common" side effects, though they were not as bad as those that had led soldiers to throw out their atabrine. Even more significant, even as Alving described primaquine as "harmless," he knew that, in a small subgroup of human beings, it could be lethal.

Researchers had long known that the kinds of compounds effective against malaria—quinine, atabrine, chloroquine, and now primaquine—caused severe anemia in some people with darker skin whose genetic roots were in Africa, Asia, the Middle East, and the

Mediterranean. That's why Alving's team had limited the testing at Stateville to white men (of mostly Northern European descent), because in 5 to 10 percent of Blacks, southern Italians, Greeks, Arabs, and Sephardic Jews, antimalarials could cause a sudden and severe breakdown in red blood cells known as acute hemolysis. It was a reaction similar to favism, a condition triggered by ingesting fava beans.

The question of *why* some patients became anemic became Alving's next project at Stateville, as he pivoted from proving that primaquine worked to investigating the subset for whom it was toxic. He did this quietly, however. There were no press conferences. By this time, Alving was no longer on site at the prison and left the daily work of that lab to a rotating team of doctors who came through in shifts of two to four years. Two of those men, a biochemist named Paul Carson and a hematologist named Ernest Beutler, made it the mission of the lab to decode what it was about certain patients that allowed these drugs to destroy their red blood cells.

More imprisoned subjects were recruited. This time the emphasis was on "more highly pigmented" men: giving them primaquine, seeing who developed anemia (and stopping the drug immediately, which reversed its destructive effects), then looking for what was physiologically different in the reactive subset to explain their response.

Joe DeSalvo participated in this newest round of trials. His Italian heritage qualified him as Mediterranean, and while he had spent years listing himself as Swedish on his intake forms, he was willing to embrace his father's side of the family in exchange for the perks, which now included unlimited access to the newly installed TV and the rumored possibility of early parole hearings for the volunteers. He became moderately ill during his turn with malaria, was cured with primaquine without incident, and had his blood examined every which way.

In time, researchers confirmed that the subjects who suffered acute hemolytic anemia did not have enough of an enzyme known as glucose-6-phosphate dehydrogenase (G6PD). The normal role of the enzyme is to protect red blood cells from being stressed by whatever it was that primaquine and fava beans (and aspirin and mothballs) had in common. Without G6PD, the red blood cells burst when exposed. That discovery would prove key to understanding the fundamental process of all genetic aberrations and create an entirely new field, pharmacogenetics, to study how genetic differences affected individuals' responses to medication. Eventually its findings would guide doctors in their choice of everything from cancer drugs to antidepressants.

The primaquine anemia trials had broader implications for Joe DeSalvo as well—ones that went beyond the usual certificate for his wall and the standard note in his prison file. During his time on the hospital ward, Joe caught the attention of Charles Ickes, the armed robber turned favored lab tech, who found him to be several notches smarter than the Stateville norm. Ickes introduced Joe to Alf Alving, and Joe used the few words of Swedish he remembered learning from his mother to charm Alving. With the warden's okay, Joe was soon the newest trainee in the Stateville malaria project.

Ickes taught Joe general laboratory work—how to draw blood, make slides, view them under a microscope, and enter findings in a log—as well as more specific malaria lab procedures, including the care and feeding of the mosquitoes. Joe learned nursing skills too, caring for the feverish patients, doling out experimental medications, and checking that each man swallowed the pills he was given. He added books about biology, medicine, and tropical disease to his withdrawals from the library.

The work was tedious and repetitive, but it suited Joe, giving him a place, a routine, and a sense of purpose for the first time in his life. He fell asleep while reading in his cell and slept soundly through the night. This was much of the reason he looked healthier to his parents even as they looked sicklier to him.

As he got better at his work and was given more responsibility, he dared to think of himself as the man of science he had once hoped to be. Joe knew that Charles Ickes had a job waiting in Alf Alving's University of Chicago lab when and if he was paroled. Joe would be eligible for his first hearing in 1958. Perhaps he could find that kind of mentorship, too.

Charles Sr. responded to his younger son's dreams by sharing the latest news about his older son, a familiar pattern that still had the power to wound. Charles Jr. had married, had two daughters, and worked at a good job as a cross-country trucker. He kept a motorcycle on the back of his rig so that he could ride at his various destinations.

Ruth, by contrast, brightened when Joe talked about his future. She was thrilled that something she'd taught him in childhood had helped to impress the Swedish scientist. And she nodded encouragingly when he vowed to use this assignment to start fresh back in the world. She assured him that he would always have a home on LaPorte Avenue when—not if—that time came.

✦

IT TOOK THIRTY-THREE YEARS, but Nathan Leopold had decided to stop doing the math. He had finally come to understand that his parole had very little to do with math. Nor was it a matter of statistics, or the ability of an individual to change, or using his past to predict his future. After decades of studying how to tell when a man was ready for parole, he realized that the State of Illinois didn't care if he was ready. They cared only about how his release might play with the public.

One bit of math was in his favor. Twelve years did not actually mean twelve years in prison tabulations. Under the rules, Leopold was permitted to submit regular requests for earlier rehearings, and he did so in 1955 and 1956. Both were denied. During the summer of 1957, with the help of attorney Elmer Gertz, he filed a nine-thousand-word application for clemency from Governor Stratton. That, too, was denied, but in a way that provided a sliver of hope. Clemency was not the best way to release a prisoner such as Leopold, Stratton said in his denial. Parole would be a better option because it included several years of supervision to ease adjustment to the outside world.

Leopold disagreed with Stratton's description of parole as provid-

ing meaningful support for ex-convicts. He kept that to himself, however, and saw Stratton's words as an invitation to apply for parole yet
again. That request was granted, and his hearing was scheduled for
February 5, 1958.

Again there were war councils, the solicitation of letters, and exclu-
sive interviews to national magazines. The job offer from the small
hospital in Puerto Rico was still open, and Leopold didn't solicit any
more. He had completed an autobiography, *Life Plus 99 Years*, that had
been in process since 1954. It didn't include an account of the actual
crime, but it did fit neatly into what he and Gertz decided would be
Leopold's best strategy for this next hearing. He would do two things
he had never done before: first, he'd appear to be fully, deeply, and
completely penitent; second, he'd put his opponents on the defensive.
To their argument that his release would tarnish belief in the penal
system, he would say the opposite—that failing to release him would
suggest that the system was not capable of rehabilitating any man.

The few new letters in his parole file stuck to that second theme—
that he was a success story for the State of Illinois Department of Corrections and that keeping him behind bars would make a mockery of
that world-class system.

"What a feather in the cap of the Illinois penal institutions, if they
could point with pride to the complete rehabilitation they were able
to accomplish with Nathan Leopold," wrote C. L. Burdick, who had
been a reporter at the 1924 trial and was now teaching biology at the
University of Arizona. "Due to the publicity, the world would soon
applaud their success. On the other hand, if he is not paroled, the
world will wonder if the penal institution failed in its goal."

As to the other prong of the plan—the expression of profound
remorse—Leopold would have to do that part himself. He wrote a
draft of what he thought he should say. Gertz made suggestions, then
gave it back to Leopold for a rewrite. They did this until the statement
was half its original length and shorn of anything that might sound
arrogant, flippant, or harsh.

"Now memorize it," Gertz instructed.

✦

ONCE AGAIN JOE DESALVO did almost no preparation for his parole hearing. He had done his best to stay out of trouble, and the three minor disciplinary tickets in his file showed he'd succeeded for the most part. He tried not to stand out, be memorable, or attract attention from guards or fellow prisoners, and he had succeeded there as well. But he'd served barely six years of a ten-to-seventy-year sentence, and he had no reason to get his hopes up. If you were prepared for disappointment, were you truly disappointed? He would give pessimism a try.

At nine a.m. on January 9, 1958, Joe took his seat in the conference room at Stateville. He brought neither a lawyer nor witnesses; even his parents failed to come this time. He had not prepared a statement, and he certainly hadn't memorized one.

"How many armed robberies did you commit?" one of the board members asked. Joe knew his file suggested that the police thought he was guilty of several stickups for which he was not charged, and he wasn't going to start confessing here.

"I really couldn't number them," he said. "There were three in Rock Island and several in Chicago." But, he added, "I never shot anyone. Once I shot a bullet in the wall more or less to enforce my demands, but I never shot at anybody or struck anybody."

The panel moved on to Joe's military record.

"It was pretty dismal," he agreed.

Changing the subject, he described how he'd made better use of his time in prison than in the army. He'd completed fourteen correspondence school courses in languages, mathematics, and literature, he said, and he'd received his GED. "Right now, I am working in the hospital as a laboratory technician," he continued, "and . . . I have managed to get registered by the American Medical Technologists.

"I have really tried to make something of myself since I got here," he continued. Before Stateville, he said, "I have never had any work which I enjoyed. I wanted to be a machinist at one time because my father was a machinist. I didn't like being a machinist. I tried working on a drill press which is just a mechanical job, nothing interesting in it. You don't have to use your mind. They tell you what to do and you do it. But medical technology is the field I am going to follow when I leave here, whenever I leave here."

His American Technologists certification should open doors, he added, and he was now working toward his chief technician's license, which required five years of training.

He regretted that last part almost as soon as he'd said it, lest it gave the board a reason to keep him for five more years.

"I think that now that I have something that I really like my heart's really in it," he said, then stopped talking.

✦

EVERYONE INVOLVED WITH NATHAN Leopold's hearing seemed to believe that this would be the last chance for his release—he was a fifty-three-year-old man with heart disease, kidney disease, and diabetes. He had effectively been turned down for parole five times. If not now, when?

On Wednesday, February 5, 1958, several dozen reporters stood in the cold outside the gates of Stateville for most of the day, while only one from the Associated Press and one from United Press International were permitted inside. There, all five members of the Illinois Parole and Pardon Board were present, a rare gathering befitting a one-of-a-kind parole applicant.

Leopold's witnesses went first, and like a greatest hits album, or maybe a broken record, they touched on the correspondence school, the library, the sociology research, and the malaria project. They alluded to Leopold's impressive IQ and to Loeb's greater responsibility for the crime. Some guessed at what Judge Caverly might have been thinking upon sentencing and speculated about whether his views would be changed were he still alive. Others listed Leopold's proffered jobs. Throughout, they talked about how the board could choose between the archaic path of revenge or the enlightened path of faith in a man's ability to change.

"The Leopold case should be ended at long last," Gertz said, "and ended in the only morally defensible way that it should end—with the parole of Nathan Leopold as vindication of the rehabilitation system in this state."

The theme articulated by the defense witnesses was that parole itself was on trial. John Bartlow Martin, who had written the *Saturday Evening Post* series, took the "stand" to say that "Leopold making good on parole would do more to advance the cause of parole than all the other convicts who will come before you this year put together."

Carl Sandburg came in person this time, to repeat, as he had on letterhead in previous hearings, that he would be delighted to invite Leopold to his home. He then waxed poetic, explaining that Leopold "was in darkness when he came here. I think there has been a struggle toward the light," and he warned that those who disapproved of his being paroled were "those who believe in revenge. They are the human stuff of which mobs are made."

Leopold's supporters were followed by the sitting state's attorney of Cook County, Benjamin B. Adamowski. He said what his predecessors in that position had said: that it was because Leopold was a celebrity, not because he was a danger, that he should be kept in prison for the rest of his life. After gushing a bit about how he'd chatted with Carl Sandburg during the lunch break, Adamowski assured the board that despite his specific objections today, he was a fan of parole. "More and more people are becoming reconciled to the idea that given proper direction and supervision, persons should not be permitted to languish in prison without any hope of ever again returning to society," he said.

But he was very much against *this* parole because of the message it would send. "If it were not for the consistent spotlight and attention this man has received, I might conclude otherwise," he said. "Because of the attention . . . this Board will be doing a disservice to every prosecutor in Illinois if you permit the release of this prisoner at this or some future time."

After more than six hours and 181 transcript pages of testimony, Leopold was called into the room. He spoke for about a half an hour without looking at his notes.

"It is not possible to compress into a few minutes the thoughts and feelings of thirty-three years," he began, "especially if those years have been spent in prison. For here, we have long hours to think, to think painfully, to regret bitterly, to repent fervently."

He then addressed the question he had been unable to answer five years earlier: Why?

"I admired Richard Loeb extravagantly, beyond all bounds," he said. "I literally lived and died on his approval or disapproval. I would have done anything he asked even when I knew he was wrong, even when I was revolted by what he suggested.

"I had no desire to do this terrible thing," he insisted. "The idea was repugnant to me. For weeks and weeks, until only a day or two before the crime, I was sure we would never go through with it, that it was only something to talk about and plan but never actually carry out."

But carry it out they did. "Loeb made sure that we would do it," he said. "I could not back out of the plan without being a quitter and without forfeiting Loeb's friendship. Hard as it is for me now to understand it, then, at nineteen, it seemed the most important thing in the world to me."

Over the decades he had developed a theory, but it was only that, he said, not an excuse or even a definitive explanation. His act had been, he hypothesized, an unintended consequence of choices made for him, ones that viewed him only as a precocious mind, not as an emotional being. Entering college at the age of fifteen, he said, "I was always in the company of boys three or four years older than I. You might say I skipped completely the early teens, and with that skip I lost the growth of character and the personality that normally goes with them. My emotions were at least five years behind my thinking.

When they finally did catch up, which was not until I had been here in prison for five years, I was shocked that I had not been able to feel things more deeply earlier."

Then remorse set in, and the only path he could see toward redemption was by helping others. That was the reason for all of it, he said— the teaching, the volunteering, the research. They were his attempt to make amends and to live with what he'd done.

"Show me the mercy I did not show" Bobby Franks, he said to the board. "Give me a chance to justify my existence."

If released, he promised to disappear. He would give no interviews, make no speeches, accept no TV appearances. "All I want is to find some quiet spot with some organization where I can live quietly and modestly," he said. "All I want is to get out of the spotlight, to live decently, respectfully and quietly."

He certainly sounded as if he meant it. He was a man pleading for the rest of his life.

"Gentlemen, you see before you today not the arrogant, conceited, smart-alecky kid of nineteen who came to prison," he said, winding down. "I am an old man, a broken man, who humbly pleads for your compassion."

✦

ONCE AGAIN JOE DESALVO had to wait for a letter. It came a month after his January hearing, sent without urgency through interprison system mail. His parole request had been denied.

Had he had access to his file, he would have seen that the state's attorney of Rock Island had argued against his release, saying, "It is . . . highly improbable that the subject will again become a law-abiding citizen."

The sociologist-actuary who wrote his parole progress report disagreed: "It is our opinion that he now has sufficient insight, which, along with the benefits of parole supervision, would be adequate to stabilize him in the free community."

The committee decided to split the difference. "This inmate was quite impressive in the interview situation," its report read. "He was quite frank in talking about his faults and stated that he has now found what he wants to do in life, and he certainly is an intelligent talking person. The main question is whether, if paroled, he would direct his energies in the right direction.

"Frankly," the committee chair concluded, "I feel that he should do a little more time as the professionals claim that he is maturing, which is certainly evidenced by his good record here. . . . It would be my recommendation that parole be denied and he be continued to October 5, 1963."

✦

ONCE AGAIN NATHAN LEOPOLD did not have to wait for the usual letter. This time he didn't have to wait for a radio report, either. On February 20, 1958, he was summoned to Warden Ragen's office where Springfield was "on the line." An official there told the warden the verdict, then the warden put his hand over the mouthpiece and repeated it to Leopold.

A few minutes later a bulletin was carried on the newswires: "Nathan Leopold has been paroled by the State of Illinois."

He issued a statement to the seventy-five news reporters who had spent much of the day gathered at the gate—one that unknowingly echoed the warning Darrow had issued more than forty years earlier at Joliet. "I am deeply conscious that more than my own future hangs in the balance. Thousands of prisoners look to me to vindicate the rehabilitation theory of imprisonment. I will do my best not to fail that trust."

That was the tone of many editorials in the afternoon editions. "Leopold can help the parole system by demonstrating that no error was made in releasing him," opined the *Decatur Daily Review*. "The future functioning of the parole system in Illinois may well depend to a large extent on his conduct."

Leopold was not released immediately. It took several weeks for the board to approve his move to Puerto Rico, where he would take the job at the Church of the Brethren, about eighty-five miles from San Juan.

On March 13, 1958—the twentieth anniversary of Clarence Darrow's death—Leopold donned the ill-fitting suit given to every newly released prisoner. He covered that with the stylish herringbone-tweed topcoat brought over by his brother. Warden Ragen handed him fifty dollars and walked him out to the car in which Gertz was waiting.

As they traveled east along I-80 toward Chicago at ever-increasing speed—90 miles per hour, 100 miles per hour—dozens of press vehicles raced to keep up. Leopold had never been in a modern car at highway speeds, and Gertz watched his client turn "pale, ashen and then green," finally motioning that they needed to pull over. With cameras clicking, Leopold spent his first minutes of freedom kneeling by the side of the road and throwing up.

1959
David Troy and Al Tarlov
Stamford and Fort Sam Houston,
Texas

IT WOULD NEVER BE CLEAR WHEN THE RIGGING FIRST CAME loose on the M-7 Bullet as it hurtled along the New Haven line. It might have happened 150 miles north of Stamford, in Worcester, Massachusetts, where the twenty-seven-car freight train had picked up its latest load of cargo before heading south to New York. More likely it happened closer to the Stamford overpass at Atlantic Street, where the flapping length of cord finally caught on the railroad ties, then jammed a switch. Fourteen cars jumped the track at fifty miles per hour. They whipped from side to side, then arced toward an approaching mail train, which burst into flames.

Three of those runaway cars tumbled down an embankment onto South Frontage Road, landing on two burning oil tankers and igniting a shipment of rubber tires. The flaming, acrid mess blocked four lanes of auto traffic below and four lanes of train track above. Live wires, which had been yanked to the ground along with the towers that held them, snaked and sputtered as if alive and very angry.

Had the rigging caught any later than five-thirty a.m. or on any day but Saturday, it would have been disastrous. Had the weather been warmer, or the passenger car heater been working, then the conductor and the flagman almost certainly would have died. But it was barely thirteen degrees the morning of January 10, 1959. Car traffic was sparse. The only two employees aboard had decided to ride up front in the engine car, to keep warm. Absent that choice, "I wouldn't be here now," the conductor told reporters, looking over the dangling remains of the coach, entombed in ice from the firefighters' hoses.

Patrolman David Troy was among the first to arrive on the scene. He would spend a good part of the next week there, directing cars through detours and passengers to buses that were substituting for the trains, keeping curious spectators away. Thirty officers and one hundred firefighters were working at the site the first day, all bundled in whatever coats, hats, and gloves were standard issue. Over the coming month, eighty-seven policemen would keep watch as three hundred track repairmen worked.

This was not what Dave Troy had had in mind when he joined the Stamford Police almost exactly a year earlier. Leaving his job at the service station had been a wrenching decision but also an obvious one. Even working nights and weekends, Dave's percentage of the pumps and repair bays had not been enough for Rosie to quit her part-time shifts at Riverside Hair Stylists over on Post Road. Rosie hated that job; what had been fun during school was tedious and monotonous in the real world, and she chafed at the lack of imagination of her customers, who all wanted a hairstyle like the movie star in the photo they'd torn from a fan magazine. She also hated leaving first newborn Doreen, then her sister Diane, in the care of their teenage cousins.

Dave, by contrast, loved his work. But he came to realize he was a better mechanic than he was a businessman. He would discount his repair fees for a pal, a family in need, a stranger just passing through town. His station was not only a centrally located place to stop for gas and a snack but also a gathering spot for his friends. And when his contract with the gasoline company came up for its latest renewal, the terms were even less favorable, as was the trend in the business at the time. His family deserved better. What good was a husband and father who was never around?

Dave was still in touch with Thomas Troy, who was now one of the longest-serving members of the Stamford Police and who periodically promised he could put in a good word for Dave with the big brass, get his name to the top of that civil service list where it had been inching up, slowly, for four years. In the fall of 1957, he was told the job was his.

After two months of training, Dave was sworn in, issued his badge and his .38 special, and given his blue uniform: two winter- and two summer-weight trousers (navy blue), five short-sleeve and five long-sleeved shirts (light blue), black shoes (that had to be polished nightly), and an eight-point hat. He was also issued one heavy winter coat, which would be replaced every five years, and one spring-weight "blouse" coat, which was replaced every three. He would earn about $6,000 a year and work staggered shifts: five days from seven a.m. to three p.m., then a day off; five days from three to eleven p.m., with another day off; and five nights from eleven p.m. to seven a.m. with three days off.

✦

IN JANUARY 1959, Al Tarlov was looking for his next job. He had completed his one-year internship in internal medicine at the University of Pennsylvania, during which Joan had paused her library science studies and given birth to Richard in May 1957. Then the small family moved back to Chicago, where Al began a two-year internal medicine residency and Joan returned to school, swaddling Richard into a pram, the number of blankets depending on the weather, and parking him outside an ivy-covered classroom. By September 1958, another baby, Elizabeth, had joined them. Two children in two years. The Tarlovs were well on their way to the life they'd plotted while dating.

That winter Al began to apply for jobs at medical centers around the country, hoping Dr. Alving's warnings were wrong and that times had changed enough that his religion wouldn't stand in his way. He didn't even practice Judaism anymore, though he also didn't attend mass with Joan, who went weekly with the children.

His world had shrunk to include only his family, his work, and his job search, but that was about to change. In Washington, American military officials watched with alarm as tensions with the Soviet

254 GENEALOGY OF A MURDER

Union grew over Soviet buildups in Berlin, and Congress responded in March 1959 by extending the draft.

That would have had nothing to do with Al; nearing thirty, he was about to age out. But then another vote reinstated the Doctors Draft, which had been used to keep the military staffed with medical personnel during World War II and the Korean War. It had been allowed to lapse in 1953, but now that the Soviets were threatening to heat up the Cold War, it was brought back. This didn't worry Al, either—at first. The scant news coverage in the Chicago papers said the Doctors Draft was more a precaution than a priority and that the army planned to order only five dozen medical men into service. Sixty doctors from among the quarter of a million in the United States—what were the odds?

The letter arrived that spring at his parents' house in Norwalk, the address he'd given when he first registered at age eighteen. "You are hereby directed to present yourself for Armed Forces Physical Examination to the Local Board," it read. He passed that medical exam, then received another letter, this one addressed to his Chicago apartment, where Joan was pregnant for the third time. "Greetings," it began, "You are hereby ordered for induction into the Armed Forces of the United States."

Days after he completed his internal medicine residency, he reported to a Chicago bus station and left for Fort Sam Houston, long the center of army medicine in the United States, for basic training. Told he would be sent to West Germany for twenty-one months of service in a military hospital, Al withdrew his applications for jobs in academia.

✦

DAVE TROY HAD JOINED the Stamford police force at a moment of transition for cities and for policing. After World War II, returning GIs took their families and moved to the greener parts of town, leaving the formerly bustling city centers behind. Storefronts now stood empty on what had once been crowded shopping streets, and apartment buildings crumbled, owned by landlords who refused to invest further in property with little value.

Where poverty goes, crime follows, and in 1956 even the Stamford Police Department itself left downtown. Headquarters was moved out of the third-floor walkup on East Main Street and into a brand-new building at the corner of Hoyt and Bedford, one that included a recreation room and a firing range for the 175-member force. It was a facade. It looked modern. But the officer training manual had been written in 1923, and the booking forms and time sheets were almost as old. The force was facing a new reality with aging tools.

By 1958, Dave's first year as an officer, the demolishment of Stamford's downtown was nearly complete. The neighborhoods where Dave's brothers had delivered newspapers, where Rosie's brothers had shined shoes, where Dave and Rosie had gone to the movies were all but gone. Now there was talk of knocking down even more in the name of urban renewal. A plan was forming to raze 130 acres in the city's center, uprooting thousands of people and hundreds of businesses. Dave had stepped into a tradition but also onto a moving train. This was no longer the police force Tom Troy had experienced. Exactly what this was, however, was still a work in progress.

A few months after Dave received his badge, a banner headline across the front page of the *Stamford Advocate* read: POLICEMEN CHARGED WITH BURGLARIES, USED SQUAD CARS TO CARRY "LOOT." (It was far larger than the headline halfway down the page that read LEOPOLD RELEASED FROM ILLINOIS PRISON.) Three officers had been arraigned in court that morning. A fourth had been hospitalized after collapsing upon hearing he was being arrested.

The cops had been stealing from downtown stores and reselling what they stole. They'd been caught when two rookies saw two off-duty patrol cars at the rear door of the Kitty Kelly Shoe Store at four-fifteen a.m., with several long-time officers on the scene but no official reason for either the cars or the cops to be there. A search of the officers' home garages found fourteen pairs of men's shoes, seventeen pairs of children's, seventy-five pairs of hose, sixty-two ladies' handbags, a stack of TV sets, and boxes of tampons. ("They're great for polishing shoes," one suspect explained.) The nature of the crimes made every officer on the force a target of mockery and mistrust.

For the rest of his rookie year, Dave went about his job as best he could, taking his gun from its hiding place in the cabinet above the fridge before each shift, adjusting his cap in the front hall mirror, and heading out to keep Stamford safe. When a drunken man fell asleep on Maureen Groves's porch over on Walnut Street, she flagged Dave down, and he brought the man a strong cup of coffee before driving him home. When Joseph Walajtyz collapsed in the middle of a crosswalk, banging his head on the asphalt and losing consciousness, Dave visited him in the hospital the next day, not to ask questions but to answer them and fill in some of the memory gaps caused by the fall. His knowledge of cars came in handy one night when the tires and wheels were removed from four new Plymouths in the lot of the Hayden Automobile Company on Main Street. Ditto when he stopped to help drivers stranded with a broken axle or a sudden flat or an empty tank due to a faulty fuel gauge.

Dave found the work satisfying, and the pay was enough for Rosie to finally quit the salon, but what he didn't find was the brotherhood of officers he'd come to expect. His first few weeks he'd been paired with a patrolman named Bruce Williams, who was just a few years his senior and who "broke Davey Troy in," teaching him the essential something you could not learn in the academy—how to assume the persona of "officer." For a while, you pretend, Williams said. One day you realize that the title fits.

Williams had other advice, too. Just think of the job, he said, not about getting hurt, never about getting killed. Perhaps big city cops have to worry, he said, but in Stamford you are a public servant, not a soldier. Williams had been close to Angelo Sabia, the only Stamford officer ever shot in the line of duty, and spoke about him often to Dave. Every child at the school where Sabia had had crosswalk duty had sent a card to the hospital after he was shot, Williams said, and that outpouring, more than any bullet scar, was the badge of a good policeman. Even after he'd retired early, on account of his injuries,

Sabia had stayed involved and, technically a civilian, had still hosted the department's annual police Christmas and Halloween parties. Now Sabia's twin sons, eighteen-year-old Peter and James, were talking about joining the force. An officer is something you are, Williams said, not something you do.

They'd walked and talked and would even describe themselves as friends, although not the kind whose wives would ever meet or who would go out for beers when off duty. After Dave "broke in," he walked his beat alone. When he saw other officers, it was at the change of shift meetings, where he was assigned his territory (usually in the Cove, where he was already a familiar face) or at the firing range, where he worked on his aim. But for whatever reason—maybe the shoe scandal, maybe the changing world—his fellow officers were not his community.

Then the M-7 Bullet ricocheted into a mail train. Nearly every uniformed man in the department did overtime at the frigid accident scene. They brought each other coffee and traded tips about how using newspapers as shoe liners kept the cold out. (His wife's brother, Dante, had taught him that one.) He learned names that had been only faces. The title began to fit.

Come summer, the municipal gossip column noted that "young David Troy" had been "identified by the 'brass' as a man with a future." By Christmas, he would be on the refreshment committee for the yearly children's party that Angelo Sabia ran. Come New Year's Day 1960, Dave and a very pregnant Rosie would have an open house, and many of Dave's fellow officers would stop by. Bruce Williams couldn't make it, but Angelo Sabia visited with his twin sons. A long-timer, Edwin "Red" Corbin, came too and was a huge hit with Dave's daughters and nephews, handing out one-dollar coins to celebrate the New Year.

✦

WITH THE BUTT OF his rifle pressing into the now-familiar spot on his right shoulder, Dr. Alvin Tarlov cradled the front handhold, looked through the rear sight, breathed in then halfway out to slow his heartbeat, and finally squeezed the trigger—smooth and steady, no jolting, not a jab—with the fleshy pad of his right index finger. There was a loud crack, a moment of recoil, and then a small round hole appeared midforehead on the faceless outline of a man across the practice range.

Al was good at this. He had never shot a gun before this week, but he now ranked first in riflery among those in his squad at Fort Sam Houston, an army base in Texas. True, there were only sixty-six others, all medical men like himself, not exactly typical of basic training. Sixty of the others were physicians, four were dentists, and two were veterinarians. Still, Al was better at shooting than the rest, and he was first in the group when it came to crawling through an obstacle course on his belly. He loved the sportsmanship, the precision, the dirt. He also loved the fact that it came so naturally. The distinction was all the more satisfying because he didn't look the part of a soldier. He appeared to be playing dress-up in his big brother's uniform, a schoolboy with a gun.

He didn't get to play for long. When Al arrived in San Antonio in July 1959, he'd learned the length of basic training was being cut by two weeks. It would be cut another two, and then two weeks more. The army really needed medical staff in Germany. In the end, the drafted doctors (and dentists and veterinarians) spent just ten full days learning the most rudimentary military skills, on the assumption that they would never see combat from the safety of a U.S. Army hospital on the west side of Berlin.

After their "graduation," the new soldiers were given their official orders to ship out. The list was read in alphabetical order. Each of the A's was told they would be headed for "Medical and Dental Activities, U.S. Command, Berlin." Then the B's, with the same destination. Al stood ramrod straight in his brand-new dress blues, wondering why it was necessary to go through the entire identical list while standing in the Texas sun.

He was the first among the T's.

"Tarlov, Alvin R," the squad leader barked. He held his breath.

Two years away from his family, who had already moved in with his parents in Shorefront Park.

"Walter Reed Army Hospital, Washington D.C., with Duty Station Stateville Penitentiary, Joliet, Illinois."

Al was not leaving the country. He was not leaving Joan and the children. He would move them all back to Chicago—to a town south of the city called Joliet—where he would oversee the army's ongoing malaria drug trials at Stateville.

1960

January 28, 1960
David and Rosie Troy
Stamford

DAVID TROY SAT ON HIS LIVING ROOM FLOOR, PLAYING CAN-
dyland with his two daughters and hoping that this third baby
would be a boy. His niece Lynne was playing, too, and listening
almost as nervously as Dave for the phone. Dave's sister Agnes,
who was Lynne's mother, should be calling any minute now. A
senior nurse at Stamford Hospital, Agnes was on the maternity
ward with Rosie. Fathers did not stay for the births of their babies
at Stamford Hospital in 1960. Dave was sent home to play game
after game of Candyland.

The plan was that Agnes would call, and Dave would return to the
hospital to see his wife and newborn while Lynne stayed with his girls.
This network of extra hands was one of the reasons Dave and Rosie
lived in the Cove. Dave knew his wife missed her clan in Cos Cob. But
his mother *had* offered to help pay for the house. And he and Rosie did
still spend every Sunday with all the Cosentinos. And at least one of
her siblings had moved nearer to Rosie. When her youngest brother,
Frank, returned from the service, Dave rebuilt the attic into a small
apartment for his brother-in-law, which also led to a warm friendship.
Dave was proud of the work—a good use of his carpentry degree from
Wright, built for Frank in the near term and for a fourth or even fifth
child in years to come.

Eventually Frank became engaged and moved a short distance
away, but he was still a regular visitor to 33 Palmer Avenue. Frank
had even considered joining the Stamford Police, but his bride-to-be
nixed the idea, fearing for his safety as crime was rising in Stamford. So Frank had taken a job at a car dealership, but he had also

joined the auxiliary police force, meaning he got to wear a uniform, train with the full-timers, and be called if support was needed. He and Dave sometimes practiced together at the shooting range, where Dave shared the advice that Bruce Williams had given to him: Don't imagine the target as someone who is trying to hurt *you*. Imagine it is someone who is trying to hurt your *family*.

Dave doted on that family. He built a swing set in the backyard and added a wading pool the previous summer. He brought home a collie, named Tinker, who sat at the children's feet all the time and not *just* when they were eating and might drop a few crumbs. As Dave became ever more content at work, he was increasingly joyful at home. He would walk in the door, put his gun back in its kitchen hiding place, then take Doreen and Diane on piggyback rides through the carpet of toys in the yard. That went over particularly well on nights when Rosie had already settled both the girls and the dog, and Dave excited everyone again.

Delighting in his daughters' company, he brought them with him everywhere, not always mentioning the destinations to Rosie. One summer evening all four of them headed over to Boots' Seaview Restaurant, a short walk away in the Cove. It was a treat for the girls, the first time they had dined at a grown-up restaurant—or so Rosie thought. The dining room was in the back, and as they passed through the front bar, the gathered regulars greeted both girls warmly. "Hi Doreen!" "Hi Diane!"

"How do all these men know my girls?" Rosie asked, suppressing a smile. Dave muttered something about sitting on the stools and drinking Shirley Temples. Not for nothing that all their friends said she was the grown-up in this marriage while her husband was still a kid at heart.

Now Rosie was about to deliver their third child. If this baby was a son, he would be named David. They hadn't decided on a name for a daughter, because Dave was certain this would be a boy; if he happened to be wrong, her name would obviously begin with a D.

Finally, the phone rang on the evening of January 28. David

Daniel Troy, Jr., had arrived. He was healthy, and he looked just like Rosie—dark hair, Mediterranean skin, full lashes, and deep brown eyes. Dave left the girls with Lynne as planned and drove the 2.5 miles to Stamford Hospital, where he could stay for less than an hour before visiting time was over. It was more than enough time for him to be smitten.

February 1960
Al Tarlov
Stateville Penitentiary

AL HAD TAKEN TO GETTING HIS HAIR CUT EVERY FRIDAY AT THE Stateville barbershop. He could have chosen any of the local barbers in the small downtown strip of Joliet, all of whom would have been able to maintain his close-cropped military cut. But he'd become fond of and fascinated by this place, where the barbers were either practicing a trade they'd done before they'd come to prison or learning one that might keep them employed when they left. Perhaps it should have given Al pause to spend part of his lunch hour surrounded by prisoners holding scissors and razor blades, but he never felt nervous. The men were courteous and calm—and they gave a very good haircut and shave.

Friday became Al's chosen day because of what it meant in the rhythms of Stateville. The barber chairs all faced the glass wall that looked out onto the hallway. Friday at noon was when the weekly "delivery" of new arrivals took place, and from here Al had a front row seat. Vans and buses arrived from the processing center over at Joliet, filled with men who had spent several days being evaluated and sorted. The newcomers, about fifty at a time, entered stage left and marched in a line to the wardrobe distribution rooms to receive new uniforms and cell assignments. That path took them right past Al's barbershop chair.

By February 1960, Al had been stationed at the army's research labs for about eight months, and as each week's prisoners walked through, he recognized more of them. Some even waved with shackled hands. "Hey, doc!" "How ya' doing, doc?"

"Doc" couldn't have conjured most of their names. He knew their faces, though, because they'd been subjects in one of the two projects he was overseeing. The men with lighter skin were likely part of the continued search for new malaria drugs in preparation for the inevitability that the parasite would develop resistance to primaquine—a scenario of great military concern as tensions grew in Southeast Asia. The men with darker skin were likely part of Al's new research, exploring exactly what happens inside a G6PD-deficient red blood cell when exposed to primaquine—a question of great military interest as the recent desegregation of the armed forces led to an increased number of Black troops. At the time, the percentage of Black prisoners nationwide still mirrored the population of the country, as the use of prisons as a weapon in the race wars had not fully begun. Al spent time with the men in both sets of trials, sometimes weeks if they were ill with malaria symptoms and recurrences. He studied their blood under microscopes, charted their fevers, and mapped where their ancestors hailed from.

He did not pretend this meant he *knew* them. Prison was not a place where friendships were formed. Al's introduction to Stateville had been quite clear on that fact, beginning with a story he was told of a warden's wife killed by a prisoner she'd befriended, followed by a framed photo he saw hanging on the wall of the staff dining room. It was of a former guard named Charles Wheeler, and beneath it was a small plaque that told his story.

"He started in a small way to trade and traffic with an inmate," it said. "First it was cigarettes and tobacco. Then, letters to be carried in and out, and finally he was persuaded to carry a gun, which resulted not only in the death of an inmate but also in the death of a fellow officer" during an attempted escape. Wheeler had been given a life sentence for that crime in 1920. He had died in Stateville just four years before Al arrived, having been refused parole four separate times.

There were other stories, some with lessons specific to the Stateville lab Al was there to run. Most memorable was the time in 1939 when four inmates put a strong sedative and hypnotic into the coffee of the guards manning the watch towers. The escape plan might have worked but for the one guard who wasn't in the mood for coffee. After that, Warden Ragen, who never did determine exactly how the would-be escapees came to possess one hundred grams of hyacine, tightened several rules. Guards were no longer permitted to eat or drink while on tower duty, and medications were put under stricter control in the infirmary. And it wasn't just the medications in the malaria trials that were counted, recounted, and double-checked, Al was told. It was every drug on the Stateville campus.

All this was on Al's mind as he watched the weekly parade of returnees from his barber's chair near the window. When he began at Stateville, there had been two incarcerated men running the day-to-day work of the lab. The most senior was Charles Ickes who, despite having completed only third grade, had become an excellent lab tech. Alving had long ago promised Ickes a job at the University of Chicago whenever he was granted parole. In October 1959, three months after Al arrived, Ickes was released, and Alving made good on the offer. Ickes was now on the staff of the University of Chicago Medical School. Every Wednesday, Al took the train to Chicago to report to Alving, and there he would often see Ickes, dressed in regular civilian clothes and a white lab coat, his name embroidered over the breast pocket.

With Ickes freed, the most senior prisoner-trainee on the Stateville malaria project was Joe DeSalvo. "He has good hands on the glass" was how Joe had been described to Al, something also said about Al over the years, meaning his results were accurate and clean. Joe, who had already received his American Medical Technologist's certification and was working toward his chief technician's license, was promoted into Ickes's place.

All Al knew of Joe's life before Stateville was that he was originally from Chicago and that this was his second prison term for armed robbery. Al found Joe to be soft-spoken and conscientious, with the vocabulary of a well-educated man. He seemed to spend much of his downtime reading in his cell. He was partial to science fiction, particularly H. P. Lovecraft, whose message was that the human race was insignificant in a yawning cosmos. Joe also read about malaria, enjoyed history and philosophy, wanted to know more about sociology and science, and would occasionally quote poetry—often in sly counterpoint to the goings on in the lab. "To know even one life has breathed easier because you have lived," for instance, quoting Emerson to the remains of a mosquito being squashed onto a microscope slide.

Al was careful not to pry, in part to respect the warnings he'd been given that staff not befriend prisoners, and also to avoid any impression that he was somehow spying for the warden. Joe spent more time on the G6PD project than on the malaria research, which meant he spent a lot of time with Al. Their work was based in a tiny room, a former prison cell. When anyone, staff or prisoner, wished to leave, a guard needed to unlock the iron doors from the outside.

Most of the conversation inside the cramped space was about the science, but sometimes it wandered to current events or to how the Chicago teams were faring this season. Lately, they also talked about parole, as Joe explained the math to Al. He had served nine years of a ten-to-seventy-year sentence, and although the board had ruled two years ago that he would not be eligible again until 1963, with good behavior that meant his parole hearing was scheduled for March of this year.

No one knew exactly what might sway the board, Joe said, but prisoners spent time trying to handicap their own odds anyway. The fact that he'd volunteered as a test subject would help his, Joe guessed, and his continuing training as a lab tech and a ward nurse couldn't hurt. He'd heard that rules prohibited staff from weighing in on a particular inmate's case, but he wondered if that included medical personnel. Everyone knew Dr. Alving had written a letter in support of Charles Ickes, which clearly helped, but had refused to do the same earlier for Nathan Leopold, which likely delayed his release for several years.

Joe never asked directly, but Al understood this was a request. He approached the question as he would any scientific problem, beginning with existing data. Nathan Leopold had assembled a collection at the Stateville library, and Al read nearly all of it, along with the work of such Leopold mentors as Ferris Laune and Ernest Burgess. Al was taken with the idea that a man can change in and be changed by prison. That would explain a mystery: how the sophisticated, gentle man he saw in the lab six days a week was also so dangerous that he'd been sentenced to up to seventy years. Al had no access to the details of Joe's original crime, and he chose not to ask. It was not his role to pass judgment on what Joe had done in the past, he'd decided. A letter of support, should he choose to write one, would be based on Al's best prediction of how Joe would do in the future.

That prediction, in turn, would be based on the only part of the question Al felt qualified to answer. Not the broad one of whether Joe had changed sufficiently, or been punished adequately, or whether a "two-time loser, armed-robber with a childhood history of delinquency" could be trusted out in the world, but a more specific one: Was Joseph DeSalvo, trained behind bars, in fact prepared to do the work of a laboratory technician?

Two years earlier Al's uncle Isadore had gone for an early morning run in Central Park. He did this every day, always wearing a pair of shorts under his street clothes as he left his apartment, then shedding his pants in the park and leaving them folded on a bench while he jogged. On this morning, he'd returned to his starting point and saw two teen boys running off with his trousers. Police were summoned, a search ensued, and both boys were apprehended. Isadore's watch, which had been in his pants pocket, was recovered, but the pants themselves were never found.

The sixteen-year-old boy caught holding the watch was returned to the children's correctional institution from which he had recently escaped. The other boy was seventeen and stood trial as an adult. He was defended by a lawyer from the Legal Aid Society who argued that because his client was not technically in possession of either the pants or the watch, he could not be guilty of larceny. The judge agreed. He gave the teen a stern lecture and told him to "go home."

This outraged Isadore enough to write a long letter to the editor of *The New York Times*. He was not angry at the boy, but on the boy's behalf. Isadore had learned that the defendant came "from a broken home, that the whereabouts of the parents was unknown, that the boy therefore had no home to go to, no job, and no money." The judge, Isadore said, did not care about any of this. "Without bothering to discover whether the boy had a home to go to," his letter continued, "the judge told him to 'go home.'"

Isadore tried to follow the boy from the courtroom but lost him on the street. "What has [he] been doing since his dismissal?" he wondered. "How has he been living? By petty thefts? Has he by now committed a major crime? And if he has, whose immediate fault is it? It seems to me that it is the fault of custodial negligence."

That way of thinking stuck with Al as he prepared to give Joe an answer. If the prison system had done its job (to punish and/or rehabilitate him) and the parole board then did its job (to recognize him as penitent/rehabilitated), who was responsible for the next logical step—making sure that he had the means to succeed when he got out? Watching the revolving door from the barbershop window, Al wondered what each of these men did once the system told them to "go home." Parole was touted as protection for the ex-con, a resource to help them readjust to the outside world. Based on the number of returnees he knew by sight, and the fact that 50 percent of the Stateville population were repeaters, whatever guidance they'd been given was not enough.

Yes, Joe had the technical skills to be a lab technician anywhere. The parole board would insist that he have a job waiting, which was a start. But what of the other things he needed—a place to live? A chance to get out of the water in which he swam—away from the environment that initially led him to crime? Not just an admonishment to "go home" but some structure and guidance once he got there?

Without those things in place, Al reasoned, Joe was an experiment destined to fail. Without those things in place, Al could not write a letter supporting his parole. So he set out to find them.

May 30, 1960
David Troy
Stamford

THE PLANNERS OF THE MEMORIAL DAY PARADE HAD POSITIONED the blue-uniformed officers between the khaki jumble of the Boy Scouts and the orange and black exuberance of the high school marching band. Dave Troy grinned beneath his blue-tinted motorcycle sunglasses and department-issued crash helmet as he slowly rolled along Main Street, waving at the crowds.

With two years on the force, he was a man on his way up. The Stamford Police Department assigned badges in order, so that the longest-serving man wore number one and the newest recruit wore whatever number reflected the current size of the force. When a man retired, everyone stepped down one badge number. Back in 1958, Dave had been number 145, and his great-uncle Thomas had been four. Now Thomas had the top spot, and Dave had moved up the ranks to 127. As fond as Dave was of anything that contained a lucky seven, Thomas was rumored to be announcing his retirement this summer, which would give Dave a new badge and the distinction of being the only "Officer Troy."

He no longer felt like an imposter when someone called him that. The children on his beat had always done so earnestly, and the adults—many of whom had known him since he was a child in the Cove—no longer did so with the sly smile that was a cross between disbelief and pride. Within the department, he'd continued to develop a reputation as the one with a soft touch, a knack for calming someone belligerent or frightened or hurt. He was a good officer, not because he was tough, but because he was kind. Drawn to the job for its old-fashioned public service elements, he practiced that kind of policing even as the city around him was becoming more complicated and police work more confrontational.

Dave was particularly effective with children and teens, a professional use of his tendency to be a kid himself. As his nieces and nephews grew, he was ever more the cool uncle, showing up on a random weekday to sign out Evelyn's sons, Billy and Don, from middle school in his silver two-door 1957 Chevy Bel Air wagon and drive them to Yankee Stadium. His own children were also growing so quickly. Already Doreen was being fitted for the uniform she would wear to kindergarten at St. Mary's in a few months.

His brood was waiting, as planned, near the end of the parade route. As he approached the intersection of Atlantic and Main, there was Rosie, pushing baby David in a buggy while holding the girls by the hand. Dave waved, then turned and followed the parade into Veterans Memorial Park. He would attend the memorial service there, watch as the wreath was placed at the plaque listing more than 5,500 names of Stamford residents who had served (including his father and older brother), and bow his head for a reading of the names of those who had died. His children were too little for that kind of grief, so they would not join him. He would meet them back home when the ceremony was over.

June 1960
Joe DeSalvo
Norwalk

THE LETTER HAD LANDED IN DR. NORMAN BOAS'S MAILBOX SEV-
eral months earlier, on stationery bearing the letterhead of the Army
Medical Research Project, The University of Chicago, Stateville Penitentiary. It was written by a Dr. Alvin R. Tarlov, the lab director at
Stateville, who had worked in a research lab at Norwalk Hospital
one summer when he'd been in medical school. Drs. Tarlov and Boas
had never met, but Al had been asking around at Norwalk Hospital
for anyone who might need a new technologist, and as it happened,
Dr. Boas did. A Harvard-trained rheumatologist, Boas had spent the
prior four years doing research at the National Institute of Arthritis
and Metabolic Diseases outside of Washington, D.C. He had been
given lab space at Norwalk Hospital as part of his recent recruitment.
Because he would spend most of his day seeing patients, he was looking to hire a lab assistant with enough training to go about his work
with little supervision.

The detailed note from Dr. Tarlov explained that he might have
just the man:

> The purpose of this letter is to discuss with you an inmate,
> Joseph DeSalvo, with the possibility of obtaining employment
> for him upon his discharge. He had an unfortunate beginning
> in life, and at the age of 15, he was given a prison sentence
> for a robbery he committed in the State of Illinois. Since that
> time, he has been paroled only to have violated the regulations
> of his parole and to be again incarcerated here.

Since his second admission to this penitentiary, he has been a model inmate. He received training here as a medical technologist and is now chief of the clinical laboratory in the General Hospital of this institution. I can personally vouch for his technical proficiency, having worked with him closely day in and day out. From this aspect I believe he would be a tremendous asset in anyone's laboratory.

Because he has been in jail since his early teens, he has not been given a chance on the outside to find his place in this world. However, I believe in the past five to seven years, Mr. DeSalvo has matured emotionally and intellectually, and that he is ready to assume his place as a useful citizen in society. His IQ is 142, one of the highest in the institution.

As I said, he has been a model prisoner and is well-liked and respected by the administration as well as by his colleagues. I personally have seen men leave this institution and I have seen the same ones return. However, I have a great deal of faith in Mr. DeSalvo and would like very much to see him usefully employed.

It turned out that Norman Boas, who was just a few years older than Al, was a good person to approach with this request. Like Al, he had been deeply influenced by a relative whose career was spent going far beyond providing medical care. Norman's father, Dr. Ernst P. Boas, had spent years fighting the American Medical Association's position against universal health insurance. He'd worked to increase the numbers of Black doctors and nurses on hospital staffs. After World War II, he founded the National Committee for the Resettlement of Foreign Physicians, and he brought thousands of doctors to the United States from Europe. He was on the side of anyone who needed a boost or a second chance.

Dr. Boas was reassured that a system was in place to determine whether an inmate was ready for parole, that it was not just Al's opinion. "There are others in this institution, such as the sociologist, the parole officer, and any one of the wardens who are more expert than I at predicting a man's outcome," and all of them were on board, Al had written.

Dr. Boas's questions for Al, therefore, were more about Joe DeSalvo's skills than about his crimes. Al assured him not only that Joe was a natural but that Al had used Norwalk Hospital's *Manual of Laboratory Procedures* in his Stateville lab, so Joe already knew the routines. After receiving a (pro forma) letter of support from Warden Ragen and checking with Norwalk Hospital administrators, Dr. Boas had sent a written offer of employment to Joseph DeSalvo, contingent upon his parole. Boas also thanked Al, sincerely, for the chance to "help someone who needed help."

Joe DeSalvo's final parole board hearing had been on April Fool's Day 1960. The tone was far more encouraging this time; the job offer seemed to make the difference. From the Illinois penal system's perspective, it was a chance for them to boast about his redemption arc while also moving a two-time loser to another state.

"You have got a telegram here from this hospital and they will give you a job and I want you to make good on it," the board chair told Joe. "You will probably meet a lot of fine people there and you will have a lot of opportunities to really go ahead, and don't blow them, and above all, don't carry any arms on you, don't carry or tote any guns or deadly weapons of any kind."

"No, I don't think I will ever do anything like that again."

"You can't afford to. You couldn't afford to violate your parole. You couldn't commit another offense unless you want to spend the rest of your life in an institution, so you have a big opportunity if you will just take advantage of it."

This time Warden Ragen called him into his office to give him the news.

"We believe that at this time he possesses both the capacity and disposition to adjust on parole," the board's April 14 decision said. The parole prediction report, it noted, placed Joe in a category where

"29 percent may be expected to violate the parole agreement. 16 percent of the persons in this class may be expected to commit serious or repeated infractions of the parole agreement, and 13 percent may be expected to commit new offenses on parole," but his "excellent" job offer meant he would be well positioned to go straight.

On Friday, May 20, Joe had said his goodbyes to Al—a strong handshake, a promise to keep in touch. A goodbye to Warden Ragen came next, and like the superintendent at St. Charles, the warden admonished him not to return. Then Joe shed his prison denim for a suit from the prison tailor shop and was given bus fare to Chicago and the small amount of money left in his canteen account. He walked out of Stateville, his few belongings in the small cardboard suitcase his mother had dropped off.

From Chicago, Joe took a second bus to New York and an early-morning train to Norwalk. Al had arranged a stay for him in the dorm—the men's side of the same place Joan had stayed during her nursing training. His single room wasn't much larger than his Stateville cell, with a bathroom down the hall and showers he could use whenever he chose. He couldn't cook in the room, but then again, he didn't know how. He got a discount in the Norwalk Hospital cafeteria and ate nearly every meal there, with occasional visits to Tarlov's Minute Chef's down the hill, where Al's father was always welcoming. With his first paycheck he invested in a new set of luggage, which doubled as his dresser.

On Joe's first day of work, his parole officer came to visit, checking out the lab and the dorm and reminding him of the rules. He was required to check in with the officer weekly and obtain permission for such things as leaving the state, changing his address, buying a car, changing jobs, and getting married. He was not to drink or own a firearm. He could not stay out past nine-thirty p.m.

He loved the work and was good at it. He extracted something called mucopolysaccharides from the body tissue of humans and animals—umbilical cords, cockscombs—to study their role in biological development and their potential as medication or treatment.

Dr. Boas was pleased. As he reported to Al in early June, he found Joe to be "extremely conscientious, competent, report[s] to work on time, and the results of his work [are] precise." Joe began to develop friendships within the hospital and took his regular coffee break with a nurse's aide who worked on the floor, a twenty-five-year-old woman with an eight-year-old son.

One June morning, as Dr. Boas was readying to leave, Joe lingered. He seemed to have something on his mind, and Dr. Boas waited patiently. In the weeks since the tech had arrived on an overnight bus from Chicago, there had been other liminal pauses like these, where he seemed to be navigating the difference between the old rules of his life and the new ones. For years, he had rarely been allowed to initiate conversation or to speak unless spoken to. Dr. Boas would give him a moment.

Eventually Joe began. The job was everything he had hoped, he said, but during his time away from work, he found himself unexpectedly restless. He was grateful for the room in the dormitory, but it was isolated and he had no transportation. While he could eat at the luncheonette down the hill during the week, Tarlov's was closed all day Sunday. Joe hoped to move into an apartment of his own, or at least find a room for rent in an actual house, but for that he needed a car. He had gotten permission from his parole officer—it might have helped that he did so during a week when the AP carried a story about how Nathan Leopold had been given permission for a car in Puerto Rico—but he was hoping Dr. Boas might help with the actual purchase. He would be buying a used vehicle and taking out a loan. Since he had no credit history, might Dr. Boas serve as a guarantor?

After the workday ended on Wednesday, June 15, Dr. Boas and his new lab tech went to a car lot and bought Joe a 1953 Chrysler two-door hardtop, in two-tone gray, VIN #T232583, license plate number 33C 053. He paid $267.48 with a check from the Fairfield County Trust Company, which he had been given when he signed an agreement to make monthly payments of $22.29 beginning on July 7,

1960, and ending on June 15, 1961. Joe was earning $292 a month. Dr. Boas had done the math and agreed this was something Joe could afford, and so he countersigned, agreeing to pay off the loan should Joe default.

Joe thanked his boss for the chance to own a car for the first time. What he didn't mention was that it was the first car he'd driven that had not been stolen.

July 4, 1960
David Troy
Stamford

INDEPENDENCE DAY FELL ON A MONDAY, MEANING THE NATION had the entire weekend to celebrate. Dave Troy was slotted to work that night, supervising traffic around Cummings Park Beach in the Cove, where crowds gathered for the fireworks. But first he made it to the annual Troy gathering at his sister Mary's house that afternoon, for his family's favorite holiday.

It wasn't just America's birthday that they celebrated but also Dave's birthday a week earlier. (He proudly showed off his new Benrus wrist-watch, inscribed TO DADDY, 6-24-60, which he vowed to wear for the rest of his life.) And the day was an early anniversary party for Dave and Rosie. As always, someone repeated the story of the earlier party, now seven years ago, when the couple announced their engagement and Bridget wrote a check as the down payment on a house.

The afternoon passed quickly, a swirl of grilled hot dogs, ice-cold beer, and Bridget's freshly baked apple pie. Dave played tag with the little kids, talked about movies and baseball with the older ones, and carried five-month-old David everywhere for most of the day. When the sparklers came out, Dave put on his policeman's voice and warned the teens to be careful, describing how he'd spent one Fourth of July in the emergency room. And in the hour before he left for work, he sat on a webbed folding chair holding his son and happily cleaning his plate of the last of his pie.

"My life is complete," he said.

July 4, 1960
Al Tarlov
Norwalk

AL AND JOAN TARLOV AND THEIR THREE CHILDREN SPENT THE holiday in Shorefront Park. They had driven 950 miles over two days to get there. As always, they'd stopped in Beaver Falls, Pennsylvania, for dinner at the Italian place with "spider web spaghetti," so named because the pasta was covered with cheese and put under the broiler, making it as fun to play with as it was to eat. Then they spent the night at a nearby motel, one that met Joan's requirement that it not rent rooms by the hour, a lesson learned the hard way a few years before. They left early the next morning, made a short stop for lunch, and rolled up to Al's childhood home as it started to get dark on Saturday evening, July 2.

The long drive was harder with three small children than it had been with two. Everything was harder with three. Ever since Jane was born in January, joining three-year-old Richard and two-year-old Elizabeth, the house had felt stuffed to bursting. It was crammed with kids and also with sadness. Joan, who had so badly wanted a big family, and who had bonded with Al over that dream, had been flattened by postpartum depression.

The spiral seemed to have begun with an argument over breastfeeding, with Al believing formula was a marvel of science, and Joan seeing it as an abdication of maternal responsibility. She insisted on nursing through a series of excruciating breast infections, soldiering on even as her tears slipped onto her newborn daughter's head. Then when she had no choice but to introduce the baby to a bottle, the squalling infant rejected it. Joan was disturbed and debilitated, and Al worried she might never recover. He began to fear she might hurt herself. He even tried to have her hospitalized for psychiatric care. When she refused medical help, he planned this trip to Norwalk, a vacation born of desperation. The plan was to leave all three children with Al's parents and spend five days at a lovely beachside inn. He hoped that physical distance from the baby, and a few nights of real sleep, would help.

Sunday, July 3, was a swirl of tricycles on the quiet streets of Shore-front Park and splashes and giggles at the tiny beach. Isadore had made the half-hour drive down from his weekend house in Ridgefield, Connecticut, and he and Al spent time catching up on the sand while Grandpa Charlie waded with Richard and Elizabeth, and Grandma Mae doted on Jane. Isadore shared Al's worries about Joan's mental health. Hadn't her father suffered from depression? he asked. And hadn't her mother been ill for months after giving birth? He also asked about the latest happenings in the Stateville lab. Al described the incremental progress being made toward understanding the role of G6PD and developing a test to determine who lacked the enzyme. Sitting in the same place where they'd once discussed the Nuremberg trials, Al admitted he had been wary when he'd started at Stateville, thinking such experimentation on prisoners could too easily tip into unethical territory. "But I am completely persuaded that the men are not coerced, they volunteer enthusiastically," he told Isadore. "We have more volunteers than we need, and they repeatedly tell us they are grateful to be useful."

Monday the fourth was much the same as the day before—beaches, bicycles, barbecues. Even Joan seemed more relaxed, willing to allow Mae to care for her in addition to the baby. With his family safe and occupied, Al excused himself shortly before lunch and headed to what had once been Merwyn's bedroom but was now his parents' study. A few weeks earlier Al had written to Joe DeSalvo to say he'd be coming to Norwalk and that he would call once he'd arrived. So he did.

They began with pleasantries and updates. Al sent regards from Charles Ickes. Joe explained that he'd moved out of the dormitory and rented a room with bath in the home of a couple named John and Frances Fitzgerald and their four school-age children. It was a comfortable enough place, certainly compared with his "room" at Stateville.

"Can I see you while you are here?" Joe asked.

"My wife and I are going to take a short vacation. Let's get together when we return on the eleventh?"

"Can't we meet before you leave here? I'd love to see you, for a short time, and then we could meet again for a longer time when you get back. There's so much to talk about."

Al paused for a long while. Joe had never directly asked him for anything—not this job, not the recommendation to the parole board—and here he was pressing Al to change his plans. Al was confused, as this was not the usual tone of their conversations, and a bit annoyed, because who was Joe to be telling him how to spend his vacation? Also, he was concerned. What was Joe leaving unsaid?

Al could have fit in a quick visit with Joe, but it would not have been simple. Already his tendency to put work ahead of family was a cause of tension in his marriage. He had kept to their agreement to be home every night for dinner, but he also went into the lab at least six days a week and read medical journals late into the night. Joe was work, and interrupting this vacation to see him would give Joan more reason to feel abandoned. There were details to be settled and errands to run before leaving all three children, and he could not go wandering off so that Joe could—what, thank Al again for arranging the job? Or share his pride that his lab skills were improving? Joe would have to wait.

"I just can't meet with you before I leave," Al said finally. "But we will definitely get together when we return. I was hoping you might come for a barbecue and to meet my family?" As he said it he wondered if Warden Ragen would consider such a visit an overstep. What are the rules about friendship with *former* prisoners?

They agreed they would see each other in a week.

During the car ride from Chicago to Connecticut and the first two days at Shorefront Park, Al had been entertaining his children with stories of the wonderful fireworks they would see on the Fourth of July. Standing on the beach, he pointed toward the expanse of shoreline and sky. Every town along the water would be sending rockets into the air, and they would all be visible from right here, he said, just as they had been when he was a child.

By dusk, all the Tarlovs were waiting on blankets, watching as the sky grew dark and the first stars appeared. At nine-thirty, as scheduled, the starting rockets whooshed and boomed overhead. Al looked toward his children for a glimpse of the excitement he had felt way back when. They were all fast asleep.

July 4, 1960
Joe DeSalvo
Wilton, Connecticut

"JOE, SO GLAD YOU COULD MAKE IT," DR. NORMAN BOAS SAID
as he clasped Joe's hand in welcome.

It was the first time the doctor had invited this lab tech to his home.
It was also the first time Joe had been invited to dinner at anyone's
home, anywhere, and the first time he had approached the Fourth of
July as a patriotic celebration, not as a chance to buy explosives on
the black market. His father hadn't been big on patriotic celebrations.
Charles Sr. had had a few stories of racing his motorcycle on the holiday and of the huge crowds that filled the new stadiums, but Joe was
not entirely sure those stories were true.

Joe brought flowers that he'd cut, with permission, from his landlady's garden. Handing them to Dr. Boas, he apologized that they were
not beer, or a pie, or something that he suspected would have been
more appropriate to the occasion, but the rules of parole said he was
not allowed to buy or consume alcohol, and even if the kitchen at the
Fitzgeralds' had been available to him, he had no idea how to bake.

Then he took in the house. The Boas family had been a presence in
Wilton, Connecticut, since 1926, when Norman's great-grandfather,
an anthropologist, purchased eighty acres of an area called Nod Hill.
Norman had been raised in Manhattan but spent summers in Wilton, the town next to Norwalk, and as a child he had planted what
had grown to be a fifty-foot redwood outside the window of what
had become his youngest daughter's bedroom. It was not the only tree
with a family story. The row of hemlocks on the left of the driveway
had been dug up and replanted by a much younger Dr. Boas when a

swamp on the property had been drained, dammed, and transformed
into a pond.

The house itself, 25 Partrick Lane, had begun as two prefab military barracks that Dr. Boas had bought for $1,200 and shipped north
from Maryland. Over the years they had been expanded and transformed into a graceful contemporary, with floors made of reclaimed
barn boards and a picture window that overlooked the hand-dredged
pond and the woods beyond.

While Doris Boas found a vase for the flowers, her husband took
Joe on a quick tour. They paused at the stone wall around the veg-
etable garden, which Norman had also built. Just seven years older
than Joe, Boas was happiest when working with his hands, restor-
ing, repairing, and building. The tasks Joe's ancestors had considered
work, Norman's considered leisure.

The afternoon passed quickly. Dr. Boas barbecued on the new
Weber grill, the first one Joe had seen. Dr. Boas had chopped the
kindling with his hatchet. They ate in the forest-green dining room
at the huge oblong table that Debbie, two, Steven, three, and Barbara, seven, loved because it was shaped like a racetrack. The
weekend was hot, but there was a breeze off the pond, and the attic
fan drew it through the opened windows. At nightfall the children played with sparklers, and Joe performed a few magic tricks.
(When he'd learned them in prison, it was a small rock that he'd
made appear and disappear; here it was a quarter.) He taught Debbie to stand on her head (a useful way to exercise in tight quarters,
like a prison cell). Everyone found him charming and made him
promise to come again.

Something about the visit disquieted Joe, though, and by the time
he reached his room at the Fitzgeralds' house, he was somewhat panicked. It was nearly ten p.m., not an appropriate time for a phone call,
yet he made one anyway, from the household phone in the Fitzgeralds'
kitchen. When Al answered at his parents' house, Joe kept his voice
low as he murmured apologies for the late hour. Was there a note of

fear in Joe's voice, Al would later wonder, replaying the conversation in his mind? Or was it just that they were both whispering?

"I thought maybe your plans had changed and we could meet tomorrow?" Joe asked.

"My plans have not changed," Al said. "But we will definitely get together next week, after I get back."

Thursday, July 7, 1960
2 p.m.
David Troy
Stamford

DAVID TROY GRINNED AS HE DRESSED FOR HIS SHIFT, ONE HE
had agreed to work in place of his friend Red Corbin, who had decided
to take a short weekend away at the shore with his family.

Rosie was relieved by her husband's good mood. Two nights earlier
he'd had a fitful sleep, filled with dreams so dark he wouldn't tell her
the details, creating a sadness so thick that it had stayed with him for
days. Dave believed that dreams were omens—not predictions necessarily, but warnings. Rosie feared that dreams were self-fulfilling
prophecies; it was belief in dreams, not the dreams themselves, that
had power.

But today the grip of that memory had clearly loosened, and Dave
was all but humming to himself as he checked his reflection in the
front hall mirror. He was twenty-seven years old, pinning badge number 127 onto his uniform on this seventh of July. Lucky number seven.
It couldn't help but be a good day.

He kissed Rosie and the kids and walked toward the door. Then,
with his hand still on the knob, he turned back and smiled at his wife.

"I had the *best* dream last night," he said. "I'll tell you about it
when I get home."

Thursday, July 7, 1960
7 p.m.
Joan and Al Tarlov
Madison, Connecticut

THE MADISON BEACH HOTEL WAS ALL IT WAS ADVERTISED TO BE—white clapboard wood, a balcony on each room, and an elegant restaurant off the lobby. Al and Joan arrived near bedtime on Wednesday night, having tucked the children into bed in Norwalk, then driven the fifty miles up the coast. They had both slept soundly for the first time in months, maybe years, and spent an idyllic day being waited on while lounging in beach chairs and dipping their toes into Long Island Sound.

At dinner they ordered a feast: four courses, sublime palate cleansers, perfect wine pairings, a heavenly dessert. Al brought a critical eye to restaurants because his father had taught him to judge not only the food but the experience: Did the waiter hover? Disappear? Clear plates too quickly? But tonight everything was perfect. Or maybe it was just that across the table, Joan was smiling.

Sometimes, Al thought, all that was needed was a change of scenery. Sometimes that was enough for a fresh start, a new perspective, an interruption of unhealthy patterns. Or so he hoped. He lifted a rare digestif—neither of them drank much—and toasted Joan's health.

Thursday, July 7, 1960
9:45 p.m.
Rosie Troy
Stamford

IT WAS NEARLY TIME FOR ROSIE TO REMOVE THE ROLLERS FROM her hair, when there came a sharp knocking at her front door. She almost didn't hear it, as her regular Thursday-night television program, *The Untouchables*, was playing in the background, and she was listening more than watching as she waited for the neutralizer to work its magic. The episode was a rerun, about a series of brazen bank robberies in the Midwest in the days of Al Capone and Eliot Ness, and its special guest star was Dan O'Herlihy, whom Rosie knew from a few recent westerns. A good shoot-'em-up was her favorite kind of movie. She liked that the heroes always won.

Dave's shift was not scheduled to end until eleven p.m. It was barely nine-forty-five, which was why she was fitting in a home perm. Some things were best done when the children were tucked in bed and your husband was at work. Time for primping, a dose of good guys versus bad guys (and handsome ones at that). In all, it was a lovely way for a young mother to spend an evening.

The door rapping continued. Rosie peered through the peephole as she'd always promised Dave she would and saw two uniformed police officers on the front step.

What happened next was a blur. She must have removed the rollers and put on something other than her robe. One of the officers stayed with the sleeping children, while the other drove her by squad car to the emergency room at Stamford Hospital, a 2.5-mile trip that normally took eleven minutes and that they covered in five. Everyone stared as she entered. Her brother, Frank, appeared from . . . somewhere . . . took her by the arm and walked her into a . . . private room? Curtained bay? Quiet corner?

And he told her.

He had been with Dave when he'd died, just a few minutes before she'd arrived. Frank's new father-in-law was the deputy chief of the fire department and had called from the scene. The first thing Frank did was pound on Evelyn's door and frantically ask her to get over to Rosie and Dave's because a squad car was on its way to take Rosie to the hospital. Then he broke the speed limit and arrived in the emergency room at about 9:55 p.m., in time to see Dave on a gurney, barely breathing, blood everywhere. He was being given last rites by Father Anthony Intagliata of the Sacred Heart RC Church. He was pronounced dead at 10:02 p.m.

Rosie screamed, just once. Then she cried, and her tears would continue to fall for days. Frank, who had just lost the man he was closest to in the world, held his sister, who had lost even more. "You know how Dave is," Frank said. "Right now, he's right up there with Saint Peter, protecting the pearly gates." Years later she told him that image helped.

Eventually, she was allowed in to say goodbye. Her husband's body had been cleaned up in the twenty minutes since Frank last saw it, a white sheet now covering him from the neck down. He did not look like he was sleeping. He looked gray and cold.

She tried to listen to what the medical people were saying. At least two bullets. Wounds on both his legs: a single bullet seemed to have entered through the left upper thigh and exited though the right. That did far less damage than the one that struck him in the right chest and may have traveled out the back. He'd lost a lot of blood, so very much blood. They didn't know yet that it had pooled in his lungs, more than four liters of it, nearly all the blood man has in his body. But they knew it was blood loss that had killed him.

Rosie spent some time alone with Dave, as Frank, Father Intagliata, and an ER doctor hovered nearby, just out of her sight. Then there was nothing for her to do but leave. She had arrived a wife but departed a widow. She couldn't take anything with her from the before to help her through the after. Not his watch, still on his wrist, inscribed TO DADDY, from children who would remember him only through stories. Not his badge, with his lucky number 127, still attached to the shirt that had been cut off him minutes ago. It was all evidence. She would also never know the content of his last, *"best"* dream.

Driving home, Frank told her what little he'd heard. There had been a holdup at the Skipper, a bar on Main Street, and Dave had chased a suspect into an alley called Greyrock Place. Shots were fired. Dave had managed to empty his gun before collapsing, and it seemed likely that he had wounded his assailant, which, Frank assured her, would make him easier to catch. Gerome had been more than familiar with the Skipper. Dante had stolen empties from behind the building and cashed them in. Now Dave had been mortally wounded there.

Two officers were stationed outside her home on Palmer Avenue when she and Frank arrived, the first of a regular rotation that they promised would continue at least until Dave's killer was caught. Evelyn was in the kitchen. Dave's mother, Bridget, sat in the living room, winding a tear-soaked linen handkerchief around and around in her lap; Father McCarthy of St. Mary's was by her side.

Valentino was upstairs on the phone with Dante, who was living in North Beach near San Francisco, having moved from Detroit and bought himself a bookstore. Surrounded by old books all day was his way of making up for the hundreds of volumes his mother had tossed out along with his father. He was also attending San Francisco State to earn a graduate degree in philosophy.

"Dave was killed in a gun duel," Valentino told him.

Dante didn't have enough cash in his bank account or cash drawer for a plane ride across the country. It was the first time in his life that he desperately wanted to be back "home."

Near midnight, Frank slipped away to his house, where he put on his auxiliary police uniform, laid his gun in the back seat of his car, and drove to the scene. There were barricades everywhere—Main

Street was blocked off, fire department rescue trucks played search-lights over the area, roadblocks had gone up on every possible route out of town. Eventually Frank made it to a checkpoint and flashed his badge. He was not waved through.

A superior walked to his open driver side window instead. "You armed?"

"I am."

"What are you going to do if you find him?"

"That's between me and my God."

"Go home, Frank. Go take care of your sister."

Throughout the night people came and went in a carousel of grief. They brought updates in snippets, which they only shared when Rosie had left the room. But the house was small and sound traveled, and so she would learn about her husband's last hours from whispers.

"The biggest manhunt in the history of Stamford," they murmured in the kitchen when she was in the living room.

"Looking for a suspect who was six feet tall, weighed approxi-mately 175 to 185 pounds, had blond hair and a cowlick," they mut-tered in the living room when she was in the kitchen.

An APB was issued for a two-tone green 1952 model Oldsmobile that had been seen speeding away from the area. There was mention of a disguise, some sort of bandage or medical tape on the robber's face. He'd ordered a beer from the bartender, John Yates, gone to the men's room, and come back with a newspaper draped over his arm. "Hey, Mac, look at this," then a jiggle of his right hand. Yates cleared out the cash drawer—forty-nine dollars, it turned out—and handed it over. The bar's owner, Dominick Tamburri, and his son, John, had been sitting just a few feet away but noticed nothing. They were engrossed in *The Untouchables*, which was playing on the TV at the back of the room.

When the man left, Yates yelled, "We've been robbed," and he and the Tamburris ran out into the street. As it happened, both David Troy and Christopher Kanel were standing nearby. They weren't sup-posed to be there. Riding together in Radio Patrol Car 21, they had answered an 8:50 call to pick up an unconscious drunk at Main Street and Greyrock, but before they could find him, they'd been detoured to the railroad station, where a pedestrian had supposedly been hit by a car. They'd completed that call by nine-thirty (the pedestrian was fine) and continued back to the drunken man, who was not unconscious, just sleeping. As they tried to rouse him, they heard shouts about a holdup and ran down the alley, Kanel to the front of Main Street and Dave Troy to the back. Shots were fired, but only two people knew what happened next. One was dead. The other was on the run.

The search went on all night. Every officer in Stamford, including every auxiliary officer except Frank, was asked to report, an eventual force of 205 men. The Greenwich Police Department and the Connecticut State Troopers sent teams. The Fairfield Police sent several dozen bulletproof vests. Bruce Williams, Dave's old mentor, told his wife he might not be home for several days, not until they "caught the guy." Edwin "Red" Corbin, who had entertained the Troy children with quarters last New Year's Eve, whose shift Dave had taken tonight, drove back from the beach and went directly to the scene; he spent hours shining his flashlight along walls and across asphalt looking for bullets, holes, or casings. Angelo Sabia, still suffering back pain from a shooting in a different alley twelve years earlier, and officially retired, said he was there because he wanted to help, but he also felt an overwhelming need to check in on his son, Peter, a Stamford Police rookie who'd also been on duty that night.

The police ordered the manager of the Main Street movie theater to raise the lights on the 9:40 showing of *Pollyanna*, and patrons filed through a double line of officers, given the once-over. Twenty-five men were picked up and questioned overnight; three were held as suspects. At twelve-fifteen a.m., Robert Byrne was stopped a block from the Skipper and found to have a dagger concealed under his pant leg in a leather sheath. When two officers brought him to the bar, so Yates and the Tamburris might identify him, a mob gathered, and police had to form a strong-arm circle to protect the suspect and themselves.

At two-thirty a.m, another man, whose name was never released, was found on the roof of the Skipper, where he punched and kicked the officers who began to question him. He was finally dragged into police headquarters with blood streaming from the back of his head. While being fingerprinted, he refused to cooperate, and it took five officers to subdue him. It turned out he had an airtight alibi for earlier in the evening but was arraigned for resisting arrest. The judge asked him why he had been so violent. "I don't like cops," he said.

Small bits of potential evidence were found—strips of adhesive tape on a staircase, a folded copy of the *Stamford Advocate* in a trash bin, a pair of sunglasses, one green lens shattered, that was dusted, unsuccessfully, for prints. All this and more was discussed in the rooms Rosie had left. "Wasn't there a famous case that was solved because the killer owned an unusual pair of glasses?" "These were cheap, run-of-the-mill, nothing special."

Near dawn Rosie went upstairs to "rest," and the downstairs talk grew freer.

"He was filling in for Red Corbin."

"Otherwise he wouldn't have been there."

"Wrong place, wrong time."

In the early morning, word came that Corbin was now hospitalized. He'd finally gone home for a bite to eat and was sitting in his kitchen telling his family that their vacation had caused his friend to die, when he collapsed. He was rushed to the hospital where he was in "grave condition" from a cerebral hemorrhage, receiving last rites. Corbin, thirty-three, had survived four years in the navy during World War II and had been at both Iwo Jima and Okinawa. Now guilt nearly killed him.

Tinker barked to announce that Doreen, Diane, and David were awake, and they were brought downstairs, while the dog crawled under the kitchen table and waited for his master to come home. The children were hugged, entertained, and marveled at by adults grateful for an excuse to smile.

Someone handed five-month-old David to Bridget—babies make

everything better. He stretched out his chubby arms and kicked his pudgy little feet, but his grandmother did not reach back.

"He may have my son's name, but he's not my son's son," she said, out loud, a thought she might have had before but hadn't voiced. Her other grandsons looked like her, felt familiar, matched her family. She refused to accept that this was all that was left of her favorite child.

"That's not Dave's boy," she said. Those who heard her, pretended they hadn't—including Rosie.

Friday, July 8, 1960
Joe DeSalvo
Norwalk

FRANCES FITZGERALD CHOSE JOSEPH DESALVO AS A BOARDER for many reasons, but top of the list was that he was a quiet man. Aiming to find someone responsible and unassuming, she did not place her ad in the "Rooms for Rent" section of the local paper. She mailed it directly to businesses that were likely to employ respectful, respectable people, hoping it would make its way to their staff bulletin boards and lead such a person to rent her "Room, with Bath" for ten dollars a week.

For a while, her new tenant was all she could have hoped for. He paid his rent on time. He made almost no noise as he came and went. He took most of his meals at work or at a local restaurant he seemed to like; when he did use her kitchen, it was never while she needed it, and he always cleaned up after himself. He never entertained women in his room. In fact, he never brought anyone to the house at all.

But today, Friday, July 8, Joseph, as she called him, suddenly became her full-time job. This was inconvenient, as she already had a job—taking care of her house, her husband John, and their children—that took up all her time. Her first hint that something was amiss came at two a.m., when her husband went to check on a crying child (it was just a bad dream) and noticed that the light on the back porch was lit. The rule of the house was the last one home turned off that light, but Joseph's car was not in the driveway, meaning he had not returned from wherever he had gone the evening before. Four hours later, when John Fitzgerald headed for the factory and Frances began preparations for breakfast, that porch light was still on, though Joseph's gray Chrysler was back.

He had not come down by seven-thirty. She knew his workday at the hospital began at seven, so she tapped on his door, concerned he had overslept. He called out that he was feeling ill and would be starting work late, if at all. Midmorning, as she hung the wash on the line, Joseph appeared at his back window and asked where he might find some Band-Aids. In the family bathroom, she said, then decided it would be simpler to send seven-year-old Timmy up than to have her boarder rummaging around in her medicine cabinet.

After that, strangers began appearing. A Dr. Weinberg showed up at about four p.m., introducing himself as a chemist at Norwalk Hospital, also employed by Dr. Boas, whom Joseph had periodically mentioned. He was carrying a bottle of white liquid—Kaopectate, it turned out. Frances showed him the stairs at the end of the kitchen that led to Joe's room, and Dr. Weinberg came back down several minutes later, without the medication. At five p.m., Frances sent Timmy in again, and the boy relayed back a request for some broth, cigarettes, and a newspaper.

At about six-fifteen, Frances carried up a tray herself, including the afternoon edition of the *Norwalk Hour*, its front page filled with the story of a policeman who'd been shot in Stamford the night before. She did not send Timmy with these because little boys should not be reading about murder. Joseph was, to her relief, fully dressed, though his outfit was unusual: a heavy woolen bathrobe (in July) over street trousers. He was shivering in a warm room with the windows closed, and sweating as he shivered, appearing extremely pale. At seven p.m. she returned for the tray, told Joseph how sorry she was that he was sick, and asked if there was anything else she might do for him. He asked, again, for cigarettes. She brought them, though she did not think they were likely to cure whatever it was that ailed him.

At eight p.m. Dr. Boas was at the door, saying Dr. Weinberg had been concerned after his earlier visit, and so he had come to see for himself. Joseph was still sitting in his easy chair, robe still over his clothes, still pale and sweaty. He assured Dr. Boas he'd be fine—just a touch of food poisoning from his lunch the day before at the little diner down the road from the hospital. He'd been up most of the night with GI symptoms, he said. (*You weren't here most of the night,* Frances thought.) He had vomited several times and suffered severe abdominal pains.

"Get on your bed so I can examine your abdomen," Dr. Boas said, but Joseph shook his head. His appendix had been removed several years ago, he said (he did not say "while in prison," Boas noticed, meaning Frances did not know about his past?), and therefore what was the point of an abdominal exam? If this was just a GI upset, it would run its course. He was exhausted, he told Boas, and would "rather not make the effort to get up and into bed."

Dr. Boas was late for an eight-thirty staff meeting, so he said goodbye, asking Joe to promise to call if his symptoms failed to improve and inviting him to his home in Wilton for the weekend where he could rest, teach his children more magic tricks, and have home-cooked meals. He passed Frances Fitzgerald as he came downstairs and suggested she might bring up ginger ale, tea, or more broth. When she did so a few minutes later, Joseph told her he was expecting a visitor, a nurse's aide named Roseann Perry, who would be arriving shortly, after she put her son to bed.

Indeed, there was a knock on the door at about nine p.m., far later than the Fitzgeralds were accustomed to receiving guests. Roseann Perry turned out to be a young woman in her twenties who took pains to explain that she and Joseph were work friends (a *just* seemed implied). He had asked her to bring over some cigarettes, she said, even though the paper bag in her hand was shaped like a bottle, not a carton. Frances showed her the way to Joseph's room. About twenty minutes later the younger woman walked back into the kitchen and asked for tonic or soda water. Frances could find only a bottle of Tom Collins mix, which was certainly not on the list of fluids Dr. Boas had recommended. Roseann Perry brought it up the stairs, and Frances went up to bed.

Saturday, July 9, 1960
Joe DeSalvo
Norwalk

THINGS DID NOT IMPROVE OVERNIGHT AT THE FITZGERALD HOUSE. Joe made it from the chair to the bed, which was where Frances found him when she brought up yet another tray, this one with dry cereal, tea, and milk. Roseann Perry had left. The forecast was for a scorcher in the nineties, and already the radio was reporting that parking at some area beaches was full. Yet Joe was still in his woolen robe, lying under a cotton blanket, shivering. He lifted the cup of tea and wrapped his hands around it, as if for comfort and for warmth.

The phone rang, yet again, and Frances left to answer it, returning to say it was a person-to-person call for Joseph DeSalvo, and the operator had said it was urgent. To her surprise, he did not jump out of bed. He made no move at all. "I'll be there in a minute," he said, in a tone that made it clear she was expected to leave.

When he did appear, he was walking with noticeable difficulty. He grimaced with each step, taking several minutes to navigate the stairs and cross the kitchen. His landlady gave him his privacy, and when she heard the phone click back in its cradle, she reappeared and helped him to a nearby chair.

His brother had died, he told her. His name was Charles, same as his father's. That was his mother calling. There'd been a motorcycle accident Thursday night. He laughed, but not with amusement. His family's curse was motorcycles, he said.

Frances expressed her condolences, then asked about his difficulty walking. He looked abashed and said he had fainted while walking to the bathroom in the middle of the night and had apparently wrenched his knee as he hit the floor. He'd be fine, he said, but admitted that he was worried about getting to Chicago for the funeral on Monday. How would he navigate airports and an airplane with such a bad sprain? And what if he had a relapse of his stomach ailment? He did not want to arrive ill and be a burden to his parents.

Just then, Roseann Perry knocked on the screen door. She had brought a bottle of ginger ale, along with the money from the paycheck Joe had given her to cash last night. She had also brought her eight-year-old son, which puzzled Frances Fitzgerald. She told her children to play in the yard with the boy. While they did, Roseann helped her work colleague back up to his room, where they sat and talked for a while—about the logistics of returning home, about the sole decoration on his walls, a certificate awarded to him by the U.S. Army for agreeing to contract malaria.

"You were in the army?" she asked.

"Navy," he answered. "But I volunteered for this army experiment."

Roseann invited him to her home for dinner that night; she'd come pick him up, and it would do him some good to get out of the house. Eventually her son came up to say it was time to leave. Frances was making lunch for her own children, and she had not invited him to join them.

At four-thirty Dr. Boas called, and Joe inched his way back down to the phone. He told his boss about his hurt knee, though this time Frances heard him say he had slammed it against the toilet while being sick, not that he had fainted. Then he told Dr. Boas about his brother's death and his concerns about getting to Chicago for the funeral. He couldn't drive to the airport because his injury was to his right knee. Lowering his voice, he added that he would need to get permission to travel and was not sure how to go about it.

Dr. Boas offered to reach out to the parole officer himself, sparing Joe from having that conversation on the phone in his landlord's kitchen. Over the next several hours, Dr. Boas had a taste of what it was like to jump through the hoops of the prison system. He dialed Charles Hewes, the name on Joe's employment file as his parole officer, but it was Saturday and there was no answer. Then he tried the general number for the Connecticut Prison Association in Bridgeport, where Hewes worked, but there was no answer there, either. His next call was to the Westport Police Barracks, where he asked the desk sergeant for general information on how to contact a parole officer— any parole officer. The sergeant's only suggestion was to contact the nearby Wethersfield Prison, where an operator gave him the names of two parole officers who might direct him to the proper authorities. The first man he dialed told him to call a Charles McGrath, who worked for the Connecticut Prison Association, which was where Dr. Boas had begun hours earlier.

Charles McGrath answered his home phone. Dr. Boas described the situation. McGrath said that as the "employer of record," Dr. Boas could authorize a parolee's departure, as long as Joe sent McGrath a letter "indicating the purpose of the trip, the date and time of departure, where he would stay while in Chicago, and the date and time of return." After jotting down McGrath's address, Dr. Boas called the Fitzgeralds and asked for Joe.

He's not here, Frances said, and for a moment the doctor thought Joe was already on his way to Chicago. No, the landlady said, Roseann Perry had returned and picked him up a short while ago, but he'd left her number in case Dr. Boas called. Then Frances hung up and went back to preparing the onion dip for the dinner guests who would be arriving any minute.

When Dr. Boas called Roseann Perry's number, Joe told him that he'd made a reservation for the next morning on TWA Flight 215, departing from LaGuardia at eleven-thirty. He accepted the doctor's offer to drive him to the airport, and they agreed to meet at nine o'clock Sunday morning.

Meanwhile, as the Fitzgeralds' small Saturday-night gathering began, the telephone rang yet again. It was another doctor, one named Tarlov, who Mrs. Fitzgerald remembered calling months earlier to offer a reference for Joe.

"Is Joseph DeSalvo at this number?"

"I'm afraid he is out with his lady friend," she said, more brusque than usual. She did not offer to take a message.

Sunday, July 10, 1960
6 a.m.
Al Tarlov
Madison

AL TARLOV WAS RUNNING ON THE BEACH, BARELY AWARE OF THE beauty of the rising sun. Running was what he did to clear his mind. In Joliet he ran eight miles every day before work. But here on vacation, each footfall seemed only to muddle his thoughts, not to settle them. Ever since he'd seen the newspaper headlines on Friday, he could think of nothing other than the murdered Stamford police officer and the possibility that he might know the man who killed him.

The priests on the neighboring blanket that afternoon had seemed determined to linger over those papers, and Al sat feigning nonchalance until they finally folded the pages and placed the squared pile beside them. Ever so quietly, in order not to startle his wife, who was asleep in the sun, he had crossed the short distance and asked, "May I borrow this if you're through?"

Nothing he'd read made him feel any better.

"A man about six feet tall weighing approximately 175 to 185 pounds."

"Blond hair and a cowlick."

"Dressed in a white shirt, tan or beige sports jacket, grey trousers . . . white scarf around his neck."

So he had walked back up to the hotel and called the Norwalk Hospital, where Joe DeSalvo should have been at work on a Friday afternoon. Facts, Al thought, would be the antidote to his imagination; a quick phone check would prove that Joe was where he should be, at the lab bench, not on the run from the law. The purpose of science was to separate coincidence from cause and effect. *"Correlation is not causality"* had been drilled into him over the years. Also popular with his professors: *"When you hear hoofbeats, think horse, not zebra."* By that they meant that the most likely explanation was almost always the simplest one, and "the man I helped parole is wanted for murder in Stamford" was neither likely nor simple.

The call to the hospital had not been of much help. "He's out sick today," a Dr. Weinberg told Al. "Stomach bug. I brought him some Kaopectate. The boss is heading over later today to check on him."

He kept his fears to himself as long as he could, finally sharing them with Joan at dinner Saturday night, breaking their promise that they would not discuss work while on vacation. She tried her best to reassure him. Surely Dr. Boas would notice if something were amiss? If Al was really that concerned, she suggested, why not call Joe directly and see how he was feeling?

Skipping dessert, the couple returned to their room, where Al dialed the Fitzgeralds' number. Joe's landlady answered, a voice Al recognized from when he'd offered a reference for Joe a few months ago. Al reintroduced himself and asked if her tenant was at home.

"He's out," she'd said a bit curtly. "With his lady friend."

Joan was delighted by this news. "Told you not to worry," she said, teasing Al a bit. "Who shoots a policeman and then goes out on a date?"

They would laugh about it later, she predicted. Al would tell Joe how his imagination had run away with him, and they would chuckle at the absurdity. Before long Joan fell into a sound untroubled sleep, tired from the sun and sand, knowing she would not be awakened by the needs of children. Al, however, had barely slept at all, replaying his wife's words and realizing he had never once heard Joseph DeSalvo laugh. How could he have missed that? How well did he really know the man?

That was how he came to be running along Madison Beach at dawn on Sunday, trying and failing to put the whole mess out of his mind. He arrived back at the hotel as the morning papers were delivered to the lobby. Lifting one off the top of the pile, he found himself staring at a police sketch that seemed to be staring back.

It could be him.

It couldn't be.

Al had no choice but to check for himself.

He approached the front desk and told the clerk, "I'm afraid we will be checking out this morning. Something has come up, and we will need to get back home sooner than we'd planned."

Sunday, July 10, 1960
Joe DeSalvo and Al Tarlov
Norwalk

JOE HAD RETURNED TO HIS RENTED ROOM IN THE EARLY HOURS of Sunday morning, still in pain, still wearing too many layers for a hot summer, now carrying a roll of ACE bandage. Roseann Perry had tried to wrap his knee but could not push his pant leg high enough, so she sent him home with supplies to do it himself. John Fitzgerald excused himself from the dinner party to offer Joe both an ice bag and a heating pad. That left Frances to explain to their guests who the injured man was and how he had been a very bland tenant until yesterday, when he became an embodiment of misfortune.

Dr. Boas arrived the next morning to find Joe still limping. He offered to take a look, and Joe raised his khakis up to the level of his knee, which looked swollen even from across the room where the Fitzgeralds were standing. Dr. Boas tapped and palpated it, reporting fluid beneath the kneecap. Joe would need crutches, and since Dr. Boas was already planning to stop by Norwalk Hospital on the way to the airport, he would have Joe checked out in the emergency room there.

Dr. Boas and John Fitzgerald carried Joe's two bags to the car and put them in the trunk while Joe walked slowly and tentatively behind. It took a full minute for him to get his injured leg up into the front passenger seat. He grimaced the entire time.

"You hungry?" Dr. Boas asked as he pulled onto Ward Avenue and suggested a stop at Mar-Sam's diner, a few blocks away. Joe said he was not hungry and would sit and wait in the car. Dr. Boas had some toast and a cup of coffee and was back within ten minutes.

They drove on to the hospital, where Dr. Boas asked an orderly to bring a wheelchair from the emergency entrance. "After considerable agonizing effort," as Dr. Boas described it later, Joe was able to transfer himself into the chair. The doctor was becoming increasingly worried. He didn't see how this man, who could hardly walk, was going to navigate his way to Chicago.

While Dr. Boas went off to see patients, Dr. John Wilson, an ER surgeon, was looking at Joe's leg and not liking what he saw. Once Dr. Boas returned, Wilson instructed Joe to lower his trousers once again so they could both examine the area. As the surgeon would write in the chart, there was "a massive hemorrhage extending along the inner aspect of his right thigh from the groin down several inches above the knee. On the inner aspect of the thigh, approximately four or five inches below the groin, there was a large firm swelling which appeared yellow in contrast to the deep reddish-purple appearance of the remainder of this area. There was no break in the skin at this point. Since we were in a rush to catch his airplane, the examination was not pursued any further. He was not asked to remove his undershorts. His abdomen was not examined, nor was the [groin] region on the right side examined."

Joe left the ER with a wrapped thigh, a pair of crutches, and a packet of pain pills. He inched his leg back into the car, and Dr. Boas headed south on the Connecticut Thruway. As they crossed into New York, Joe realized he had not mailed the letter to Charles McGrath at the Connecticut parole office. Fishing it out of his pocket, he read it aloud to Dr. Boas, who agreed it met the requirements outlined by McGrath and promised to mail it when he returned home.

They took the Hutchinson River Parkway to the Whitestone Bridge, through Queens, to LaGuardia Airport. Dr. Boas got out of the car first and secured yet another wheelchair. The porter suggested driving the car directly to gate nine, at the back of the building. It was 11:15 when Joe handed the doctor eighty-four dollars in cash to pay for the pre-reserved ticket, and 11:20 when the doctor returned with the ticket, a boarding pass, and a baggage claim receipt. Dr. Boas helped Joe to the gate and watched him limp toward the plane. Then he got back on the road, arriving home at twelve-thirty. Finding a stamp in his desk, he put the letter in the mailbox in front of the house, to be picked up the next morning.

Late that same afternoon came yet another knock on the Fitzgeralds' door. Frances opened it to a compact man, about her age, wearing spectacles, a business suit, and a polite smile. She predicted what he would say before he said it.

"I am looking for Joseph DeSalvo. Is he at home?"

"You just missed him. And you are . . . ?"

The man extended his hand. "Dr. Alvin Tarlov. I believe we have spoken before. Do you know when Mr. DeSalvo might return?"

"I do not. He was on his way to the hospital to get some crutches."

"Crutches?"

"He sprained his knee. Or banged it. Maybe a boil? It became infected. He was having trouble walking, so Dr. Boas drove him to the emergency room."

"Dr. Boas is there with him?" Al asked.

"Doubt it. That was hours ago. Then they went to the airport, and I think his plane would have left by now?"

"The airport?"

"LaGuardia."

"Dr. Boas was traveling?"

"No. Joseph. He is flying to Chicago."

Al must have looked as confused and concerned as he felt because Frances added, "For a funeral. His brother died on Thursday night in some sort of accident."

Al mumbled his thanks, backed down the steps, and headed for his car, all the while wondering whether he was hearing horses or zebras.

Joe happened to get hurt at the same time a police officer was shot? Coincidence. The police sketch of the gunman looked a lot like Joe? Those sketches look like everyone. The knee injury caused by a fall in the bathroom was so severe that it required crutches and caused an infection? Highly unlikely, but possible.

That Joe—a man on parole, who was not permitted to leave the state, and who had never been on a plane—absolutely needed to travel halfway across the country just as a manhunt for someone who looked like him ramped up near his new home? And that the reason he had to leave town so suddenly was because of a brother who just happened to die on the very same night as the officer? What were the odds of all that?

They were, Al decided, impossible. He drove back to Shorefront Park, headed up to his parents' study, and called the Stamford Police.

Sunday, July 10, 1960
5 p.m.
Leo P. Gallagher Funeral Home
Stamford

THE WAKE HAD BEEN UNDERWAY FOR TWO DAYS NOW. MORE than one thousand people had signed the guest book, then filed past the casket where Dave lay amid hundreds of floral arrangements, wearing his blue uniform, holding his cap in his hands, his badge pinned above his heart.

The fatal bullet had hit the right side of Dave's chest, and as Bruce Williams stood over the open casket, he found himself wondering— what if he'd been hit on the left side instead? Would the badge have stopped it? But you could play that game forever, he decided. What if Dave had paused to scratch his nose before running into the alley? What if he had wrenched his back while trying to lift the unconscious drunk on Main Street, or gotten up fifteen minutes earlier or later that morning. What if—as every single person he'd spoken to in the past forty-eight hours had speculated—Dave had not filled in for Red Corbin? Would Dave and Rosie be having their usual Sunday dinner with her mother right now? There were so many things that, had they happened differently, would have changed everything. With all those *maybes*, you simply had to accept that there was only one way that anything was ever going to happen, that it was all meant to be, Bruce thought. Otherwise you could lose your mind.

Both Dave's shield and his hat, Bruce guessed, had been sent over from the evidence room, where they would be returned, to be used if there was ever a suspect and a trial. That must be the protocol when a Stamford officer was killed. Then again, maybe there was no protocol, as this was the first time it had happened in the city's history. Dave's uniform, he noticed, looked somewhat worn; the blue of his "blouse," his summer-weight jacket, was faded slightly, and one cuff was fraying. The department issued officers a new set of uniforms every three years, and Bruce had just picked up his own a few weeks ago. It looked like Dave had been almost due for a replacement as well.

Rosie Troy sat on the far side of the room, crying. One thousand people walked past the casket, then to her chair. Many were familiar— colleagues of Dave's from the department, former classmates from Wright Tech, old customers from the gas station, friends from the neighborhood. Others were complete strangers. They wanted to tell her about the time Officer Troy rescued their cat or winked in place of writing them a parking ticket or held their hand while waiting for an ambulance. Some had never met Dave, didn't recall if they'd ever seen him, but they wanted to come anyway, to pay their respects. His twenty-five-year-old widow clasped hundreds of hands, listened to thousands of words of condolence, accepted kisses and hugs, and received offers of help. "If there is anything we can do," Bruce heard them say again and again. "Anything at all, just ask."

Bruce had been one of those people earlier in the day. He had never met Dave's wife before. He had introduced himself to Rosie, told her he had trained Dave in his early months, said that even as a rookie he had had all the makings of a good cop. "If there is anything I can do," he said, then let the sentence trail, because he knew how empty it sounded.

Unless.

Bruce Williams went home, took off his brand-new summer-weight blouse, and hung it gently on a hanger. Then he dressed himself in the older version that was still in his closet. He returned to the funeral parlor, asked to speak with whoever was in charge, and handed over the brand-new garment. Dave was about his size. He would be buried wearing the crisp uniform that he deserved.

Monday, July 11, 1960
Rosie Troy
Stamford

THIS TIME THE MOTORCYCLE OFFICERS LED THE PROCESSION.
Half a dozen riders, all of whom had been trained and befriended
by David Troy, donned their helmets, lowered their sunshields, and
let their sirens wail. It was a quarter-mile from the funeral home to
St. Mary's Church. More than six thousand people lined the route
along Elm Street, bowing their heads as the cortege passed. Police
Chief Joseph Kinsella walked behind the motorcycles and ahead of
the hearse, followed by members of the board of public safety and
other Stamford officials. The six pallbearers in the procession were all
fellow officers. Christopher Kanel was among them. Red Corbin was
not—he was still in critical condition.

The rest of the Norwalk Police force, more than two hundred men,
marched behind the hearse, which was barely visible beneath the
mounds of flowers. Behind the Norwalk officers were three hundred
others, from elsewhere in Connecticut and New York City. A police
officer never dies alone.

At the corner of Elm and Shippan, the uniformed men saluted
toward what used to be the Troy Service Station. Then they took their
seats in the church, creating a sea of blue. The pallbearers lifted the
casket and entered the stained-glass-and-stone sanctuary in silence.
This was the church in which Dave had been raised, where he had
served as an altar boy, where his oldest daughter, Doreen, was readying to start kindergarten in the fall, and where his mother, Bridget,
prayed every Sunday. Now his sobbing mother was following his
weeping wife down the center aisle, a bride in reverse. Rosie was leaning on the arm of her brother-in-law, Agnes's husband. Bridget was

clinging to her son, Patrick. Dave's children were home in the care of their teenage cousins, playing in the yard with Tinker. Rosie had not found a way to tell them yet.

Eulogies were not the norm for a solemn requiem mass, but the Rt. Rev. Msgr. John J. Hayes made an exception and gave one at the end of the service. He offered the sympathy of the entire city to the "inconsolable widow." He praised Dave as "a solid Christian young man" and a "devoted father and loyal husband," who had met a "hero's end."

"I could not wish for him a fairer death," he said, slightly altering *Macbeth* for the occasion, then adding, "To die in the line of duty, representing law and order, is the greatest thing that can be said for any policeman."

Rosie, sitting stoically, could certainly think of a fairer way for him to die: at home in bed well into his eighties with his grown children and grandchildren beside him, for instance. Still, she took comfort in the fact that Dave was a believer. She prayed that he was doing what Frank had described—helping Saint Peter protect and serve.

An eternity and a moment later, the service ended and everyone marched back out—the five hundred officers, the dignitaries, the family and friends, the pallbearers, the priests. At the corner of Elm and Main, not far from where Dave had waved to his family during the Memorial Day parade, the officers formed lines on either side of the road and saluted as the hearse passed between them. Then the smaller group proceeded another three miles to St. John's Cemetery, where Dave would lie forever near his father and his baby brother.

A motorcycle escort led the way.

July 11 to 13, 1960
Al Tarlov
Norwalk

DAVID TROY WAS BURIED ON AL TARLOV'S THIRTY-FIRST BIRTH-
day. The Tarlovs spent the day doing birthday things at Shorefront
Park, taking the kids to the beach, teaching the older ones how to
ride bikes in the driveway, singing "Happy Birthday." Mae baked.
Charlie barbecued. Joan napped. Al left periodically to listen to news
reports on the radio or to drive into town to get the afternoon edition
of the paper.

"Work," he said, when asked. He hadn't told his parents of his suspicions, and although he had shared them with Joan, he didn't tell her
that he had given Joe's name to the Stamford Police. He said nothing
because he might be wrong, though he didn't really think he was. A
dispassionate look at the available facts said he was right, but then
again, his reading of available facts had led him to mentor Joe in the
first place. One way or the other—trusting Joe earlier, suspecting him
now—he had made a terrible mistake.

Al had spent his thirty-one years trying not to make mistakes. He
believed they were avoidable with the right amount of thought and
deliberation. Even when you took a best guess based on the odds, it
was because you first took the time to establish those odds and to
know what you were risking. Such was the nature of science: there
was a best answer and a way to find it. It wasn't that he didn't recognize complexity or uncertainty; rather, he delighted in them, saw
them as challenges to be conquered. If something was complicated or
unpredictable, it was because you hadn't studied it enough to make
it simple. But this wasn't complexity. This was an error. And a man
had died.

Al's Sunday-night call had been relatively simple. He told the officer what he'd learned—Joe's injury, his sudden announcement that he was leaving the state for a funeral, his TWA flight number. Al had Joe's file with him and supplied whatever phone numbers were inside: Dr. Boas. John and Frances Fitzgerald. Charles and Ruth DeSalvo. Al also provided his own parents' number, assuming there would be additional questions. But three days had passed, and no police had called. Nor did news reports contain even a hint that anyone was interested in an ex-con in Chicago.

As Sunday became Monday and then Tuesday, other men were named. By now seventy suspects had been investigated, many turned in by acquaintances who seemed interested in the reward money. The three who had been held the night of the murder had been set free, all fined for minor crimes that would likely not have merited police attention had Dave Troy not been killed. A parade of others took their place, as detectives followed up anything and everything, just in case.

Twenty-seven-year-old Vincent Engdall was briefly questioned. He was on a list of regulars given to the police by the bartender at the Skipper, but he was released when his wife swore he had done his drinking early on the night of the shooting and by nine o'clock had been too drunk to leave the house. H. L. Cromwell, also twenty-seven, also fit the physical description and was also an alcoholic who often loitered in the area, but the bartender at another bar, over on Atlantic Street, said he had been there until at least nine on the night in question. Also, his jaw had been wired shut from a recent operation, so he wouldn't have been able to say "Hey, Mac, look," in any intelligible way.

A painter with the Reliable Paint Company in Darien was described as "a suspicious type" by a former customer, but he was taller than the man police were looking for and spoke with a heavy accent. A man with known mob connections was picked up in Westchester at the request of the Stamford Police. His alibi, that he was at a family cookout from four to eleven p.m., was corroborated, and he had no sign of scrapes or wounds. "He was told of the reward offer

316 GENEALOGY OF A MURDER

and was very co-operative," a police spokesman said to reporters; the mob man had even supplied a list of names of people "he believed would be capable of committing this type of crime." All of them had alibis, too.

When it was not chronicling suspects-who-weren't, the *Stamford Advocate* gave over its front page to a detailed daily account of the Troy Fund, created by the publisher to help the slain officer's children. Its first contributions had come from Chris Kanel ($50) and Stamford mayor J. Walter Kennedy ($50). By Tuesday the total had reached $1,927.32, including $32.25 in dimes, quarters, and nickels from the piggy bank of twelve-year-old Sandra Tulinski and her brother Joseph, six. On Wednesday morning, the fund was up to $2,787.38, including several gifts from local businesses that had put collection jars out by their cash registers. A groom's friends at his stag dinner at the Genovese Steak House collected seventy dollars and sent it in honor of the soon-to-be Mr. and Mrs. Robert Grogins. The employees of Food Fair pooled $94.25. Mary Ronan gave two weeks of her allowance, a total of two dollars. The patrons of Boots' Seaview Restaurant, where Rosie had once discovered that Doreen and Diane were regulars, gave $102. Peter Castelluzzo, whose daughter had been dubbed "Stamford's Blue Baby" by this same newspaper in 1946, and who had died despite the city's generosity, gave ten dollars in her honor.

It was minutiae masquerading as news, Al thought, as each edition told him nothing. (It did prompt him to make his own anonymous donation to the Troy Fund, however.) Then on Wednesday morning, as the fund total topped $3,000, local front pages blared the fact that police were "more than casually interested" in an out-of-state suspect. The state was not Illinois, and the suspect was not Joe DeSalvo.

POSSIBLE NEW JERSEY LINK REPORTED IN TROY SLAYING, the headline read. Al read with fascination, frustration, and a touch of relief. Reading the coverage, he could certainly see why the authorities were focusing on this "possible link" rather than following his own leads.

Michael Fekecs was a twenty-five-year-old Hungarian immigrant who, two days after David Troy's murder, had been stopped for driving wildly in Franklin Township, New Jersey. The police who chased and caught him charged him with driving with a suspended license, the third time he'd been so charged in less than a year. The two young officers impounded Fekecs's late-model Lincoln Continental and headed with him toward the Somerset County Jail, where they and their prisoner assumed he would be ordered released on $250 bail. Fekecs charmed the officers into detouring past his apartment, though, so he could get cash for his bond. At about six-thirty Sunday evening, both officers were found dead in that apartment, each with a single shot through the back of the head.

A ballistics check showed that the .32-caliber pistol that killed them had also been used in a sensational unsolved murder in New Jersey in January of that year. Four victims had been found bound and dead in a wealthy doctor's home, also from a single bullet to the brain. Cash and jewelry were missing. Failure to solve that case had been a political albatross for the mayor and police chief at the time. Now two police officers were dead by the same gun, and a manhunt was underway that rivaled the one in Stamford.

Were they perhaps searching for the same man? Had Fekecs, having spent the money from the January robbery, somehow made his way to Stamford and sought to replenish his funds by robbing local taverns? He certainly had been leading a flashy life in recent months. Described by one friend as "a real nut with big cars and fancy clothes," he owned a black jaguar convertible, a pea-green Edsel convertible, an MG, and two Lincolns, some of which he had actually paid for. He loved jazz clubs and was a self-taught talent, taking the stage periodically to jam with the band. A search of his apartment found five cummerbunds, in red, gold, black and silver, and twenty-two LPs, most of them jazz. He earned eighty dollars a week at the Westinghouse plant in Edison, New Jersey, which was not enough to pay for even one of the cars.

Police also found several additional guns, although they would not say whether any were 9-mm, which would match the bullets found at the scene on Greyrock. They learned that Fekecs had a knowledge of weapons or claimed he did—he had purportedly gained entry to the United States after describing himself as a Hungarian freedom fighter, fleeing the Communist government after participating in a failed revolt, a story the police now doubted.

Newspapers ran photos of Fekecs, who fit the description of the Troy shooter. Articles noted an eerie similarity: one of the officers he'd slain had, like Troy, been filling in for a colleague on vacation. To Al, Fekecs, in the photo, looked exactly like Joe DeSalvo—the same oblong face, the same high forehead, even, looking closely, the same acne scars. Al rooted for this man's capture, the questioning that would follow, and the possible answers it would provide.

Then he opened Wednesday's paper and read that a woman in Union, New Jersey, had called police to report a shirtless man, matching the fugitive's description, hiding in the woods near her house. The first officer on the scene fired three shots, one of which hit the man, who was indeed Fekecs, right between the eyes. He was taken to Elizabeth General Hospital, where he remained in a coma, with two officers standing guard. He was not expected to survive.

Connecticut reporters peppered Stamford Police about a possible link between the hospitalized man and the Troy case.

"We haven't sent any men to Union yet," Chief Kinsella said, "but I have been in contact with the Union Police Department. The description of Fekecs matches Troy's killer very closely."

As for the captain of detectives, William J. Lynch, the *Stamford Advocate* reported that he was "not at his desk in the Detective Bureau this morning, and it was not stated where he was. No one would say whether he had left for Union."

Maybe Joe wasn't guilty after all, Al thought. Maybe he did have food poisoning, did faint on the way to the bathroom, did not take a bullet to the leg. Maybe his brother really had died in a motorcycle crash, and perhaps he had raced off to Chicago the next day for the funeral. Maybe Al's instincts weren't wrong after all, and Joe really was a changed man who deserved a fresh start. Maybe Al was not a woeful judge of character but just a by-the-book doctor who lived in a world of parasites and genes, not one of killers and con men. Maybe anything otherwise was his imagination.

Wednesday, July 13, 1960
Joe DeSalvo
Chicago

JOE REALLY DID GO TO CHICAGO FOR HIS BROTHER'S FUNERAL. On the night of Thursday, July 7, Charles DeSalvo, Jr., had been a passenger on a motorcycle in downtown St. Louis, flying along without a helmet and above the speed limit. The driver was twenty-two-year-old Clarence Miller, with whom Charles worked at Allied Van Lines. At nine-fifteen p.m., a woman stepped off the curb directly into their path. Clarence swerved to avoid hitting her and smashed head-long into a concrete pylon.

Both men died en route to the hospital. The coroner listed their time of death as nine-thirty Central Time, which was ten-thirty in Stamford, where Rosie Troy had been saying her last goodbyes to Dave.

It had taken Ruth a while to contact Joe. They had not spoken since he left Chicago for Norwalk. She had the phone number for the hospital where he worked, but when she called there on Friday morning, July 8, she was told he was out sick. On Saturday she tried again, and this time the hospital switchboard operator looked up the number for the Fitzgeralds. Ruth did not ask Joe to come home but was pleasantly surprised when he said he would. She was even more surprised when he said he would pay for his airline ticket himself.

Things had not been going well for Joe's parents. Charles Sr. was essentially bedridden with an ailing heart; Ruth was experiencing symptoms that she preferred not to discuss, involving her digestive tract, her appetite, and severe abdominal pain. They had not shared these things with Joe, but he could tell they were ill the moment he walked through the door. His father was short of breath, his feet so swollen he could not wear shoes. His mother was frail to the point of being skeletal, had no appetite, and showed a yellow tinge to her skin.

While he did a visual scan of his parents, they were doing the same to him: the crutches, the fact that he winced anytime he was inadvertently jostled. The neighbor who had brought Joe from the airport had offered to carry his bags into the apartment because Joe couldn't begin to lift them himself. Two large heavy bags. How long did he plan to stay? Ruth had to choose which version of the story she preferred: the one where Joe was a success who could pay for his own flight and who would soon return to his excellent job in Connecticut; or the one where he had missed his family and was coming home to stay and help his parents through their grief. She did not fantasize a version where he was in trouble and fleeing the law.

Joe explained that he had suffered ptomaine poisoning, fainted, and injured his leg. He spent all of Sunday on the couch, and that afternoon, when his brother's ex-wife, Doris, came to visit with her two daughters, she tried to help him change the bandage on his knee. He moaned and bit his lip, so she gave up. Some friends of Doris arrived later, one of them a nurse, and she and Joe went out that evening for a few hours to find him a better pain medication. He came home looking even more drained than when he'd left, and he slept on the couch because it would have taken too much out of him to climb the stairs to his old bedroom.

On Monday, Charles's body arrived from St. Louis, and the DeSalvos went to the funeral home for the wake. Joe could not stay still during the hours he was there, standing up every few minutes to hobble around on his crutches and then sit down again. His leg ached terribly if left in one position too long, he said.

Tuesday was the funeral. Joe was clearly suffering, and Ruth suggested he stay home. "I came into town to go to the funeral, and I'm going," he snapped. The same neighbor who'd picked him up from the airport drove him to the Mount Carmel Catholic Cemetery, and during the ride Joe lay lengthwise in the back seat, holding his leg.

The man drove as slowly as he could, but even the slightest bump caused Joe to cry out.

The funeral was particularly bleak. This Charles Jr. was buried under the same five-foot pillar that marked the grave of the first Charles Jr. Annunziata and Michal's headstones were within view, as were those of the Volpe and Iannucci families, into which the DeSalvo sisters had married. There were far more dead DeSalvos looking on at the service than living ones. Still alive, but not in attendance, was Charles Sr.'s brother, Joseph. The twins had not spoken in years.

During the short service, Ruth seethed silently at her husband. Their boy had died on a motorcycle. The sins of the father. Charles Sr., meanwhile, felt disappointment bordering on shame. His son had not even been at the wheel when that motorcycle crashed. He had been riding on the back of the bike, arms around the driver like a girl. Joe, in visible pain from his injured leg, did his best to make small talk with his ex-sister-in-law and his nieces once the ceremony ended. But he had little to say.

The group returned home in the same two-car caravan that had brought them. Doris drove ahead, with Ruth, Charles Sr., and the girls. When she turned onto LaPorte Avenue, she saw a police wagon in front of the house, flashing lights signaling they meant business. As she pulled to a stop at the driveway, at least a half-dozen officers swarmed her car, guns drawn.

"Hands in the air, get on the ground!" the men yelled, and even Charles Sr., as frail as he was, managed to comply, sliding off the passenger seat and onto the patchy lawn.

The officers were shouting for Joe—*Where is Joseph? Which one of you is Joseph?*—when a second car appeared and stopped behind the first. Several officers turned their attention to the new arrival, pointing their weapons at the back passenger door.

"Hands where we can see them!" the policemen yelled, and Joseph Eugene DeSalvo stretched his arms out in front of him, holding a crutch in each one. Then he rose, very slowly, and stood by the opened car door, trying to balance on his one good leg.

✦

CAPTAIN OF DETECTIVES WILLIAM J. Lynch had not been at his desk
in police headquarters in Stamford when local reporters came by,
because he had been on a plane to Chicago. Michael Fekecs had never
been a suspect—he was a convenient coincidental diversion.

The information that Al Tarlov shared had swiftly made its way up
the chain of command. Stamford detectives called Joe's parole officer, Charles Hewes, who had just heard from a fellow officer, Charles
McGrath, about the same man. McGrath had received a letter from
DeSalvo that morning, requesting permission to attend a funeral out
of state. McGrath had pulled DeSalvo's file to add the letter when he
noticed it contained a photo of the parolee—one that looked quite a bit
like the newest drawing on the "Wanted" bulletin board in the hall. In
McGrath's experience, parolees on the run from a murder charge did
not check in with their parole officers for permission to leave town.
But just in case, he called the parole officer of record, Charles Hewes,
who agreed to investigate further. Before Hewes could alert the Stamford Police, the Stamford Police were calling him, based on Al Tarlov's tip. Everyone in this game of telephone was now very interested
in Joseph DeSalvo.

Captain Lynch was soon on a plane, accompanied by County Detective Frank Bowes of the state's attorney's office. Al had told them that
the suspect was traveling to Chicago for the funeral of a brother, who
had died in an accident in St. Louis. The St. Louis Police provided the
information that the body of a Charles DeSalvo, Jr., had been shipped
to the Iannucci Funeral Home in Chicago, and the standard funeral
home newspaper announcement said the burial would take plce at
ten a.m. at the Mount Carmel cemetery. The officers briefly considered making the arrest during the funeral, but there are unwritten
rules against police action in places of burial and of worship. Instead,
Lynch, Bowes, three members of the Chicago homicide squad, and
three local patrolmen arrived at 217 LaPorte Avenue, the address of
the suspect's parents.

For a few hours, Joe DeSalvo denied he'd had anything to do with the shooting of Officer David Troy. But as he had during his two previous arrests, he failed a polygraph test and, confronted with that fact, confessed to everything. He gave a seven-page statement admitting to his part in the killing and said he would not fight extradition.

"This is a senseless, useless life," he said of himself as he signed that statement.

Next, the officers took their suspect to retrace his steps during this brief trip to Chicago. They began at an apartment he'd visited his first night in town, the home of the woman he had met via his ex-sister-in-law. The run-down flat on West Fulton Street was rented by a Carol Dwyer and Mary Ellen Gregoria, who, when questioned, described their joint attempts to help remove a bullet from Joe's thigh. He had told them he'd been shot in a bar fight. They had sterilized a razor blade in a pot of boiling water, then swabbed Joe's skin with a bottle of rye. When they sliced into the wound and felt metal hit metal, Joe had screamed so loudly, they had to stop.

Next the suspect directed the officers to the bedroom dresser, where they found a Radom 9-mm Luger pistol, serial number Z-4970, hidden amid the undergarments in the top drawer. The Radom had been produced in a Polish factory that had been seized by the Nazis during the war, and this one was probably a souvenir picked up by an American GI. There was a swastika drawn on one side of the handle and a sketch of Adolf Hitler on the other. Joe said he had bought it that way from a Norwalk pawn shop and insisted that he was attracted not by the drawing but by the twenty-two-dollar price. Police found five cartridges in the automatic's clip, a live cartridge in the chamber, and a box of 9-mm cartridges in the top of a kitchen closet, at the bottom of a box of winter clothing.

At Joe's request, the officers then drove to his parents' house, so he could collect the suitcases he'd brought to Chicago and explain everything to Ruth and Charles, who had been lying facedown in their front yard when he was taken away. Perhaps learning from the story of Fekecs, officers did not permit DeSalvo to enter the house or even leave the car. His mother was brought out to see him.

With Detective Bowes sitting in the front seat, Ruth was allowed to climb into the back with her handcuffed son.

"Joe, what's the matter? Are you in trouble?" she asked.

"Yes, Mom, I'm in serious trouble."

"What did you do?"

"I shot and killed a policeman in Stamford."

"Oh Joey! What's the matter with you? I tried to bring you up to do what is right. We can't help you. You know your father is seriously ill, and this might finish him."

"Don't do anything. Don't spend any money."

Thursday, July 14, 1960
Al Tarlov
Norwalk

AL GOT THE NEWS ALONG WITH NEARLY EVERYONE ELSE IN CON-
necticut, from the morning headlines on what happened to be Joe
DeSalvo's thirty-first birthday.

SAY LOCAL MAN ADMITS KILLING, blared the *Norwalk Hour.* The
subhead said: JOSEPH DESALVO, EX-CONVICT AND LABORATORY TECH-
NICIAN AT NORWALK HOSPITAL, HELD IN CHICAGO FOR MURDER OF
STAMFORD COP.

There were several versions of how the arrest had come about. The
Associated Press story said that the suspect "was seized in the west
side home of his parents after a photograph of him was identified by
a witness of the Stamford tavern robbery." *The New York Times* said
that "Detective William Trefny of Greenwich drew the portrait of
the suspect. Sgt. Daniel Hanraham of the Stamford police then went
through the rogues' gallery of the Connecticut state police until he
was able to match the sketch with a photograph of DeSalvo." The
Stamford Advocate said, "The suspicions of a prison association official and leg work by two policemen are reported to have 'cracked'
the July 7 shooting. . . . Charles McGrath, field director of the state
prison association, became suspicious when the parolee requested
permission to go to Chicago after the shooting" and contacted several other officers who "began checking Norwalk Hospital and after
a day's work, were convinced that DeSalvo was implicated."

None of the descriptions made any mention of Al.

His first call was to Warden Ragen, whose main concern was that
this might bring Stateville's parole process into question. Ragen knew
Darrow's prophecy: "If something serious were to happen under the

system that the warden is trying to carry out . . ." And, in fact, Illinois state's attorney was now bellowing at reporters, "Someone goofed. When he got ten to seventy years, it was the understanding of the court that he . . . would be an old man before he got out of prison. And now he gets out after only nine years?"

Ragen's advice to Al was simple: "Don't talk to the press. Refer all questions to me."

Alf Alving, in turn, was concerned for the future of the army's malaria research. This was the first Dr. Alving had heard about Al securing a job for a prison lab tech upon release, and he was displeased. That surprised Al, who had essentially been following his mentor's lead. After all, Alving had done the same for Charles Ickes, who had been productively employed at the University of Chicago for nearly a year by that time. Dr. Alving conceded the point, with a qualifier. He had known Ickes for fifteen years before vouching for his character. How long had Al known Joe?

"It takes time to really understand a man," Alving said. Still, he assured Al, "You didn't pull the trigger, he did."

Isadore, to whom Al placed his final call, was predictably philosophical. "Trust is a tricky thing," he said. "Too much, and you can get burned. Too little, and you can burn others. But do you want to live in a world where there's no trust?"

Later that day, a reporter from the *Norwalk Hour* called the house. He'd learned it was Al who had arranged Joseph DeSalvo's employment at Norwalk Hospital. Did Al have any comment? Al did as he had been told and directed the caller to the warden. Then Al's father got on the extension and asked to speak to an editor. Years in the restaurant business meant Charlie knew everyone in Norwalk. Al hung up. He didn't want to hear what was said next.

The following morning Al and Joan were packing the station wagon, preparing to drive back to Chicago and whatever was left of his job. Charlie came out with the morning edition of the *Norwalk Hour* and pointed wordlessly to the front page. The lead article was about how Democratic presidential nominee John Kennedy had chosen Texas senator Lyndon Baines Johnson as his running mate, infuriating the South. The offlead was headlined DESALVO BACK, ADMITS TO SLAYING YOUNG OFFICER; HOSPITAL SAYS WARDEN, OTHERS RECOMMENDED HIM FOR JOB HERE. Much of the piece was about how DeSalvo had been flown back to Connecticut the night before, then brought to Stamford Hospital, where a surgeon removed a 9-mm slug from his thigh under local anesthesia. The slug was undergoing ballistics testing to determine whether it had come from Officer David Troy's gun.

Near the end, the writer turned his attention to Al. "DeSalvo's employment at the local hospital resulted from a recommendation by a research physician at the Illinois State prison at Joliet who was formerly associated with Norwalk Hospital and the recommendation of the warden of the prison," the article said. "Both vouched for his technical ability, and both felt that this man's conduct during the past five to seven years was such as to convince them that he had rehabilitative potential."

Then there was a lengthy quote from the recommendation itself— the letter Al had written to Dr. Boas. "A model inmate." "Well-liked and respected." "A tremendous asset in anyone's laboratory." "I have a great deal of faith in Mr. DeSalvo." "Ready to assume his place as a useful citizen in society."

Al read every word but didn't see the two he'd most feared. He wasn't sure if it was the persuasiveness of his father or the influence of his warden, but the name Alvin Tarlov did not appear in this article. It would not appear at all in the coming months, neither in this newspaper nor in any others. Al would not be questioned by police. He would not be called to testify. It would almost be as if his actions had never happened. Only he would know that every day he wondered whether he somehow could have saved David Troy.

Summer 1960
Joe DeSalvo
Bridgeport, Connecticut

PRISONERS HAVING TOO LITTLE TO DO WAS A LONG-STANDING problem at the Fairfield County Jail, although it was less of a problem than it used to be. Before the new wing was completed a year earlier, the eighty-five-year-old building had been overcrowded, understaffed, and prone to escapes. A $650,000 construction project was intended to correct that, bringing in new thinking with the new wing. At the building's dedication, the outgoing sheriff noted that when he'd begun the first of his six terms, his job had been "to make jail tough and terrible." In the decades since then, he said, he'd come around to the view that "confinement itself does not correct anything" and that prison's purpose should be "to help persons who are confined so they can leave feeling their lives have been reconstructed and rebuilt."

Now Fairfield's prisoners tended corn and tomato crops in the jailhouse garden, rebuilt engines in the new machine shop, and worked on the fifteen-man kitchen detail. But Joe, as a "bind-over" who had not yet been tried or sentenced, was not eligible for any of these, though he suspected he would not have been assigned them anyway, as his guards seemed to have separate rules for a cop-killer. The prison had a brand-new nine-bed infirmary, but he didn't even ask about working there. Nor did he volunteer when the Pfizer company enrolled twenty-two inmates in a tolerance trial of medication for diabetes, paying them six dollars for a day during which their blood was drawn seven times after they swallowed large white chalky pills. They didn't want his experience or his blood.

So, Joe spent all his time in his five-by-eight-foot cell or in the common area right beyond it. Up to ten prisoners could be housed in each communal space, but whether on purpose or by happenstance, all the other cells around his were empty. Alone most of the day, he read the books sent over from his room at the Fitzgeralds', wrote in his journal, and replayed how he'd gotten himself into this mess.

He wasn't miserable at first. The rhythms of prison were more familiar, more comfortable, than those of the outside world. In here there were schedules—breakfast at seven-fifteen, lunch at eleven-thirty, dinner at four, Catholic services on Sunday at seven a.m., Protestant services at eight. Here things were given to you—clothes, food, a public defender, a stretch of time to think, a nightly sleeping pill when you needed to stop the thoughts—and there was no need to impress a boss or decide whether to come clean about your past to a young lady or stretch a paycheck to take that young lady to dinner and a drive-in while having enough left over to cover the rent. In here it was easy to make resolutions; out there you had to keep them.

At the start, this was a relief. But as the hours became days and then weeks, the realization grew that this time was different. Even if, by some miracle, Joe were not convicted of (and executed for) first-degree murder, he would still be locked up again for all the parole violations he had committed that the authorities knew about—owning a gun, drinking alcohol with Roseann Perry, staying out past nine-thirty at night. He would have no more parole hearings; whatever the number on his prediction report, he'd made it clear he was a parole risk. Looking into the small mirror over his metal bunk bed, he had to face the fact that the man looking back, in the denim pants and shirt, had become all he was ever going to be. If there had ever been a time when he could change his future, it had passed.

By late July, Joe had stopped eating. He no longer went to the dining hall, and he barely touched the food that was brought to him in his cell. Before long he just sat on his bunk all day, staring straight ahead, not saying a word. The deputy warden called the jail psychiatrist, reporting that the prisoner was "acting peculiarly" and "seemed catatonic."

He was taken by ambulance to the Fairfield State Mental Hospital in Newtown and involuntarily committed for thirty days. He had no idea where—or who—he was until he "woke up" at the end of August, or so he insisted to his doctors. Then he tried to escape by threatening to stab an attendant in the neck with a piece of glass; he was subdued and heavily medicated. He somehow unscrewed a lightbulb, smashed it, and tried to cut his wrists with the shards; he was medicated again and put on suicide watch. Every time, when the drugs wore off, he denied remembering anything.

In September he was returned to the Fairfield County Jail, many pounds thinner and sufficiently subdued. At the end of the month, a grand jury spent a day hearing testimony from twenty-five witnesses, then spent three minutes indicting Joseph DeSalvo for the first-degree murder of Officer David Troy. Joe pleaded not guilty because that was his only option. His court-appointed attorney, a seemingly capable and thorough man named John F. James, explained that in a capital case, state law requires a not guilty plea and a full trial. If he was found guilty at that trial, the penalty would be death, unless the jury recommended mercy, in which case the penalty would be life with no possibility of release. Technically the board of pardons could vote to commute his sentence one day. But James warned that in recent years the board had clamped down on parole for recidivists, tired of freeing people only to have them return.

"You're looking at death or perpetual imprisonment," James said.

Summer 1960
Al Tarlov
Stateville Penitentiary

RETURNING TO STATEVILLE, AL FOUND EVERYTHING EXACTLY AS it had been when he left. But also everything was different. The plaque with the cautionary tale of the guard who'd paid the price for befriending a prisoner now felt personal. Conversations with the prisoners currently training in his lab now felt strained. Was it his imagination, or did Warden Ragen rush past when they crossed in the halls, rather than waving hello? On Al's weekly trips to the University of Chicago, was Dr. Alving monitoring his work more closely, as if he needed more supervision? Was Charles Ickes more eager to update him on how well he himself was faring, as if to emphasize that he would never be Joe?

Al went through his days sorting data, following procedures, unlocking puzzles, but a part of his brain often drifted to the data he'd misread, the process he'd mangled, the puzzle of Joseph DeSalvo that he had failed to solve. How had he been so wrong? Sometimes he blamed his blind spots—his tendency to confuse "intelligent" with "exemplary"; his assumption that if someone was smart, like him, they were in every other way like him, too; his inability to imagine the view from a place he had not stood. Other times he blamed his ego. Was he trying to be like Isadore and play the hero?

Over the weeks he came to blame the system. It preached rehabilitation, but it took people who'd failed to manage in the world, locked them away for years, then sent them back to do what they had failed at in the first place. This thought caused such despair that he changed his haircut appointments so he no longer had to watch the weekly busloads of newcomers (and returnees).

Mostly he blamed his timing. What if he had agreed to see Joe in

Norwalk? Al's parents had been sending newspaper clippings about
the case, from which Al learned that Joe had purchased his Luger
on July 5—the day after the ten p.m. call when Joe had begged Al
to reconsider and meet before going to the beach. Had Al's no been
Joe's final straw? Perhaps Joe had been feeling unmoored without the
scaffolding and structure of prison and was seeking an anchor in Al,
who had come to represent those things. When Al let him down, Joe
looked for that security in a gun.

Near the end of July, Al wrote a letter. He rewrote it many times,
then showed it to Warden Ragen and Dr. Alving. Typed on the same
Army Medical Research Project stationery as the job recommendation for Joe, it was sent to the same address. It was a bit overwrought,
but so was Al, for one of the few times in his life.

Dear Dr. Boas,

*No words can tell the tremendous disappointment and dis-
gust that I have in my heart because of the dreadful tragedy
which Joseph DeSalvo has committed. Similarly, I judge, no
words can tell the grief that shakes the bodies of the surviv-
ing members of the police officer's destroyed family, to say
nothing of the waste of time that you had invested in Joe or
the public embarrassment which has befallen the Norwalk
Hospital.*

*The administration of the penitentiary has told me that in
twenty-five years, although they make recommendations only
for those men in whom they have the greatest confidence, this
case has had an outcome worse than any. The morale and
aspirations of the inmates of this and of other penal institutions have been severely damaged by this tragedy because the
doors to employment have been in general closed to them and
now are closed even tighter.*

*The fact that so many of us working so close to the problem
have erred so badly in predicting the outcome of this parolee
points up the wide gaps that must exist in our knowledge of*

*human, particularly criminal, behavior. There are undoubt-
edly undesirable factors in our socio-economic structure
which breed such a large class of deranged personalities; our
system for handling these problems is surely inadequate and
is, apparently, misdirected.*

I am profoundly sorry for everyone concerned,
Most regretfully,
Alvin R. Tarlov, MD

Summer 1960
Norman Boas
Wilton

DR. BOAS ALSO SPENT THE SUMMER REPLAYING EVENTS IN HIS mind. He had invited this criminal into his home, to dine with his children. Shouldn't a parent have some sort of sixth sense for danger? And the morning after that barbecue, when Joe left the lab during his lunch hour and bought himself a gun—had that been a response to his visit to Nod Hill the day before? Dr. Boas prided himself on his generosity and hospitality, and he had enjoyed giving Joe a look at what could be. Was there a line, though, between sharing and taunting? What must this home have looked like to a man who owned so little and had few tools with which to change that?

Those kinds of thoughts came during the day; night was for darker visions. He had invited this armed, desperate felon to come stay with him and recuperate. He had examined his leg wounds but didn't insist when Joe balked at taking off his pants completely. What if he or the ER staff had been firmer? What if they had found a bullet wound? (And how on earth had all of them missed a bullet wound?) Would Joe have turned his weapon on anyone who got close to the truth?

Near the end of the summer, two letters arrived for him at Norwalk Hospital. The typed one was from Dr. Tarlov, who seemed to be suffering similar thoughts; Dr. Boas couldn't bring himself to respond. The other was written in the round, careful, almost juvenile script he'd come to recognize as Joe's, on a single page of white loose-leaf paper, covered front and back.

Dear Dr. Boas:

I can only imagine how you felt when you learned what I had done ~ how I had repaid your trust and confidence. Would that this act of mine could be undone. This can never be, though in time, retribution of sorts shall be exacted. The moving hand writes, and having writ moves on, and no entreaty will suffice to erase one word.

Although nothing I can say can alter what has been, I want to tell you this:

The last four or five years I spent at Stateville were spent constructively, and with the aim of becoming a useful member of society upon my release. When I was finally released there was no doubt in my mind that I was going to lead a decent life. There was no doubt, not the slightest, in my mind, that I was going to "go straight." I knew I was never going to return to crime. I am telling you this so you will know that at the time you placed your trust in me it was not misplaced.

What subsequently came to pass must have an explanation, but it is not to explain nor excuse what has happened that I am writing, I just want you to know that when I was paroled, I wanted and intended to follow an honest life.

What you have done for me, I can now never repay. What I have done to you I can never undo.

I would like to pay you back, though, as well as I can, for the loan you cosigned for me. I have an excellent set of luggage and a nice wristwatch I want you to have. I shall not need the civilian clothes I own anymore either. Will you please let me send you these things? If my return flight ticket is still valid when the authorities release it to me, I will send the money on to you.

Respectfully,
Joseph E. DeSalvo

Summer 1960
Rosie Troy
Stamford

WITHOUT TRAINING OR WARNING, ROSIE TROY WAS CAST IN THE role of young widow, and she was to play it beneath a blazing spotlight. The newsmen did not disappear after the funeral but called (or just showed up) several times a week, asking for her thoughts on the search, the capture, and the mental health of the man who had shot her husband. Her responses were calm and temperate, which is how she thought a grieving police widow should sound.

She was pleased to hear of the arrest and confession, she said, "because it will ease the hurt of the police department. For myself, I could never work up any feeling about the man, bitter or anything. But it will help them a little bit, knowing that they have captured the man."

Keep the focus on the department, not on herself or her children. They'd had more than enough attention.

She tried to strike the same tone in her written words. The Troy Fund had officially closed on July 30, reaching a total of $33,002, which was more money than Dave could have earned in six years on the police force. (She would also receive a pension equal to half Dave's salary for the rest of her life, or until she remarried.) To mark the date, Rosie wrote another letter to the editor of the *Stamford Advocate*.

I would like to try to express my deep felt thanks to all of you
who have been so kind to me. Words would be so inadequate
in expressing the gratitude I feel toward each and every one
of you. A person cannot look directly at the flaming sun in
the sky. All he can do is feel it. The warmth of the sun's rays

can soothe a man if his body aches. The sun's shining light
can push frightening darkness away from him. All of you
have been the sun in my time of sorrow. I cannot look directly
at you, but I have felt your presence. Your light has shone
through to me in my darkest hours. I have felt your warmth
and it has comforted me. You have given me the strength I
need to do the work my late husband and I set out to do. I can
never thank you enough.

With the fund closed, at least she no longer faced a collection can-
ister at the market checkout, with a photo taped around it, usually the
one of Dave and her holding just the girls, not the baby; it had been the
only picture she could find to give the newspaper reporters, because
there were no photos yet of them as a family of five. Even without the
canisters, she was still recognized, and more unnervingly, so were her
children. It was a magnified version of the night they'd gone to Boots'
Seaview Restaurant for dinner, and the regulars had waved to Doreen
and Diane from the bar. Now strangers stopped Rosie on the street,
wanting to touch her son or give candy to her daughters. Doreen especially liked the spotlight and began to strut about in public, waiting
for someone to notice.

Not all the attention was unwelcome. The mayor and the police
chief called periodically to check on how she was faring. Rabbi Samuel Silver and Rev. Hendricks Osbourne, who hosted the local radio
show *The Reverend and the Rabbi*, invited her on their program as
a guest. Neighbors shared casseroles and their own experiences of
loss. All the messages were the same: you will always miss him, but
you need to get back to normal as soon as possible, for the sake of
the children.

That advice was a conundrum. What *was* normal when the mayor
and police chief were calling? When even your nephews were collecting bottles to donate the refunds to a fundraiser for your family?
When your daughters' new favorite game was dressing up in the pile
of ribbons they'd found in a closet—the ones Rosie had shoved there,

that had decorated Dave's casket? Normal might have been sending Doreen to kindergarten at St. Mary's in the plaid jumper with the SMS crest that she'd been fitted for before Dave died. That would have pleased Bridget, who went to St. Mary's every day to light a candle for her son. But Rosie could not see the magnificent building as anything other than the place her husband's funeral had been held. Rosie feared the sisters would treat Doreen too strictly, as was their reputation, or too gingerly, reinforcing that she was different. The other parents would talk to her in that soft, empathetic tone that had begun to make her flinch.

Rosie could have used advice from Bridget. The two very different women shared the experience of being left alone by husbands who'd suddenly died, so if anyone could truly inhabit Rosie's pain, it was her mother-in-law. But Bridget was in no shape to help anyone. Rosie never brought up the night Bridget had refused to hold baby David ("not my son's son"). Still, it hung between them like a thick fog.

And there were other moments, too. Unlike Rosie, who kept her grief in her bedroom, Bridget let it spill all over the children. One afternoon Doreen was visiting Granny Troy, playing in the back room off the kitchen. There was a newspaper on the floor nearby, and Doreen was looking at the pictures when she came to one of a lanky man with a long face, leaning on crutches. "That's the man who killed your father," Bridget snapped. For the rest of her life Doreen would remember lying on her stomach on her Granny's floor and pounding on the newspaper with her fists.

Also unlike Rosie, who was trying valiantly to remain composed, Bridget made her hatred clear. "You know he's one of *them*," she'd said, a Mafia reference, upon first learning the last name of the suspected shooter. "They all are," seeming to mean all Italians. Rosie shared that conversation with Dante, who was becoming her long-distance sounding board, removed enough to be objective. How could a grandmother say that, knowing she had three children with Italian heritage? she fumed.

Dante was now a business owner and well on his way to a master's degree, eventually a Ph.D.—a world away from where he began.

Yet he came from a dysfunctional home with a drunken absent father and no model of how to aim toward a future. When Rosie was small, Dante had been a thief and a truant who told lies as easily as the truth and thought rules did not apply to him. Today he was a philosopher and a teacher, a source of comfort and wisdom for his little sister.

"Why did I turn out differently than DeSalvo?" he said during one long late-night phone call. He answered his own question by reaching back to his psychology class at Wayne. "One person who believes in you as a child," he answered. "That makes all the difference."

Soon after the Troy Fund closed, Bridget asked Rosie for $5,000. The money she had given Dave and Rosie toward the deposit on the house had not been a gift, she said, though she might have erroneously used that word when she presented it to the newly engaged couple with such ceremony. It had always been a loan, Bridget said. And now it was due. That was news to Rosie, who had never asked her husband questions about their finances and, like so many young wives of the day, was so protected from the mechanics of the world that the first time she pumped her own gas was after Dave died. She had not yet received a cent of the donated *Stamford Advocate* funds, and when she did, it would be in trust for the children. But she wrote Bridget a check anyway, hoping it gave her mother-in-law whatever it was she so clearly needed.

In late September, on an unseasonably hot autumn day, Rosie joined her sisters and their families on a trip to the beach at Coney Island. They had a glorious time, the children digging in the sand and chasing the waves, the adults happy simply to watch them. No strangers stopped Rosie to offer their condolences. At the end of the day, as her sisters began readying for the trip home, Rosie left her children in their care and went for one last dip. Striding back to the group, she looked down at her hand and realized her wedding band was gone, lost to the sea.

Panic caught in her chest then rose to her throat where, to her surprise, it melted into something warm and certain. Dave was with her. He had a message. She would live a long full life without him, and she would be fine.

December 1960
Joe DeSalvo and Rosie Troy
Fairfield County Courthouse

"THERE IS NO MORE IMPORTANT TRIAL BEING CONDUCTED IN Connecticut at this time," said Judge Thomas E. Troland, as he took the bench in the case of *State of Connecticut v. DeSalvo*. It had taken four full days to seat a jury at the superior court in Bridgeport—six women, all describing themselves as "housewives," and six men, all with jobs like milling machine operator, life insurance underwriter, a tax collector, and lab director. More than eighty people had been questioned, with sixty-eight excused for reasons that ranged from doubts about the death penalty to certainty that being on trial is evidence of guilt. Many said they had read about the case in the newspapers and formed an opinion about the defendant. One had a son who was a police officer.

Joseph DeSalvo sat through the jury selection as he would sit through nearly all of the trial—ramrod straight at the defense table, oddly dwarfed by his six-foot-four public defender, John James, who sat on one side of him, and six-foot-one co-counsel Samuel Freedman, who sat on the other. The defendant wore khakis, a sport jacket, and a tie, and "the only variation in [his] expression has been from brooding to glumness," the *Stamford Advocate* reported. "He has maintained a tight-lipped calm in the trial for his life."

On the other side sat State's Attorney Lorin W. Willis, with his deputy, Otto Saur. Seven years earlier the same team had appeared before Judge Troland to prosecute the last police shooting in the county—a parolee who shot a state policeman on the Merritt Parkway. That man had died in the electric chair. The prosecutors looked somber but confident.

Altogether thirty witnesses would testify. Rosie did not attend for the first few of those because her friends and family persuaded her it would be too painful. She was not there when the bartender told of the adhesive tape on the holdup man's face and the newspaper draped over his arm; or when the pawn shop owner described selling a gun decorated with a swastika and a picture of Hitler to a man who had said his name was Joe E. Sansone, but who looked exactly like the defendant; nor when the Tamburris and a number of their bar patrons described running after the bandit themselves, then calling for help from the two officers who happened to be at the corner of Main Street and Greyrock Place.

But when Judge Troland gaveled the court back into session on the morning of Tuesday, December 6, Rosie Troy was there. She was flanked by her sister Evelyn and Dave's sister Agnes, and they had chosen seats near the back, not wanting to attract attention. Several dozen policemen were among the sixty to eighty people in the audience every day, and those who recognized Rosie nodded but kept their distance, respecting her privacy. The reporters who'd come to know her by sight did the same and did not reveal her attendance until the trial ended. She didn't want to affect the jury with her presence, to be seen as putting on a performance. Their "job was hard enough without them having to think about me," she would say when it was over. "God knows best, I don't want to interfere."

And yet on this day she needed to be there. Chris Kanel was testifying, and Rosie would have her first chance to hear everything he had seen that night, things she knew he could not bear to tell her directly. Kanel was the last person her husband had spoken to before he died. She had come to listen.

Kanel's voice was shaky from the start and became more so as State's Attorney Willis walked him through the events of the evening of July 7, starting with the ones Rosie already knew: Kanel rode solo in a patrol car until 8:30, when Dave Troy, who had been assigned to a motorcycle earlier in the shift, joined him. At 8:50 they answered a call to "pick up a drunk" at Main Street and Greyrock Place, but then detoured to the train station to check on a pedestrian who'd been hit by a car. There were no real injuries, so they returned downtown, to the drunk, and had been there for just a moment when bar patrons interrupted to report that a holdup man had run into the alley. Kanel shouted to Dave that he should "cover the rear, while I ran out to Main Street to get this fellow supposedly coming through the building."

Then Kanel described hearing several shots and running back into the alley toward the sound.

He yelled for his partner in the darkness. Dave called back, saying he'd last seen the shooter on the back porch of a building, on the second or third tier, hiding behind a partition.

"I shone my flashlight onto the second floor, but I couldn't see anything," Kanel said on the stand. The veteran officer was slouched in the witness box, pressing a wadded handkerchief to his eyes.

"I heard a groan," he continued, tears streaming. "That was the first I realized he was in pain. I yelled 'Where are you, Dave? What's the matter?'"

Kanel began to sob. Judge Troland called a recess so the witness could compose himself. About fifteen minutes later everyone returned to the courtroom, including a shaken Rosie.

Kanel resumed his testimony: "Where are you, Dave? What's the matter?" He described Dave's answer: "I'm hit. It's bad."

The exchange of fire Kanel had heard moments earlier had been between Dave, shooting up from the second floor of the multistory back porch, and the gunman, shooting down from the third. Hit several times, Dave had stumbled back and fallen ten feet to the asphalt, where he crawled under the only shelter he could find—a six-wheeled Sleep Shop delivery truck.

"I . . . half carried and half pulled him out," Kanel testified. "He told me he was shot, and [I saw] his shirt was covered with blood. I held him in my arms and loosened his tie and tried to make him as comfortable as possible. I heard sirens and then I knew help was on the way."

The first to arrive was Patrolman Rodney L. Varney, who drove his police station wagon as close to Dave as possible, and then he and Kanel lifted their wounded friend into the back. Asked if he had seen his assailant, Dave responded that it was dark, and the man was wearing a mask. Varney drove like a madman, sirens wailing.

Kanel steadied Dave as best he could.

"I'm hit Chris, I can't breathe," Kanel quoted Dave as saying. "I'm not going to make it."

And then, "You have to save me, I have three kids." He didn't say anything else. By the time they reached the emergency room, he was unconscious.

"You have to save me. I have three kids." For as long as she lived, Rosie would never be able to bring herself to tell her children those were their father's last words.

Several more witnesses testified that day and the next, but they were a blur to Rosie. Witnesses who had seen the gunman run from the building. The landlady who took the phone call telling the gunman his brother had died. The doctor who hired him in the first place, saying he'd come highly recommended by an army doctor at an Illinois prison. The three separate doctors who'd examined him and somehow missed the bullet wounds. The two police officers who traveled to Chicago and were present for the arrest and confession, and three other police officers who scoured the scene and mapped the bloodstains and bullet casings.

On Thursday, December 8, at twelve-thirty p.m., the state rested its case, and the defense would present theirs starting tomorrow. Rosie prepared to go home and stay there; she had no interest in hearing anyone try to defend this clearly guilty man. But just then the defendant himself rose and asked to address the judge. It was the first she had ever heard his voice.

"Mr. James and Mr. Freedman have advised me not to take the

stand," he said calmly. "And I have advised them that I wish to take the stand in my defense."

The next morning, when John James called the first defense witness, Rosie was in her seat once again. She was there for Dave, she told herself, to face down the man who'd taken him away. She sat patiently through the procedural jousting—the request to have the charges dismissed (the judge refused), the argument that the defendant's Fourth Amendment rights had been violated because doctors had not gotten proper consent before operating on him to remove the bullet (the judge disagreed).

Throughout the morning, the gallery had been filling steadily. By noon, nearly one hundred spectators crammed into pews designed for far fewer. The show they'd come for began at twelve-fifteen, when Joseph DeSalvo, who was dressed for the occasion in a dark blue suit, placed his hand on a Bible and swore to tell the truth. Four police officers flanked the witness box while he spoke. His attorney stated one more time for the record that his client was testifying contrary to advice of counsel. Then his questioning began.

The late editions tried to do justice to the drama.

JURY STUNNED BY HIS 3 HOURS OF TESTIMONY read the headline in the *Bridgeport Telegram*.

"Coolly he recounted in detail the story of a life whose 31 years have been filled with crime and violence," the article continued. "His Superior Court recital was delivered without hesitation, in precise, measured tones and impeccable grammar, and gave evidence of an extensive vocabulary."

"A tale of pain was projected on a background of family tragedy this morning . . . in the murder trial of Joseph E. DeSalvo," said the *Stamford Advocate*.

And the *Norwalk Hour* pulled out all the stops.

The headline: PACKED COURT HELD BREATHLESS BY DESALVO'S LURID CONFESSION; HISTORY MADE IN BRIDGEPORT AS NORWALKER ADMITS KILLING POLICEMAN, BARES LIFE OF CRIME IN THREE-HOUR RECITAL.

The opening paragraph: "In one of the most amazing scenes ever enacted in a courtroom on or off stage, Joseph DeSalvo . . . told a spellbound jury . . . how he killed Patrolman David D. Troy in a gun battle July 7 after a holdup. For three solid hours the jammed courtroom sat galvanized by a situation without precedent in the history of justice, as DeSalvo confessed to a life of crime and violence, starting at the age of eight and indirectly indicted society as his accomplice. His life story was like a chapter ripped from a modern version of Les Misérables. Even Judge Thomas E. Troland stopped taking notes and followed the tale in a sort of fascinated horror."

Joe began with his beginning—a volatile father, an overprotective mother, an eat-or-be-eaten schoolyard ethos where he was once beaten by a baseball bat as part of an argument during a recess pickup game. He listed his early acts of truancy and theft, his first arrest, for stealing a pocketbook, his years at the St. Charles School for Boys. At seventeen he joined the navy, then went AWOL. Stealing more cars. Making his way back to Chicago. Being sentenced to "two-to-ten" at Pontiac.

He'd had a chance for a new start upon release, he said, but the available work was low-paying and monotonous, leaving him frustrated and angry. "I never seemed to get ahead," he said. Then came the holdups with Keck, Clair, and Hultin, their capture, his escape. Months spent "driving aimlessly" around the country. His eventual arrest in Moline while playing the piano.

The crime reporters in the room had never heard a criminal speak this frankly. He admitted to thirty robberies—far more than he'd ever been charged with. He rattled off his record—where he'd done time, how long, what for—the way other men do their work résumé.

While at Stateville, the witness continued, he was assigned to the research laboratory where he conducted all the chemical and blood studies for the prison. His antimalarial research there was instrumental in his being granted parole, he said. Then he talked about Al, though not by name.

He told of meeting "a doctor at the Army Hospital, who had

formerly lived in Norwalk," and who supported his application for parole. "He suggested that I come East," he said, "that I leave the environment of Chicago," unlike another released trainee (apparently Charles Ickes) who had stayed in town to take a job at a University of Chicago research lab. "He thought that would be too static for me," Joe said, providing too much temptation to return to old ways.

Judge Troland finally ordered a lunch break at two p.m. Testimony resumed at three with a description of Joe's several suicide attempts. He had tried to slash his wrists while at St. Charles, he said, but had been rescued by an on-site nurse; he'd tried to hang himself with a belt while in the Kane County Jail and even lost consciousness but was revived; after his arrest at Rock Island, he again slashed his wrists, with a broken lightbulb, but was found by a guard. He was told he tried again while at the psychiatric hospital in Newtown, he said, though he had no memory of that.

His lawyer returned the conversation to the days before the shooting. On July 5, 1960, Joe said, he left the lab during his lunch hour, went to the Thrift Shop, and chose a gun. He was told he could not take possession for two days, a cooling-off period required by state law. He picked up his purchase on July 7, then returned to work, the gun safe in a holster he'd fashioned out of two belts twisted around his waist.

"What purpose did you have in buying the gun?" his lawyer asked.

"I guess it was in my head to hold someone up, but I didn't know who."

He had dinner with Roseann Perry after work that night, he said, then returned to the Fitzgeralds', where he cut five strips from the roll of adhesive bandage he'd brought home from the lab. He dressed in a black T-shirt, a blue dress shirt, a brown suitcoat, blue sharkskin trousers, and black shoes and took a sports cap. He seemed to take some satisfaction in the fact that not a single eyewitness had described his outfit correctly to the police.

He drove without a destination, thinking, at first, that he might scout a bar in Darien, then New Canaan. Eventually he found his way to Stamford, parked in a municipal lot, walked out toward Main Street, and passed the Skipper. He peered through the window to get a sense of the place. "If it had been too boisterous, I wouldn't have done anything," he said. "A drunk doesn't know too much what he's up to and might react in a manner dangerous to me."

He ordered a drink. Went to the men's room to ensure no one was there. Listened as a TV played some crime show right outside the bathroom door. Stuck tape on his face as a disguise, draped the gun in a newspaper he'd found on the back of the toilet, went back to the bar. Told the bartender to empty the cash drawer. Walked briskly out of the Skipper.

Rounding the corner to Greyrock Place, he somehow took a wrong turn. He had intended to retrace his steps to his car, but "soon discovered that I had never seen this alley before. I didn't know where I was."

Sitting in the crowd, Rosie suddenly realized a chilling truth. Her husband had died because Joseph DeSalvo had a terrible childhood, and a talent for lab work, and a predilection for guns. But also because Joe DeSalvo had gotten lost.

It was very dark, the defendant continued, but he made out a staircase at the rear of a building, climbed to the third floor, and sat behind a metal partition, listening to voices and footsteps below.

"I was tired out and just sat there," he said, "hoping they might not see me. A flashlight was being waved. The light seemed to play around a little bit, a man . . . came into the space at the foot of the stairway and the light glowed on my face.

"I jumped up and started to throw up my hands," he said. "I said 'don't shoot, don't shoot.' And. He. Shot."

The last three words were like bullets themselves, a staccato burst into the silent courtroom.

Rosie did not believe them. Her husband would not shoot a man who'd begged him not to. He would not shoot first.

After a pause Joe described being hit twice and thrown against the stairway. He pulled out his own gun and returned fire. He knew he'd hit his mark, he said, when the man "staggered back and fell."

He could have stopped there. Rosie wanted him to stop there. He had just admitted killing Dave—what more was there to say? His lawyer also hoped he would stop there. But he went on.

He described finding a door into the building and passing a couple on the second floor. "I noticed two colored people standing near the stairs, the woman was looking at me, so I said, 'I'm with the police.' She said, 'You're not with the police, you're the man the police are looking for.'"

He admitted that he had thought of killing them.

"Was there a reason you did not kill them?" his lawyer asked.

"Certainly, there was a reason!" he shouted. "I'm no butcher!"

While he worried that the two might identify him later, he said, "they offered no danger to my person at that time."

He finally found his car, fainted for the first of a half dozen times, then drove around Stamford with his windows open and the air on his face. Again, he got lost, spending half an hour driving near a body of water. He knew he was going in circles because he kept seeing the same sign for the Cove. A news report on his car radio told him that the man he'd shot was a police officer named David Troy, and that the officer had died.

It was well past two a.m. when Joe arrived at the Fitzgeralds', and he spent the rest of the night trying to will himself to make the short trip from his car into the house. His landlord, who left early for work, would discover him if he stayed where he was. As the sky began to lighten, he pushed himself upright, braced himself against the car, and made his way to his room by leaning on anything he could find—the walls, the kitchen table, the stairway railing—for support.

For two days he suffered, using his limited nursing knowledge to tend to his injuries: the entry wound in his right side, the exit wound on the left portion of his back, and the more serious one above his right knee where a bullet had lodged in the fatty tissue of his thigh.

He was surprised at how concerned his co-workers seemed to be, but he wished they would stop offering to examine him. When they did, he somehow held his pant leg in such a way that his entire thigh was not visible "because I didn't want to take the chance of their finding I had been wounded by gunfire." When he received the news that his brother had died, he marveled at the coincidence, then seized on it as a reason to leave town.

His lawyer walked him through his trip to Chicago, his attempt to remove the bullet himself, his arrest at his parents' when returning from the funeral.

Finally, it was the state's attorney's chance for a cross-examination, and he approached it with the energy of a man who never got to question a defendant who had just confessed all.

They squabbled over words.

"You murdered him, didn't you?" Willis asked.

"Not murdered, killed," he replied.

They debated details.

"You needed that gun to assure you of escaping?"

"I wouldn't say that."

"Well, you brought it along to avoid arrest, didn't you?"

"I hadn't even thought of being arrested."

"But you loaded that pistol so as to assure you that you wouldn't be arrested, isn't that right?"

"No, I've said I thought I wouldn't be arrested. Sometimes a person does not want to be held up, and then it is often true that a shot into the ceiling or floor is sufficient to intimidate the victim and make him realize that the gun is loaded and not fake."

After several hours of verbal combat, Willis had no more questions, and Judge Troland dismissed the witness and called a recess.

Rosie made her way home, unable to shake the feeling that for much of his testimony, her husband's killer had been talking directly to her, offering the only thing he had to give. He couldn't raise Dave from the dead, but he could fill in the gaps of what she knew, so she could move on without any more questions.

Her sister Evelyn felt it too. "He looked at Rosie. I don't know how he knew she was there, but he looked right at her and had a sorrowful look on his face."

Rosie did not go back to court, and so she didn't hear the final defense witness, Dr. Earle L. Biassey, a psychiatrist who had visited Joseph DeSalvo three times at the Fairfield County Jail. Using the now-common approach that Darrow had invented to defend Leopold and Loeb, John James was not pleading insanity for his client but was presenting him as not exactly sane, either.

DeSalvo suffered from a "deep-rooted, deep-seated character neurosis" that had been present since the age of eight, Dr. Biassey said. "His emotional development has been extremely deprived. He had very little contact with both his parents. As far as I know he had no close friends from the age of eleven."

Like many people with high intelligence but a lack of experience with "normal" social interactions, he was good at mimicking the behavior expected of him, the doctor said. But he did not internalize it, and when threatened, he returned to "primitive type, at one moment a deliberate thinking machine, and at the next a panicked, fleeing figure who loses all ability to deliberate further.

"There were attempts to show emotion, but they were studied attempts," the doctor said. And yet, he added, there was evidence of some real emotions beneath his detachment—guilt and self-loathing. The murder had forced him to face the fact that, at his core, he was the criminal that was chronicled in his record, not the erudite-man-just-waiting-for-his-chance that he had persuaded himself he could be.

The defendant's attempts to kill himself were his way of destroying the beast he was within, the doctor concluded. Taking the stand, he said, was a fifth suicide attempt. He had tried and failed at St. Charles, in Kane County, in Rock Island, at the psychiatric hospital. By testifying, he all but guaranteed a guilty verdict, assuring the state would do to DeSalvo what he had not been able to do to himself.

He was sentencing himself to death.

Wednesday, December 14, 1960
6:55 a.m.
Joe DeSalvo
Fairfield County Jail

SNOW FELL THROUGH THE NIGHT ON SUNDAY, AND BY MONDAY morning nearly the entire eastern seaboard was paralyzed. It was an epic storm, made worse by the fact that it had not been predicted. Weather reports had said there would be flurries, but the accumulations were measured in feet. From the Carolinas to Maine, schools, factories, roads, and businesses were closed as temperatures dipped below zero and winds gusted to fifty miles per hour. At least two hundred people died.

The misery continued into Tuesday. In Connecticut, the speed limit on the Merritt Parkway stayed lowered to twenty-five miles per hour, and local governments began carting snow to the sound in dump trucks. Fifty cars had been abandoned by their drivers at the peak of the storm and had to be removed before roads could be plowed.

For the first time in weeks, local papers made no mention of David Troy or his killer in local papers. Instead, there were stories of other kinds of victims. The two seventy-six-year-olds who died while shoveling. The thirteen-year-old boy with epilepsy who was found dead in a snowbank near his house. The sixty-year-old who collapsed and died as he waded from a grocery store to his car.

Joe did not read any of this because no newspapers made their way to the Fairfield County Jail on Monday or Tuesday. Nor did he see much of the snow himself because Superior Court was closed and he never left the building. "Live to die another day," he'd said when a guard told him his trial had been postponed.

Joe expected that was a relief to his lawyer, who was supposed to begin his closing argument this week and who, Joe knew, was at a loss for what to say. "How do you defend a man who has confessed to everything?" John James had asked a reporter. "I've never seen anything like it."

The new wing of the jail was hushed and serene under its white blanket. It might even have been described as cozy, with a Christmas tree in the communal area decorated by prisoners, all atwinkle with tiny white lights. Joe spent most of his two snow days in his cell, reading and writing. He was completing a treatise about death and had shown an early draft to John James, in case the lawyer wanted to borrow from it for his summation.

"Death is a state which all men must face," it began. "As I at this time find myself in the odd and rather distressing circumstance of seeing the transition of my own death from inevitability to evitability, my thoughts are necessarily commenced to center on this macabre situation. Fortunately, or no, depending on one's point of view, I have knowledge relative to the cause and agency of my demise."

Dinner on Tuesday was frankfurters and beans. Court would reopen the following morning, Joe was told, and prison staff would deliver him there, even if they had to bring him in a snowplow. By the ten p.m. check, his single caged lightbulb was off, and he was reported to be asleep.

At 6:55 a.m. on Wednesday, December 14, jailer Robert Lanse came running out of the new wing, looking for Lt. Miles McLaughlin.

"Mac, come in the wing right away. I think DeSalvo is dead."

McLaughlin could not find a pulse, though the body was still slightly warm. A priest was called to give last rites. Guards found a piece of lined loose-leaf paper in Joe's sock, folded into a one-inch square. On it he had scribbled poetry.

"There is no road, hath not a star above it," he wrote, quoting Ralph Waldo Emerson.

Below that he had copied the first stanza of a 1918 poem titled *Nemesis* by H. P. Lovecraft:

I have seen the dark universe yawning
Where the black planets roll without aim
Where they roll in their horror unheeded
Without knowledge or lustre or name.

At seven-thirty the coroner estimated that the prisoner had been dead for about an hour. At eight-thirty the body was removed by ambulance and taken to St. Vincent's Hospital for an autopsy. Public Defender James arrived at the jail at nine a.m., and from a telephone in the office, he broke the news to Charles DeSalvo, Sr.

"Oh no!" Joe's father said. "How will I tell his mother?" Ruth was due home from the hospital that day, Charles told his son's attorney. She had undergone exploratory surgery, and the finding was cancer of the gallbladder, but the doctors had not told her, and had advised her husband not to tell her, because she was so distraught over Joe's trial.

Joe's death knocked the snowstorm off the front pages of the afternoon editions.

"World Weary and despairing, accused murderer Joseph DeSalvo, 31, was found dead in his cell at the County jail this morning, apparently a suicide," read the *Bridgeport Post*.

Al's father called to read him the *Norwalk Hour*:

Joseph DeSalvo, 31, a Chicago boy who lived a life of crime by his own admission, became a resident of Norwalk through the faith of a physician who hoped that he would be able to go straight after he was released from the penitentiary. But the path he followed led to the slaying of Policeman David Troy in Stamford, for which he was on trial in Superior Court, Bridgeport, when he was found dead in his county jail cell this morning of an overdose of barbiturates.

December 1960
Al Tarlov
Joliet

THE LATE DECEMBER PHONE CALL TOOK AL TARLOV BY SURPRISE. The caller was a Fairfield County Police Department investigator, and Al did not write down his name. He was so startled that he didn't take any notes at all.

The coroner's report was about to be released, the man told him. It would say Joe DeSalvo had died of the equivalent of fifty-eight Seconal. Investigators had found a tiny slit in Joe's mattress, and they suspected, though could not prove, that he had used it as a hiding place for the sleeping aids he'd been given during the fifty-eight days he'd spent in the jail. Guards watched him swallow the pills each night, the man said, but somehow this convict had fooled them.

Al realized that he had taught Joe more than he'd intended. Part of the job of a nurse in the malaria trials was to make certain that every subject took his medicine. Joe knew how to follow the pill with a full glass of water, make sure it was downed, then have the man open his mouth to show he had swallowed. But clearly he also knew that a coated gelatin capsule, tucked just so between back molar and gum, could stay in place long enough to fool a guard. The coating might dissolve, but the core of the pill—the part that, when multiplied, could kill—would stay intact.

There was more, the caller continued. A back side to the suicide note, which had not been released to the press. It included messages from Joe to his parents and lawyers, which the caller would not share. And one final line was addressed to Al Tarlov.

"I'm sorry," was all it said.

Today
The Belkins, the Tarlovs, and the Troys
Stamford

SOON AFTER THE DESALVO TRIAL ENDED, ROSIE TROY LEFT FOR California with her children to join her brother Dante in San Francisco. In part, she left because she feared what the spotlight was doing to Doreen, Diane, and David. In part, it was to get away from Bridget, or so her children came to believe. Having paid back Bridget's $5,000, she sold her Stamford house to her younger brother Frank. Eventually he and his first wife divorced, and he remarried a woman who had a son who, by coincidence, had the first name Troy.

Bridget died in 1981, at age eighty-two. Rose died in 1997, age one hundred one, leaving twenty-seven grandchildren, forty-eight great-grandchildren, and seven great-great-grandchildren; the proceeds from the half of the house she'd persuaded Tony to leave her paid for her nursing home care.

Rosie married Sidney Johnson, a philosopher friend of Dante's. The blended family moved to Europe for two years; Rosie's fourth child, Jessica, was born there. Diane and Doreen became fluent in German while living in Salzburg, Austria and Rosenheim, Germany. Doreen would go on to major in German in college.

"It's a lot of feelings," Doreen said during our first conversation, "knowing we had a life we would probably never have had if my father hadn't died."

"I would have loved him to have walked me down the aisle," she continued. "I would have loved to have heard him laugh or heard him sing. I would have loved for him to meet his grandchildren. But I also would not be the person I am."

Returning to the States, Sid and Rosie's marriage crumbled. She divorced her alcoholic husband, changed her last name back to Cosentino, and moved into a two-family house in Santa Barbara with Dante, his wife, and their young children. There Rosie developed an interest in painting, eventually getting her master's in fine arts; she would spend decades teaching art to middle school students.

Rosie Cosentino died in 2002, age sixty-seven, hit head-on by a teenager who'd fallen asleep at the wheel. Her children had to decide where to bury their mother: With her first husband and all the Troys at St. John's Cemetery? Or with her mother and all the Cosentinos at St. Mary's? They chose the latter, separating Rosie and Dave but trusting that souls can find their way to each other regardless of real estate.

Doreen would have four children, three grandchildren, and build a business with her husband in Rhode Island. Diane would have a daughter and become a social worker in Stamford. David would marry, raise three children in Washington, D.C., and work as an IT manager. Jessica would move to California, become self-employed, and continue along her mother's path with her interest in art.

The land where Cove Mills once stood is now Cove Island Park, a waterfront recreational complex. The baseball fields are named for David Troy. Every July 7 the Stamford Police Department holds a memorial service for him there. The Troy children have attended nearly every year, and strangers regularly approach them with stories of selling lemonade and collecting cans back in 1960 to contribute to the *Stamford Advocate* fund.

There are no memorials for Joseph DeSalvo. His body was shipped to Chicago, and only his parents seem to have attended his funeral in December 1960. Ruth died in February 1961, of the cancer her doctors had advised her husband not to mention, which had metastasized from her gallbladder to her liver and lungs. Charles Sr. died in 1965, of the heart disease that had left him weak for years. Charles Jr.'s two daughters both died young, in their forties or fifties. Some families completely disappear, and while Annuziata and Michal, with their many children, have hundreds of descendants by now, the family Ruth and Charles tried so desperately to build have almost none.

Al Tarlov served at Stateville for nearly two more years. He and Joan had two more children, for a total of five. Over the next three decades, Joan descended into schizophrenia. She died in 1994. Al went on to hold prestigious positions—chairman of medicine at the University of Chicago, president of the Henry J. Kaiser Family Foundation, professor at the Harvard School of Public Health and at the Tufts School of Medicine, director of health policy studies at Rice University. The through line in all his work is how nonmedical factors determine an individual's physical and psychological health. And the root of that work, he says, is all the thinking he has done since July 1960 about genetics, environment, nature, nurture, and the social determinants of health. He met my mother in 2005, a year after my father's death, when they were seated next to each other at my niece's bat mitzvah. Al had been my sister-in-law's mentor at Tufts.

Warden Joseph Ragen retired from Stateville in 1965, lauded as one of the leading penologists of his day. He worked as marketing director for a Joliet bank until his death in 1971.

Nathan Leopold took the job with the Church of the Brethren Hospital in Puerto Rico, where he lived until his death in 1971, of heart and kidney disease that may have been a result of toxic malaria drugs. He had earned his master's degree in social work from the University of Puerto Rico and married the Baltimore-born widow of a Puerto Rican physician. A framed photograph of Clarence Darrow was given a place of honor in the couple's small apartment. A smaller picture of Richard Loeb was reportedly displayed in the bedroom. Leopold never again got in trouble with the law.

Charles Ickes, Alf Alving's favorite lab tech, did not stay "outside" for long. Three years after his release from Stateville, he robbed a motel at gunpoint, netting $437, and was captured when his car stalled on some ice in the parking lot. Alving was quoted in Chicago papers saying Ickes was an "excellent technician" and that his arrest came as a "tremendous shock." Al was silently relieved that Alving's judgment wasn't infallible either. Alf Sven Alving died in 1965; Al Tarlov was his personal physician near the end of his life.

Isadore Max Tarlov died of the big heart that brought him so much pride. The cardiac enlargement he bragged about to Al had been caused not by a lifetime of exercise but by untreated hypertension, which led to congestive heart failure. In June 1977, Isadore bumped his head against a bedpost. By then he was taking blood thinners because of his heart condition, and that bump resulted in a subdural hematoma—essentially a clot on the brain. His son Edward, also a neurosurgeon, knew his father would not want brain surgery under the circumstances, and Isadore died a few hours later. He was buried in a Quaker cemetery in Nantucket. He was seventy-two years old.

Dr. Norman Boas died in 2016 at the age of ninety-three. An obituary in the local paper, written by his children, read, "He will be remembered for his quick wit, generous heart, ethical standards, and the belief in the goodness of mankind."

The Stateville malaria trials were halted in 1974, as a result of reports of abuse at other research sites around the country. In Tuskegee, Alabama, *The New York Times* uncovered a thirty-year-long practice of withholding penicillin from hundreds of poor Black men who had syphilis, so that researchers could observe the progression of their disease, which they were not told they had. At the Holmesburg Prison near Philadelphia, a whistleblower revealed that, for more than twenty years, prisoners had been used as guinea pigs in the testing of consumer goods—shampoos, moisturizers, eye drops, suntan lotions—some of which contained dioxin and other cancer-causing or radioactive chemicals, and caused burns and allergic reactions. Retin-A was a result of those experiments, earning billions for the pharmaceutical industry. There was no way to portray this research as patriotic, and it contributed to a deep vein of suspicion of science among many Americans that is still present today.

None of the most publicized trials had anything to do with Stateville, but the resulting shift in public perception certainly did. Senate hearings chaired by Senator Edward Kennedy of Massachusetts eventually led to a national standard: experimentation without consent was unethical, full stop, and experimentation on prisoners was unethical even with consent, because a prisoner cannot, de facto, give consent. The hearings also opened the door to a new system where every hospital and laboratory had an ethical overseer. Under this lens, the Stateville program looked "immoral," the director of the Illinois Department of Corrections said, and he shut the research down.

That left unfinished business. There was still no perfect weapon against malaria. Chloroquine was increasingly ineffective, as the parasite had become resistant. A vaccine was said to be on the horizon, but the World Health Organization would not actually approve it for use until 2021.

Over the years, former Stateville researchers, including Al Tarlov, insisted that "their" prisoners had been fully informed; that the risk to subjects was completely explained; and that there were more volunteers than spaces for them, so how could coercion have been a factor if people were being turned away? Over the years ethicists and academics such as Bernard Harcourt of Columbia University and Karen Masterson of SUNY Stony Brook have agreed—to a point. The malaria experiments at Stateville were likely as close as research could come to getting full consent from prisoners, they have written. But close is not enough.

The other "experiment" being done at Stateville—testing instruments of parole prediction—has also been phased out since 1960. That is because parole itself is largely a relic of the past. In 1978 the State of Illinois eliminated parole and substituted indeterminate sentencing: a formula that judges must follow with terms that convicted criminals must serve. Illinois is now one of sixteen states in the country where prisoners have no way of being paroled.

That does not mean the system has stopped trying to predict behavior. "Risk assessments" are the new "parole predictions," with Silicon Valley creating software to foretell how a defendant will act in the future. Most of the new questionnaires have 100 to 150 questions, reminiscent of the ones Leopold and Loeb came up with in their cell: "Was one of your parents ever sent to jail or prison?" "How often did you get in fights while at school?" There are also agree/disagree questions: "A hungry person has a right to steal" and "If people make me angry or lose my temper, I can be dangerous."

The resulting "risk score" is used for everything from setting bail to determining sentence length. Investigations by groups like Pro-Publica have shown that those scores tend to be higher for defendants of color than for white defendants, resulting in stiffer sentences for convicted defendants who are Black, Hispanic, and Indigenous when other factors are statistically equivalent.

Joliet Prison was finally closed in February of 2002. By then it had been immortalized in the movies *The Blues Brothers* and *Natural Born Killers* and the TV show *Prison Break*. Once the building was emptied of prisoners and film crews, it stood vacant for more than a decade, allowing vandals and vagrants to rip it to pieces. Then the Joliet Historical Society began to repair the ricketiest sections and give twilight tours, complete with ghost stories.

One evening near Halloween I took a tour, accompanied by a young woman named Katharine Dryden, Warden Allen's great-great-granddaughter. I had told our guides who she was, and they were particularly generous with tales of the Allens' grand hopes and dashed dreams. Our tour group stayed outside the building, because it was too dangerous to go inside, but as darkness fell and the other sight-seers headed for their cars, the guides held us back. Using industrial power flashlights, they brought us in through the front door I had spent years looking at in photos, then up what was left of the grand staircase to the family's quarters. Katharine could not actually visit the room where her great-great-stepgrandmother had died, because that uppermost floor had caved in years ago. But the second floor was identical, and she wandered through the shadows where the present met the past.

Decades also collided the day I brought Al to meet David Troy's children. One summer afternoon we drove up to Norwalk where Doreen and David and their families had gathered at Diane's house.

What Dave's descendants most wanted to know was something Al could not tell them. He had never met David Troy and could not fill in the gaps of what their father had been like. But they also wanted to learn about Joseph DeSalvo. What had made Al trust him? Then what had made Al suspect him? Al wanted to know about their lives too, ones he had completely changed.

The time neared for us to leave, and as we started saying our good-byes, Al raised his hand like a schoolboy with a question.

"May I say one more thing?" he asked. "I just want to say I am sorry. I am sorry for the pain you've suffered because of an action of mine."

"What would you have done differently?" one of Dave's grandchildren asked.

"If I had it to do over again, I would still write the parole letter, because I made the best choice I could with the information I had. What I would have done differently was, I would have gone to see DeSalvo when he called."

Joe had been struggling with his freedom and needed an anchor, Al said. "Maybe if I had seen him, talked to him and reminded him of who he could be, he wouldn't have bought the gun."

He took a deep breath. "I realize it's likely he might have bought another gun, another day, held up another place, and shot another person. In fact, that's very likely. But it would not have been that day. And it would not have been your father."

Acknowledgments

THE TROY AND COSENTINO FAMILIES—ALL THE CHILDREN AND grandchildren, siblings, in-laws, nieces and nephews—have been as welcoming, supportive, and marvelous as I could possibly have hoped. From my first email, they embraced this project and opened their hearts and their memories. Most of all, my deepest gratitude to Doreen Troy Dolan, Diane Troy, and David Troy, for answering my initial email and the years of questions that followed.

I also want to give special thanks to Dante Cosentino for writing his own memoir, *Pride and Memory*, and allowing me to borrow from it. And thanks to the many members of both families for their endless sharing of stories, finding of photos and checking of facts, particularly: Evelyn Davidson, Frank Cosentino and Val Cosentino; Serenella Cosentino and Antonia Cosentino; Charlotte Nelson, Ingrid Lenihan, Lynn Bisceglia, Patti Silverman, and Rosemary Curcio Matson; Billy Anderson and Donald Anderson; Jim Troy, Peter Troy and Charlie Troy; Linda Masten and Carla Troy.

The Tarlov family also treated me as one of their own, and not just because—technically—I am. They too embraced this story and graciously trusted me with the telling. So many thanks to Al's children, Richard, Jane, and Elizabeth, and the late Suzanne and David, as well as to Isadore's children, Edward, Anne and Susan, and Jay's wife, Marina. Also to John Perfetti and Arliss Perfetti for filling in some important blanks in Joan's life.

The DeSalvo family was harder to find. I am grateful to have connected with some distant cousins on Ancestry.com, particularly Niki Hatzenbuehler, who was Dora-the-midwife's great-granddaughter. Two others I interviewed have asked not to be named here, reluctant to talk publicly about their cousin the cop-killer. I am grateful for the time and the facts they anonymously shared.

It took a team to do all this digging, and I had the best: my dogged researchers Kristen Hussey, Ray Johnson, and Currie Engel. It took another team to make a smooth read out of all that they found; mine included my incomparable editor, John Glusman, and agent, Barney Karpfinger. Then there were my secret weapons, the deft Peter Griffin and the precise Jerry Adler, along with my husband, Bruce Gelb, the king of commas. Also copious thanks to Helen Thomaides, Robert Byrne, Janet Biehl, Kyle Radler, Meredith McGinnis, and the whole magnificent team at W. W. Norton.

That said, I spent eight years reporting and writing, and there are, conservatively, a gazillion facts in this book; despite best efforts, I fear there will be some details I have inadvertently gotten wrong. Which leads to the traditional yet heartfelt disclaimer: while I had a lot of help with research and fact-checking, the ultimate responsibility for any mistakes is all mine. And I offer a more modern corollary: if you find any errors, please let me know via social media or direct email so I can correct them, both in cyberspace and in subsequent editions.

I had so many wise, patient, sounding boards over the years, and every one of them made this book better: Nick Kristof and Sheryl WuDunn; David and Sherill Sanger; Allison Fine and Scott Freiman; Al and Cathy Cattabiani; Bob and Amy Sommer; Barron Lerner and Cathy Seibel; Roxana Klein and Iair Rosenkranz; Todd Kessler and Sharon Hall; Vered Vinitzky-Seroussi; Shari Rosen Ascher; Brooke Reinfeld; Heather Rafter, Lynda Clarizio, Mary Throne, and Kim Quinones.

Then there were the writers who let me talk their ears off: Karen Stabiner, Sam Freedman, Laura Muha, KJ Dell'Antonia, Mary Laura Philpott, Jessica Lahey, Christina Baker Kline, Jennifer Mendelsohn, Erik Larson, Mimi Swartz, Sharon Fairley, Allison Gilbert, Alison Cowan, Farah Miller, Lori Leibovich, Emma Mustich, Emma Gray, Lori Fradkin, Laura Schocker, and Margaret Wheeler Johnson, the whole Portland gang, and my talented Columbia Journalism School students who were subjected to more than a few impromptu riffs about the joys and the grind of writing books. Note: the train crash stayed.

For informal legal advice on how courts work, thanks to Lisa Tucker. For advice on FOIA, thanks to the Chicago Journalists for a Free Press.

A FOIA officer at the Illinois Prisoner Review Board, whom I shall not name, spent nearly a year refusing to give me Joseph DeSalvo's prison files despite my legal right to have them. To him I say, truth will out. To the very sane and logical lawyer in the Illinois State's Attorney's Office who finally told said FOIA officer to hand the files over already: So. Many. Thanks.

I am indebted to every author in my bibliography, as well as to some experts who went beyond and educated me in person (well, by phone and Zoom). For clarifications of neuroscience: Dr. Edward Tarlov. For clarifications of traumatic brain injuries: Dr. Daniel Perl. For the history of pediatric cardiology: Dr. Bob Sommer and Dr. Bruce Gelb. For everything to do with malaria: Karen Masterson. For everything about medical experiments on prisoners: Dr. Barron Lerner. And about modern surveillance and prediction: Bernard E. Harcourt.

For the history of motorcycles: Don Emde, Mark Mederski, Diane Hall, and Daniel K. Statnekov. For all things railroad and trains: the Railroad Museum of Pennsylvania and Frank DeStefano. For prison and parole history in general and Stateville and Joliet in particular: John Maki, Joanne Kantrowitz, and Morgan Shahan. For the Nuremberg Code: John Harkness, the man who figured out the story behind the story. For the tale of Pompey: Dolores Natale and Elizabeth Ofiero. For the economics of gas stations in the 1950s: Michael Fox at the Gasoline and Automotive Service Dealers of America, and J. Lenard at the National Association for Convenience and Fuel Retailing.

When it comes to Leopold and Loeb, Simon Baatz literally wrote the book. And Erik Rebain is a walking encyclopedia, and a generous one at that.

For history of Dartmouth College, Clark University, Johns Hopkins, Wright Tech, and Stamford High School, many thanks to their alumni associations. Researchers at Wayne State found me Dante's protest activities, and archivist Danielle Nista and researcher Amina Frassi found Al Tarlov's footprints at the Jefferson School by digging through NYU's special collections at the Elmer Holmes Bobst Library.

For a deep dive into the genealogy of the Troy family, deep thanks to the Irish Family History Center in Dublin, and to Melanie McComb in Boston. For the history of the DeSalvos in Italy, I am indebted to George Ott of Ancestry ProGenealogists.

I could not have written this book without Ancestry.com and Newspapers.com. Thank you for your very existence.

In Stamford, Connecticut, I had so much help from Tom Lombardo at the Stamford Police Department, along with Sgt. John Scalise, Amy LiVolsi, and Elizabeth Joseph. I owe thanks to Ron Marcus at the Stamford Historical Society, to so many of the staff at the Stamford Library, and to Bruce Williams, his daughter, Cynde, and Emilie Blackwell.

In Norwalk, Connecticut, deep thanks to Ralph Bloom, Paul Keroack, Dr. Norman Boas and his children, and the Family Service Bureau of Norwalk. In Greenwich, Tod Laudonia, Christopher Shields, Carl White, and Bob Mowbray. In Madison, Connecticut, the Madison Historical Society and the staff of the Madison Beach Hotel.

In Chicago, Allen Ramsey; Katharine Lee Dryden; the rare documents staff of the extraordinary Chicago History Museum; Nathan Parker at the Chicago Public Library Help Line; and the staff of the Northwestern University Library. In Moline, Neil Dahlstrom, the archivist at the Moline Plow Company. In Joliet, Heather Bigeck, Elizabeth Covelli, Jessamyn Moore, Audra Kantor, and Steven J. Wright, staff past and present at the Joliet Area Historical Museum. In Rock Island, the Rock Island Historical Society and the Swenson Swedish Immigration Research Center at Augustana College.

To my own dear family: Gary Belkin and Kate Burch, Kira Belkin and Saul Fishman, Dana Gelb Safran and Alan Safran, Debbie Isaacson, and all my nieces and nephews. I am so happy that we share a family and a history.

To my stepfather, Alvin Tarlov, without whom this book literally would not be possible. Your life story is one of always trying to do the right thing, and I hope I have done right by that story. And my love to Al's wife, my mother Janet Belkin, who cared for his tale and for her daughter's book, as though they were her own.

Sending my whole heart to my boys, Evan Gelb and Alex Gelb, and to the spectacular women in their lives, Melissa Purner and Courtney Kassel. The love of family that I tried to put on every page of this book is, I hope, my legacy to you.

And finally, my husband, Bruce Gelb. This is a story about all the things that have to happen before all the other things can happen. If I had not forced myself off my couch on a ridiculously cold December night and shown up at an obscure French film, my own story would be completely different. I can't begin to guess what that alternative path might look like. But I do know, with absolute certainty, that it would not have been as magical as the one you have made possible for me.

Notes

Introduction

xix *More people died from the 1918 flu:* This is true even after the recent Covid-19 pandemic, with some caveats. The 1918 flu is estimated to have killed 675,000 Americans; as I write this, the "official" death toll from Covid-19 in the United States has passed 1 million. Adjusted for population, the 1918 death rate was 1 in 150 Americans, while Covid is 1 in 500. Globally, the 1918 flu is thought to have killed between 20 million and 50 million worldwide, and Covid 4.5 million.

May 1906 ✦ Max and Raisel Tarlov ✦ On the No. 18 Train

11 *The No. 18 train, also known as:* Nearly all the schedule details in this chapter were found with the help of the Railroad Museum of Pennsylvania. And all the bits of train lingo—e.g., one "steers" a train, one does not "drive" it—are courtesy of the very knowledgeable hobbyist Frank DeStefano.

12 *paused in Hollidaysburg:* All details of what happened before, during, and after the crash are from local papers in Altoona and Norwalk and the legal hearings that eventually followed.

13 *the coastal town of Norwalk, Connecticut:* I never did find Max Tarlov's arrival information. I estimate that he came in 1887 or 1888. I suspect the exact answer was lost in the 1897 fire at Ellis Island, which destroyed a large percentage of immigration records dating back to 1855. Although these records were stored at Ellis Island, most predated that center, which did not open until 1892. Before that, immigrants passed through Castle Garden, on the southernmost tip of Manhattan Island, which is almost certainly where both Max and Raisel arrived. Castle Garden was a neither a castle nor a garden. Built as a fort during the American Revolution, it was an intimidating space, where rules were unclear and noise levels were overwhelming. It made such an impression that a new word took root in American Yiddish over the decades, *Kesselgarten*, meaning "a place of chaos."

13 *back when he was Max Tarloffsky:* A common misconception holds that at Ellis Island, capricious immigration clerks wielding powerful pens simplified or Americanized ancestors' surnames. But while there were a few misspellings or misunderstandings, for the most part newcomers' names were entered as they appeared on their ship's arrival manifest—the names they used when they boarded, ones they provided themselves. Yes, millions of Americans currently

have names that are different from those of their ancestors, but it was almost always the holders of a name—the immigrants themselves—who changed it, not faceless bureaucrats.

15   *In 1900 only eight thousand cars:* When Max took his last train ride in 1906, the word *automobile* was relatively new to the English language. January 4, 1899, was the first time it appeared in *The New York Times*, on the editorial page, and the unbylined writer was a fan neither of the machine nor of the word:

> There is something uncanny about these new-fangled vehicles. They are all unutterably ugly and never a one of them has been provided with a good, or even an endurable, name. The French, who are usually orthodox in their etymology if in nothing else, have evolved "automobile," which, being half Greek and half Latin, is so near to indecent that we print it with hesitation.

17   *"The engines reared up":* I love newspaper reporters of old. Because there were more of them, and their focus was local, I can know what seat Max Tarlov was in when he died. Their day has come and gone, but I am ever grateful that it existed and that we are left with their effusive purple prose. Here's one sample from the *Altoona Mirror*:

> The crash sent a convulsive thrill through the two trains. The engines reared up like fighting stallions and fell over on their sides. A scene of indescribable horror ensued and to add to the confusion the splintered timbers held prisoner some of the people. The scene presented after the collision was one never to be forgotten by those who saw it. The shrieks of the injured, the groans of the dying and the escaping steam of the engines were all mingled together in the confusion and the darkness.

19   *the large white shingled farmhouse:* The sole existing photograph of that farmhouse was taken sometime in 1905—the child who at the time was named Morris is shown as an infant in his mother's arms. The livery stables are visible to the right of the house. And my favorite detail is on the porch: a handmade dollhouse that is apparently a replica of the larger one. This was a family where someone took the time to make a child a dollhouse that looked like home.

1914 ♦ Charles and Joseph DeSalvo ♦ Chicago

23   *a hundred-mile, eleven-hour slog:* According to the sports page of the *Inter Ocean*, a Chicago newspaper, the headlights didn't operate because the generators ran on water and froze, so they rode in the dark "from midnight to dawn." At one point, "DeSalvo hit a sharp stone and wrecked his rear tire," which he essentially wrapped with duct tape and continued on, stopping periodically to replace the tape as it wore off on the frozen roads. Charles stopped in Aurora at eight a.m. "for breakfast and a general thawing out," then continued on to Chicago "without incident" arriving "well ahead of a number of the automobiles participating in the run." DeSalvo, the paper noted, rode an Excelsior model "autocycle," which gave "Excelsior local credit for the first

century to be finished in 1909 and possibly the first to be finished anywhere in the country."

25 *to propose to his girl "Snooks"*: Nearly all the information about the motor-cycle stars comes from news reports in local papers and in *Motorcycling* magazine. One exception is the story of Fearless Balke and his wife Snooks, whose great-grandnephew Bill Bradford found her scrapbook in an attic in 2004, leading to the charming paperback book *Fearless: The Lord of the Murder-drome* by Rick and Lane Ongstad.

29 *terms like* traumatic brain injury: I'm grateful to Dr. Daniel Perl for an informative discussion of these conditions, and for his opinion as to whether Charles Sr.'s injuries and behavior changes were consistent with these diagnoses.

1914 ◆ Rose Cufone and Bridget Reilly ◆ Rose, Italy, and County Cavan, Ireland

32 *the county of Cavan, parish of Drumlumman:* For years, Bridget's early life was a mystery to me. Her children and grandchildren knew only that she was from Northern Ireland and that her parents had sent her to America when she would have preferred to remain at home. Bridget Reilly is an extremely common Irish name, and without other facts, such as the town in which she lived or the year she left, all I had were dead ends. Then Melanie McComb, a genealogist with the New England Historic Genealogical Society, and Stephen Peirce, with the Irish Family History Center in Dublin, helped me through this brick wall, guessing correctly that as a girl Bridget went by the nickname Delia. There she was on a ship's manifest, with the name of her father, her home address, and the name and address of the uncle who had paid her ship's fare.

35 *Antonio also came from the village of Rose:* Antonio Belmont, aka Anthony, gave an oral history to the Greenwich library in 1977, and much of this information about Rose's early years in America comes from there.

35 *on the night before Independence Day:* Independence Day became a leitmotif in this story. Sabato's birth is but the first of many events on the day itself or on the weekend surrounding the day. So a bit of context: In the first decade of the 1900s, immigrants were literally maiming and killing themselves on the holiday. One reason was that in that decade firecrackers had become more available, varied, and powerful, and therefore more fun. Another was that the country's newest arrivals took to the tradition with gusto, a literal interpretation of "rockets' red glare" and "bombs bursting in air." Because they lived in the most densely populated neighborhoods, they were likely to set themselves or someone nearby aflame.

This led to the Safe and Sane Fourth movement, which aimed to get fireworks off the streets and provide substitute ways of celebrating. It was originally championed in 1908 by the City of Cleveland, where a fireworks factory had exploded a few years earlier, leveling twelve buildings and killing three people. Soon after that, in a crowded Kresge's store, a boy playing with a sparkler accidentally ignited a sales display of rockets, setting off a chain reaction. In 1909, twenty cities participated in the Safe and Sane Fourth campaign, and the national casualty rate was 5,307. In 1910, ninety-one cities participated, and the death and injury rate was down to 2,923. And in 1911, it was 160 cities, and the total rate was 905.

38   *she would believe that some immigrants:* I struggled mightily with how to write about Bridget. Who she was depended on which of her descendants I talked to. I know the descriptions I have chosen may cause pain to some of her grandchildren, but they are the stories other grandchildren were raised on, and it is entirely possible that Bridget was as both sides of the family remember her—the good-hearted grandmother who would do anything for those she loved, and the bigot with blind spots who believed certain "kinds" were lesser than others.

1915   ✦   Warden Edmund Allen   ✦   Joliet Prison   ✦   Joliet, Illinois

39   *her "houseboy," Joseph Campbell, wasn't answering:* News accounts at the time referred to Joseph Campbell as "Chicken Joe," a racist and demeaning nickname of uncertain origins.

40   *a tin bucket that they emptied once a day:* Electricity came to Joliet Prison long before indoor plumbing, so as soon as the lights went on in the morning and the cell doors were opened, the men would march, latrine pails in hand, to the west wall of the yard. There they would dip the pails into a trough filled with water, swirl it around a few times, then fling the watered-down contents into a huge open cesspool. Next the pails were rinsed in a smaller trough and emptied into a smaller cesspool. Finally they were hung on a numbered nail that corresponded to that prisoner's cell. Task complete, everyone marched into breakfast with no opportunity to wash their hands.

40   *How a nation treats its prisoners:* I relied on many excellent general histories of prisons for this summary: Philip Goodman, Joshua Page, and Michelle Phelps, *Breaking the Pendulum: The Long Struggle Over Criminal Justice*; Norval Morris and David J. Rothman, eds., *The Oxford History of the Prison: The Practice of Punishment in Western Society*; Ashley T. Rubin, *The Deviant Person: Philadelphia's Eastern State Penitentiary and the Origins of America's Modern Penal System, 1829–1913*; and Rebecca McLennan, *The Crisis of Imprisonment: Protest, Politics and the Making of the American Penal State, 1776–1941*. The Selected Bibliography at the end of the book gives more information. The abundant press coverage of Camp Hope informs this chapter as well.

42   *In his off-the-cuff hour-long speech:* Perhaps the only coverage of Darrow's visit to Joliet is in *The Joliet Prison Post*, the prisoner-run newspaper that Edmund Allen founded. So all the information about the speech comes from an unbylined prisoner.

43   *"panopticons," a word first used:* Bentham's idea for a panopticon was laid out mostly in letters—no actual building of such a structure was realized in his lifetime. He had great aspirations for his vision, writing in a letter that would become his treatise *Panopticon; or The Inspection House*, in 1787:

> Morals reformed—health preserved—industry invigorated, instruction diffused—public burthens lightened—Economy seated, as it were, upon

a rock—the gordian knot of the Poor-Laws are not cut, but untied—all by a simple idea in Architecture!

In the centuries since his death, the panopticon has come to represent none of these things but rather an all-seeing state, an analogy made by French philosopher Michel Foucault in the 1970s. More recently, critics of corporate surveillance of employees have compared that electronic monitoring to a panopticon.

47   *"We've had a little accident":* A reporter from the *Chicago Tribune* was in the office with Ryan when he made the call, which is the source of these quotes.

48   *Even though evidence was circumstantial:* In the end, Joe Campbell was convicted and sentenced to hang not because of anything he or anyone else said but because of what he didn't say. The guilty vote was unanimous by the fourth ballot, but the jury then spent hours debating between life and death. The last holdout, August Borms, was persuaded to change his vote on the twenty-first ballot when reminded that Campbell, on cross-examination, could not recall the name of the employer he had shot and killed to land him in Joliet in the first place. "When Campbell said he could not remember the name of that man, I decided he was unworthy," Borms said. Newspapers covering the trial apparently couldn't verify that fact either, some reporting it was Steven Sephus and others that it was Henry Stevens.

49   *He still trusted his prisoner:* There is no way to prove that Joe Campbell was charged only because he was the one Black man present at the time of the fire, but there are many reasons to believe that was the case. He was represented in his appeal by Ida B. Wells and her husband, Ferdinand Lee Barnett, of the Negro Fellowship League, who succeeded in reducing the sentence from death to life.

After the Great War • The Tarlovs and the DeSalvos •
Norwalk, Connecticut, and Chicago

53   *Something apparently happened:* Impossible as it is to prove a negative, what I did was this: Aime was born in 1887. Max left for America sometime that year. Aime's next sibling, Esther, was born in the summer of 1889. That meant Raisel had to have arrived with Aime sometime in 1888 (when she was all of eighteen). I have never found her arrival information, as it was likely lost in the same Ellis Island fire as Max's. But I pulled all the shipping news from the *New York Times* archives that year and did not find any describing fires or sinkings or mothers threatening to swim ashore.

54   *Raisel had inherited:* Max's will, the probate records, and the land deeds are all still on file with the State of Connecticut and the City of Norwalk. These came from *Norwalk Probate Records* 44 (1906). I mapped where the family lived in the years after his death by examining the city's directories—precursors to phone books—which listed the names, addresses, and occupations of residents before there were telephones.

55   *taken her younger brother:* Ruth's family disappeared from the Moline directory at about the time of her marriage. Joe's cousin said he never saw any members of Ruth's family, and Joe never mentioned the names of any of the

Swedish members of the family on any of the many forms he filled out over the years.

56   *every Sunday when the extended family:* Generalizations about Swedish life in Chicago come from Lilly M. Setterdahl, *Swedes in Moline, Illinois, 1847 to 2002*, and from the archives at Augustana College in Rock Island, which Swedish settlers established before the Civil War. Generalizations about Italian life are from books such as Dominic Candeloro and Fred Gardaphé, eds., *Reconstructing Italians in Chicago: Thirty Authors in Search of Roots and Branches*, as well as Hull House records. The tiny detail that Ruth was tall comes from a comment her son once made to Al, that he took after his mother, who was taller than anyone else in the family.

57   *In 1917 America went to war:* A word about the 1918 influenza pandemic that overlapped with the war. Though these particular families and their immediate circles were barely touched by the virus, it was all around them. In Norwalk, Connecticut, the death toll was 281, or 2.9 percent. The town had just built a new building for Norwalk Hospital, and in response to the epidemic, it accelerated the construction schedule by several months so it could open early. In Chicago, the death rate in October 1918 was twelve hundred a day, and by November ten thousand were dead. And Joliet, the city of forty thousand that surrounded the prison, had eighteen hundred cases of the flu and 263 deaths. Joliet schools were closed, along with movie theaters and restaurants. Church services were called off. Funerals were limited to immediate family. Clarence Darrow, scheduled to address a union organizing meeting in the Joliet civic center, was asked to please stay home.

57   *Like many immigrant parents:* The immigrants' reasons differed from one nationality to the next. Those who'd come from Germany were in favor of neutrality, for fear of a backlash were they to find themselves living in a country that was fighting Germans. Those who'd come from Ireland, in turn, were not eager to support the British because the United Kingdom refused to allow Irish independence. Eastern European Jews also tended toward neutrality, not wanting to support Britain, which had refused the creation of a Jewish state in Palestine, and not wanting to oppose Germany, one of the strongest enemies of the tsar.

58   *"Get into khaki":* After Aime died, the *Norwalk Hour* quoted some of his letters home.

58   *The bombardment began:* This account is drawn from Lt. Col. John Abram Cutchins and Lt. Col. George Scott Stewart, Jr., *History of the Twenty-ninth Division, "Blue and Gray," 1917–1919*, published by McCalls & Co. in 1921.

62   *That was not what killed him:* With thanks to my husband, Bruce Gelb, a pediatric cardiologist.

1929 ❖ Rose Cufone Cosentino and Bridget Reilly Troy ❖ Cos Cob and Stamford, Connecticut

65   *The fourteen-year-old she rescued:* For a long time, Pompey was a rumor. Then I was introduced to Elizabeth Ofiero, a descendant of Charles Troy's (aka Patrick's) sister Agnes Jr. Now ninety-two years old, Elizabeth had distinct memories of the man. She led me to three bits of information that made

Pompey real. First, he was from North Carolina. Second, he was mentioned in a book about the Cove, which turned out to be Jeanne Majdalany, *The History of the Cove in Stamford Connecticut*, published by the Stamford Historical Society in 1979. Third, during the time he lived with the Troys, he was baptized (Majdalany's book says by Bishop Nilan of Fairfield County). Not long after that, I had the census listing of his sharecropper family back in North Carolina, and the certificate of his baptism.

67   *None of their children:* The Troy family was certain that Bridget and her husband wed sometime in 1919. I spent years trying to find the record of the 1919 wedding, which I assumed was in Stamford, as that was where they both lived and attended church. One day, on a hunch or a whim, I searched in New York instead. There they were, marrying at a Manhattan church on August 26, 1920 (which happened to be the day the Nineteenth Amendment was ratified, giving women the right to vote).

The Roaring Twenties ♦ Nathan Leopold and Richard Loeb ♦ Stateville Penitentiary ♦ Joliet

72   *when they kidnapped and murdered:* I do not describe the murder of Bobby Franks in this book. I've stuck to the parts of the Leopold and Loeb story that changed the lives of the Tarlovs, DeSalvos, Cosentinos, and Troys. For those who are interested in learning more about the crime itself, two books stand out amid a wealth of literature: Simon Baatz, *For the Thrill of It*, published in 2008; and Hal Higdon, *Leopold and Loeb: The Crime of the Century*, in 1999. The website *The Lives and Legends of Richard Loeb and Nathan Leopold* (https://loebandleopold.wordpress.com/) is deeply sourced and meticulously curated. Its creator, Erik Rebain, has written a full biography, *Arrested Adolescence: The Secret Life of Nathan Leopold*, due out at about the same time as this book.

73   *Arkhe kakon:* With thanks to Daniel Mendelsohn, who wrote at some length about *arkhe kakon* in *An Odyssey: A Father, a Son, and an Epic* (2017).

80   *they hatched a new project:* Most of the information about the prison school comes from Nathan Leopold's papers archived at the Chicago History Museum, which is the museum of the Chicago Historical Society, and from Leopold's autobiography, *Life Plus 99 Years*.

82   *"Dear Warden":* Fernekes's note, which was reprinted in newspapers nationwide, is confusing. "Too many men my reason for giving more room," it says. He seems to have meant something like: "there were too many men at Stateville, and that's my reason for leaving, to provide more room there."

Summer 1935 ♦ Joseph DeSalvo and Alvin Tarlov ♦ Chicago and Norwalk

87   *It felt as though the trophies:* Joe DeSalvo did not like his father. He made that clear to prison intake officials and social workers, all of whom wrote reports mentioning his overbearing father and his overly enmeshed mother. Both of the cousins I spoke to seemed to think the dislike was warranted, describing Charles Sr. as a man who belittled his children and would not let his wife buy

new clothes. They both described bookshelves that were full of trophies but
no books.

1936 ✦ Bridget Troy and Rose Cosentino ✦ Stamford and Greenwich, Connecticut

95 *On the night of July 14:* All accounts of Gerome's arrests come from Greenwich Police archives and local newspaper articles. The financial details of the
Cosentino family were found in the city's property records, while their list of
residences comes from Greenwich and Stamford directories.
96 *"We were among the poorest":* This quotation comes from Dante's self-
published autobiography, *Pride and Memory*. Much of what I have written
here about the childhoods of the Cosentino children also comes from Dante's book, as well as from interviews with him and his wife Antonia and their
daughter Serenella, from Evelyn and her daughter Charlotte, and from Frank
and Valentino.
96 *"The Farm" was part of an effort:* I was continually struck that all these people might have been treated differently for the same problem had they stumbled
at another point in history, and that their lives might have been different as a
result. Gerome and "the Farm" is but one example. Its history can be found
in newspaper accounts and in *The Mentally Ill in Connecticut: Changing Patterns of Care and the Evolution of Psychiatric Nursing 1636–1972*, published
in 1974 by the Connecticut Department of Mental Health, as well as archived
reports from the hospital board to the governor.

1930s ✦ Nathan Leopold and Richard Loeb ✦ Stateville Penitentiary

103 *Joseph E. Ragen had always:* For the history of Ragen and of Stateville, I
relied on contemporaneous news reports and on two books. The first one,
Gladys A. Erickson's *Warden Ragen of Joliet*, was written in 1957. Erickson,
who covered crime and prisons for the *Chicago Herald American* at a time
when women reporters were almost always relegated to the society pages,
clearly liked the warden. (So did her husband, Charles Finston, the warden's
co-author for *Inside the World's Toughest Prison,* which is theoretically the
warden's biography but is really a 952-page collection of memos, documents,
and procedure manuals from his tenure.) The other was Nathan Leopold's
autobiography, *Life Plus 99 Years*, published in 1958. Leopold wrote it to sway
public opinion on the question of his parole. Despite the biases of their authors,
both books offer detailed accounts of events at Stateville from insiders.
    Two more critical books are James B. Jacobs, *Stateville, The Peniten-
tiary in Mass Society* (1975), and Nathan Kantrowitz, *Close Control:
Managing a Maximum-Security Prison: The Story of Ragen's Stateville
Penitentiary* (1996). Kantrowitz wrote his book during the 1960s, when he
was the sociologist-actuary at the prison, but he could not get it published
until 1996 because, he says, "liberal academics" who were fans of the warden rejected it.
112 *remained tacked above Leopold's workspace:* Einstein's letter is now in the

archives Leopold left to the Chicago History Museum. Also in those archives is Leopold's correspondence with a large number of people about parole prediction research. That, along with Leopold's biography, was the source of nearly everything I've written here about his parole prediction project.

The War Years ◆ Al Tarlov and Joe DeSalvo ◆ Norwalk and Chicago

121 *Brooklyn Dodgers:* Yes, there was a Brooklyn Dodgers *football* team. They played from 1930 to 1943, in the National Football League. You can learn more about them in Roger A. Godin, *The Brooklyn Football Dodgers: The Other "Bums."* But for this book, all you need to know is that those Dodgers were playing the New York Giants on December 7, 1941, and that Al Tarlov was listening on the radio. The audio he heard when that game was interrupted is now widely available on YouTube.

127 *sentenced to the St. Charles School for Boys:* I never received Joe's juvenile records, because of privacy protections for minors. I did receive his adult records, but only after a yearlong fight with a Freedom of Information Act bureaucrat in the State of Illinois Prisoner Review Board. Notations in his adult records that refer to his years of juvenile delinquency are the source material for this chapter.

127 *The school was created:* Like Gerome at the Farm, Joe's experience at St. Charles was a product of the times. Had he arrived when it first opened in 1901, he would have found a paternalistic institution, yet one dismissive of immigrant parents who needed the state to step in and raise their children like real Americans. Had he arrived a decade later, he would have found a militaristic tone; the "families" would now be called "companies," required to participate in daily marching drills and a dress parade twice a week. But even with this more rigid overlay, St. Charles still would have viewed Joe as a wayward boy who simply needed a guiding hand.

Ten years further along, he might have found the place would have been downright fun. Col. Frank Whipp (who would go on to oversee Stateville when Fernekes escaped) built a lake, a park, and a zoo for his St. Charles "boys." The Depression years saw a return to discipline, including the use of "twenty licks" across bared buttocks with a rigid leather strap. And by the time Joe got there, the legislature had effectively given up on "fixing" the boys and was warehousing them instead, surrounding the place with a forty-foot fence to prevent escapes.

The War Years ◆ Dante Cosentino and David Troy ◆ Stamford

134 *David often saw signs, connections:* How to assess the importance of faith to someone you have never met? Dave was described this way by his wife to their children. She also told them of his belief in dreams and the lucky number seven. He was an altar boy and none of his brothers were, so likely it was his choice, not the result of pressure from his mother.

134 *collected scrap metal and paper:* This comes from a photo and caption in the *Stamford Advocate.*

The War Years ✦ Warden Ragen, Alf Alving, and Nathan Leopold ✦ Stateville Penitentiary

138 *They could use canteen funds:* Which leads us to the story of Arthur St. Germaine, a twenty-seven-year-old prisoner at a small Massachusetts prison who died in the early stages of the war. His parents were not told much about how he died, and they were a bit mystified when the governor attended their son's memorial service, as did the commissioner of corrections. They gave his mother a proclamation pardoning her son. The document, quoted in newspaper stories nationwide, praised the young man's participation in "vitally important research . . . that involved possible savings of thousands of lives not only on the battlefront but among society itself."

It took four decades for Arthur St. Germain's death to be unclassified, showing him to have been part of an experiment to find a safe substitute for human blood plasma. Eventually the work would lead to the isolation of serum albumin in human blood, which made it possible to give shelf-stable transfusions on the battlefield. But in its initial stage, Arthur St. Germain and twenty-two others were given albumin from a cow to see how they would tolerate it. They did not. A dozen men became severely ill, and Arthur died. The laudatory funeral, with the accompanying pardon, was designed to keep his family from asking questions. It had the added benefit of sending the message to prisoners that they could be heroes even while behind bars.

At the time of Arthur's death, the War Department was conducting a "Buy-a-Bomber" drive, in which groups of individuals—schools, businesses, entire towns—pooled their war bond purchases until they had enough to fund a single B-17 war plane. The inmates of America's prisons were one such group, collecting $983,000 (including $6,200 from Stateville). That was enough for three separate bombers, and because the donors were given naming rights, the prisoners were asked to send their suggestions. "Their" planes became *The Fighting Felon*, *The Striped Lady* (after the nation's female inmates), and *The Spirit of St. Germain*.

No bombers with these names ever fought in the war. Their missions are not recorded in air force records; a search of obituaries, battle histories, and news articles turns up no word of them (beyond the initial naming announcements). The "Buy-a-Bomber" drive was a marketing campaign, not a purchase order, and though at first actual planes were christened with donor-chosen names (a charming history of one such plane is told in Sandra Warren's *We Bought a WWII Bomber: The Untold Story of a Michigan High School, a B-17 Bomber and the Blue Ridge Parkway*), there was a war going on, and production quickly outpaced the pomp.

Instead of witnessing a fly-through by an actual plane, schools, businesses, towns, and prisons received photos of "their" bomber, its chosen name painted on its nose. The photos, though, looked more than a bit alike, because a "ruse was carried out in the photographic department" of the North American Aviation factory in Kansas City. In his book *Warbird Factory: North American Aviation in World War II*, John M. Frederickson writes: "A master photo of a generic B-25 was prepared. . . . [with] no serial number or other identifying marks. A calligrapher then inked the name of the contributing group onto paper. The image was photographed so the small cursive was then overlaid onto the generic negative. The resulting 8x10 photo implied that there was an actual B-25 with white paint decorating the nose in celebration of their monetary contribution. Every group received a photo of the same airplane and nobody at the factory bothered to dab a brush into paint. Many people have attempted to research the combat fate of 'their' bomber, only to be frustrated when told that no such airplane ever existed."

To recap: Arthur St. Germain's death as part of a prison medical experiment was covered up, and the plane that was named for him, paid for by prisoners, probably never existed.

139   *The mosquito-borne tropical disease:* My best sources for the malaria trials were Nathan Leopold's autobiography; Alvin Tarlov's one-on-one tutoring sessions in the early days of my research; Karen M. Masterson, *The Malaria Project: The U.S. Government's Secret Mission to Find a Miracle Cure*; and L. A. Webb, Jr., *Humanity's Burden: A Global History of Malaria*.

145   *Alving tried to hide his discomfort:* Alving was apparently quite vocal in private about his dislike of Nathan Leopold. Al recalls hearing stories. Karen Masterson attributes some to Alving's son, Carl. But Alving did not make any disparaging *public* statements about the man that I could find.

145   *"How many volunteers":* Leopold described this conversation in his autobiography. It is retold often in other books, but all the retellings seem to originate with Leopold.

146   *Kenneth Rucker, who was serving:* According to Masterson, Rucker said this to Alving's young son, Carl.

1945 ✦ Al Tarlov and Joseph DeSalvo ✦ Norwalk and Chicago

152   *Isadore would write a book:* That would be *Autologous Plasma Cloth Suture of Nerves*, in 1943, which he later expanded into *Plasma Clot Suture of Peripheral Nerves and Nerve Roots: Rationale and Technique*, in 1950.

153   *Two separate war crimes trials were underway:* Göring, Hess, and Schilling were all convicted. Göring was sentenced to death by hanging but committed suicide before the punishment was carried out. Hess was sentenced to life in prison. Schilling was hanged at Landsberg Prison in Bavaria in 1945.

155   *Isadore would write the first:* This would become *Sacral Nerve-Root Cysts: Another Cause of the Sciatic or Cauda Equina*, which he published in book form in 1953.

157   *Joe filled out form upon form:* Because Joe was no longer considered a minor, and so not part of the juvenile system, I was (finally) granted access to his prison files (known as "jackets") starting with this one in 1946.

1946 ✦ Dante Cosentino and David Troy ✦ Stamford

161   *Tom Troy was a beat cop:* The fact that Tom Troy mentored David Troy comes from Bruce Williams, the cop who "trained Dave up" once he entered the department. The stories about Thomas's early days on the force are from newspaper accounts; local police blotters were big news back in the 1920s and '30s.

162   *The Stamford Police had been a welcoming:* Tom Lombardo is the institutional memory of the Stamford Police Department. What he does not know about its history, he knows where to find.

163   *part-time job at Woldan's Service Station:* Woldan's had been there, in some form, since the 1910s. It belonged to Ferdinand Woldan and his wife Emilie. Ferdinand had been a butcher before emigrating from Czechoslovakia, so he initially opened a butcher shop on the site, at the corner of Elm and Shippan Avenue. It became the Park View Market, which in turn became the side-business for a service station. It had a two-bay garage (back when mechanics climbed down into pits to look beneath a car, rather than raising it up hydraulically). The station also had a two-pump island.

In 1941, Ferdinand Woldan advertised in the *Stamford Daily Advocate* that his "MEAT and grocery store" was for rent. His asking price was seventy-five dollars. Apparently he received no offers, so he leaned into the gas station instead, as his granddaughter, Emilie T. Blackwell, described it in an interview. But he wanted to find others to run things so he could go fishing. He contracted with Texaco to provide the gasoline and shiny new pumps. With a share of the profits, he hired hourly help to fix cars and pump gas. By 1949, Dave Troy was one of those employees.

1946 ♦ Warden Ragen, Dr. Alving, and Nathan Leopold ♦
Stateville Penitentiary

166   *"bite day":* An account of the *Life* magazine photo shoot as viewed by Nathan Leopold is in his autobiography. An account through the eyes of Warden Ragen is in Gladys Erickson's *Warden Ragen of Joliet.*

167   *"For a firsthand report":* The full script can be found, of all places, in the transcript of the Doctors Trial at Nuremberg, placed into evidence by the defense. Every word spoken at Nuremberg can be found online and searched by keyword, courtesy of the Harvard Law School Nuremberg Trials Project.

171   *That fact would remain secret:* John Harkness, Ph.D., scoured the Nuremberg transcript and pieced together Andrew Ivy's partial truths and fudged timeline. His account can be found in the November 27, 1996, issue of the *Journal of the American Medical Association.*

171   *Ivy's testimony was hardly covered:* His testimony wasn't mentioned in *The New York Times,* and although his name appeared often in the Chicago press that summer, it was not because of Nuremberg or the Green Committee, but because of a research grant he'd received to put apes in corsets to determine whether restrictive women's undergarments caused ulcers.

1950 ♦ Cosentinos ♦ Cos Cob

191   *nearly knocking down Frank:* This story was related to me by Frank Cosentino.

1950 ◆ David Troy and Rosie Cosentino ◆ Al Tarlov and Joan Hylton ◆ Stamford and Norwalk

193 **J. M. *Wright Technical School*:** The school is still in operation and still provides a mix of career training and academics. Much of its history as described in this chapter (and the wins and losses of its baseball team) comes from the *Stamford Advocate*, dating back to 1919.

195 ***Joan was not like any other girl:*** The story of the Hylton family could fill its own book. The descendants I spoke to, specifically John Perfetti, traced their lineage back to Norman times. Joan's great-grandfather, Theodore Marmaduke Hylton, and his brother Thomas, were not only West Indies plantation owners but also doctors who considered themselves adventurers. When Theodore left for California, it was with his wife, Sarah Cunningham Melmouth, who was also a child of wealthy landowners; they settled in Petaluma, California, where they had their son, George, in 1860 and a daughter, Kitty, four years later.

Theodore never found much gold, but he did establish a local newspaper, one of the original "scandal sheets," which made him a lot of money and a lot of enemies. One of those enemies shot him in broad daylight on Front Street, wounding but not killing him. Nearly every lawyer in town offered to represent the shooter at little or no charge because Theodore was so universally disliked. Eventually, the judge declared a mistrial for lack of evidence, since not a single witness would come forward to testify.

Theodore went on to divorce Sarah and claim custody of both their children, citing her alcohol problem and her dalliances with other men. She moved to San Francisco, where, in the census of 1870, she is listed as a thirty-eight-year-old "servant out of place," living in a boardinghouse with six other women, all similarly described, all likely working as prostitutes. Theodore moved back to New York, where he began keeping company with a wealthy widow, Rossanna Brewster, who had teenagers of her own. She did not particularly want two more, so Theodore sent Kitty to live with relatives and deposited George in the orphanage. Rossanna and Theodore finally married in 1889. By 1891 he was dead.

196 **"*female complications*":** Carole's birth was hard on Eleanor. She never recovered physically or emotionally. Every month she suffered severe menstrual pain and took aminopyrine, a pain reliever and fever reducer. In November 1935, she became even more exhausted than usual, with a sudden and severe sore throat and a high fever. Doctors at the Hunts Point Hospital watched her organs begin to shut down and diagnosed agranulocytic angina, which results in a virtual wipeout of white blood cells, making it impossible for the body to fight infection. It was a rare but known reaction to aminopyrine and would soon lead to the drug being banned in the industrialized world.

196 ***He did so by marrying:*** And he didn't waste much time. Eleanor Simpson Hylton died at three p.m. on November 7, 1935. Her funeral service was held three days later at St. Peter's Church in the Bronx. She was twenty-six years old. Eleanor's youngest daughter, Carole, was baptized in the same church on December 15. She was eleven months old. Eleanor's younger sister, Lucille, held the baby during the ceremony. She was barely eighteen. Then Walter and

Lucille were married in September 1936, less than a year after Eleanor's death. Conveniently, Walter and Lucille were already living at Lucille's parents' home at 1646 Pilgrim Avenue, where Walter and Eleanor had moved when Walter lost his job during the Depression.

197   *Al began spending his summers:* His employer during those months was Leo Leonard, who was struggling with his own work identity. Leo's family had long been in the milk business, running Clover Farms Dairy in Norwalk. Founded in the 1920s, it was state of the art, with pasteurizing and bottling equipment on site. By the 1950s, it had grown to include home delivery trucks, distinctive because of the plastic cows attached to their front grilles and the unusual sounds of their horns; the trucks didn't honk, they mooed. Leo was uninterested in his family's business, but he was saved from having to enter it by his younger brother, Stewart, who was a classmate of Al's. Stew Leonard was happy to grow the dairy into a grocery chain, which left Leo free to do something that had nothing to do with cows. For decades, Stew oversaw the food and entertainment at reunions for the Norwalk High School Class of 1947, where live animals often wandered through.

November 1950 ✦ Joe DeSalvo ✦ Pontiac Prison

201   *showed his IQ to be 142:* IQ tests were created by the army, and the one Joe took was Army Alpha, the version for literate test takers. (Army Beta used drawings and other visuals for test takers who could not read.) These were early days for the tests, which became controversial over the years because of racial and cultural biases contained in the questions. They are now thought to be best for the macro—determining outliers at either end of the spectrum— rather than for the micro. Still, 142, at the time, was genius level, and all evidence about Joe indicates that word was not hyperbolic.

April 1951 ✦ Joseph DeSalvo ✦ Chicago

203   *Joe did not say a word:* Everything about Joe's 1951 robbery spree comes from news reports, trial testimony, witness statements, and the DeSalvo prison file.

1951 to 1953 ✦ Nathan Leopold ✦ Stateville Penitentiary

213   *When Joe DeSalvo arrived:* X-rays were taken of Joe when he arrived, as was noted in his file. And in Leopold's autobiography, he boasts that he took almost all the films during every yearly TB screening. Given these two facts, I made a leap to a third. As for the size of the X-rays, four by five inches seems small for a lung X-ray, but Leopold specifically gave that measurement, so I defer to him.

214   *A "war council" of relatives and friends:* The details in this chapter come from news accounts, Nathan Leopold's autobiography, and his papers at the Chicago History Museum; and from Elmer Gertz's *A Handful of Clients* and his papers at Northwestern University.

April 1954 • Dante Cosentino and Al Tarlov • Detroit and Manhattan

220 *the campus of Wayne University:* Two years later, in 1956, the school's name would be changed to Wayne State University.

223 *Al certainly knew the school's reputation:* The Jeff School did not keep its origins a secret. It was openly founded by the American Communist Party during the 1930s, one of several the party established around the country. All the information about the school in this chapter comes from its archived papers in the special collections at NYU's Elmer Holmes Bobst Library.

223 *New York Medical College:* The unwieldy name resulted from decades of mergers and new buildings. When Al attended, the school and hospital occupied a huge Beaux-Arts building, a mix of limestone and terra cotta, on Fifth Avenue, between 105th and 106th streets. Eventually it would be converted to the Terrance Cardinal Cooke Health Care Center, a long-term care and rehabilitation facility, still an affiliate of the New York Medical College, which moved north to Westchester County.

227 *It would be fifty years before he would see:* My several FOIA requests for Al's FBI file came up empty. FBI FOIA requests often come up empty even when there is every reason to believe that a file exists. My request for the file on the Norwalk VFW was also denied, yet I know from contemporaneous news accounts that there had to have been one.

In response to my request for Isadore's file, I received twenty-four pages. Most of them were concerned with "Espionage Agent with Mentally Deficient Wife"—a government search to find the neurosurgeon who operated on the wife of a suspected Communist infiltrator, on the theory that the surgeon was probably a Communist, too. Isadore was not found to be that surgeon, but his political beliefs and activities were scrutinized. Among the morsels: Dr. I. M. Tarlov attended a dinner of the Committee for a Democratic Far Eastern Policy on Wednesday evening April 3, 1946, at the Hotel Roosevelt in New York City. Dr. Tarlov's name, address, and phone number were included on a fund-raising list for the *National Guardian*. Clarence Green, an English teacher for the personnel office of the Soviet UN delegation, had been attempting to locate Dr. Tarlov. I. M. Tarlov gave a five-dollar contribution to the American Committee for the Foreign Born. Oh, and Dr. Tarlov was born in 1905 in Latvia. Which, as you know, he was not.

July 1954 and June 1956 • The Troys and the Tarlovs • Cos Cob and Chicago

235 *standing directly in front of the portrait:* According to Evelyn, that photo hung in the front hallway until Tony's death in 1973, when his children asked for it back and Rose willingly gave it to them.

1957 to 1958 • Joe DeSalvo and Nathan Leopold • Stateville Penitentiary

238 *Joe could follow Leopold's trail:* Joe took out his full allotment of library books, but we have no existing record of exactly what books those were. Al

recalls discussing books with him, particularly ones on science and philosophy. Al also recalls reading Leopold's scientific papers, out of curiosity, and thinks it likely that Joe did as well.

239 *small subgroup of human beings:* Race is not a central theme in this book, but as with most of American history, it is ever present. Here we see it in the casual lack of interest in the potentially fatal effects of primaquine on patients with roots in Africa and the Mediterranean. Attention was not paid until the percentage of Black soldiers increased, making this a practical problem for the military.

242 *he filed a nine-thousand-word application:* Details about the "campaign" for clemency are from Gertz's memoir; his papers in the Elmer Gertz Collection at Charles Deering McCormick Library of Special Collections at Northwestern University; Leopold's autobiography; and Leopold's papers at the Chicago History Museum.

1959 ✦ David Troy and Al Tarlov ✦ Stamford and Fort Sam Houston, Texas

252 *he was a better mechanic:* In 1956 the sign at the gas station changed yet again, from TEXACO to SHELL, as the Woldans looked for the best deal from suppliers. "David Troy invites his customers and friends to the GRAND OPENING of Troy's Shell Service Station, Elm Avenue and Shippan Avenue," read the ad in the *Stamford Daily Advocate*, which added that there would be lollipops for the kids and giveaways for their parents—six "golden iridescent" plastic tumblers with every purchase of eight gallons of gasoline. Despite the name, Dave still did not own the station, but rather ran the day-to-day at the pumps and the repair bays in exchange for a percentage of each.

February 1960 ✦ Al Tarlov ✦ Stateville Penitentiary

267 *former guard named Charles Wheeler:* Al remembered the photo and the various legends. Erickson's *Warden Ragen of Joliet* provided the details.

268 *H. P. Lovecraft, whose message:* Born Howard Phillips Lovecraft, the writer of dark, creepy fiction and poetry died in 1937. But he has had posthumous popularity, "experiencing more commercial success now than he ever sought while he was alive," culture writer Michael Calia wrote in *The Wall Street Journal* in 2014. The H. P. Lovecraft community on Reddit has more than 200,000 members. Joe DeSalvo's tastes were ahead of his time.

270 *a long letter to the editor of* The New York Times: The letter, published in "Letters to the Times" on August 18, 1958, under the title "Fight Against Delinquency," made a lasting impression on Al, like so many things his uncle did.

June 1960 ✦ Joe DeSalvo ✦ Norwalk

274 *landed in Dr. Norman Boas's mailbox:* Dr. Norman Boas kept a thick file of everything that had to do with the DeSalvo case. This letter, and the others

sent to Dr. Boas, were in that file some sixty years later, along with all the paperwork for Joe's car loan.

July 4, 1960 ♦ David Troy ♦ Stamford

280   *"My life is complete"*: Here we are at Independence Day again. Frank is absolutely certain he heard Dave say this at a backyard party surrounded by his children. He is fairly certain it was this Fourth of July picnic.

July 4, 1960 ♦ Al Tarlov ♦ Norwalk

282   *"But I am completely"*: I asked Al many times whether he'd had any questions or reservations in real time about his research. This was always his answer.

July 4, 1960 ♦ Joe DeSalvo ♦ Wilton, Connecticut

285   *It was the first time the doctor:* Details of the visit are based on interviews with Dr. Boas and his children, Debbie, Steven, and Barbara. Descriptions of the house, and its history, come from the Boas children and from a memoir written by Dr. Boas in 1996, *Nod Hill, Wilton, Connecticut: Reminiscences.*

Thursday, July 7, 1960 ♦ 9:45 p.m. ♦ Rosie Troy ♦ Stamford

290   *time for Rosie to remove the rollers:* This chapter relies on interviews with the Troys and the Cosentinos who granted them, as well as news reports (and TV listings) from several Connecticut newspapers; David Troy's death certificate and autopsy report; the complete Stamford Police file on the case; witness statements and eventual testimony; and a drive I made from 33 Palmer Avenue to Stamford Hospital, to time a typical trip and compare it to the times in the police file from that night.

296   *"That's not Dave's boy"*: One afternoon early in my research, David and Rosie's three children, their children, and many of their aunts and uncles all gathered to meet with me at Evelyn's house. They fed me a mountain of delicious food and spent hours telling me stories. Near the end of the gathering, talk turned to Bridget. Doreen started to speak, then stopped and said, "I don't know if I should tell this. Should I?" and looked at her sister Diane.

Seeing the look, their brother asked. "It's not about me, is it?"

"Yes, it is," Doreen said, took a deep breath, and then continued. "Mom said that Granny was holding you, and she said—what did she say? It was like basically saying 'He may have my son's name, but he's not my son's son.' Because you look Italian."

That boy, by then a man in his fifties, had never heard that story before. He looked as though he had been slapped.

Doreen also looked stricken. "You were always your father's son," she reassured her brother.

Later, Evelyn, Rosie's older sister, would confirm hearing Bridget say something like that the night David Troy died. "That's not Dave's boy," was her memory. "That's not my grandchild."

Friday, July 8, 1960 ✦ Joe DeSalvo ✦ Norwalk

297 *Frances Fitzgerald chose Joseph:* This section, and the next several, are constructed from the police interviews, affidavits and courtroom testimony of the Fitzgeralds, Dr. Weinberg, Dr. Boas, Mrs. Perry, and Charles McGrath, and from Joe's 1960 police file.

Sunday, July 10, 1960 ✦ 5 p.m. ✦ Leo P. Gallagher Funeral Home ✦ Stamford

310 *As Bruce Williams stood:* Officer Williams told me this story not long before he died.

Monday, July 11, 1960 ✦ Rosie Troy ✦ Stamford

313 *Rosie, sitting stoically:* Connecticut newspapers provided much of the information here about the funeral.

July 11 to 13, 1960 ✦ Al Tarlov ✦ Norwalk

316 *the* Stamford Advocate *gave over its front:* The wide-net collection of funds has now become a familiar part of the public grieving process, but it was new for Stamford in 1960.

Wednesday, July 13, 1960 ✦ Joe DeSalvo ✦ Chicago

320 *he could tell they were ill:* Charles and Ruth DeSalvo's death certificates indicate that they would have already been quite ill when Joe arrived home. So he would have been able to tell if he had been paying attention.
321 *the crutches, the fact that he winced:* The DeSalvos' impressions of and interactions with Joe come from their police statements.
322 *The officers were shouting:* Details of the actual arrest come from the police reports filed by the officers at the scene.

Thursday, July 14, 1960 ✦ Al Tarlov ✦ Norwalk

327 *"Don't talk to the press":* The quotes from Warden Ragen, Alf Alving, and Isadore Tarlov are as Al Tarlov remembered them.

Summer 1960 ◆ Joe DeSalvo ◆ Bridgeport, Connecticut

330 *By late July, Joe had stopped eating:* This chapter comes from news coverage
of the new Fairfield County Jail and of the DeSalvo case during the summer of
1960. I have gone back and forth on whether Joe truly lost his mind and had
no memory of his actions, or whether he was using it as a ploy.

Summer 1960 ◆ Norman Boas ◆ Wilton

335 *how on earth had all of them missed:* That was inexplicable to me until I saw
Joe DeSalvo's police file with photos of him standing in his tighty-whities, a bullet
wound halfway up his outer thigh, farther up than any pant leg would stretch.
Thinking they were looking at a wrenched knee, the docs would have no reason
to look farther up his leg. And the one time he was asked to drop his trousers in
the ER, I imagine his shirttail hid the wound. But that is just my best benefit of the
doubt. I really can't believe that two bullet wounds managed to go unnoticed.

335 *almost juvenile script:* Al received almost exactly the same letter from Joe, but
with no mention of the car loan as that was specific to Dr. Boas. Joe's hand-
writing was heartbreaking. It was that of a child, with big loops, trying to be
perfect, stuck, at least emotionally, in adolescence.

336 *I would like to pay you back:* Joe DeSalvo didn't make a single payment on
his car. The first one was due on July 18, 1960, by which time he was in jail.
As the guarantor, Dr. Boas owed the balance of $257.48 to the Fairfield Trust
Company, which he paid. He then sued DeSalvo in Oct. 1960, and, in January
of 1961, was awarded his employee's last paycheck, for $58.36, and the car
itself. But by the time Boas could take possession the tires were flat, the battery
was dead, and it wasn't worth the price of towing it to the junkyard.

Summer 1960 ◆ Rosie Troy ◆ Stamford

339 *"That's the man who killed":* This is one of Doreen's earliest memories.

340 *"Why did I turn out differently":* From my conversations with Dante amid the
floor-to-ceiling books in his home library in California.

340 *she wrote Bridget a check:* Whether the original $5,000 was a gift or a loan
still divides the family. Dave's children had little to do with their Troy cousins
growing up, a distance that began with Bridget's request for repayment. They
have reconnected as adults and work hard not to talk about the money. Rosie
paid Bridget back, but her children are not sure with what. It was not the money
from the Troy fund. That remained in trust until they were young adults, and
they used it for such things as the down payment on their own houses.

December 1960 ◆ Joe DeSalvo and Rosie Troy ◆
Fairfield County Courthouse

341 *"There is no more important trial":* All the descriptions and quotes from
the trial were found in the coverage of Connecticut newspapers, particularly

the *Norwalk Hour* and the *Stamford Advocate*. The actual trial transcript is long gone.

346 *"In one of the most amazing scenes":* The coverage of DeSalvo's testimony reminded me a bit of the news circus during the Leopold and Loeb trial. Rather than using the phrase "the crime of the century," they invoked *Les Misérables*.

348 *Rosie did not believe them:* The Troy children still vehemently reject this part of Joe DeSalvo's testimony. "We find it hard to believe that Dad shot first and that Dad shot at someone who said 'Don't shoot,'" Doreen said. "It seems to go against everyone else's description of Dad as a man and an officer. Is there anything to corroborate those two statements in his testimony? And, if not, shouldn't that be noted?"

There is of course no way to corroborate what happened in the darkness of Greyrock Place. All we have is the killer's description. He was known to be a liar. And yes, that should be noted.

Wednesday, December 14, 1960 ◆ 6:55 a.m. ◆ Joe DeSalvo ◆ Fairfield County Jail

353 *"Mac, come in the wing":* This is how Al originally began telling me this story, with a question about suicide. "Do you think there is such a thing as a noble suicide?" he had asked me, then began to tell me about his fatal friendship with Joe DeSalvo.

By that morning in his kitchen, Al had spent fifty years trying to decide whether what Joe did, in the end, was noble or cowardly. He knew Joe was determined never to return to jail, which would have made his suicide self-serving, a personal escape. But in his decisions right before he killed himself, to give his victim's widow the closest thing he had to an explanation, Al saw in that act something more. Al believes that Joe had concluded that this— a criminal, a murderer, a prisoner—was all he was, *what* he was, the only thing he would ever be. So he looked directly at Rosie in court, gave as close to an apology as he could manage, and decided to remove himself from the world because he was too damaged to be permitted to live in it.

Selected Bibliography

Motorcycle Racing

Emde, Don. *The Speed Kings: The Rise and Fall of Motordrome Racing*. Emde Books, 2019.

Ongstad, Rick, and Lane Ongstad. *Fearless: Lords of the Murderdrome*. Doubleday, 2017.

Parole Prediction and Practice

Abadinsky, Howard. *Probation and Parole: Theory and Practice*, 12th ed. Prentice-Hall, 2015.

Angwin, Julia; Surya Mattu, and Lauren Kirchner. "Machine Bias," *Pro Publica*, May 23, 2016. https://www.propublica.org/article/machine-bias-risk-assessments-in-criminal-sentencing.

Laune, Ferris F. *Predicting Criminality: Forecasting Behavior on Parole*. Greenwood Press, 1936.

Ohlin, Lloyd E. *Selection for Parole: A Manual of Parole Prediction*. Russell Sage Foundation, 1951.

Petersilia, Joan. *When Prisoners Come Home: Parole and Prisoner Reentry*. Oxford University Press, 2009.

Schauer, Frederick. *Profiles, Probabilities and Stereotypes*. Belknap Press of Harvard University Press, 2003.

Wickersham Commission Report No. 9. *Report on Penal Institutions, Probation and Parole*. 1931; reprint by Patterson Smith, 1968.

Prison History

Alexander, Michelle. *The New Jim Crow: Mass Incarceration in the Age of Colorblindness*. New Press, 2012.

Altgeld, John Peter. *Our Penal Machinery and Its Victims*. 1886; collection of University of Michigan Library.

Baldi, Frederick S. *My Unwelcome Guests*. J.B. Lippincott, 1959.

Conover, Ted. *Newjack: Guarding Sing Sing*. Vintage Books, 2001.

Erickson, Gladys A. *Warden Ragen of Joliet*. E.P. Dutton, 1957.

Foucault, Michel. *Discipline and Punish: The Birth of the Prison*. Translated by Alan Sheridan. Vintage Books, 1995.

Friedman, Lawrence M. *Crime and Punishment in American History*. Basic Books, 1993.

Jacobs, James B. *Stateville: The Penitentiary in Mass Society*. University of Chicago Press, 1977.

Morris, Norval, and David J. Rothman. *The Oxford History of the Prison*. Oxford University Press, 1995.

Pisciotta, Alexander W. *Benevolent Repression: Social Control and the American Reformatory-Prison Movement*. New York University Press, 1994.

Ragen, Joseph E., and Charles Finston. *Inside the World's Toughest Prison: How a Prison Housing Thousands of Tough Convicts Is Kept Literally Free from Riots and Escapes*. Charles C. Thomas, 1962.

Samenow, Stanton E. *Inside the Criminal Mind*. Crown, 1984.

Shaw, Clifford R. *The Natural History of a Delinquent Career*. University of Chicago Press, 1931.

Steidinger, Amy Kinzer. *Joliet Prison Blues: A Century of Stories*. History Press, 2021.

Sykes, Gresham M. *The Society of Captives: A Study of a Maximum Security Prison*. Princeton University Press, 2007.

Medical Experiments, Malaria, and the 1918 Flu Epidemic

Harcourt, Bernard E. *Against Prediction: Profiling, Policing, and Punishing in an Actuarial Age*. University of Chicago Press, 2007.

Lederer, Susan E. *Subjected to Science: Human Experimentation in America Before the Second World War*. Johns Hopkins University Press, 1995.

Masterson, Karen M. *The Malaria Project: The U.S. Government's Secret Mission to Find a Miracle Cure*. New American Library, 2014.

Moreno, Jonathan D. *Undue Risk: Secret State Experiments on Humans*. Routledge, 2001.

Rothman, David J. *Strangers at the Bedside: A History of How Law and Bioethics Transformed Medical Decision Making*. Basic Books, 1991.

Spinney, Laura. *Pale Rider: The Spanish Flu of 1918 and How It Changed the World*. PublicAffairs, 2017.

Immigration

Bull, Bonnie K. *Images of America: Stamford*. Arcadia, 1997.

Dolan, Jay P. *The Irish Americans: A History*. Bloomsbury, 2008.

Gordon, Milton M. *Assimilation in American Life: The Role of Race, Religion, and National Origins*. Oxford University Press, 1964.

Handlin, Oscar. *The Uprooted: The Epic Story of the Great Migrations That Made the American People*, 2nd ed. University of Pennsylvania Press, 2002.

Vans-McLaughlin, Virginia, Marjorie Lightman, and the Statue of Liberty Ellis Island Foundation. *Ellis Island and the Peopling of America*. New Press, 1997.

American and World History

Graham, John W. *The Gold Star Mother Pilgrimages of the 1930s: Overseas Grave Visitations by Mothers and Widows of Fallen U.S. World War I Soldiers*. McFarland & Co., 2005.

Lepore, Jill. *These Truths: A History of the United States*. W.W. Norton, 2018.

Mendelsohn, Daniel. *The Lost: A Search for Six of the Six Million*. HarperPerennial, 2013.

Sandler, Martin W. *1919: The Year that Changed America*. Bloomsbury Children's Books, 2019.

Squire, J. C. *If It Had Happened Otherwise*. St. Martin's Press, 1972.

Leopold and Loeb

Baatz, Simon. *For the Thrill of It: Leopold, Loeb, and the Murder That Shocked Jazz Age Chicago*. HarperPerennial, 2009.

Darrow, Clarence. *Attorney for the Damned: Clarence Darrow in the Courtroom*. Edited by Arthur Weinberg. Simon & Schuster, 1957.

———. *Crime, Its Causes and Treatments*. 1922; reprinted by Kessinger, 2010.

Gertz, Elmer. *A Handful of Clients*. Follett, 1965.

Higdon, Hal. *Leopold and Loeb: The Crime of the Century*. First Illinois, 1999.

Leopold, Nathan F. *Life Plus 99 Years*. Doubleday, 1958.

Levin, Meyer. *Compulsion, A Novel*. Fig Tree Books, 2014.

McKernan, Maureen. *The Amazing Crime and Trial of Leopold and Loeb*. Signet Books, 1957.

Shapiro, David L., Charles Golden, and Sara Ferguson. *Retrying Leopold and Loeb: A Neuropsychological Perspective*. Springer, 2018.

Tarlov Writings

Tarlov, Alvin, and Michelle Precort Debbink. *Investing in Early Childhood Development: Evidence to Support a Movement for Educational Change*. Palgrave Macmillan, 2008.

Tarlov, Isadore M. *Plasma Clot Suture of Peripheral Nerves and Nerve Roots: Rationale and Technique*. Charles C. Thomas, 1950.

———. *The Principle of Parsimony in Medicine, and Other Essays*. Charles C. Thomas, 1969.

———. *Sacral Nerve-Root Cysts: Another Cause of the Sciatic or Cauda Equina Syndrome*. Charles C. Thomas, 1953.

———. *Spinal Cord Compression: Mechanism of Paralysis and Treatment*. Charles C. Thomas, 1957.

City History

Bull, Bonnie K. *Images of America: Stamford*. Arcadia, 1997.

Bulmer, Martin. *The Chicago School of Sociology: Institutionalization, Diversity, and the Rise of Sociological Research*. University of Chicago Press, 1986.

Bundy, Chris. *West Baden Springs: Legacy of Dreams*. Self-published, 1999.

Feinstein, Estelle F. *Stamford in the Gilded Age: The Political Life of a Connecticut Town, 1868–1893*. Stamford Historical Society, 1973.

Gordon, Maggie. *The Gilded Age on Connecticut's Gold Coast: Transforming Greenwich, Stamford, and Darien*. History Press, 2014.

Grant, Lisa Wilson. *Images of America: Norwalk*. Arcadia, 2014.

Huntington, E. B. *History of Stamford Connecticut from Its Settlement in 1641, to the Present Time*. Oxford University, 1868.

Majdalany, Jeanne. *The History of the Cove in Stamford, Connecticut*. Stamford Historical Society, 1979.

Masters, Edgar Lee. *The Tale of Chicago*. G.P. Putnam's Sons, 1933.

Pavia, Tony. *An American Town Goes to War*. Turner, 1995.

Sterling, Robert E. *Joliet Then and Now*. G. Bradley, 2004.

Other

Cosentino, Dante. *Pride and Memory*. Xlibris US, 2013.

Frederickson, John. *Warbird Factory: North American Aviation in World War II*. Quarto, 2015.

Rosner, Elizabeth. *Survivor Café: The Legacy of Trauma and the Labyrinth of Memory*. Counterpoint, 2017.

Tracy, Sarah W. *Alcoholism in America: From Reconstruction to Prohibition*. Johns Hopkins University Press, 2005.

Index

Many secondary characters are indexed by their maiden names.